Receiver, Bearer, and Giver of God's Spirit

Receiver, Bearer, and Giver of God's Spirit

Jesus' Life in the Spirit as a Lens for Theology and Life

LEOPOLDO A. SÁNCHEZ M.

☙PICKWICK *Publications* • Eugene, Oregon

RECEIVER, BEARER, AND GIVER OF GOD'S SPIRIT
Jesus' Life in the Spirit as a Lens for Theology and Life

Copyright © 2015 Leopoldo A. Sánchez M. All rights reserved. Except for brief quotations in critical publications or reviews, no part of this book may be reproduced in any manner without prior written permission from the publisher. Write: Permissions, Wipf and Stock Publishers, 199 W. 8th Ave., Suite 3, Eugene, OR 97401.

Pickwick Publications
An Imprint of Wipf and Stock Publishers
199 W. 8th Ave., Suite 3
Eugene, OR 97401

www.wipfandstock.com

ISBN 13: 978-1-62564-282-0

Cataloging-in-Publication data:

Sánchez M., Leopoldo A.

   Receiver, bearer, and giver of God's spirit : Jesus' life in the spirit as a lens for theology and life / Leopoldo A. Sánchez M.

   xxvi + 272 p. ; 23 cm. —Includes bibliographical references and index(es).

   ISBN 13: 978-1-62564-282-0

   1. Spirit christology. 2. Jesus Christ—Person and offices. 3. Holy Spirit. I. Title.

BT205 .S34 2015

Manufactured in the U.S.A. 03/20/2015

Scripture quotations, unless otherwise stated, are from the New Revised Standard Version Bible, copyright 1989, Division of Christian Education of the National Council of the Churches of Christ in the United States of America. Used by permission. All rights reserved.

The original version of the last section of chapter 6 appeared as "The Holy Spirit in Christ: Pneumatological Christology as a Ground for a Christ-Centered Pneumatology," in *Propter Christum: Christ at the Center*, edited by Scott Murray et al., 343–56. St. Louis: Luther Academy, 2013. Used with permission.

The original version of chapter 7 appeared as "God against Us and for Us: Preaching Jesus in the Spirit," *Word & World* 24 (2003) 134–45. Used with permission.

The original version of chapter 8 appeared as "Praying to God the Father in the Spirit: Reclaiming the Church's Participation in the Son's Prayer Life," *Concordia Journal* 32 (2006) 274–95. Used with permission.

The original version of chapter 9 appeared as "Life in the Spirit of Christ: Models of Sanctification as Sacramental Pneumatology," *LOGIA* 22 (2013) 7–14. Used with permission.

For my dear Tracy

and our precious children, Lucas and Ana

Contents

Preface | ix
Acknowledgments | xv
Abbreviations | xviii
Introduction | xix

1 The Eclipse and Promise of Spirit-Oriented Christologies: Early Church Responses to Heterodox Views of Jesus' Anointing | 1

2 Reading the Story of Jesus as Receiver and Bearer of God's Spirit: Invigorating Logos-Oriented Approaches to the Conception, Anointing, and Exaltation of Jesus | 30

3 Reading the Story of Jesus as Giver of God's Spirit: Invigorating Logos-Oriented Approaches to the Paschal Mystery and the Atonement | 65

4 The Joint Mission of the Son and the Spirit: The Holy Spirit's Proper Work in the Incarnation and the Reciprocity of the Son-Spirit Relationship | 86

5 The Son's Eternal Life in the Spirit: Person, Relation, and Models of the Immanent Trinity | 110

6 The Holy Spirit in the Incarnate Logos: Toward the Complementarity of Logos and Spirit Christologies | 148

7 Preaching Jesus in the Spirit: Pneumatological Christology as a Lens for Proclamation | 181

8 Praying to the Father in the Spirit: Reclaiming the Church's Participation in the Son's Prayer Life | 195

9 Living in the Spirit of Christ: Models of Sanctification as Sacramental Pneumatology | 219

Conclusion | 238

Appendix: A Comparison of Logos and Spirit Christologies | 241
Glossary | 243
Bibliography | 249
Subject Index | 259
Name Index | 265
Scripture Index | 269

Preface

"But who do you say that I am?" (Matt 16:15).[1] In this work, I assess the productivity of a Spirit Christology as a theological model for reflection on Jesus' perennial question. A traditional and correct answer to the question has been to confess that Jesus is the God-man, the Word made flesh, the incarnate Logos or Son. Yet the incarnate Word also lives "in the Spirit." Jesus has a pneumatological identity. I propose to investigate more closely the usefulness of such a Spirit-oriented dimension of Jesus' life as a lens for Christology itself, Trinitarian theology, and three areas of the Christian life—namely, proclamation, prayer, and sanctification. I argue that reading the life and mission of Jesus as receiver, bearer, and giver of God's Spirit (i.e., a "Spirit Christology")[2] invigorates or complements classic Logos-oriented approaches to Christian theology.

Like many proposals in systematic theology, mine has both critical and constructive tasks. Critically, I investigate the partial eclipse and budding promise of the place of the Holy Spirit in the history of theological reflection on Jesus Christ, paying particular attention to representative church fathers and theologians. Constructively, I propose a revitalization of the pneumatological dimensions of Christology in view of their partial relativization by the church's dominant but necessary apologetic interest in Logos-oriented approaches to the person of Christ. My investigation shows that a rediscovery of the historically weakened and at times forgotten pneumatic aspects of Jesus' identity can assist theologians immensely in recovering key soteriological, Trinitarian, and ecclesial dimensions of the mystery of God's salvation in Christ.

Against the heterodox Arian denial of Jesus' divine nature, a Nicene Logos-oriented Christology defines Jesus' identity in terms of his essential equality or consubstantiality (Gk. *homoousios*) with God the Father. Moreover, in

---

1. Unless otherwise noted, biblical references are to the NRSV.

2. Some interchangeable terms include pneumatological or pneumatic Christology, and Spirit-oriented or pneumatologically-oriented Christology.

reaction to Nestorian (Logos-man) and Eutychian (one-nature) Christologies, a Logos-oriented Chalcedonian approach defines Jesus' identity in terms of his personal (hypostatic) constitution from the first moment of the incarnation without dividing (against Nestorius) or confusing (against Eutyches) his divine and human natures. In all these apologetic moves, the emphasis falls on the "static" and "individual" dimensions of Jesus' identity, namely, his "being-from-before" and his "being-in-himself." A Spirit-oriented Christology, as I envision it, defines Jesus' identity in terms of his acts and relation to the Father "in the Spirit" (Lat. *in spiritu*), both for us and in the divine life. By placing the question of Jesus' identity in the context of his acts and relations, a Spirit-oriented Christology complements, but does not replace, the static and individual emphases of a Logos-oriented Christology.

From a pneumatological angle, we can then speak of Jesus' identity in "dynamic" and "relational" (social or ecstatic) terms—namely, according to his "being-in-act" and "being-in-relation" (or "being-in/through/with/for-another"). This ontological adjustment allows us to give full weight to the defining place of the Spirit of the Father in the humanity of the Son and the events of his life and work for us (Christology and atonement), and in the Son's identity before the Father in the Spirit (economic and immanent Trinity). Furthermore, because the saints share with Christ a Spirit-indwelt humanity, a Spirit-Christology also leads to reflection on the church's present-day participation by grace in the Son's pneumatological identity through his Spirit's work in our lives. By focusing on the relative continuity between the presence and activity of the Spirit in Christ and his saints, in the only-begotten Son and the adopted sons, a Spirit-oriented Christology also serves as a bridge between Christology and ecclesiology. As the receiver and bearer of the Spirit, the Son is also the giver of the Spirit to the church. The Spirit of Christ shapes Christ in the saints. This work explores the implications of this insight for reflection on the Spirit's work in Christian proclamation, prayer, and sanctification.

In formulating my thesis, I use the language of invigoration and revitalization as part of a conscious methodological decision to think of Spirit Christology as a complement to Logos Christology. Rather than two opposing models, I envision two aspects of Christ's life pointing to the same person of Christ. From this angle, the reader should note that the terms "static" and "individual" are not to be seen as negative or pejorative ones, but rather as designations that best describe the ontological priorities of a Logos-oriented approach—namely, preserving the integrity of the Son's divine unity with the Father and the unity of his person. Conversely, the terms "dynamic" and "relational" are not to be seen as positive ones because they are "better" than their Logos-oriented counterparts. In a full Trinitarian context, these terms are complementary dimensions of Jesus' identity that must not be interpreted unilaterally or set in opposition to each other.

In a broader philosophical perspective, my project could be seen as a critique of Western logocentrism. In short, "logocentrism" denotes any attempt to see or explain reality in one way alone or according to an exclusive logic or metanarrative. I admit that the critical part of my work serves at first as a deconstruction of the exclusive use of Logos-oriented approaches to Christology in the history of dogma. However, the crucial problem that necessitates as a methodological strategy such an initial decentering of the predominant narrative does not have to do so much with a critique of the centrality of Jesus' identity as the incarnate Word clearly attested in the Scriptures, the ecumenical Councils, and the patristic tradition as a whole. Instead, the danger lies in logomonism, that is to say, the tendency to make of such a centrality the exclusive and absolute biblical and theological paradigm to the exclusion of its broader biblical and Trinitarian implications for Christian faith and life. We shall see that a Spirit Christology can invigorate Logos-oriented approaches to Christian theology without falling into an unhealthy pneumatocentrism that might lead to an adoptionist view of the Son or a view of the Spirit without a central christological trajectory. My overall goal is to develop the implications of a theology of the *joint mission* of the Son and the Holy Spirit in the Father's economy of salvation.

In a work that deals with Trinitarian theology, a few comments on God-language are appropriate. I acknowledge both the danger of the univocal use of masculine language for God and, on biblical and theological grounds, the possibility of employing feminine language analogically to speak about the Father and the Son in their relationship to the church (e.g., Isa 49:15, 66:13, and Luke 13:34). However, I also agree with LaCugna's observation that calling God "Father" does not necessarily amount to patriarchalism, just as calling God "mother" instead of "father" does not necessarily safeguard against the potential danger of trading Trinitarian monotheism for a unitarian theism.[3] For this project, I engage on its own terms the language of the Gospels, where Jesus addresses God as "Father" or "Abba" and teaches his disciples to do the same (e.g., Matt 6:9, Luke 11:2, John 17:5 and 20:17; cf. Mark 14:16, Rom 8:15), as well as the classic Trinitarian language of the creeds where the first person of the Trinity is confessed as the "Father." In dialogue with the East, the Nicene identification of the one God (Gk. *ho theos*) in the first article of the Creed with the person of the Father in particular has the added benefit of addressing a certain Western-Augustinian tendency in Trinitarian theology to take the unity of the divine substance as its ultimate ontological principle.

3. LaCugna, *God for Us*, 18.

When I refer to the triune God, and thus all three persons of the Godhead at once (not just the person of the Father), I use expressions like "God reveals Godself" and "God in Godself." When using the first expression, the reference is to the economic Trinity, that is to say, the divine persons in their relationship to us in history. When using the second expression, the reference is to the immanent Trinity, namely, the divine persons as they relate to each other. When referring to the "Trinity," I use the singular pronoun "it" in order to point to the *oneness* of the three persons, since the term's prefix "tri" already points to the *three* persons of the Godhead.

What of the Spirit? In this work, I often use neuter pronouns to refer to the Spirit (Gk. *pneuma*). I am aware that this decision is not without its problems, particularly, the potential dangers of thinking of the Spirit too impersonally or using language somewhat foreign to the person in the pew. The latter issue is alleviated primarily in the last three chapters of the work, where I use traditional masculine pronouns to refer to the Holy Spirit. My use of the neuter is thus not meant to be exclusive. A practical advantage of the use of the neuter for the Spirit in sentences where a reference is also made to the Son with a masculine pronoun helps the reader to distinguish between the two persons. As to the potential danger of an impersonal view of the Spirit through the use of the neuter, this need not be a cause of major concern since the personal character of the Spirit's work in the economy of salvation is evident in many biblical descriptions of his activity, even apart from the use of pronouns. For instance, the Holy Spirit defends the disciples against the judgment of the world (John 16:7–11), intercedes for the saints when they do not know how to pray (Rom 8:26–27), and is grieved by sin (Eph 4:30). These activities describe the Spirit in personal terms. While I am open to the use of feminine metaphors to speak of the Spirit's work, I have chosen not to use feminine pronouns to refer to the Spirit.[4]

I would like to suggest an additional theological reason for the non-exclusive use of the neuter. Speaking of the Holy Spirit in the neuter highlights an element of elusiveness to the mystery of its personhood alluded to some degree in the biblical language itself, which uses images of things such as wind, breath, fire, power, and water to speak about the Spirit's activity.

---

4. While I certainly do not have all the answers on this issue, I confess trepidation with the use of feminine pronouns for the Spirit. While the feminist critique against the univocal use of male language for God (God = male) is correct, I fear that the attempt to bring balance into God-talk by introducing female pronouns for the Holy Spirit can lead to the logical introduction of a female principle in God. This move creates a certain male-female duality in God that creates problems for the church's Trinitarian monotheism. Such a move is also likely to make too much of gender in God-talk (hyper-genderization), which defeats the purpose of the original feminist critique against the univocal use of language for God in the first place.

Moreover, unlike the Son who is incarnate and relates to God as his Father in the biblical narrative, the Holy Spirit has no visible face of its own and no filial relation to God as Father. The Spirit is neither Father nor Son, but the one in whom Father and Son relate to one another and to us. As Augustine once noted, the Spirit appears to be a certain bond of communion between the Father and the Son. Apart from the Father and the Son, it is hard to ascertain who the Spirit is for us. Yet the Spirit's modesty does not take away from its important role in the life of Christ and Christians. The Spirit indwells, leads, and empowers the incarnate Son in his redemptive mission as the breath of God who accompanies the Word in the creation of the world. As an audible wind blows where it chooses while hiding from us its origin, so the Creator Spirit freely gives us the breath of life in our mothers' wombs, imparts to us rebirth to new life in Christ through the waters of baptism and the Word, and as the purifying fire of God's love shapes our lives of witness, prayer, and holiness in the world.

Yet for all of the Spirit's concrete descents or comings, and even as the closest point of contact between the other divine persons and us, there is still a certain anonymity to the Spirit of God's dwelling in Christ and his saints. Even though the Spirit inhabits and sanctifies the saints, it does not come to us "in the flesh" in the same way the Son of God dwelt among us. The Spirit is faceless in that it does not draw undue attention to itself, but rather points us to Christ and the neighbor. There is, in other words, a certain "it-ness," a self-effacing character to the Spirit's person and works, even if the Spirit also takes on a sort of "subtle corporeality" for us—a material, sacramental, or incarnational quality because of its close association with the incarnate Word.[5]

The Spirit's paradoxical closeness in hiddenness escapes us and grasps us at once. In all this, the person of the Holy Spirit remains quite active, but takes a behind-the-scenes persona, pointing us to another, namely, to Christ, and through Christ to the Father in prayer and the neighbor in service. As a provisional theological strategy, therefore, the non-exclusive use of the neuter to refer to the Spirit throughout parts of this work can bring out some of these aforementioned dimensions that make the third person unique in its distinction from and relation to the Father and the Son.

    Leopoldo Antonio Sánchez Merino
    St. Louis, Missouri

---

5. On the self-effacing character of the Spirit, see Sánchez, "Pneumatology," 122–24; for the expression "subtle corporeality," see Congar, *Holy Spirit*, 1:3; on the materiality of the Spirit's sanctifying presence in the saints through Word and sacrament, see Sánchez, "Life in the Spirit of Christ," 7–11.

Acknowledgments

THIS WORK IS AN expanded revision of my doctoral dissertation, which I completed in the spring of 2003. Since then, I have conducted doctoral seminars, offered workshops to pastors and laity, and written articles in the field of Spirit Christology. Over the years, a number of my graduate students have begun to test the usefulness of the framework I lay out in this work for reflection on the Trinity, ethics and mission, spiritual warfare, the theology of the Word, and preaching. Their creative use of Spirit Christology and the growth of my own ideas over time on the topic have encouraged me to update and publish my research.

Three additional essays that I published after the original dissertation have been included in the current revision. The last section of chapter 6 represents my latest thinking and proposal on the complementarity of Logos and Spirit Christologies. The last two chapters represent proposals for using Spirit Christology as a critical framework for promoting a robust theology of prayer (chapter 8) and sanctification (chapter 9). Many thanks to the editors of the *Concordia Journal* (chapter 8), the Luther Academy and its journal *LOGIA* (last section of chapter 6 and chapter 9), and *Word & World* (chapter 7) for allowing me to include slightly revised versions of these previously published essays.

I am indebted to the Graduate School of Concordia Seminary for providing me with an Anonymous Scholarship and an Overseas Study Grant during my last years of doctoral work. The latter stipend allowed me to pursue dissertation research at the Gregorian University in Rome, where I engaged in consultations with Drs. Philip J. Rosato, Luis F. Ladaria, and John J. O'Donnell. I wish to thank these Roman Catholic scholars for their ecumenical spirit, theological insights, and advice. At various stages of my argument, I acknowledge Ladaria's influence in my initial thinking on the complementarity of Logos and Spirit Christologies. The reader will note that one of the contributions of the present work is its ecumenical engagement with literature on Spirit Christology from the East and the West, including works from the Roman Catholic Spanish-speaking theological world.

During my doctoral studies, I benefited much from my involvement with The Hispanic Theological Initiative (currently HTI Consortium), a program of The Pew Charitable Trusts for advancing theological reflection from a Hispanic perspective. I thank HTI directors Zaida Maldonado Pérez and Joanne Rodríguez for their support during my years in the program. Through generous Doctoral, Special Mentoring, and Dissertation Year grants, writing workshops, and other networking opportunities, HTI facilitated my growth as a Latino theologian and strengthened my commitment to our communities. I am appreciative of my HTI mentor, Dr. Samuel Solivan, with whom I had the honor to work as a teaching assistant for a pneumatology course during the 2000 Hispanic Summer Program at Princeton Theological Seminary, learning from his experiences as educator, pastor, and theologian. Our relationship resulted in Dr. Solivan's gracious participation as a reader for the original dissertation.

Among faculty at Concordia Seminary, I wish to express my gratitude to Dr. Jeffrey Gibbs who served as a dissertation reader, and to Drs. Charles Arand, Paul Raabe, and Robert Kolb for providing comments on earlier drafts. I am also thankful to Drs. James Voelz and Bruce Schuchard, deans of the Graduate School during my years as a student, for their encouragement and collegial assistance. Last but certainly not least, I am deeply thankful to my colleague and friend, Dr. Joel Okamoto, for his service as my dissertation advisor. I count it a blessing to have been his first doctoral advisee and to have been working alongside him for the past ten years with the systematic theology faculty at Concordia Seminary. I thank God for his critical eye, generosity, commitment to this project, passion for theology, love for the church, and influence in my professional and personal growth as a theologian. Given my theological formation, the reader will note that one of the contributions of this work is to offer what is to my knowledge the only major contribution to date written by a Lutheran in the field of Spirit Christology.

About twenty-four years ago I arrived in the United States, leaving my mother Conzuelo, my father Carlos, and my sister Dayana behind in the city of Panama and embarking on a journey that took me to this country. I thank them for teaching me the value of family, solidarity, and service. God used a number of people too high to mention to lead me on a vocational path to a career in the church. Heartfelt gratitude goes to the family of Mr. and Mrs. Larry and Pat Dellamuth. Their unconditional devotion to Jesus Christ and their unassuming service to the church, their families, and their neighbors served as a key witness resulting in my becoming a Lutheran and, later, a seminarian. A most special thanks goes to the family of Mr. and Mrs. Tom and Kathy Von Behren for their love and support in ways too great to describe, but especially for their help in securing a top quality computer and volunteering for babysitting services to enable me to work on and complete the original dissertation in a timely fashion.

To my dear wife Tracy and our precious children Lucas and Ana, I owe a profound debt of gratitude that words can neither repay nor fully express. I am speechless. You give me love and joy that moves me to do meaningful things and serve others. I often reflect on and attempt to imagine the Spirit's role in Jesus' life and mission, but at home I see with my own eyes in all three of you the gifts of the Spirit of Christ. Through you, as the members of Christ's body closest to me, I approximate the mystery of Christ, God's faithful Son and suffering Servant. And I smile and say to myself, "God is love."

Abbreviations

ANF *The Ante-Nicene Fathers: Translations of the Fathers down to A.D. 325*. Edited by Alexander Roberts and James Donaldson. 10 vols. Peabody, MA: Hendrickson, 1994.

BC *The Book of Concord: The Confessions of the Evangelical Lutheran Church*. Edited by Robert Kolb and Timothy J. Wengert. Minneapolis: Fortress, 2000.

    CA The Augsburg Confession (Confessio Augustana)

    Ap Apology of the Augsburg Confession

    SA Smalcald Articles

    SC Luther's Small Catechism

    LC Luther's Large Catechism

    FC Formula of Concord

    SD Solid Declaration of the Formula of Concord

LCC *The Library of Christian Classics*. Edited by John Baillie, John T. McNeill, and Henry P. Van Dusen. 26 vols. Philadelphia: Westminster, 1953–66.

LW *Luther's Works*. American edition. Edited by Jaroslav Pelikan and Helmut T. Lehmann. 55 vols. Philadelphia: Muhlenberg and Fortress Press, St. Louis: Concordia, 1955–86.

NPNF *The Nicene and Post-Nicene Fathers*. Edited by Philip Schaff. 28 vols. in two series. 1886–90; reprint, Grand Rapids: Eerdmans, 1983–87.

ST Thomas Aquinas, *Summa Theologiae: Latin Text and English Translation, Introductions, Notes, Appendices, Glosaries*. Translated by the Fathers of the English Dominican Province. 61 vols. London: Blackfriars, New York: McGraw-Hill, 1964–1980.

TDNT *Theological Dictionary of the New Testament*. Edited by Gerhard Kittel and G. Friedrich. Translated by Geoffrey W. Bromiley. 10 vols. Grand Rapids: Eerdmans, 1964–76.

Introduction

"SPIRIT CHRISTOLOGY" IS A term with many meanings. Teachings about "Spirit" (Gk. *pneuma*, Lat. *spiritus*) have informed both orthodox and heterodox views of Jesus. An ante-Nicene type identifies Spirit as the divine principle in Christ or the name of the preexistent Logos.[6] There are also early adoptionist narratives that speak of the Spirit's presence in the man Jesus, while denying his divine preexistence.[7] Broadly speaking, we may call the aforementioned attempts pre-Chalcedonian types of Spirit Christology. Some recent proposals substitute a Spirit Christology for the Logos Christology of the church Councils by arguing for Jesus' divinity on the basis of his unique possession of Spirit, revisiting the question of his personal identity as the Logos.[8] In these post-Chalcedonian (and post-Trinitarian) proposals, the term "Spirit"—like "Logos" or "Wisdom"—functions merely as one of many possible biblical "metaphors" or "symbols" for describing in general terms God's presence in the world or in his creatures.[9]

My approach to Spirit-Christology is Nicene and Chalcedonian. It assumes a theological understanding of Spirit as an agent and person in its own right, distinct from and related to the Father from whom it principally proceeds, and to the Son upon whom it rests and through whom it is given. Within this Trinitarian framework, we can further speak of a twofold

---

6. A classic study is Simonetti, "Note di cristologia pneumatica," 201–32.

7. Rosato, "Spirit-Christology," 429–38; see also Pannenberg, *Jesus—God and Man*, 116–23.

8. Lampe, "Holy Spirit and the Person of Christ," 111–30, later expanded in *God as Spirit*; Haight, "Case for Spirit Christology," 257–87, and his subsequent treatment in *Jesus—Symbol of God*.

9. Lampe, *God as Spirit*, 37, 115–16; and Haight, "Case for Spirit Christology," 257, 267–68; Schoonenberg's approach to the presence of the Logos and the Spirit in Jesus' "human reality" assumes a similar position, but allows for a bit more differentiation between these modes of presence. Schoonenberg, "Spirit Christology and Logos Christology," 360–75.

self-differentiation in God's self-giving to the humanity of Christ in the person of the Son *and* in the person of the Holy Spirit. The former narrative yields a Logos Christology, which speaks of the Son as the Word (Logos) made flesh; the latter, a Spirit-oriented one, which speaks of the Son as the receiver, bearer, and giver of the Spirit. Even though I see both christological orientations as distinct but complementary aspects that draw us closer to the one and same Jesus Christ, the history of theological reflection on Christ shows a partial eclipse of the pneumatic dimensions of his life and mission. At times, the tradition also shows promising ways of bringing out the Spirit's role in Christology. My proposal shows that a revitalization of these pneumatic aspects is crucial to recover the economic dimensions of Jesus' identity for the sake of fostering rich reflection on Christology, soteriology, Trinitarian theology, and themes in the Christian life such as proclamation, prayer, and sanctification.

Against the Arian problem, Logos Christology in Nicene key defends the unity Jesus and God the Father, confessing the Son's divine consubstantiality (*homoousios*) with the Father. Against Nestorian and Eutychian Christologies, Chalcedonian Logos Christology safeguards the personal or hypostatic unity of the Son against attempts at dividing or confusing his divine and human natures. The ontology of the Logos-oriented approach stresses the "static" and "individual" dimensions of Jesus' identity both as eternal and incarnate Son, that is, his "being-from-before" and his "being-in-himself." As an approach "from above," according to which a person's existence is established before his acts in history (Lat. *ordo essendi*), Logos Christology proceeds from the Son's eternal and divine preexistence to his assumption of a human nature at the hypostatic union. It argues that the divine Logos assumes a human nature and, therefore, the Logos is none other than the man Jesus. Methodologically, a Logos Christology argues that Jesus saves us *because* he is God, thereby establishing who Jesus *is* ontologically before moving on to what he does for us and for our salvation.

A study of God's self-giving to the humanity of the Son in the Spirit, as I articulate it, invigorates and complements—and, therefore, does not replace—Logos Christology by reflecting on the broader soteriological, Trinitarian, and ecclesial implications of the incarnation. As an approach "from below," a Spirit Christology proceeds from a consideration of Jesus' relation to his Father and works for us as faithful Son and suffering Servant in the economy of salvation—namely, his life and mission in the Spirit—to an affirmation of his lordship and divinity in light of the paschal mystery. In view of the glorified Son's sending of the Spirit to us, a Spirit Christology argues that the man Jesus, the receiver and bearer of the Spirit, is none other than the Logos. As an approach "from below," according to which a reality is confessed on the basis of our knowledge of it (Lat. *ordo cognoscendi*), a Spirit Christology shows that Jesus is Lord and God *because* he saves us, thus revealing who the Son is on the basis of what he *does*.

An outline of my proposal follows. In chapter 1, I argue that the pneumatic dimensions of Jesus' identity suffered a partial eclipse in the history of dogma due to the church's apologetic interest in preserving Logos-oriented approaches against heterodox groups. Using Jesus' baptism as a locus for assessing heterodox views of his relationship to God's Spirit, I show the influential character of orthodox responses to the heterodox prior to the Council of Constantinople (AD 381) in the church's partial relativization of the pneumatic aspects of Christology. Reaction to the adoptionist principle in Jewish, Gnostic, and Arian views of Christ led early church fathers to defend his divine preexistence and incarnation to the extent that in some cases the Spirit's descent on Christ became only revelatory or exemplary *for others* but not constitutive *for himself*. I also show that some of these responses offer promising insights in the early Christian tradition that can deal positively with the Spirit's role in the life of Christ and his saints. I focus on views of the anointing of Jesus by Justin Martyr, Irenaeus, and Athanasius, looking for the eclipse and promise of a Spirit Christology in their insights.

Under the rubrics of Jesus as receiver and bearer of God's Spirit, chapter 2 assesses critically three classic Logos-oriented readings of main events in Jesus' life and mission (i.e., conception, anointing, and exaltation) and argues for the need to recover the Spirit-oriented dimensions of such events on biblical and Trinitarian grounds. A proposed pneumatic reading of events in Jesus' life then serves as a biblical springboard to describe systematically the major issues any Nicene and Chalcedonian Spirit-oriented Christology must deal with in order to function adequately as a complement to, rather than a replacement for, the classic Logos Christology of the ecumenical Councils. All these issues arise from a consideration of the nature and purpose of the Holy Spirit's presence in the Logos, and the christological, Trinitarian, and soteriological implications that follow from such a pneumatic presence. The chapter serves as a preliminary look into the potential complementarity of Logos and Spirit Christologies.

Logos-oriented readings of the life of Christ tend to see events in Jesus' life and mission as revelatory, confirming, declarative, or proclamatory of either his prior identity as God from eternity or his possession of the Spirit as God-man from the first moment of the incarnation. In the case of Jesus' baptism, the Jordan event can also be seen as exemplary of Christian baptism for the church. Either way, the focus is on what the events reveal about the Son's *prior* identity or about *us*, but not on what the events mean for the Son *himself* either in his humanity or in his person. All such readings highlight the prominent place of the Logos as the subject of acts in and through his assumed and sanctified humanity from the first moment of the hypostatic union.

A Spirit-oriented Christology reads events in Jesus' life and mission as special instances of the Father's sending of his Spirit upon his incarnate Son in the economy of salvation. A pneumatic reading of the story of Jesus highlights the dynamic presence of the Spirit as an agent in its own right in the humanity of the Son throughout his life and work as obedient Son, suffering Servant, and risen Lord. Such a Spirit-oriented reading establishes an economic-Trinitarian ground for Christology and soteriology, as well as a christological ground for the Christian's participation by grace in the Spirit, who is given to us by the Father through Christ. A Spirit Christology also underscores the place of the Father as principal source of the Spirit given to his incarnate Son, an insight that does not receive due attention in a Logos-oriented reading.

Whereas chapter 2 deals with the contributions of a Spirit Christology for reflecting on the mystery of the incarnation, chapter 3 focuses on its contributions for our understanding of the paschal mystery and atonement theories. In chapter 3, I show how a Spirit Christology centered in the paschal mystery offers a strong biblical basis and economic trajectory for grounding human reception of the Spirit in Christ's identity as receiver, bearer, and giver of the Spirit. I also test the usefulness of a Spirit Christology as a lens to assess and strengthen three Logos-oriented readings of the atonement associated with Anselm (Latin), Abelard (subjective), and Aulén (classic). Logos-oriented readings of atonement theories work within the framework of Christ's inner constitution as divine and human, and therefore tend to contrast the theories in terms of how much weight they give to the divine or human element in salvation to the point that it is hard to conceive their integration. A Spirit Christology focuses on how the Spirit of the Father is involved in all dimensions of the Son's identity and work as vicar (Anselm), victor (Aulén), and example (Abelard). By doing so, my proposal sets the stage for integrating various salutary insights of each atonement narrative into a broader economic-Trinitarian account of Christ's identity as receiver, bearer, and giver of the Spirit.

In the next two chapters, I demonstrate how the joint mission of the incarnate Son and the Holy Spirit in God's economy of salvation provides a fruitful ground for reflection on Trinitarian theology. In chapter 4, I argue for the defining place pneumatology plays in assessing the nature and implications of the incarnation, seen both as hypostatic union and as the entire life and mission of Christ (incarnating), for reflection on the economic and the immanent Trinity. Using Rahner's axiom ("the economic Trinity is the immanent Trinity, and viceversa") as a point of departure for establishing the proper work (Lat. *proprium*) of the person of the Holy Spirit, I propose a way of speaking about the Spirit's sanctification of the Logos's humanity from conception and its continuous indwelling in all fullness in the same humanity, while preserving the logical priority of the Son's hypostatic union over his sanctification. There is a reciprocal relationship between the Son and Holy Spirit in the mystery of the incarnation. The Spirit indwells and sanctifies the humanity that the Logos alone assumes and acts through in or by the same Spirit. Yet the notion of reciprocity in this joint mission deserves qualification so that the economic priority of the hypostatic union is established vis-à-vis the Spirit's indwelling of the Son's assumed humanity. A Spirit Christology that functions as a complement to Logos Christology is sensitive to the issue of priority in the missions of the Son and the Spirit, particularly to avoid adoptionism or the logic that a Spirit-indwelt Jesus is united to God on the basis of his prior holiness.

In chapter 5, I employ a Spirit Christology to assess the Trinitarian concepts of person and relation (especially as these apply to the Son), the relationship between the social (or perichoretic) *and* processional character of personal relations among the divine persons, and models of the immanent Trinity. What emerges is my proposal for an *in spiritu* model of the Trinity. Such a model highlights the person of the Son's eternal existence "in the Spirit" before his Father in the inner-life of the Trinity and for us in the economy of salvation. It also leads us to a conception of the Son as one upon whom the Spirit of the Father rests, and thus as one who is begotten of the Father "in the Spirit." While this model yields a social or perichoretic view of Trinitarian relations, it does so without harming the Logos-oriented *filioque* and *per filium* models of the Trinity, which defend the logical priority of the Son over the Holy Spirit in the immanent order of Trinitarian processions.

The complementarity of Logos and Spirit Christologies receives due attention in chapter 6. I offer four proposals towards a systematic synthesis of approaches, highlighting the fourth one in particular as a Lutheran contribution to the discussion. Such proposals may be described under the following categories: 1) the Trinitarian distinction and relation between the personal or hypostatic "identity" of Jesus and the Logos, and the personal "non-identity" between Jesus and the Holy Spirit, 2) the philosophico-theological distinction and relation between the order of knowledge (*ordo cognoscendi*) and the order of being (*ordo essendi*), 3) the conciliar distinction and relation between the human and divine wills and operations in the person of Jesus Christ, and 4) the proposal for a *genus pneumatikon* or *genus habitualis* in Lutheran Christology, namely, the inclusion of a way of speaking about the incarnation from a pneumatological perspective in the context of a two-natures Logos Christology.

The fourth approach highlights the ecumenical promise of a Christology that could bridge the gap between Eastern-Alexandrian and Western-scholastic approaches to the mystery of Christ.

As an initial attempt to move from a pneumatological Christology to the broad field of christological pneumatology, the final three chapters test the usefulness of my thesis for promoting three Christian practices or ways of life—namely, proclamation, prayer, and sanctification. These chapters develop the argument that the Christian's life in the Spirit is shaped after or takes the form of Christ's own life in the Spirit, allowing us to explore the pneumatological continuity between the mystery of the Christ and his church. Interacting with the work of Lutheran theologian Gerhard Forde's thesis on the function of systematic theology to promote proclamation, chapter 7 proposes that the telling of the story of Jesus in word and sacrament from a pneumatological perspective fosters the present-day Spirit-led plunging of hearers into the anointing, death, and resurrection of Jesus. I show that a Chalcedonian Spirit Christology is better suited than a Logos Christology alone or a post-Chalcedonian (post-Trinitarian) Spirit Christology to incorporate hearers into the mysteries of Jesus' life in such a way that they are continually convicted of their sins against Jesus (law) in order to be liberated from them through the forgiveness of sins and the promise of the final resurrection in him (gospel). It is through conviction, forgiveness, and hope that the Holy Spirit addresses us today in order to shape and incorporate our life-stories into Jesus' own life-story. Since the Spirit makes us participants of this story by killing and making alive, through our dying and being raised with Christ, we may aptly describe such life in the Spirit as a cruciform or cross-shaped life.

In chapter 8, I explore the potential benefits of Spirit Christology as a critical tool for assessing and developing a solid Trinitarian basis for a theology of prayer.[10] I do so by entering the contemporary debate on the God-world relation between classical and open theists, particularly among Evangelicals in the English-speaking world. Engaging in a critical analysis of Thomas Aquinas's Logos-oriented approach to the nature and purpose of Christ's prayer, in which prayer is basically revelatory of his divinity or an example to the church, I move on to propose a theology of prayer that is grounded in the church's participation by grace in the sonship or filiation of Christ and thus in his prayer life in the Spirit. Prayer is then seen less in a substantialist framework that defends either God's necessary transcendence (classical theism) or immanence (open theism) as the ultimate theological

---

10. For an expanded Spanish version of this chapter, see Sánchez, *Teología de la santificación*, 185–220.

principle, and more in personalist terms as the adopted sons' relationship and access to their Father in the Spirit of the Son. The church's prayer in the Spirit of the Son is best seen as a divine gift, in terms of filial trust, and as a hopeful eschatological cry for the life of the world to come.

The last chapter looks at the implications of a Spirit Christology for sketching a theology of sanctification. It does so by arguing that a pneumatology in Nicene key, whose focus lies in the works of the Spirit in creation, through Christ in the flesh, through word and sacrament, and through the saints, lays the groundwork for a material and embodied account of the Spirit. Otherwise stated, by making Christ the privileged locus of the Spirit, a Spirit Christology offers an incarnational and sacramental view of life in the Spirit. In dialogue with the Western Lutheran tradition, three models of life in the Spirit of Christ are laid out—namely, baptismal, dramatic, and eucharistic models of sanctification. This section of the work is the least apologetic of all the chapters dealing with the Christian life. Its intent is not to complement a Logos-oriented reading of the Christian life with a Spirit-oriented reading per se, but simply to illustrate the possibilities of using a Spirit Christology as a lens to enrich reflection on yet another theme in Christian theology. In particular, the reader will note how the Lutheran historic emphasis on God's justification of humans by faith in Christ does not have to take away from a robust theology of sanctification or holiness.

1

The Eclipse and Promise of Spirit-Oriented Christologies

Early Church Responses to Heterodox Views of Jesus' Anointing

IN THIS CHAPTER, I show how three classic orthodox reactions to heterodox views of the baptism of Jesus paved the way for church theologians to defend his divine preexistence and incarnation to the extent that in some cases the place of the Spirit of God in his human life and mission became only revelatory *for others* but not constitutive *for himself*. These responses represent foundational arguments for, and at times influential instances of, a broader problem in the history of dogma, namely, the partial but significant eclipse of the pneumatological (and thus economic-Trinitarian) dimensions of Christology. In some cases, however, these responses also offer promising insights towards an inclusion of the Spirit in the mystery of Christ.

In his treatise on the baptism of Christ, Cantalamesa argues that the rise of Gnostic, Arian, and "adoptionist" (more specifically, Samosatenian) views of the relationship between Jesus and the Holy Spirit contributed to a weakening of the pneumatic aspects of Christology.[1] His comments serve as an instructive guide and point of departure to pursue the causes for the partial eclipse of Spirit-oriented Christology in the early church:

> In the Gnostic view, Jesus was one person and the Christ another: Jesus denoted the man born of Mary, whereas Christ denoted

1. Cantalamessa, *The Holy Spirit in the Life of Jesus*, 7.

the deity that descended on Jesus at the moment of baptism. Thus the baptism came to negate the reality of the incarnation and this could not but give rise to a strong reaction on the part of the Church. Other heresies came later to reinforce the reasons for "discrediting" the baptism of Jesus: Arianism used Jesus' baptism as a pretext for asserting that if any change occurred in Jesus at the moment of baptism, this meant that he was subject to change and therefore not a changeless God like the Father; the adoptionism of Paul of Samosata made Christ's actual divinity depend on the coming of the Holy Spirit, as though Jesus were one of the prophets, though certainly the holiest one, in whom the power of God had worked.[2]

At a methodological level, Cantalamesa proposes that Jesus' baptism serves as a fruitful locus to investigate and analyze heterodox views of Jesus Christ's identity and orthodox reactions to the same. Following the lead of this patristic scholar, I elaborate further on Christian responses to a Jewish question, Gnostic views (at times combined with Ebionite elements), and Arian theology.[3] All these responses deal to a significant degree with the issue of the proper use of biblical texts pointing directly or indirectly to the anointing of Christ at the Jordan.

First, I look at the arguments of the Christian philosopher Justin Martyr (ca. 100–ca. 165) in his *Dialogue with Trypho, a Jew*, an apology on the Old Testament's witness to Christ's messiahship and divinity. Second, I study the major extant apologetic work of Irenaeus (ca. 130–ca. 200), bishop of Lyons (beginning ca. 177), namely, his extensive refutation of various Gnostic systems entitled *Against Heresies* (written between ca. 182 and 188). Finally, I deal with one of the most significant and mature works of Athanasius (ca. 296–373), bishop of Alexandria (beginning in 328), namely, his first of four *Discourses Against the Arians* (written between ca. 356 and 360).

The reason for exploring these particular patristic sources lies in the conviction that any proposal for a Spirit-oriented Christology today

---

2. Ibid.

3. González argues that Paul of Samosata (third century) does not hold to an adoptionist position in the strict sense because he affirmed that Jesus is Son of God (although not the Word) from birth. An adoptionist trend surfaces in his teaching that the Word who dwells in and makes Jesus the Son of God at the incarnation represents only the reason, purpose, or power of God but not God as such. Since the substantial identity of the Word and God and the personal identity of the Word and Jesus are severed, Jesus is only a man. Thus there is also a disjunctive principle in Paul's adoptionism. González, *A History of Christian Thought*, 248–51; I do not include Paul in this chapter because his adoptionism seems to focus more on the relation Word-Jesus at conception than on the relation Jesus-Spirit or Son-Spirit at the Jordan.

The Eclipse and Promise of Spirit-Oriented Christologies 3

must learn from history, especially from dangers inherent in adoptionist Christologies. In general terms, adoptionism sees Jesus as a mere man made worthy of sonship and/or elected by God to be his son by the grace or indwelling of the Spirit in him.[4] The problem of Jesus' preexistence and divinity becomes irrelevant, meaningless, or simply denied. Of those mentioned in our study, Trypho, Cerinthus (a Gnostic with Ebionite leanings), and the followers of Arius represent the adoptionist principle in various ways. Indeed, an in-depth examination of post-Niceno-Constantinopolitan adoptionist Christologies in their complete historical development and as a dogmatic problem needs more elaboration and precision than this chapter requires. Such a study would have to include, for example, the problem of Nestorianism[5] and the Spanish adoptionism of the late eighth century.[6]

---

4. "[T]he generalization can be made that this Christology was in effect no Christology at all, but rather a blend of Father theology and Spirit theology to the exclusion of Son theology . . . Emphasis on a strict monotheism on the one hand and on a theology of grace on the other made any assertion about Jesus Christ's unique ontological role in the very nature of God superfluous. Instead, God's absolute transcendence and man's universal participation in grace through the Spirit reduced the Messiah to the model of man's own relationship to God, to the paradigm of man's own adoption as son of God." Rosato, "Spirit-Christology," 435.

5. Adoptionism can relate to so-called "disjunctive" Christologies, which separate the divine and human natures in Christ. After the Council of Ephesus, adoptionist/disjunctive Christologies were suspected of being Mopsuestian or Nestorian. This judgment is clear in Constantinople II (AD 553) and its twelfth sentence or anathema against Theodore's teaching "that the Word of God is one person, but that another person is Christ . . . as a mere man was baptized . . . and obtained by this baptism the grace of the Holy Sprit, and became worthy of Sonship." *The Capitula of the Council* (*NPNF*² 14:315); cf. Pope Vigilius's letter in confirmation of Constantinople II, in which he condemns Theodore for teaching "that it was a mere man who was baptized . . . and that he received through his baptism the grace of the Holy Spirit and merited his adoption." *The Decretal Epistle of Pope Vigilius in Confirmation of the Fifth Ecumenical Council* (*NPNF*² 14:322). The problem of an adoption into sonship lies in the disjunction in the person of Jesus Christ that it either seems to require as its condition or can in effect promote.

6. Beginning with Alcuin, the judgment of the Councils is passed on to the Spanish Elipandus of Toledo and Felix of Urgel, since they had taught that according to his assumed humanity Jesus was the "adoptive" Son of God (especially Elipandus). But Cavadini argues that Alcuin (mis-)interpreted their uniquely Western approach to Christology through Eastern categories (i.e., the Nestorian-Eutychian polarity) foreign to the context in which it arose. He explains that the Spanish teaching on Jesus' "adoptive" sonship as the firstborn *for others* was necessary to ensure *our* participation in the same by grace. The rationale behind this move was the impossibility of humans to share in the divine sonship of Jesus as the only-begotten of the Father, which belongs to him alone and thus cannot be communicated unto others. In summarizing Elipandus's views, Cavadini writes: "There is never, finally, a point at which the Father (e.g.) is said to have 'adopted' the Son or a human nature or a man, etc. The point is much more subtle, namely, that *by assuming* flesh or a body, etc., the Word, the 'Only-begotten' with

Here I am only interested in three early heterodox views of Jesus' reception of the Spirit at his baptism that called forth some alternative explanations from the orthodox for the first time in the history of dogma. I focus on the orthodox responses as such, leaving the issue of their accurate portrayal of the heterodox positions to other scholars. It is the relatively distinct, articulate, and lengthy answers of the orthodox to the controversies at hand that provide hermeneutical building blocks for the church's later judgment on similar issues.

THE JORDAN REVEALS THE SON'S ETERNAL ANOINTING: JUSTIN MARTYR'S ANSWER TO TRYPHO

Justin's *Dialogue with Trypho* is of great significance in the history of dogma for later reflection on Jesus' baptism in the face of threats to his messianic claims and divine preexistence. He gives us a key second-century response to a question concerning the appropriate manner to reconcile belief in Christ's preexistence with his reception of the Spirit's gifts as cited in Isaiah 11:1ff. Concerning Christ, Trypho asks how

> He can be demonstrated to have been pre-existent, who is filled with the powers of the Holy Ghost . . . as if He were in lack of them?[7]

Justin answers that Christ did not need the anointing for himself, but rather was anointed for our knowledge of his messianic or divine power. Indeed, if Jesus is God from eternity and then also from the first moment of birth (as incarnate God), what could he possibly need for himself from the Spirit (even in his humanity) that he does not already have? Instead, Justin focuses on the pretemporal anointing of Christ as God in view of his creation of the world (cosmic anointing) or his messianic fulfillment of the offices of priest, king, and prophet (titular anointing). Divine preexistence and messiahship become intrinsically related realities that converge under Christ's *eternal* anointing as God and are thus grounded in the Logos's eternal divine being from God the Father. Justin's teaching on the cosmic and titular functions of Christ's eternal anointing eclipses in some measure the unique significance

---

regard to nature, becomes the 'First-born' in adoption and grace." Cavadini, *The Last Christology of the West*, 33.

7. Justin, *Dialogue* 87 (*ANF* 1:243); Arians ask the same question in the fourth century, as Cyril of Alexandria notes in the early fifth century: "How then can the Son be of the same substance as the perfect Father since he himself is not perfect and that is why he is anointed?" *Commentary on John* 175 (trans. Maxwell, 78).

of God's historical anointing of Jesus with the Spirit for his messianic mission at the Jordan. As a result, Jesus' baptism mainly reveals *to* or *for others* the saving knowledge of his prior ontological identity as Christ or Messiah (= God). A partial eclipse of the pneumatological dimension of Christology occurs.

Let us look at the development of Justin's arguments more closely. Prior to Trypho's question above, Justin had acknowledged that "some . . . of our race"—very likely some "Christians" of Judaizing persuasion—spoke of Christ as nothing more than a "man of men."[8] Trypho is willing to allow for "this Jesus . . . born man of men" to achieve dignity and honor as Christ, but only by election "on account of having led a life conformed to the law."[9] Yet such a concession assumed a denial of Justin's witness to the fulfillment of the prophecy of Isaiah 7:10ff. in the birth of Christ (= God) from a virgin: "Behold, the virgin shall conceive, and shall bear a son, and they shall call his name Immanuel" (v. 14b). Since Trypho finds the fulfillment of this passage entirely in Hezekiah's birth from "a young woman," he sees the Christian interpretation of the prophecy as "monstrous" and dismisses the virgin birth of Christ (= God) as Greek mythology.[10] Trypho suggests that an adoptionist view of Christ is less offensive than an incarnational view of God. Over against Trypho's conception of the anointing of Jesus as the consequence of his fulfillment of the law, Justin argues that Jesus' anointing is a reference to his divinity.

When Trypho asks for an answer to his seemingly insurmountable question on the way of reconciling Christ's divine preexistence and possession of the Spirit's gifts, he simply assumes—but only for the sake of argument—what Justin defends, namely, that Jesus is the Messiah or Christ and thus the preexistent God made incarnate for us by being born of a virgin. But then Trypho takes Justin to task for affirming at the same time that this Christ, who is God, is also the "rod from the root of Jesse" upon whom the Spirit of the Lord shall rest.[11] Does not the resting of the Spirit and its powers upon Christ imply a necessity or lack unbecoming his nature as preexistent God? Significantly, Justin had previously cited Psalm 45:6ff. to support God's (= the Father's) witness to his incarnate God (= Son or Logos) "as deserving to be worshipped, as God and as Christ."[12] The crucial words

8. Justin, *Dialogue* 48 (*ANF* 1:219).

9. Ibid., 67 (*ANF* 1:231).

10. Ibid. Justin explains the prophecy at length in other chapters (esp. 68, 77, 78, and 84).

11. Ibid., 7 (*ANF* 1:243).

12. Ibid., 63 (*ANF* 1:229); Justin quotes the psalm earlier to show that Christ receives adoration (see ibid., 38 [*ANF* 1:213–14]).

of the psalm in the same manuscript read as follows: "Thy throne, O God, is for ever and ever: a scepter of rectitude is the scepter of Thy kingdom.... [T]herefore God, even Thy God, hath anointed Thee with the oil of gladness above Thy fellows" (vv. 6–7). Herein lies the key text Justin uses to link the language of anointing to Christ's divine dignity. Thus the incarnate Christ, who is born from or begotten through Mary's womb in history by the Father's will or intention, receives our adoration because of his being "from above" or preincarnational anointing as Christ (= God) from the Father.[13] For Justin, the Son or Word

> who also was with Him [i.e., the Father] and was begotten before the works . . . is called Christ, in reference to His being anointed and God's ordering all things through Him.[14]

Thus Justin argues that the Father anoints the Son in eternity as God with a view towards the creation of the world (cosmic anointing). What happens in time has its ground in a pretemporal unction. Justin also returns to Psalm 45:7b to point out that "all kings and anointed persons obtained from Him [i.e., Christ] their share in the names of kings and anointed: just as He himself received from the Father the titles King, and Christ, and Priest, and Angel [= Prophet]."[15] Justin interprets the idea that God anointed Christ "above" his fellows in the sense that Christ's preincarnational status as King and Christ (= Anointed One) already set him "above" kings and anointed people of the Old Testament who shared in his unique unction from God. What takes place in time in the Old Testament has its ground in a pretemporal anointing of Christ into various offices, names, or titles. The author has ascribed to Christ divine preexistence and, closely linked with such pretemporal dignity, his unparalleled reception of God's anointing into

---

13. Ibid. Quoting Psalm 110:3-4 as a prophecy of the nocturnal virgin birth of the preexistent Christ by the Father's will, Justin writes, "And then, what is said by David, 'In the splendours of Thy holiness have I begotten Thee from the womb, before the morning star . . . Thou art a Priest for ever, after the order of Melchizedek,'—does this not declare to you that [He was] from of old [or, in Greek, 'from above'], and that the God and Father of all things intended Him to be begotten by a human womb?" See also Justin's similar use of Psalm 72:5, 17: "And David predicted that He would be born from the womb before sun and moon, according to the Father's will, and made Him known, being Christ, as God strong and to be worshipped." Ibid., 76 (*ANF* 1:236); for my parenthetical use of the Greek phrase "from above" (instead of the Latin "from of old") in *Dialogue* 63, and for a study of the texts cited above, see Orbe, *La unción del Verbo*, 22–29.

14. Justin, *Second Apology* 6 (*ANF* 1:190); on the cosmic anointing, see Orbe, *La unción*, 61–72.

15. *Dialogue* 86 (*ANF* 1:242); "Angel" is synonymous with prophet and apostle. See ibid., 75 (*ANF* 1:236).

The Eclipse and Promise of Spirit-Oriented Christologies

all titles—e.g., King, Priest, and Angel (= Prophet or Apostle). He has also ascribed to Christ the subsequent dispensing of his anointing from God to others such as kings, priests, and prophets in the Old Testament church (titular anointing). It is crucial to remember that, for Justin, all these types are not simply fulfilled later in the incarnate Christ (although this is true), but already derive before time from the preexistent Christ due to his eternal anointing as God (= Messiah) by God the Father.[16]

Let us return to Trypho's question: If Christ fulfilled the prophecy of Isaiah 11:1ff., he must be the messianic receiver and bearer of the Spirit of God in history, namely, the one on whom the Spirit will rest and who will be filled with the Spirit's powers. But then Christ cannot be God, for the descent of the Spirit upon him—that which can make him the Christ by election—belongs only to the world of humanity. Receiving and bearing the Spirit of God may make a great "man born of men," but is still unbecoming the nature of God. So goes Trypho's implicit argument in his question to Justin, leaving the Christian philosopher with the task of reconciling his belief in Christ's divine dignity with his identity as receiver and bearer of the Spirit of God in history.

Justin held that the "powers of the Spirit" do not supply a need in Christ. To say that they do would suggest that Christ as preexistent God lacked something. Instead, our author affirms that these powers "find their accomplishment in Him [i.e., Christ]" as the fulfillment of all the Old Testament prophets who only received the Spirit's powers in piecemeal fashion.[17] After John the Baptist, the last Old Testament and Jewish prophet, the Spirit's prophetical gifts now come to rest in Christ "so that there would be no more prophets in your nation."[18] Yet Christ is also the one in whom the prophetic Spirit rested or "ceased" as his definitive bearer, so that—under the new dispensation—he may be the giver of the Spirit's gifts to the worthy after his ascension (Ps 68:18 and Joel 2:28–29).[19] Even though Justin does not explicitly mention Psalm 45:7b at this point in the argument, he clearly extends his previous thoughts on God's eternal anointing of Christ "above" his fellows to the title of prophet and the gifts of prophecy. These title and gifts find their historical fulfillment in the incarnate Christ from whom New Testament believers in turn receive the "prophetical gifts" that Jews once

16. Orbe, *La unción*, 61.

17. *Dialogue* 87 (*ANF* 1:243).

18. Justin speaks of the Baptist as "a prophet among your nation; after whom no other prophet appeared among you." Ibid., 49 (*ANF* 1:218); Justin also writes, "[T]he powers enumerated by Isaiah would not come upon Him [i.e., Christ], not because He needed power, but because these would not continue after Him." Ibid., 88 (*ANF* 1:243).

19. Ibid., 87 (*ANF* 1:243); cf. Eph 4:8 and Acts 2:17–18.

possessed.[20] In short, Christ receives and bears the Spirit of God (with all its powers) who once rested among the anointed ones of the Old Testament. Consequently, Christ has the Spirit in order to impart in the new messianic era inaugurated by him "the grace of His Spirit's power . . . to those who believe in Him, according as He deems each man worthy thereof."[21]

If the incarnate Christ-God imparts his Spirit and accompanying gifts after his ascension, then, when does he receive the fullness of the Spirit of God, along with its powers, to do so? Not at the Jordan, "for even at His birth He was in possession of His power," as the worship of the Christ-God child by the Magi illustrates (see Micah 5:2 and Matt 2:11).[22] Only after Justin has placed the full reception of Christ's "power" at the moment of his virgin birth (because of his preincarnational anointing as God) does the apologist speak of the Holy Spirit's descent upon Christ "when He came out of the water."[23] Since Christ has the fullness of power already from birth (as the Magi's worship of the Christ child proves), his possession of the Spirit and its powers at the Jordan seems superfluous.

Christ did not need baptism or the Spirit's anointing for himself (or his own preexistent person) but for the sake of humanity's sin inherited from Adam. The Spirit's descent upon this otherwise humble son of Joseph serves as "proof" to others that he is their saving Messiah (= God).[24] When Christ went into the Jordan "a fire was kindled in the Jordan," and when he came out of the river "the Holy Ghost lighted on Him like a dove."[25] Above all, such expressions underscore the epiphanic or revelatory character of the Jordan event for the sake of the race of Adam.

Is the descent of the Spirit of God upon Christ only a sign or epiphany *for others* or is it in some way constitutive for Christ *himself*? At first, when Justin refers to the Jordan event as a new generation or birth of Christ for

---

20. Justin tells Trypho that "[the gifts] formerly among your nation have been transferred to us." *Dialogue* 82 (*ANF* 1:240); "Now, it is possible to see amongst us women and men who possess gifts of the Spirit of God." Ibid., 88 (*ANF* 1:243).

21. Ibid., 87 (*ANF* 1:243).

22. Ibid., 88 (*ANF* 1:243). Thus the Magi's worship of the child proves his divinity; Justin also refers to the Magi to buttress his argument in favor of a fulfillment of Isaiah 7:10ff. in the virgin birth of Christ, the preexistent God. Ibid., 78 (*ANF* 1:237–38).

23. Ibid.

24. Ibid., 88 (*ANF* 1:243–44); similarly, Justin argues that it was not Jesus' riding into Jerusalem on a donkey (see Zech 9:9) "that empowered Him to be Christ, but it furnished men with a proof that He is the Christ" (ibid. [*ANF* 1:243]; cf. ibid., 53 [*ANF* 1:222]).

25. Ibid., 88 (*ANF* 1:243); cf. Justin's reference to the manifestation or epiphany of Christ in the Old Testament as "the glory of fire" in the burning bush (ibid. [*ANF* 1:128, 264]).

the sake of humans (by appropriating the language of Ps 2:7 or the variant reading of Luke 3:22b), he seems to have in mind only that "time when they [i.e., humans] would become acquainted with him."[26] As Kilian McDonnell notes, in this case "to be known is to be born."[27] Jesus' baptism confirms for others what he has always been, namely, the Christ (and thus God, for the Magi worship him from birth), but does not appear to affect Christ himself even in his humanity. Should we qualify this judgment? Unlike McDonnell, Antonio Orbe argues that the anointing of Jesus at Jordan is not just a "sign" for others of a prior reality, but is actually "real" in a salvific sense because at that time (and not before) Christ receives the Spirit "in his humanity" for the sake of the church.[28] Since Christ is already anointed as God before time, he does not need to receive the Spirit for himself once again as God. This much is clear. However, Orbe argues that, according to Justin, Christ as man does receive the Spirit for others so that the church, the race of Adam, can share in his anointing and receive the Spirit of adoption. Thus far Orbe. A few reflections are in order.

Orbe correctly notes that Justin does not conceive of the incarnation as the preexistent Logos's anointing of his assumed humanity with his own divinity (as some later church fathers do).[29] In other words, he does not use anointing as a metaphor for the work of the Logos in the incarnation or hypostatic union. However, do Justin's apologies show any concern for speaking of an anointing of Jesus by God the Father with or in the Spirit from birth? Perhaps the most one could say, as McDonnell argues, is that Justin's reference to Christ's possession of his "power" from birth points to the fact that "he possessed the Spirit and the gifts of the Spirit since his birth."[30] If this is the case, then, the anointing at the Jordan becomes relativized by the emphasis on Jesus' prior possession of the Spirit from the first moment of his human existence.

However, some elements in Justin's theology make a final decision on McDonnell's judgment more elusive. Above all, for Justin, God's anointing of the Son is an eternal or pretemporal reality. From this angle, Justin's reference to the child's possession of all his "power" from birth appears to point more to the incarnation as an epiphany of his preincarnational anointing and dignity as preexistent Christ-God (as revealed *to* and *for others* in the

26. Ibid., 88 (*ANF* 1:244).

27. "When he is recognized by us as the Son of God, at that moment he . . . is born Son of God for us, for the Church. To be known is to be born." McDonnell, *The Baptism of Jesus at the Jordan*, 92–93 (cf. 111–13).

28. Orbe, *La unción*, 40–43, 634–36.

29. Ibid., 635.

30. See McDonnell, *The Baptism of Jesus at the Jordan*, 24.

Magi's act of worship) than to a total reception and bearing of the Spirit and its gifts *in his humanity* from birth. Moreover, in an allusion to Luke 1:35, Justin interprets the Holy Spirit and the "power" of God as a reference to the preexistent Word, who coming upon and overshadowing Mary "caused her to conceive, not by intercourse, but by power."[31] This means that the "power" Jesus has from birth does not appear to be the Holy Spirit and its gifts as much as the divinity and/or divine attributes of the Logos. We may recall that, in view of Trypho's adoptionist proposal, Justin argues for the virgin birth to protect Christ's divine preexistence and not really to make a point about the Holy Spirit's role in his humanity from the moment of the incarnation.

The crucial questions are: Did Justin feel that Christ's preexistence could only be safeguarded by making the Spirit's descent upon him at the Jordan *revelatory* for others (McDonnell)? Or is such a descent *constitutive* for Christ in his own humanity in view of his giving of the Spirit to the race of Adam (Orbe)? Or both? On the one hand, Justin speaks of the Jordan event as "proof" of Jesus' identity as the Christ. As we have seen, for Justin, the title "Christ," immediately points to his anointing as preexistent God before time in view of the world's creation. Furthermore, Justin states that the baptism points to Jesus' generation at the river for us insofar as *we* "become acquainted with Him." Here the language does not really make clear that *Christ* himself is reborn "in his humanity" (as Orbe says) for us or as head of the church in the Jordan, although the idea of his dispensing of the Spirit's gifts to those who believe in him after his ascension seems to presuppose this prior reception and bearing of the Spirit. A difficulty, however, arises if we consider that Christ as God already has the anointing of the Father from eternity. Strictly speaking, one could conclude that, upon his ascension, Christ gave the Spirit to the church acting as preexistent God, but not necessarily as the one who receives and bears the Spirit in his humanity for the sake of humanity. If so the baptism at the Jordan becomes only a sign to us that Jesus is the eternal Christ-God without showing that he actually received the Spirit and its gifts for himself in the flesh in order to give the Spirit to the church. If this is the case, then, even if we disagree with McDonnell on whether Justin taught or not Jesus' possession of the Spirit from birth, we can still agree with his judgment that Jesus' "birth" for us at the Jordan does not point to his messianic identity and anointing with the Spirit as much as to the church's knowledge of him as God.

On the other hand, even if the title Christ (and thus the idea of messiahship) has its roots in an eternal reality (anointing), we must also admit

---

31. Justin, *First Apology* 33 (*ANF* 1:174).

that this preincarnational unction always occurs in view of the Father's future ordering (anointing) of the world through the creative Word.³² As Orbe suggests, then, the anointing of Jesus at the Jordan may also be seen as analogous in the order of grace to the cosmic anointing of the Word in the order of nature.³³ In other words, the cosmic anointing, the titular anointing, and the church's anointing find their eternal ground in God's pretemporal anointing of his Son/Logos as preexistent Christ and God. Within this framework, however, greater care must be taken not to minimize the unique place that Scripture gives to the anointing of Jesus at the Jordan with the Spirit. As long as we keep this point in mind, we must not dismiss the possibility that Justin may actually be operating with a richer and a more nuanced theology of anointing that encompasses to various degrees Christ's identity as preexistent God, creative Word, and receiver, bearer, and giver of the Spirit to others in the economy of salvation. The eternal and cosmic anointing of the Son finds its temporal epiphanic center in the incarnation, and from that center reaches back to the Old Testament saints' participation in Christ's manifold offices (titular anointing), and then forward to the New Testament believers' reception of the Spirit lost by Adam and the Spirit's gifts that had departed from Israel (ecclesial anointing).

Still the transposition of Jesus' messianic dignity and the idea of anointing to the eternal realm of preexistence clearly relativizes the unique significance of the anointing at the Jordan for Jesus' own humanity. To this extent, Justin's comprehensive theology of anointing favors a partial eclipse of the pneumatological dimensions of Christology. On the other hand, Justin's passing claim that Christ was baptized with the Spirit because of the sin inherited by humanity from Adam points in the direction of a soteriological trajectory for the mystery of the Spirit in the life of Christ, who as the last Adam rescues man from sin by giving him the Spirit lost by Adam in the Fall. The eternal anointing of Christ as God makes this salvation from sin possible in history. What needs more development in Justin's impressive theological vision is how the anointing of Christ (= God) in his humanity, and the place of the Spirit in his humanity, relate to his identity as the preexistent Logos as well as his receiving of the Spirit and giving of its powers to humanity. The Logos-oriented approach of Justin's anointing theology, with its heavy focus on the identification of Christ's messiahship with his divine preexistence (or eternal begetting) and its tendency to see temporal events in the life of Christ mainly as revealing his divinity, seems to leave out the

---

32. This is the sense in Justin, *Second Apology* 6 (*ANF* 1:190); see Orbe, *La unción*, 63–66.

33. Orbe, *La unción*, 71–72.

role of the Spirit in Christ from the system altogether. And yet, at the same time, Justin's vision invites us to further reflection on the place of the Spirit-anointing in Christology, Trinitarian theology, and ecclesiology.

THE NECESSITY OF THE INCARNATION AND THE ANOINTING IN GOD'S PLAN OF SALVATION: IRENAEUS'S RESPONSE TO THE GNOSTICS

In this section, we look into Irenaeus's response to a common teaching among various Gnostic groups concerning the Holy Spirit's descent upon Jesus at the Jordan.[34] Irenaeus suggests that, in their similar interpretations of the Jordan event, Gnostics shared a denial of the union of Jesus' human (= fleshly) reality and the divine Word both prior to Jesus' baptism and also right before and during his passion and death. In his response to the Gnostics, and in contrast to Justin's answer to Trypho, Irenaeus gives full weight to the Father's sending of the Spirit (= unction) upon the incarnate Word both for himself and his salvific mission among us. At the Jordan river, the anointing one (= Father) sends his unction (= Spirit) upon the incarnate Word and thus constitutes him as anointed one (= Christ). Dwelling in the flesh of Christ (= anointed one), the last Adam, the Spirit becomes accustomed to dwell again in the race of Adam who lost the Spirit in the Fall. Irenaeus's move is predicated upon a logical and temporal priority of the union of Word and flesh (incarnation) over the descent of the Spirit upon him at the Jordan (anointing). Unlike Irenaeus, however, later fathers will focus almost exclusively on the incarnation as such (the nature of the union itself) to the detriment of the place of the Holy Spirit in subsequent mysteries of Jesus' life (especially his anointing, death, and resurrection). Irenaeus's response to the Gnostics gives us significant theological background for understanding concerns in later developments leading to the eclipse of Spirit Christology, as well as an early attempt to bring into some harmony the concerns of a Logos-oriented Christology (i.e., preexistence and incarnation) with those of a Spirit-oriented one (e.g., accounting for the function of Spirit narratives in the Gospels).

A few reasons led to the Gnostic (especially Valentinian) position on Jesus' baptism. To grasp such reasons, we need to describe briefly Irenaeus's

---

34. I leave aside Irenaeus's teaching on the eternal anointing of the Son with a view towards the creation of the cosmos—a doctrine which he basically shares with Justin Martyr—in order to focus on his reaction to the Gnostic interpretation of the Jordan event. For a discussion of the eternal and cosmic anointing in Irenaeus, see Orbe, *La unción*, 521–27, and McDonnell, *The Baptism of Jesus in the Jordan*, 56–59.

The Eclipse and Promise of Spirit-Oriented Christologies 13

description of their cosmological, anthropological, christological, and soteriological assumptions. Gnostics present us with a cosmology that begins "from above" in the Pleroma, a heavenly-like realm of entities called eons separated from one another by degrees of emanation from the perfect and preexistent eon known as Propator (= First-Father).[35] All "material substance" (i.e., the created world) is a defect resulting from the primordial passion of an eon called Sophia, who desired to have the impossible knowledge (gnosis) of the Father's nature ahead of the other eons preceding her in the scale of gradation.[36] To prevent a similar passion, the supreme Father wills to produce Christ and the Holy Spirit through Monogenes (= Only-Begotten). Christ and the Holy Spirit in turn make the rest of the eons aware of their inability to know the Father and of their common equality.[37] As a cosmic act of thanksgiving to the Father for strengthening the Pleroma, all eons then collaborate with one another to produce Jesus (= Savior, Christ, and Logos).[38] But who is this Gnostic Savior and whom exactly does he save?

The representative Savior basically serves as a mediator between the realm of the eons (Pleroma) that collectively formed him and especially the "spiritual substance" in the created world that derives from Achamoth, the product of Sophia's passion.[39] We say "especially" because this Savior also mediates between the Pleroma and the "animal" (in contrast to spiritual) substances created in turn by the Demiurge, Achamoth's offspring and the equivalent of God the Father and the Creator of the world.[40] In Gnostic anthropology, a human (created) being receives "his animal soul from the Demiurge, his body from the earth, his fleshly part from matter, and his spiritual man from the mother Achamoth."[41] Since the body and the flesh (= matter) cannot receive incorruption, redemption touches the animal substance to some imperfect degree and the spiritual one to the fullest measure of illumination. Not surprisingly, Gnostics reject the notion that

---

35. Irenaeus, *Against Heresies* 1.1.1–2 (*ANF* 1:316–17).

36. Ibid., 1.2.1–3 (*ANF* 1:317–18).

37. Ibid., 1.2.5–6 (*ANF* 1:318).

38. Ibid., 1.2.6 (*ANF* 1:318).

39. Ibid., 1.4.1, 5 (*ANF* 1:320, 322). The author affirms that "she [i.e., Sophia] herself certainly remained within the Pleroma; but her enthymesis, with its passion . . . was expelled from that circle. This enthymesis was no doubt, a spiritual substance, possessing some of the natural tendencies of an Eon." Ibid., 1.2.4 (*ANF* 1:318).

40. Ibid., 1.5.1–2, 5 (*ANF* 1:322); for Irenaeus's refutation of Gnostic cosmology and its identification of God the Creator with the Gnostic Demiurge, see ibid., 1.12.1 (*ANF* 1:347), and also his preface to bk. 2 (*ANF* 1:359).

41. Ibid., 1.5.6 (*ANF* 1:323).

their Savior assumed a true humanity in the material sense, for this notion undermined their principle that "matter is incapable of salvation."[42] Herein lies the docetic principle in their Christology.

In terms of soteriological implications, church members who live only by faith are seen as "animal" humans inferior to "the spiritual and perfect" (i.e., the true "Christian" Gnostics) who alone receive salvation in the fullest sense through "perfect knowledge" (gnosis) of the Father.[43] Given these anthropological and soteriological presuppositions, Gnostic Christology can speak of a cosmic Savior who assumes unto himself animal and spiritual substances in order to redeem, respectively, animal and spiritual human beings (churches)—though only the latter will eventually enter the Pleroma, together with their spiritual mother Achamoth.[44] With these basic tenets in mind, we can now approach some common Gnostic understandings of what took place at the Jordan. Let us begin with Irenaeus's description of Cerinthus's position.

> He represented Jesus as having not been born of a virgin, but as being the son of Joseph and Mary according to the ordinary course of human generation, while he nevertheless was more righteous, prudent, and wise than other men. Moreover, after his baptism, Christ descended upon him in the form of a dove from the Supreme Ruler, and that then he proclaimed the unknown Father, and performed miracles. But at last Christ departed from Jesus, and that then Jesus suffered and rose again, while Christ remained impassible, inasmuch as he was a spiritual being.[45]

For Cerinthus, Jesus and Christ are two different beings. "Christ" refers to the Savior already mentioned, the one who mediates between the Pleroma and the created world. But who is Jesus? Cerinthus seems to hold a more Ebionite view on this point: Jesus is a man born of Joseph and Mary in an ordinary way (i.e., not through a virgin birth as some Gnostics taught), and perhaps also one who perseveres in the observance of the law.[46] In Gnostic theology, this Jesus may be seen as a product (even a son) "of an animal nature" originating from the Demiurge, but also as one who possesses the

---

42. Ibid., 1.6.1 (*ANF* 1:324).

43. Ibid., 1.6.2, 4 (*ANF* 1:324–25).

44. Ibid., 1.6.1 (*ANF* 1:324); cf. ibid., 1.7.1 (*ANF* 1:235); on the other hand, the "animal" humans will enter an intermediate sphere together with the Demiurge and all matter will be destroyed. See ibid., 1.6.4, 1.7.1 (*ANF* 1:325).

45. Ibid., 1.26.1 (*ANF* 1:352).

46. Ibid., 1.26.2 (*ANF* 1:352).

The Eclipse and Promise of Spirit-Oriented Christologies

spiritual substance from Achamoth.[47] In Cerinthus's system, the Savior (= Christ) "from above" touches the man Jesus in both his animal and spiritual components by descending upon him in the form of a dove at the Jordan.[48] However, since the spiritual Savior or Christ cannot suffer, he must leave the animal substance of Jesus (along with his body and flesh) prior to the passion. There is a special type of union between Christ and Jesus at the Jordan, but the same cannot be said before the event or afterwards when the passion and death come. In this sense, Gnostic Christology does not hold to the incarnation of the Logos and therefore can be described as disjunctive.

Can we gather from the Gnostic view of the Jordan event the significance of Jesus' anointing for the Gnostic church? The answer is yes. Some Gnostics spoke of the spiritual Christ, who descended upon the spiritual Jesus, as the "power" or "sweet odour" above all things by which the spiritual church in turn participates through her baptism (along with her reception of balsam or unguent as a type of such sweet odour) for regeneration into the perfect gnosis of the Father.[49] We may say that the Gnostic rite of baptism unto perfect illumination allows for the spiritual church's sharing in the anointing (= spiritual Christ) first received by the spiritual man Jesus at the Jordan. Gnostic ecclesiology finds its ground in a Christology.

Among the orthodox, Justin had already spoken of Jesus' anointing at the Jordan as a revelatory event and perhaps condition for the church's sharing in the knowledge of the Father's Son as Messiah and God, but for Justin this participation also likely took place through Christian baptism for the sake of deliverance from death and the transgression inherited from Adam.[50] Irenaeus describes the ecclesiological import of Isaiah 61:1 in a similar way: "Therefore did the Spirit of God descend upon Him . . . so that we, receiving from the abundance of His unction, might be saved."[51] By contrast, in the Gnostic view of redemption, a crucial difference is that only the "animal" church receives the lesser baptism "for the remission of sins" instituted by the animal man Jesus.[52] For the more "spiritual" Gnostic, there is a corresponding "spiritual" baptism. Even though their interpretations of the Jordan are quite different, it is clear that both heterodox and orthodox

---

47. Ibid., 1.7.2 (*ANF* 1:325); in this context, Jesus may also be called Christ or Lord.

48. Valentinian Gnostics can also distinguish between the baptism in water for the animal Jesus and the baptism in the Spirit for the spiritual Jesus. See Orbe, *Introducción a la teología de los siglos II y III*, 655.

49. *Against Heresies* 1.21.2–3 (*ANF* 1:345–46).

50. See *Dialogue* 88 (*ANF* 1:243–44), and ibid., 14 (*ANF* 1:201).

51. *Against Heresies* 3.9.3 (*ANF* 1:423).

52. Ibid., 1.21.2 (*ANF* 1:345).

theologians see the Jordan as a link between Christology and ecclesiology, between Jesus' baptism and the church's baptism.

The Ophites came closer than Cerinthus to proposing a dualistic Spirit Christology in which the spiritual Christ (seen as the masculine principle) in conjunction with Sophia (also known as the Holy Spirit and seen as the feminine principle) descended upon and adopted the man Jesus at the Jordan, making him "Jesus Christ."[53] For the Ophites, the union Christ/Sophia produced "Jesus Christ," who as the receptacle of Sophia mediates unto her spiritual children (i.e., the church of the perfect) the Father's gnosis that only Jesus can transmit to them because of his communion with Christ.[54] Otherwise stated, the spiritual church shares in Jesus' unique anointing with the Holy Spirit (= Sophia) through baptism into the knowledge of the Father first received by Jesus through communion with the spiritual Christ. Before the cross, the conjunction Christ/Sophia departs from Jesus, but Christ still puts in him "a certain energy . . . which raised him up again in the body, which they call both animal and spiritual" (though not in the actual flesh).[55] As in Cerinthus's system, the union Christ/Jesus occurs preeminently at the baptism.

What, then, is Irenaeus's response to the Gnostic view of Jesus' anointing at the Jordan? In what way does his reaction serve as a building block for later orthodox reflection on a pneumatological Christology? For the Gnostics, the impassibility of the representative Savior does not allow for a real and permanent union between his spiritual element (= Christ) from the Pleroma and a bodily or fleshly substance from the created world. Central to the problem of a lasting spiritual-material union of sorts in "Jesus Christ" is their docetism: Jesus is not a man in the flesh (in the material sense). Neither from birth nor during his passion can Jesus' flesh and body ever be united to an impassible spiritual element from above. The same observation applies to the union "Jesus Christ" at the Jordan because Jesus does not truly possess the "material" human substance. Yet, as I have shown, Gnostics can also posit a union of an animal and a spiritual Christ with respective animal and spiritual human substances, both of which Jesus possesses. It is now time to take a closer look at the nature of the Gnostic idea of such a union in light of Irenaeus's own reaction to it and his own view of the union.

---

53. The Ophites's assertion that Jesus "was begotten of the Virgin through the agency of God" distinguishes them on this point from Cerinthus's Ebionite opinion. *Against Heresies* 1.30.12 (*ANF* 1:356).

54. On this point, I am indebted to Orbe's interpretation of Irenaeus's *Against Heresies* 1.20.11–12, in "El Espíritu Santo en el bautismo de Jesús (en torno a san Ireneo)," 681–83.

55. *Against Heresies* 1.30.13 (*ANF* 1:357).

The Eclipse and Promise of Spirit-Oriented Christologies 17

A crucial question is: Do the Gnostics posit anything more than an adoptive type of union in "Jesus Christ" at the baptism? In his discussion of the nature of the union Christ/Jesus at the Jordan according to some Ebionites, Orbe suggests that the descent of the Holy Spirit (= superior Christ)—a seed from God, but not God as such—in Jesus is not merely an "adoptive" union but rather a "substantial" one.[56] Despite this kind of "crasis" in which two substances come together without losing their distinctiveness, Orbe points out that the greater Ebionite emphasis fell on the "qualitative" union of the Spirit and the mere man Jesus.[57] In this latter sense, the union Spirit/Jesus surely differs from the union between the Spirit and the Old Testament prophets, but only "quantitatively," by degree (intensity), or "in the measure of the divine filiation."[58]

In the case of the Valentinian and Ophite Gnostics, Orbe suggests that their system could allow for a form of "hidden" and "inoperative" union between the superior or cosmic Savior and Jesus from birth that only becomes "active" and "dynamic" in Jesus (as the firstfruits of the animal and spiritual churches) from Jordan until his passion.[59] By emphasizing the latter type of union over the former, the "natural" over the "personal" one—these are Orbe's terms—the Gnostics clearly showed a stronger interest in the baptism of Jesus than in his virgin birth for the sake of highlighting the ecclesial trajectory of the Jordan event. The descent of the Christ from above upon the spiritual Jesus at the Jordan is the condition for the spiritual church's attainment of the Father's gnosis through him.

Irenaeus agrees that at the Jordan the Word of God was made "Jesus Christ," but only in the sense that the *incarnate* Word (already from birth) was at the time of his baptism (and not before) anointed in his humanity for a mission on our behalf. First, let us take up the issue of the union. Irenaeus writes:

> For Christ did not at that time descend upon Jesus, neither was Christ one and Jesus another: but the Word of God ... who did also take upon Him flesh, and was anointed by the Spirit from the Father ... was made Jesus Christ.[60]

---

56. Orbe, *Introducción a la teología de los siglos II y III*, 647; and his *La unción*, 302–23.

57. Orbe, *Introducción a la teología de los siglos II y III*, 651–52.

58. Ibid., 652; and his *La unción*, 302–23.

59. *Introducción a la teología de los siglos II y III*, 655–61, and especially Orbe's comments at 659n15.

60. *Against Heresies* 3.9.3 (*ANF* 1:423); cf. ibid., 3.16.1–2 (*ANF* 1:440–41).

By making the incarnation of the Word the logical condition for his anointing as man by the Spirit of God (not a spiritual Christ, but a distinct agent in its own right), Irenaeus prevents a separation of the Word and Jesus into two distinct beings. He writes, "For inasmuch as the Word of God was man . . . in this respect did the Spirit of God rest upon Him, and anoint Him to preach the Gospel to the lowly."[61] Therefore, the union of the Word and the flesh taken upon himself from birth (not after), even if defined as a "crasis" (i.e., something like a mixture without confusion of substances) in such an early stage of the history of dogma, still constitutes an impossible union for the Gnostics due to their low view of matter in general and their concomitant docetism in particular.[62]

For Irenaeus, the title Christ does not point to a superior being above Jesus, but rather to the incarnate Word insofar as he is anointed as man by the Spirit of God for us. Thus the title points to the Trinitarian framework and soteriological import of Jesus' own anointing as declared in Isaiah 61:1ff. (cf. Luke 4:18ff.): "For in the name of Christ is implied, He that anoints, He that is anointed, and the unction itself with which He is anointed. And it is the Father who anoints, but the Son who is anointed by the Spirit, who is the unction."[63] Since the Gnostics often identified the dove (= Spirit) with the cosmic Christ or Savior from above, Irenaeus's use of the title Christ gives its proper due to the biblical role of the Holy Spirit (seen as a distinct agent) in Jesus' life and mission.[64] Drawing from Isaiah 11:1ff. and 61:1ff., Irenaeus notes that the Spirit descends upon Jesus to anoint him for his messianic mission to preach the gospel, heal the sick, and forgive sins.[65] Upon completion of his mission, the Lord then gives the Spirit whom he received at the Jordan to the church through baptism.[66]

The Lord's identity as Spirit-giver implies that the Spirit of God actually descended upon and filled the incarnate Son of God at the Jordan.

> Wherefore He [i.e., the Spirit] did also descend upon the Son of God, made the Son of man, becoming accustomed in fellowship with Him to dwell in the human race, to rest with human

---

61. Ibid., 3.9.3 (*ANF* 1:423).

62. On the use of "crasis," Orbe cites Irenaeus's *Epideixis* 41. See *La unción*, 304 (esp. his comments in n7).

63. *Against Heresies* 3.18.3 (*ANF* 1:446).

64. "These men do, in fact, set the Spirit aside altogether; they understand that Christ was one and Jesus another; and they teach that there was not one Christ but many." Ibid., 3.17.4 (*ANF* 1:445).

65. Ibid., 3.9.3 (*ANF* 1:423).

66. Irenaeus cites Matthew 28:19 and alludes to Acts 2:17 (cf. Joel 2:28). *Against Heresies* 3.17.1 (*ANF* 1:444).

beings, and to dwell in the workmanship of God, working the will of the Father in them, and renewing them from their old habits into the newness of Christ.[67]

Although Irenaeus shares with Justin the idea of the eternal anointing of the Word as Christ in view of the world's creation (cosmic anointing), Irenaeus's language clearly stresses the constitutive role of the Holy Spirit in making the incarnate Word "Jesus Christ" at the Jordan in a way that Justin's theology does not. The cosmic anointing does not relativize the historical one. Having received the Spirit "as a gift from His Father," the Lord then does "confer it upon those who are partakers of Himself, sending the Holy Spirit upon all the earth."[68] Christ's reception of the Spirit in the flesh functions as a condition in God's plan of salvation for his giving of the Spirit to all flesh.

Irenaeus's theology of recapitulation requires the logical priority of the incarnation over the anointing. The Son of God becomes a human being (for Irenaeus, the Son of man) so that he can recapitulate in his own humanity the image and likeness of God that humans lost in Adam: "God recapitulated in Himself the ancient formation of man, that He might kill sin, deprive death of its power, and vivify man."[69] Irenaeus uses the language of incarnation as an analogy to speak of humanity's sharing in God's salvation through the Word made flesh: "[T]he Word of God . . . dwelt in man, and became Son of man, that He might accustom man to receive God, and God to dwell in man, according to the good pleasure of the Father."[70] If the Word (= Logos) accustoms human beings to receive God by becoming a human being himself (incarnation), does not this incarnation-oriented move eclipse to some extent the idea that human beings can only share in God through the gracious indwelling of the Spirit who descended upon the incarnate Word at the Jordan (anointing)? Not for Irenaeus. In God's renewal of creation, his two "hands," the Logos and the Spirit, have a role in the vivification of man and thus in his restoration to the image and likeness of God.[71] First, the Son takes upon himself the nature of Adam (incarnation)

---

67. Ibid.
68. Ibid., 3.17.2 (*ANF* 1:445).
69. Ibid., 3.18.7 (*ANF* 1:448); cf. ibid., 3.18.1 (*ANF* 1:446).
70. Ibid., 3.20.2 (*ANF* 1:450).

71. "[T]he Word of the Father and the Spirit of God, having become united with the ancient substance of Adam's formation, rendered man living and perfect, receptive of the perfect Father, in order that as in the natural [Adam] we all were dead, so in the spiritual we may all be made alive. For never at any time did Adam escape the *hands* of God, to whom the Father speaking, said, 'Let us make man in Our image, after Our likeness.' And for this reason in the last times (*fine*), not by the will of the flesh, nor by the will of man, but by the good pleasure of the Father, His hands formed a living man, in order that Adam might be created [again] after the image and likeness of God." Ibid., 5.1.3 (*ANF* 1:527).

and, second, the incarnate Son is anointed with the Spirit so that he will in turn, upon completion of his work, restore the Spirit of new life to the race of Adam.

Irenaeus understands that the church's Spirit-led participation by the Father's pleasure in the divine life happens through the church's present-day reenactment of the incarnate Word's *anointing* by the Father with the Spirit. Thus the church does not participate in the divine life through a reenactment of the divine Word's *incarnation* as such, for that event constitutes an unrepeatable and non-transferable dimension of his identity. For Irenaeus, human reception of God and God's indwelling in humans can only take place by the church's sharing in the Spirit (unction) of God who first anointed Christ at the Jordan. For only the descent of the Spirit on the Word made flesh touches his true humanity in a way that allows for people of all times to participate or share in his anointing or unction through Christian baptism, a partaking that allows for human regeneration into the image and likeness of God and thus into a sharing in Christ's incorruptibility at the resurrection of the flesh.

In subsequent years, many orthodox theologians would almost completely focus on the nature of the union of God and flesh in Christ from birth and pay little or no attention to the Spirit's descent upon Jesus at the Jordan as a defining moment in his life and his mission for us. Others will rightly point to the import of the event for the church as an anticipation or example of her Christian baptism, but once again, at the expense of its significance for Jesus himself. In his response to the Gnostics, Irenaeus provides some of the most foundational arguments early on in the history of dogma for placing the union at the moment of the incarnation—instead of placing it later at the Jordan. Our author's significance also lies in the fact that he defended such union (*crasis*), but not at the expense of the anointing. Irenaeus is able to make the union at conception (incarnation) a condition for the anointing at the Jordan without losing sight of the importance of the Jordan event for the Word as "Christ" (= anointed one), and consequently, for us who receive the Spirit from him. The pneumatic link between Christology and ecclesiology is established. Other church theologians would not be as discerning, making of the genuine stress on the language of incarnation an absolute and exclusive analogy for understanding the mystery of Christ and the church's participation in the same without considering its constitutive pneumatological dimensions. Given his rich biblical, Trinitarian, and soteriological commitments, Irenaeus's theology of recapitulation lays opens for us the possibilities of bringing Logos- and Spirit-oriented aspects of the mystery of Christ into fruitful dialogue and integration.

THE SON SANCTIFIES AND ANOINTS HIMSELF FOR US: ATHANASIUS IN THE STRUGGLE AGAINST THE ARIANS

Athanasius's approach to the problem of the anointing is significant in the history of dogma. His genuine anti-Arian concern for protecting the consubstantiality of the Son with God the Father and thus the Son's essential (as opposed to adoptive) sonship ends up contributing to a partial eclipse of the pneumatic dimensions of Christology. By making the Son the preeminent giver of the Spirit *as God* to others, Athanasius gives less weight to the Son's identity as receiver and bearer of the Holy Spirit *as man*. Above all, the emphasis falls on the ecclesiological import of Jesus' anointing for us. This is in and of itself a fine soteriological move, which he shares with Justin and Irenaeus, but one made at the expense of the full significance of the Jordan event for the incarnate Son himself. Second, Athanasius makes the Son (in contrast to the Father) the preeminent *subject* of the anointing. As God, the Son of God is the preeminent giver of the Spirit, for in the eternal order of processions the Holy Spirit logically proceeds from the Son who is one in substance with God the Father. What this ultimately means for our theologian is that the Son as such anoints or sanctifies *himself* with his own Spirit. But not exactly at the Jordan, for the Son already does this at the time of incarnation. Athanasius can even refer to the incarnation as a "chrism" (unction, anointing) in which the Son sanctifies his own humanity with his divinity. At that time, the Son also gives to his humanity his own Spirit. One notes that no distinction is made between sanctification and anointing and, therefore, the Father's sending of the Spirit in and upon the incarnate Son at the Jordan becomes basically a revelatory sign for others of the Son's prior giving of either his divinity or Spirit to his humanity from birth.

Let us now look at Athanasius's arguments more closely. In the aftermath of Nicea (A.D. 325), Athanasius arises as a staunch defender of the Council's definition of faith. In particular, he upholds the use of the term *homoousios* (of the same substance) to express the divine equality of the Son with the Father as a reaction to Arian views of the same relation in adoptive and subordinationist terms. Reflecting on the reason for the Council's *homoousios* language, Athanasius notes that the Arian party accepted the teaching that the Son is "from God," but only in the same way that human beings and all created things have their beginning from God.[72] Certainly, Arians gave the Son a higher dignity than all children of God adopted by grace, but this claim failed to put him above the level of creatures who also

---

72. Athanasius, *Defence of the Nicene Definition* 5.19 (NPNF[2] 4:162).

owe their origin and existence to God. At worst, the Son is only a man; at best, a man deified on the basis of his works.

Athanasius never disputes that "the Son was created too, but this took place when he became man."[73] The Son's incarnation can never exhaust his own self-existing (divine) nature, for he can be considered as preexistent God even apart from such an unrepeatable act of grace. Athanasius often speaks of "the Word, considered as the Word" to separate the Son's unparalleled dignity as God from his becoming man for us. Thus the creedal term *homoousios* does not deny that the Son is a creature according to his human nature, but it rejects the subordinationist principle that Arius's teaching inevitably leads to, namely, that the Son is *only* a creature willed into existence by the Father (although a greater one than the rest of us). In regard to their common nature as God, there can be no temporal distinction (or partition) between the Father and the Son who is begotten from him.[74] The Son is "begotten" of the Father in the analogical sense that the Son is—to use creedal language—"very God *of very God*," and thus "begotten, not made." As God, the Son is not of the will of the Father as the rest of the creatures, but rather of the substance (Gk. *ousia*) of the Father ("God *of God*"). If there were a temporal division between the Son and the Father as to their undivided *ousia*, the Son would have a beginning from the Father (even as other less virtuous creatures do) and this would imply his ontological subordination to God. Athanasius rightly defends the Nicene teaching on the substantial (in contrast to adoptive) sonship of Jesus Christ in relation to God the Father. The distinction between both types of sonship ends up being a hermeneutical principle for defending the Nicene teaching on Jesus Christ in disputes with Arian readings of biblical texts. Passages on the anointing of Jesus serve as a key example.

Athanasius sees Psalm 45:7-8 as neither an eternal nor a cosmic anointing, but rather as a reference to the anointing of the Word as man. He does so in reaction against the Arian interpretation of the passage. Let us review the psalm:

> Thy throne, O God, is for ever and ever; a scepter of righteousness is the scepter of Thy kingdom. Thou hast loved righteousness and hated iniquity, *therefore* God, even Thy God, hath anointed Thee with the oil of gladness above Thy fellows" (italics mine).[75]

---

73. Ibid., 3.14 (*NPNF*² 4:158).

74. Ibid., 3.11 (*NPNF*² 4:157).

75. Athanasius, *First Discourse* 11.37 (*NPNF*² 4:328); I have used the version of the psalm cited in ibid., 12.46 (*NPNF*² 4:333).

Arians put a lot of weight on the word "therefore" (or "wherefore") in their interpretation of biblical passages referring to Christ's anointing and exaltation. They argued that such conjunction signified that the Son "received a reward . . . and would not have had it, unless He had needed it, and had His work to shew for it, then having gained it from virtue and promotion."[76] Arians applied this argument by referring primarily to a text on Christ's exaltation (Phil 2:9–10): "*Wherefore* God also hath highly exalted Him, and given Him a Name which is above every name. . . ." (italics mine).[77] First, they argued that if the Son had received anything from God (i.e., exaltation, anointing), then he must have "acted from purpose" to obtain it.[78] However, to do so implies a need on the part of the Son to have (or be) what he does not already have (or is)—a creaturely quality unbecoming the nature of God.[79] Therefore, Arians argued that God exalted (and by implication, anointed) his Son as a "reward of His purpose" or "the prize of works done," thereby denying his identity as Son by nature and making him a Son by grace as those "men who have received the Spirit by participation."[80] Does the Son then share in the Spirit of God in any way?

For Athanasius, the Son is "the Giver of grace," not the receiver of grace.[81] The basic idea behind this anti-Arian contention is that *receiving* God's grace (even as a human) amounts to an adoptive (in contrast to a natural or substantial) view of Christ's sonship.[82] If the Son is substantially Son (= God), then, he must always be *giving* grace to others and not receiving it from another. Likewise, the Son is, above all, the giver of the Spirit, not the "partaker" of the Spirit as the rest of God's creatures.

> All other things partake of the Spirit, but He, according to you, of what is He partaker? [O]f the Spirit? Nay, rather the Spirit

---

76. *First Discourse* 11.37 (*NPNF*² 4:328).

77. Ibid.

78. Ibid.

79. The Arians argue that, unlike God, the Son "is altogether of an alterable nature." Ibid.

80. Athanasius also speaks of "a grace by acquisition" in the case of God's children. Ibid., 37–38 (*NPNF*² 4:328).

81. "For though the Word has descended in order to be exalted, and so it is written, yet what need was there that He should humble Himself, as if to seek that which He had already? *And what grace did He receive who is the Giver of grace?* . . . And the term in question 'highly exalted,' does not signify that the essence of the Word was exalted, for He was ever and is 'equal to God,' but the exaltation is of the manhood." Ibid., 11.40–41 (*NPNF*² 4:329–30); italics mine.

82. Ibid., 11.37–39 (*NPNF*² 4:328–29).

Himself takes from the Son . . . and it is not reasonable to say that the latter is sanctified by the former.[83]

It is acceptable, however, to affirm that *we* are "sanctified by Him in the Spirit."[84] In Athanasius's theology, God becomes man so that man can become god (or deified). The Spirit mediates our participation in the Son, but it does so because the Son *as God* supplies this Spirit to us.[85] In this argument, little attention is given to the *incarnate* Word's reception of the Spirit and the Spirit's active influence upon him. Due to the Arian polemic, the interest lies instead in the Word's consubstantiality with God the Father. Still the question remains: How does Athanasius understand the anointing of the incarnate Son with the Spirit at the Jordan? Does he receive it in his humanity?

As the psalmist states, the Son does not have a need for the Spirit's anointing "that He may become God, for He was so even before; nor that He may become King, for He had the Kingdom eternally . . . but *in our behalf*" (italics mine).[86] So goes Athanasius's view of the anointing. It is a soteriologically driven event. Just as the Son becomes man for us (incarnation), so his being anointed with the Spirit as man is an act of grace. Athanasius does not put the stress on what the incarnate Son receives from the Spirit of the Father at the Jordan, but rather on what the church receives from the Son through his Spirit in her baptism.

> [T]he Saviour . . . being God . . . and being Himself He that supplies the Holy Ghost, nevertheless is here said to be anointed, that . . . He might provide for us men, not only exaltation and resurrection, but the indwelling and intimacy of the Spirit.[87]

In this text, the salvific import of the Jordan event for the church comes to the fore in a remarkable way. Athanasius argues that "when He [i.e., the Son] is now said to be anointed in a human respect, *we* it is who in Him are anointed; since also, when He is baptized, *we* it is who in Him are baptized" (italics mine).[88] Not only are we baptized in Him, but also "by Him"—an apparent move to affirm once again the Son's identity as giver of

---

83. Ibid., 5.15 (*NPNF*² 4:315).

84. Ibid., 12.46 (*NPNF*² 4:333).

85. Athanasius works under the Trinitarian assumption that, just as the Son is begotten from God the Father without division in their common substance, so too does the Spirit take from the Son without prejudice to the Spirit's divinity.

86. *First Discourse* 12.46 (*NPNF*² 4:333).

87. Ibid.

88. Ibid., 12.48 (*NPNF*² 4:335).

The Eclipse and Promise of Spirit-Oriented Christologies 25

the Spirit, "Sanctifier," and "Lord of sanctification."[89] Athanasius articulates the connection between Christology and ecclesiology, but still seems somewhat hesitant to give too much weight to the Son's reception of the Spirit for himself in his humanity.

We may inquire further about the christological import of the baptism of Christ. What does it mean for the *incarnate* Word himself? Using John 17:19, Athanasius argues that at the Jordan "the Son is not sanctified by other, but Himself sanctifies Himself, that we may be sanctified in the truth."[90] What our theologian appears to say is that the Word, viewed or considered as *God* the Word, does not receive sanctification. This much is clear. What is not clear in Athanasius's reading of the baptism narrative is whether the Word as *man* receives the sanctification (or more specifically, the anointing) of the Spirit.

Athanasius speaks of the Word's sanctification of his own humanity with the Spirit as a reality that occurs already from the time of the incarnation.

> I, being the Father's Word, I give to Myself, when becoming man, the Spirit; and Myself, become man, do I sanctify in Him [i.e., in the incarnate Word], that henceforth in Me, who am Truth . . . all may be sanctified.[91]

Notice that the anointing of Christ at his baptism does not appear to add anything unique to the incarnate Word's identity that he did not previously possess from the time of his incarnation. Using our author's language, one can affirm that at the Jordan *we* share in the anointing (= sanctification) of the Spirit that the eternal Son already gave to himself in his humanity at the incarnation.

However, can we say that the Son *in his humanity* receives the Holy Spirit in a new way at the Jordan that is distinct from his sanctification by the same from the moment of his birth? This is unclear. It is in the Word, who already sanctifies himself with his own Spirit at the incarnation, that *we* are sanctified at the Jordan. Here Athanasius partially eclipses the significance of the incarnate Son's active reception of the Spirit of the Father at the Jordan in favor of the Son's earlier giving of his own Spirit to himself at the time of his birth. Athanasius is hesitant to distinguish between the Spirit's presence in the incarnate Word from the first moment of the incarnation

---

89. He writes, "And when He received the Spirit, *we* it was who *by Him* were made recipients of It" (italics mine). Ibid., 12.46–47 (NPNF² 4:333); cf. ibid., 12.47 (NPNF² 4:334).

90. Ibid., 12.46 (NPNF² 4:333).

91. Ibid.

and its presence in him at the Jordan in view of his giving of the same Spirit to us. Anointing and sanctification are thus synonymous realities, pointing to the Son's possession of the Spirit from birth.

Another crucial point in Athanasius's description of the anointing (= sanctification) of the Son as man has to do with the subject of the anointing. Who anoints whom? Does God the Father anoint the Son with his [i.e., the Father's] Spirit, as we see in the baptism narratives? Or does the Son anoint himself with his own Spirit? Our theologian opts for the latter expression, giving prominence to the Word as the subject of his own actions—an important contribution to Alexandrian "Word-flesh" Christology. However, making the Word the subject of his own "anointing" at the incarnation leads to lack of clarity as to what or who the "anointing" actually is. For instance, Athanasius explicitly refers to the divinity of the Word as the "chrism" that anoints his humanity.

> For I the Word am the chrism, and that which has the chrism from Me is the Man; not then without Me could He [i.e., the Man] be called Christ, but being with Me and I in Him.[92]

Here the anointing reaches the level of a metaphor for the incarnation. In other words, at the incarnation, the Word gives his own divinity to his humanity. Therefore, the Word is also the preeminent giver of his own Spirit to his humanity. Despite the apparent lack of clarity with regard to what the anointing entails—is it a reference to the divinity of the Word or the Holy Spirit?—it is probably safe to assume, in light of Athanasius's overall teaching, that in his theological approach the eternal Word communicates to his own creaturely reality both his own divinity and his own Spirit. Unlike Irenaeus's use of the term "Christ" to refer to Jesus' anointing at the Jordan, Athanasius uses it to speak of the incarnate Word. The uniqueness of the anointing at the Jordan for the incarnate Word, along with the place of the Father and the Holy Spirit in the event, is partially lost in Athanasius's overall approach. The Jordan serves basically as a *confirmation* for us of the Son's prior sanctification (= anointing) of his humanity with either his divinity or his Spirit from the time of the incarnation (incarnational anointing).

The logical priority of the Son's incarnation over his anointing (a move already made by Irenaeus), coupled with the eternal processional (not substantial) priority of the Son in relation to the Spirit, leads Athanasius to read the Jordan event in light of the Son's identity as giver of the Spirit. In this way, the theologian can affirm that the Son sanctifies and even anoints himself with either his own Spirit or his divinity at the incarnation. Yet even if

---

92. Athanasius, *Fourth Discourse* 36 (NPNF² 4:447).

legitimate in his strong opposition to Arianism, Athanasius's interpretation of Christ's baptism pays no attention to the role of God the Father as subject of the incarnate Son's anointing at the Jordan and relativizes the constitutive action of the Father's Spirit in him at different stages of his human life and mission in the economy of salvation. Furthermore, because Athanasius's account of the anointing of the Son as man at the Jordan does not quite differ qualitatively from his sanctification from birth, the Jordan event only reveals to others who the Son already is (i.e., the divine Word) or what he already has (i.e., the Spirit) at the incarnation.

Despite these critical remarks, the theologian's strong soteriological interest in the Jordan as the place where we are anointed in and by Christ remains a profound insight. By approaching the Jordan in terms of the church's participation in Christ, Athanasius links Christian baptism to Christ's own baptism. Athanasius's well-known claim that the Word became man that man might be deified can thus no longer be seen apart from man's participation by grace in the Word's anointing (= sanctification) as man for our sake. For Athanasius, this paradigmatic character of Christ's baptism for humanity is impossible without the Holy Spirit. In a profound statement on Isaiah 61:1 (cf. Luke 4:18), Athanasius notes that "no otherwise should we have partaken the Spirit and been sanctified, but that the Giver of the Spirit, the Word Himself, had spoken of Himself as anointed with the Spirit for us."[93] Regardless of whether Athanasius makes the incarnation proper or Christ's baptism the immediate condition for the church's reception of the Spirit in Christian baptism, he still paves a way for thinking about humanity's share in Christ's life through baptism in both incarnational and pneumatological terms. Thus Athanasius's theology of the anointing shows promise for mining the pneumatic dimensions of Christ's identity in the framework of an incarnational Logos Christology.

Summary

In his engagement with Trypho, Justin Martyr transposes the historical anointing of Jesus at the Jordan to his preincarnational anointing as God in view of his creation of the world (cosmic anointing). Even though all Spirit-filled offices in the Old Testament cease and are fulfilled in the anointed Son (titular anointing), they already have their ground in his eternal anointing as God. Understandably, then, the Magi worship him from birth as one who has always been in possession of his power. Overall, one notices a lack of sufficient clarification in our theologian between the Son's divinity and his

---

93. *First Discourse* 12.50 (NPNF[2] 4:336).

anointing. These realities belong so closely together in the realm of preexistence that the historical uniqueness of Jesus' anointing with the Spirit at the Jordan is relativized. Although Justin at one point refers to Jesus' baptism metaphorically as a "birth," the event appears to serve more as an epiphany of his prior identity as Christ (= God) for the sake of others' *knowledge* of his power and salvation than as a *new* historic presence of the Spirit of God in him for our sake. Therefore, the event is mainly revelatory for others, but not necessarily constitutive for Jesus himself in his own humanity. Yet Justin's grand theology of anointing, and the intricate link he suggests between Christ's baptism, his preexistence, and the reception of the Spirit by believers, invites further thinking on the place of the Holy Spirit in the events of Jesus' life and their implications for Christology, Trinitarian theology, and ecclesiology. Indeed, Justin's multi-dimensional theology of the Logos's anointing remains influential, even if indirectly, in my attempt to account for the economic and immanent Trinitarian implications of the pneumatic identity of the divine Logos.

Although Irenaeus shares Justin's cosmic view of the anointing, this insight does not take away from the significance of the Jordan event for Jesus himself. In reaction to the Gnostic conception of a "union" between the spiritual Christ (= the Spirit) and the man Jesus at the Jordan, our theologian has to posit the union of Jesus and Christ from the moment of the incarnation and defend the non-identity of Christ and the Spirit. Even though a logical priority has to be given to the incarnation over the anointing, this move does not prevent Irenaeus from giving the Spirit its defining place in the latter. Thus it is at the Jordan (neither before nor after) that the incarnate Word becomes "Jesus Christ" and thus the one anointed by the Father with the Spirit (or unction) so that others (i.e., the church) in turn may share in his own anointing as man. While Irenaeus's conception of the union as a "crasis" is an early formulation, and therefore does not benefit from later expressions of the mystery of the incarnation, his main contribution lies in offering us a sweeping Trinitarian account of salvation history that speaks to God's ongoing work through his two "hands"—the Logos and the Spirit—from creation to new creation. By doing so, Irenaeus inspires us to work towards an integration of Logos- and Spirit-oriented elements in a Christian account of salvation. His vision remains a guiding principle in my own argument for the complementarity of Logos and Spirit Christologies.

Athanasius grounds the logical priority of the divine Word's sanctification of his own flesh vis-à-vis his anointing with the Spirit at the incarnation in the priority of the Son's eternal begetting from the Father vis-à-vis the Holy Spirit's procession from the Father. Since the Word is the giver of the Spirit, he does not receive the Spirit according to his divinity. However, the

Word does not appear to receive the Spirit of the Father at the Jordan according to his humanity either. Rather, the divine Word sanctifies himself as man with his own Spirit from birth. At the Jordan, the divine Word sanctifies others in him with the same Spirit with whom he previously sanctified himself in his humanity from birth. The anointing at Jordan per se does not seem to touch the Word in his own humanity. Strictly speaking, therefore, the Holy Spirit does not descend upon the incarnate Son at the Jordan in a *new* way. For Athanasius, it is enough to point to the presence of the Spirit in the Son already from the moment of the incarnation. The anointing at Jordan seems to be a later *confirming* instance of a prior reality. Moreover, by placing the emphasis on the divine Word as the subject of sanctification and anointing at the incarnation, the place of the Father as the personal source of the anointing of the incarnate Word at the Jordan with the Spirit does not receive the same attention it does in Irenaeus's thinking. For Athanasius, the anointing (or chrism) of Christ can even become a metaphor for the incarnation, describing the Son's anointing of his own flesh with his *divinity*—a move made by other church fathers in subsequent years. All these proposals tend to eclipse in part the pneumatic and economic-Trinitarian aspects of Christology. Yet Athanasius's soteriological description of the church's participation by grace in the anointing of Christ through Christian baptism offers a vital link between Christology and ecclesiology, and invites further reflection about the place of the Holy Spirit in an account of our salvation in and through Christ. I shall return to this ecclesiological aspect of Athanasius's thought on the anointing of the Son later on, especially as I look into the implications of a Nicene Spirit Christology for sanctification.

2

Reading the Story of Jesus as Receiver and Bearer of God's Spirit

Invigorating Logos-Oriented Approaches to the Conception, Anointing, and Exaltation of Jesus

IN THIS CHAPTER, I seek to invigorate classic Logos-oriented readings of the biblical story of Jesus with its defining pneumatic dimensions. In doing so, I show how a reading of events in Jesus' life from the perspective of his identity as receiver and bearer of the Spirit raises issues that a Spirit Christology needs to deal with in order to serve as a complement to—rather than a replacement for—Logos Christology. Logos-oriented readings see major events in Jesus' life and mission as *revelatory*, epiphanic, confirming, declarative, or proclamatory of either his prior identity as God or his prior possession of the Spirit as man from the moment of incarnation. In particular, Jesus' baptism or anointing at Jordan is typically seen as *exemplary* for the church of her Christian baptism. We can thus speak of a revelatory and exemplary significance of events in Christ's life *for others*, but not of their significance for the incarnate Word *himself*. Logos-oriented readings of events in Jesus' life also highlight the work of the Logos as the subject of acts in and through his assumed and sanctified humanity from the first moment of the hypostatic union (incarnation).

A Spirit Christology invigorates these Logos-oriented accounts by placing the person of the Logos in the broader soteriological and Trinitarian context of his acts and relation before the Father and for us in the Spirit. It looks at events in the course of Jesus' life and ministry as special instances of the Father's sending of his Spirit in and upon the incarnate Son in the economy of salvation and, therefore, as *constitutive* moments for his own human life and history in the work of redemption. In ontological terms, a Spirit-oriented reading of Jesus' story strongly highlights the dynamic and relational presence of the Spirit as an agent in its own right in the Son's human existence as obedient Son, suffering Servant, and risen Lord. It does so while safeguarding the place of the Father as preeminent giver and source of the Spirit to and through his incarnate Son.

Reading the narrative of Jesus as the receiver, bearer, and giver of the Spirit helps us to look at the mystery of Christ as a series of defining moments that spans from his particular reception and possession of the Spirit for us to his universal giving of the same to us. In God's economy of salvation, Jesus of Nazareth receives the Holy Spirit of the Most High at his conception in Bethlehem, at his baptism at the Jordan, and as the risen and ascended Lord seated at God's right hand. Throughout his life and work as God's faithful and obedient Son, Jesus bears the Spirit in inexhaustible fullness. In loving freedom, Jesus also pours out this Spirit on us from the time of his glorification onwards, or, in more comprehensive terms, from the beginning of his paschal mystery—i.e., passion and death, resurrection, and Pentecost. At various times, in new ways, and for us, the anointed Son and Servant receives, possesses, and gives to others the eschatological gift of the Spirit who proceeds from the heavenly Father.

Referring to God's gracious plans to save humankind in Jesus Christ, Basil (ca. 330–79) rhetorically asks, "who would deny that it was all made possible through the grace of the Spirit?"[1] With the incorporation of the *homoousious* in the Nicene Creed, the orthodox made a decisive move in their account of Christ from what he *does* in the economy to who he *is* in substance or essence with God the Father.[2] In other words, with Nicea, a soteriological-economic understanding of Christ's sonship gave way to the more pressing apologetic issue of defending his ontological-immanent constitution as God. This was done to combat Arius's adoptionist principle in his Christology and thus his ontological subordination of the Son to God the Father. As LaCugna puts it, a historic move from *oikonomia* (God for us) to *theologia* (God in Godself) takes place at this point in the history of dogma and, consequently, "God's relationship to Jesus of Nazareth faded

---

1. Basil, *On the Holy Spirit* 16.39 (trans. Anderson).

2. LaCugna distinguishes between pre-Arian (or pre-Nicene) biblical-economic and Arian philosophical (or ontological) types of subordinationism: "Arianism . . . is a form of ontological-theological speculation that construes the salvation-history subordination of Son to Father to be a difference in nature (*ousia*) between God and Christ." *God for Us*, 24.

in importance to the Father's relationship to the Son."³ If one considers the Arian interpretation of Jesus' baptism as an influential factor for the crucial Nicene move towards "ontologization," one can see why a post-Nicene bishop like Athanasius might shy away from giving too much weight to the Holy Spirit's active role in Jesus and his earthly mission.⁴ Basil, however, does not hesitate to do so.

Although Basil holds to the consubstantiality of the Son with the Father in the spirit of Nicea,⁵ such a commitment to the Council does not prevent him from reflecting in his theology a keen sense of the pneumatological framework of God's salvation in Christ:

> [E]verything that happened since the Lord's coming in the flesh, it all comes to pass through the Spirit. In the first place, the Lord was anointed with the Spirit, who would henceforth be inseparably united to His very flesh . . . After His baptism, the Holy Spirit was present in every action He performed. He was there when the Lord was tempted by the devil . . . The Spirit was united with Jesus when He performed miracles . . . Nor did the Spirit leave Him after His resurrection from the dead."⁶

Like Irenaeus, Basil represents something of an exception in the early history of theological reflection on Christ. Both theologians see no conflict between affirming the incarnate Word's preexistence/divinity and his reception of the anointing/unction (= Spirit) from the Father at the Jordan. Others would not always follow in their footsteps, minimizing to a significant degree the

---

3. Ibid., 42.

4. Cantalamessa speaks of "ontologization" in Greek culture as a tool used by theologians to define Jesus' identity in their historical context. His comments are set against the background of a discussion of the reasons for the theological neglect of Jesus' anointing: "Added to the nuisance of all these heresies [i.e., Gnosticism, Arianism, adoptionism] there is also an external factor: the strong tendency towards ontologization, characteristic of the Greek culture to which the people of those days, including the theologians, belonged. In this view, what matters, in everything, is 'what it was at the beginning,' the *arché* of things, that is to say their metaphysical constitution, not their becoming and their history; what matters is the essence, not the existence." *The Holy Spirit in the Life of Jesus*, 8.

5. See Basil, *Letter* 8.3 (*NPNF*² 8:116–17); Zizioulas argues that Basil did not employ the *homoousios* language of Nicea for the Holy Spirit at Constantinople I in AD 381 because the original function of the term was not to make a positive statement about the divine substance but rather a more modest negative one on the created-uncreated dialectic, namely, that the Son is *not* a mere creature. See "The Teaching of the 2nd Ecumenical Council on the Holy Spirit," 33–34.

6. Basil, *On the Holy Spirit* 16.39 (trans. Anderson). Basil cites the following texts: John 1:33, Matt 3:17, Acts 10:30, Matt 4:1, Matt 12:28, and John 20:22–23; "He [Christ] comes in the flesh, but the Spirit is never separated from Him" (ibid. 19.49).

Holy Spirit's place in the doctrine of Christ. In the end, this partial eclipse of biblical pneumatology does not simply stifle a robust theology of the Spirit per se but, more broadly, our understanding of God's own loving self-giving in the economy through Christ and in the Spirit for us and for our salvation.

To recover the constitutive role of the Holy Spirit in all major events of Jesus' life and mission, I propose a systematic construction of significant biblical witnesses to the Son's identity as receiver, bearer, and giver of God's Spirit.[7] After introducing the reader to the general pneumatic contours of events in Jesus' life, I show comparative Logos-oriented readings of the same events in the history of dogma and then propose ways to revitalize or invigorate their often-forgotten pneumatic dimensions. As heirs of a partial pneumatic weakening of Christology in the church's tradition, Christians will do well to revisit Basil's question.

JESUS AS RECEIVER OF GOD'S SPIRIT: THE PLACE OF THE SPIRIT IN THE CONCEPTION, ANOINTING, AND EXALTATION OF JESUS

Three major moments highlight Jesus' reception of God's Spirit. These are his conception and birth in Bethlehem, baptism or anointing at the Jordan, and exaltation at his resurrection, ascension, and session at the right hand of God. The other side of reception is, of course, giftedness. In Trinitarian terms, Jesus' receiving of the Spirit from the Father points at once to the Father's self-giving in the Spirit to his incarnate Son. God's identity as Father and fountain of gifts is an honorable biblical and patristic theme. To quote a familiar text: "Every generous act of giving, with every perfect gift, is from above, coming down from the Father of lights, with whom there is no variation or shadow due to change" (Jas 1:17). What applies to the Father's character as origin of gifts in regard to his children in history applies by analogy to his own personal or hypostatic identity as unoriginate source of the Son and the Holy Spirit. In Greek theology, the Father is origin (Gk.

---

7. A few contemporary examples of outlines and proposals in pneumatological Christology include Kasper, *Jesus the Christ*, esp. 230–74; Congar, "Pour Une Christologie Pneumatologique," 435–42 [ET, *I Believe in the Holy Spirit*, 3:165–73 (hereafter, *Holy Spirit*)]; and Congar, *The Word and the Spirit*, chap. 6; Ladaria, "Cristología del Logos y cristología del Espíritu," 353–60; and Ladaria, "La unción de Jesús y el don del Espíritu," 547–71; O'Donnell, "In Him and Over Him: The Holy Spirit in the Life of Jesus," 25–45; Wong, "The Holy Spirit in the Life of Jesus and of the Christian," esp. 59–72; Moltmann, *The Spirit of Life*, 60–71; Welker, *God the Spirit*, chap. 4; Pinnock, *Flame of Love*, chap. 3; Habets, *The Anointed Son*; and Habets, "Spirit Christology," 199–234; Alfaro, *Divino Compañero*.

archē), source (Gk. *pēgē*), and cause (Gk. *aitia*) of the eternal generation of the Son and procession of the Holy Spirit.[8] In the Latin tradition, the historical missions of the Son and the Holy Spirit find their ground respectively in the Son's passive generation from the Father and in the Holy Spirit's passive spiration from the Father (principally) and the Son.[9] In both Eastern and Western traditions, we find basic agreement in the teaching that God the Father is sheer and full generosity, both in his intradivine relations and in his acts for us in salvation history. We get the picture that the Father openly and freely gives to others neither less nor another than himself; in short, that the Father is the first personal cause of all created and uncreated gifts. We can apply this basic biblical and ecumenical insight to our thinking by speaking of Jesus as receiver of the Father's Spirit.

Conceived by the Holy Spirit: Early Spirit Christology and Luke 1:35

If the Father gives all things to his Son and the Son receives all things from his Father, should not this give-and-take apply to Jesus' receiving of the Spirit from the Father?[10] What greater gift could the Father give to his beloved Son? It is not surprising that John should make the case: "He [i.e., the Son] whom God has sent speaks the words of God, for he [i.e., God] gives the Spirit without measure [to the Son]. The Father loves the Son and has placed all things in his hands" (3:34–35). When does God initially bestow such an uncreated gift upon his beloved Son in the economy of salvation?

Jesus' conception and sanctification by the Holy Spirit in Mary's womb comes to mind. The Holy Spirit, "the power of the Most High," comes upon and overshadows the virgin; "*therefore* (Gk. *dio*), the child to be born will be

---

8. Zizioulas has argued that the Greek teaching on the Father as source and cause of the Son and the Holy Spirit follows from the Cappadocian's move towards the ontological priority of person over substance for defining God's being-in-relation in terms of freedom and love towards another. If the person is the concrete mode of being of divine substance or existence, then, a person in particular (i.e., the Father) must also be the origin of this divine existence. *Being as Communion*, 39–41; Zizioulas also points out that the term *aitia*, unlike *archē* or *pēgē* (often used by Augustine in the West), allows for no substantialist notion of person and thus denotes personal freedom in a way that the other two terms do not. See "The Teaching of the 2nd Ecumenical Council on the Holy Spirit," 37, 47.

9. In Latin theology, John 15:26 and 20:22 illustrate the Son's participation in the sending and breathing (or spiration) of the Holy Spirit. In Greek theology, however, John 15:26 is a classic text for affirming the unique procession of the Holy Spirit from the Father in distinction from the Latin *filioque*.

10. See Badcock, *Light of Truth & Fire of Love*, 28–30.

holy; he will be called Son of God" (Luke 1:35, italics mine). Luke does not ascribe only the birth and holiness of the child to the Holy Spirit, but even his identity as Son for us. The designation "Son of God" does not refer to the child's preexistence in the Father's eternal bosom (as in John 1:1-2, 18), but to his conception by the Spirit as the Davidic Messiah-king (cf. Luke 1:32-33).[11] The Spirit is God's dynamic power in history bringing forth God's kingdom in the Son.

The Spirit is neither the mother nor the father of the Son. Mary is Jesus' mother, God his Father. As an act of God's Spirit, however, the conception of "Emmanuel" (= "God with us") in the virgin does not only serve to protect Mary and Jesus against respective charges of adultery and bastardy (see Matt 1:18-25), but also directs us to Jesus' divine origin from the heavenly Father in that Jesus has no biological father (Matt 1:16 and 2:11, 13).[12] The Holy Spirit comes upon Mary as the power "of the Most High" (Gk. *hypsistou*)—a Lukan term for the Father (Luke 1:32, 76 and 8:28; Acts 16:17)—and so her child is the Son "of God" (not "of the Holy Spirit").[13] Yet the Holy Spirit mediates the Father-Son relationship in the economy, for the holy child Emmanuel becomes the messianic Son of God for us by means of the creative, eschatological power in history of the Father's Spirit.

At times, an overriding interest in Christ's inner-constitution as human and divine led early patristic exegesis to relativize the pneumatological dimensions of the incarnation. Interpreting the identity of Christ under the twofold *pneuma/sarx* pattern (especially Rom 1:3-4), an early type of orthodox Spirit Christology fostered what later came to be known as a "two-natures" Christology.[14] Prior to the first two ecumenical Councils, one can already find a substantial or essential use of the term "Spirit" that often takes priority over the personal (hypostatic) use formally consolidated at Constantinople I (A.D. 381). Thus the biblical term "Spirit" functions as a description for the divine substance in general (i.e., God) or Christ's divinity in particular (especially to refer to the preexistent Word).[15] Cantalamesa

---

11. Congar, *Holy Spirit*, 1:16; and Fitzmyer, *The Gospel according to Luke, I-IX*, 351; Luke's theology (1:32-33) finds its roots in the Old Testament's foreshadowing of the coming of the awaited Messiah through the line of David (esp. 2 Sam 7; cf. Isa 11:1-2; Pss 89:3-4, 34-37 and 132; and Isa 9:6-7).

12. See Davies and Allison, *The Gospel according to Saint Matthew*, 1:183, 248.

13. See Bertram, *TDNT*, esp. 8:619-20; in the New Testament, "God" (Gk. *ho theos*) refers primarily to a person, namely, the Father. See Rahner, "Theos in the New Testament," 79-148, esp. 125ff.

14. See Loofs, *Leitfaden zum Studium der Dogmengeschichte*, 14, 5a, cited in Pannenberg, *Jesus—God and Man*, 119.

15. See Simonetti, "Note di cristologia pneumatica," 201-32; for Simonetti's groundbreaking study of Luke 1:35, see 217-26; Kelly writes, "It is noteworthy that the all but

has argued that the Niceno-Constantinopolitan phrase "Incarnatus est de Spiritu Sancto ex Maria Virgine" had its origins in the notion that Christ as God was born of "spirit" (i.e., of God's substance) and as man was born of "flesh" (i.e., of Mary's substance).[16] Ignatius of Antioch (ca. 35–ca. 107) shows us an early post-apostolic example of this interpretation. He speaks of Jesus Christ as "possessed both of flesh and spirit; both made and not made; God existing in flesh; true life in death; both of Mary and of God; first possible and then impossible."[17] More concretely, in a reference to Luke 1:35, Justin Martyr, for example, argues that "it is wrong . . . to understand the Spirit and the power of God as anything else than the Word."[18] In the West, Tertullian (ca. 160–ca. 225) speaks of Christ as one who possesses "the two substances, both of flesh and of the Spirit," which respectively signify his "being generated in the flesh as man" and his being "born of God" (i.e., of the Spirit).[19] The same interpretive principle applies to Tertullian's understanding of Luke 1:35:

> Now, by saying 'the Spirit of God' (although the Spirit of God *is* God,) and by not directly naming God, he wished that portion of the whole *Godhead* to be understood, which was about to retire into the designation of 'the Son.' The Spirit of God in this passage must be the same *as the* Word. . . . For both the Spirit is the substance of the Word, and the Word is the operation of the Spirit, and the Two are One (and the same).[20]

In the history of dogma, there are Logos-oriented readings of texts in which the Holy Spirit's role in effecting the conception, sanctification, and identity of the child as messianic Son in the economy are interpreted as a description of the preexistent Word's forming, sanctifying, and assuming

---

unanimous exegetical tradition of *Luke* I,35, equated 'the holy spirit' and 'the power of the Most High' which were to come upon Mary, not with the third person of the Trinity, but with Christ Who, preexisting as spirit or Word, was to incarnate Himself in her womb." Kelly, *Early Christian Doctrines*, 144–45; Lactantius is another example of such pre-Nicene Spirit Christology. See McGukin, "Spirit Christology," 141–48.

16. See Cantalamessa, "«Incarnatus de Spiritu Sancto ex Maria Virgine»," 101–9. He proposes that Luke 1:35 (along with Matthew 1:20) was read through Romans 1:3–4, which in turn was interpreted in light of John 1:14; however, if we follow Loofs's thesis, we may have to leave some room for the possibility that John 1:14 was read through Paul's *pneuma/sarx* pattern.

17. Ignatius, *Letter to the Ephesians* 7 (shorter version) (*ANF* 1:52); cf. Hermas, *Similitude Fifth* 6 (*ANF* 2:35–36).

18. Justin, *First Apology* 33 (*ANF* 1:174).

19. Tertullian, *On the Flesh of Christ* 18 (*ANF* 3:537).

20. Tertullian, *Against Praxeas* 26 (*ANF* 3:622); cf. *On the Flesh of Christ* 14 (*ANF* 3:534).

of the flesh unto himself. In his reading of Luke 1:35 (in combination with Luke 1:32 and Matt 1:21), for example, Justin speaks of the Word (not the Holy Spirit) as "this which, when it came upon the virgin and overshadowed her, caused her to conceive, not by intercourse, but by power."[21] In the East, Cyril of Jerusalem (ca. 315-86) and John of Damascus (ca. 675-ca. 749) sought to distinguish the work of the Word—for them also, "the power of the Most High" in Luke 1:35—in the assumption and formation of the flesh from the work of the Holy Spirit in the sanctification of Mary (although not the fruit of her womb) to receive the preexistent Word.[22] In the latter move, a Spirit-oriented Mariology takes priority over a Spirit-oriented Christology proper.[23]

In the West, Thomas Aquinas (ca. 1225-1274) sees "the power of the Most High" in Luke 1:35 as a reference to the Son, who is according to Paul "the power of God." He concludes that "the Power of God, which is the Son himself, according to *I Corinthians* [see 1 Cor 1:24], *Christ the Power of God*, through the Holy Spirit formed the body which he assumed."[24] Although Thomas does not identify "the Holy Spirit" with the Son (as Justin Martyr and others do), he still wants to read "the power of the Most High" as a reference to the Son who assumes a body at conception. We may say that Thomas reads Paul, and indirectly John 1:1-14, into Luke 1:35. Admittedly, the Holy Spirit does have a role in the formation of Jesus' body. Yet in line with a Logos-oriented Christology, Thomas finally has to make "the Power of God" (i.e., the Son) the personal subject of actions (including his own body's formation) taking place through his assumed humanity.

Thomas's Logos-oriented approach to Christology posits the full and perfect sanctification of the assumed humanity through the hypostatic union (or "grace of union") as an act effected by the preexistent Logos. Jesus' reception of grace and growth in holiness throughout his life and work (i.e.,

---

21. Justin, *First Apology* 33 (ANF 1:174).

22. For Cyril, see Granado, "Pneumatología de San Cirilo de Jerusalén," 446-48; for John, see *An Exact Exposition of the Orthodox Faith* 3.2 (NPNF² 9:46).

23. In contemporary Eastern theology, within the framework of reflection on the humanization of God, Bulgakov speaks of a hypostasizing of the Holy Spirit in the virgin Mary correlative to the hypostatizing of the Logos in Jesus. Just as the personal identity between Jesus and the Logos points to divine sonship as a concrete manifestation of God's humanity through the Logos's act of incarnation, so does the identity between the Mary and the Holy Spirit point to divine motherhood through the Spirit's act of sanctifying her humanity in the fullness of grace from the moment of the Annunciation onwards. See *Le Paraclet*, 236-40; studying the Russian texts, Valliere gives us an invaluable summary and analysis of Bulgakov's theology and Spirit-oriented Mariology. See Valliere, *Modern Russian Theology*, 320-28.

24. *ST* 3a, q. 32, a. 1, ad. 1.

his "habitual grace") may be attributed or appropriated to the Holy Spirit but finally depends on the grace of union.[25] In the framework of Thomas's distinction between the *gratia unionis* and the *gratia habitualis* and the dependence of the latter on the former, the Spirit's proper work of sanctifying the fruit of Mary's womb runs the risk of being seen as accidental in the sense that its work is ultimately ascribed to the Logos or his divine effects in the world.[26] We shall return to this distinction later on.

A Spirit Christology reminds a Logos-oriented one that, despite its genuine ontological interest in preserving Jesus' divine identity as God and personal identity as incarnate Logos, a robust biblical theology must still deal adequately with references to the Spirit in the life of Christ. A Spirit Christology notes, for instance, that Luke's references to "the Holy Spirit" and "the power of the Most High" do not point to the Logos, but function as parallel terms referring to the Holy Spirit and his activity in the Christ child. Evidence for this claim lies in Luke's link between "Spirit" and "power" (see Luke 24:49, Acts 1:8 and 10:38).[27] In Luke-Acts, the term "power" points to the Spirit in its work as the Father's creative eschatological presence in the life of Jesus and his disciples. The Holy Spirit is both inseparably united to God and sent from God, yet distinct from the divine nature in general or the preexistent Logos in particular. In the aftermath of Constantinople I, we can speak of the Holy Spirit as a personal agent in its own right, one whose descent upon and overshadowing of Mary makes the fruit of her womb "holy" from the first instance of his existence for us as the messianic "Son of God." Consequently, the Holy Spirit (and not the preexistent Son) effects the conception and sanctification of the Christ child in the new times of salvation, constituting or making him messianic "Son of God" (Luke 1:35), "Emmanuel" (= "God with us," Matt 1:23, quoting Isa 7:14), and the *enfleshed* Word (John 1:14). We may say that the Word alone *assumes* and *becomes*

---

25. "The grace of union is precisely God's free gift to the human nature of having personal existence in the Word, and that is the term of the assumption. Habitual grace, forming part of the special holiness of this man, is an effect following upon the union." *ST* 3a, q. 6, a. 6.

26. Classical Lutheran Christology assumes this scholastic distinction in such a way that the divine Logos confers habitual gifts on his own human nature as a result of his power or operations following from his prior communication of his divine attributes to his own flesh at the hypostatic union. Here the habitual gifts are implicitly ascribed to the divine Logos—a move that tends to relativize the defining actions of the Spirit of the Father in the humanity of the Son. See Chemnitz, *The Two Natures in Christ*, chap. 20.

27. See Walter Grundmann, *TDNT*, 2:300–301, 310–11; in Luke 1:35, *pneuma hagion* and *dynamis hypsistou* function as parallel terms. Luke links Spirit and power in phrases like *ex hypsous dynamis* (24:49) and *dynamin epelthontos tou hagiou pneumatos* (Acts 1:8).

flesh, but he does so *in the Spirit*, namely, in a manner that the preexistent Son receives from his Father in the economy of salvation, and therefore for us, the Holy Spirit who creates and perfects in holiness what the Son at once assumes.

In Thomas's Logos-oriented reading of Luke 1:35, the preexistent Word is the personal subject of acts occurring in and through his assumed humanity. The legitimate concern to safeguard the personal or hypostatic identity of Jesus and the Logos drives the reading—an important concern of Logos-oriented Christology against Nestorianizing *Logos-man* readings that tend to divide the *one* person of Christ. Maintaining a proper distinction between the presence of the Logos and the Holy Spirit in Christ's assumed humanity, a Spirit-oriented Christology helps us to affirm that the Holy Spirit in its own right is a personal agent of acts in and through the man Jesus, who is none other than the incarnate Logos. The first of such acts occurs at the conception and sanctification of the humanity of the Son, who receives the power and gift of the Spirit of the Father in the flesh for us. Other defining pneumatic events follow in the course of Jesus' human existence.

Anointed with the Spirit of the Lord: The Revelatory and Exemplary Character of Jesus' Baptism and the Incarnation As Anointing

The unique sanctifying presence of the Spirit of God in Jesus from conception should not take away from Jesus' reception of the Spirit at the Jordan. The former event constitutes Jesus as "holy" child and messianic "Son" for us. The latter one points to his anointing for mission as faithful Son and suffering Servant: "And the Holy Spirit descended upon him in bodily form like a dove. And a voice came from heaven, 'You are my Son, the Beloved, with you I am well pleased'" (Luke 3:22, cf. Ps 2:7 and Isa 42:1).[28] The presentation of the event in all four Gospels confirms its importance for the earliest church (Mark 1:9–11, Matt 3:13–17, Luke 3:21–22, and John 1:29–34). Along with Jesus' death and resurrection, Peter includes in his preaching the baptism at Jordan as a basic datum of the nascent apostolic church's faith: "[You know] . . . how God anointed (Gk. *echrisen*) Jesus of Nazareth with

---

28. The Western variant reading (D) quotes Psalm 2:7 in its totality: "You are my Son, today I have begotten you." The variant allows for the church's interpretation of Jesus' baptism as a new "birth" or "begetting" in his humanity for us. See McDonnell, *The Baptism of Jesus in the Jordan*, chap. 6.

the Holy Spirit and with power; how he went about doing good and healing all who were oppressed by the devil, for God was with him" (Acts 10:38).[29]

In terms of the economic succession of events in the Gospels, we may say that Jesus' identity as "Christ" (= anointed one) does not become a concrete reality *for us* until the Father anoints *him* at the Jordan with his [i.e., the Father's] Spirit for mission. Indeed, the child Jesus is announced as the messianic King and Savior prior to his baptism (see Luke 1:32-33 and 2:11-12, 25-26). I have already spoken of the Spirit's eschatological role in bringing forth God's kingdom on earth through the creation and sanctification of the Messiah-king from conception. But Luke never speaks of Jesus' "anointing" or "chrism" as a metaphor for the Logos's communication of his divinity to his flesh at the *incarnation*—a move made by some church fathers. Rather, the anointing of the Son is an event that takes place when the Spirit descends upon him at his baptism (Luke 4:18-19; again Acts 10:38).

Basil refers to texts on Jesus' anointing as "Christ" at his baptism (Acts 10:38, Isa 61:1, and Ps 45:7) to defend Christian baptism in the name of the triune God: "To address Christ . . . is a complete profession of faith, because it clearly reveals that God anoints the Son (the Anointed One) with the unction (*chrisma*) of the Spirit."[30] Christian baptism is grounded in Christ's own baptism. In Luke, it is Jesus' reception of God's Spirit at this moment of his life and work (and not before) that fulfills Isaiah's prophecy (61:1-2) and makes of the event—to use Congar's appropriation of biblical language—a *kairos* that adds something new to Jesus' identity as Son in the economy of salvation.[31] Our reflections thus far suggest that Scripture allows for a qualitative distinction between the sanctification of Jesus by the Spirit from the time of conception and his anointing with the Spirit later on at the Jordan.[32] The point is not to deny Jesus his full reception of the Spirit from conception and birth, but to acknowledge the Spirit's dynamic and ongoing

---

29. Given the influence of Epiphanius's shorter creed in the phrasing of the creed at Constantinople I, it seems remarkable to me that the Council did not include a reference to the baptism of Jesus from a longer creed of the saint written in his *Ancoratus* as early as AD 374. In the third article, Epiphanius's longer creed gives witness to the Holy Spirit "who descended at Jordan" (*NPNF*² 14:164). In terms of the pneumatic aspects of Christ's conception, the reader should note that whereas Nicea only spoke of the Son who "was incarnate," Constantinople I (and Epiphanius before that) spoke of the Son who "was incarnate of (Gk. *ek*) the Holy Ghost and the Virgin Mary" (*NPNF*² 14:162-63).

30. Basil, *On the Holy Spirit* 12.28 (trans. Anderson).

31. Congar defines "kairoi" as "authentic qualitative moments in which God's communication of himself in Jesus Christ and in a very real sense also *to* Jesus Christ was accomplished." *The Word and the Spirit*, 87; italics mine.

32. See Ladaria, "La unción de Jesús y el don del Espíritu," 552-53.

presence in him throughout the course of his entire life and work. At the Jordan, the Son is anointed with the Spirit to begin his prophetic mission and establish God's kingly rule in our midst. By the anointing of the Father's Spirit at the Jordan, the Son becomes, is made, or inaugurates his existence in God's plan of salvation as the obedient Son and suffering Servant.

In a Logos-oriented Christology, Jesus' baptism often appears to be only an accidental event that affirms nothing new about his own identity. Since the descent of the Spirit upon Jesus seems to threaten his previous status as preexistent Son or his full reception of the Spirit from conception, the event is only significant either as a *public confirmation* for others of Jesus' prior identity as God and Christ or as an *exemplary prefigurement* of Christian baptism. In order to reconcile Christ's preexistence with his reception of the Spirit at Jordan, we recall Justin Martyr's argument that Christ does not need the Holy Spirit at his baptism because he already fully possessed the anointing as Christ/God from eternity and thus his divine power from birth; therefore, the event basically reveals for our sake who Jesus already is. We also recall Athanasius's somewhat static view of the Spirit in the humanity of the Word, as seen in his tendency to equate the Son's anointing with the sanctification of his flesh from birth. The "Spirit" the Son already has from the time of the incarnation *as man*, he does not seem to receive in a new way at the Jordan.

In their respective struggles and reactions against Arianism and Nestorianism, Athanasius and Cyril of Alexandria (d. 444) speak of the anointing as the glorification of the divine Word, who "anoints," "sanctifies," or "glorifies"—all synonyms—his assumed humanity at the incarnation with his own Spirit. At the Jordan, the Spirit proceeds from the Word for others.[33] Like Athanasius, Cyril is somewhat hesitant to speak of a passive reception of the Spirit at the Jordan by the incarnate Christ, because he conceives of the Word above all as one who "gives" the Spirit *as God* unto others.[34] Overall, the anointing is ultimately more for us than for the Son himself—unless, of course, the Son actively glorifies himself through the Spirit's resting on his

---

33. Ibid. On Cyril's position, see Odero, "La Unción de Cristo según S. Cirilo Alejandrino," 203–8, and his more extensive study, "La Unción y el Bautismo de Cristo en S. Cirilo de Alejandría," 519–40.

34. Concerning his *Declaratio Septima*, Cyril echoes Athanasius's approach. He seems to subtly underplay Jesus' passive reception of the Holy Spirit by stressing Christ's identity as *giver* of the Spirit and the implications of the event *for the race of Adam*: "But he was named also Christ, because that according to his human nature he was anointed *with us* [then Cyril cites Ps 45:8]. For although he was the *giver* of the Holy Spirit . . . nevertheless as he is man he was *called* anointed economically, the Holy Spirit resting upon him spiritually . . . in order that he might abide *in us.*" See *The XII. Anathematisms of St. Cyril against Nestorius* (NPNF² 14:214); italics mine.

flesh. As giver of the Spirit, the divine Word must be the subject of his own glorification as man, "for it is believed that he who works through his own Spirit is God according to nature."[35] Cyril's position that the Word glorifies himself with "his own Spirit" finds its ultimate ground in the idea that the Holy Spirit receives from the Son as third in the order of eternal processions and, moreover, in the teaching that the Holy Spirit abides in and with the Son and the Father eternally in the divine unity.[36] The implications of the Jordan as a witness to the Logos's divinity and to his giving of the Spirit to the church remain important contributions of a Logos-oriented Christology in Nicene key, even if the historical dynamics of the Holy Spirit's influential presence and activity in the Son's concrete fleshly existence are not always highlighted.

Suffice it to say that, in the events surrounding the Council of Ephesus (A.D. 431), Cyril is influenced by Athanasius's prior arguments against the Arians in his own debates with Nestorius. All the basic elements of Cyril's position on the Spirit's resting in Christ are already in place in his early anti-Arian work, and thus before the Nestorian controversy. In Cyril's exegesis of John 3 and 7, for instance, he highlights that the Son has the Spirit (or holy anointing) essentially as God, and that as man he has preserved the same Spirit in his own flesh for us from the moment of his incarnation.[37] Overall, Athanasius and Cyril hesitate a bit to give the incarnate Word's reception of the Holy Spirit at the Jordan fuller christological weight, in part because of the problem of adoptionism but also due to their tendency to see human nature in more abstract or universal rather than historical or concrete terms. Otherwise stated, their soteriology stresses what the Logos does universally

---

35. *The Epistle of Cyril to Nestorius with the XII. Anathematisms* (NPNF² 14:204).

36. See Petavius's comments on Cyril's ninth anathema against Nestorius, in ibid., 215; the position of the Lutheran confessors on the anointing of Christ's assumed humanity has deep roots in Athanasius's and Cyril's Alexandrian approach. Consider the following argument: "[B]ecause according to his deity Christ is the second person of the Holy Trinity and *because the Holy Spirit proceeds from him* as he does from the Father (and therefore he is and remains forever the Spirit of Christ and of the Father, never separated from the Son), the entire fullness of the Spirit . . . is imparted to Christ according to the flesh because it is personally united with the Son of God through the personal union." FC, SD 8.73, in *BC*, 630; italics mine.

37. Cyril's heading before his exegesis of John 1:32-33 shows the influence of Athanasius in his theological language: "The Holy Spirit is in the Son not by participation or as something brought in from the outside but essentially and by nature." *Commentary on John*, p. 77; Cyril notes that the Son "did not receive anything for himself personally because he himself is the supplier of the Spirit" (82), and condemns the Arian teaching that "the Spirit is in the Son by participation or that he came to be in him when he was baptized during the time of the incarnation, and was not in him before" (83); for John 7, see pp. 308-12.

for all human nature through his own human nature, rather than what the Father does in, with, and through the Logos by the Holy Spirit through each event of his human life and history. This soteriological move is not inadequate in and of itself, and is not unique to Cyril, but can benefit from other patristic contributions that give more weight to the place of the influence of the Spirit in the Son's human existence.[38] Furthermore, their Logos-oriented readings of the anointing in terms of the Word's self-glorification of his own flesh tend to underplay the personal identity of the Father as the ultimate fountain, origin, source, and personal cause of the Spirit's anointing.[39] This is a general tendency in the Alexandrian approach to Christology.

In the West, Augustine (354–430) goes as far as denying that Christ was anointed at the Jordan and instead finds the significance of the event in its prefiguration of the church's reception of the Spirit in baptism.[40] Since Christ had all things—including "the grace of the Holy Spirit"—from the time of the hypostatic union, Thomas argues that he "did not need a baptism in the spirit.... Christ wished to be baptized in order to lead us to baptism by his example."[41] So the baptism of Jesus only has a proclamatory and/or exemplary function *for others*, not a determinative one *for Jesus*. Augustine's claim that Jesus was not anointed at his baptism is not exactly a denial of his anointing but rather its transposition to the moment of the incarnation:

> But He [i.e., Christ] is understood to have been then anointed with that mystical and invisible unction, when the Word of God was made flesh, *i.e.* when human nature, without any precedent

---

38. Bobrinskoy argues that "Gregory the Theologian was closer to the Alexandrian tradition" and "seems more reluctant than St. Basil to investigate the mystery of Christ's humanity and the mode of the Spirit's presence within that humanity. The Spirit, he affirmed, is present but not acting: a formula that expresses his fear of diminishing the personal role of the divine Word-become-man." "The Indwelling of the Spirit in Christ," 64 (cf. 60–62).

39. Alexandrian theology tends to underplay the Eastern concern for safeguarding the Father's unique hypostatic identity as ultimate cause (*aitia*) of the procession of the Holy Spirit. See Zizioulas, "The Teaching of the 2nd Ecumenical Council on the Holy Spirit," 43–44.

40. "And Christ was certainly not then anointed with the Holy Spirit, when He, as a dove, descended upon Him at His baptism. For at that time he deigned to prefigure His body, *i.e.* His Church, in which especially the baptized receive the Holy Spirit." *On the Holy Trinity* 15.26.46 (*NPNF*[1] 3:224).

41. *ST* 3a, q. 39, a. 2, ad. 1; Thomas represents the classic example of what Congar calls a "non-historical" theology in which "Christ possessed everything from the time of his conception and, in what are reported in Scripture as institutive events, there is simply a manifestation for others of a reality that is already there." See Congar, "Pour Une Christologie Pneumatologique," 436 [ET, *Holy Spirit*, 3:166].

merits and good works, was joined to God the Word in the womb of the Virgin, so that with it it became one person.[42]

A line of thinking exists in the patristic tradition that places the anointing of Jesus at the moment of the hypostatic union and ascribes such unction to the Logos.[43] In the East, after Athanasius, Gregory Nazianzen (329-89) refers to the preexistent Christ as "the Anointing of His manhood."[44] John of Damascus explains the hypostatic union as an event in which Christ "in His own person anointed Himself; as God anointed His body with His own divinity, and as Man being anointed. For He is Himself both God and Man. And the anointing is the divinity of His humanity."[45] Unlike Irenaeus and Basil, these fathers use "chrism," "anointing," and "unction" as metaphors for the Word, not the Holy Spirit; and therefore, as language pointing to the incarnation of the Logos at Bethlehem and not to the incarnate Logos's baptism with the Spirit of the Father at the Jordan.

A pneumatological Christology reminds a Logos-oriented one that, strictly speaking, its apologetic move to place the anointing at the incarnation and ascribe it to the divine Word cannot be justified on the basis of the Gospels.[46] The Jordan event does not point merely to one instance (along with and resulting from the incarnation) of the Word's self-glorification or anointing of his humanity with his own Spirit. The event is a unique anointing of the Son by the Father with his own [i.e., the Father's] Spirit for his mission. Even if Jesus receives the Spirit of God from the first moment of the hypostatic union, such a presence of the Spirit in him cannot be thought of in static terms.

Instead, the presence of the Holy Spirit in the incarnate Son has both dynamic and relational dimensions. The former aspect allows for each descent of the Spirit upon Jesus in God's economy of salvation to *actualize* or

---

42. Augustine, *On the Holy Trinity* 15.26.46 (*NPNF*[1] 3:224). Augustine's language is quite likely used against the adoptionist principle in the Pelagian (and even Donatist) idea that human nature requires "merits and good works" to be adopted by God. The analogy from the realm of grace in the case of Christology is that human merits are required to be assumed by the divine Word.

43. See Ladaria, "La unción de Jesús y el don del Espíritu," 547-53.

44. Gregory writes, "He is Christ, because of His Godhead. For this is the Anointing of His manhood, and does not sanctify by its action, but by the Presence in His Fulness of the Anointing One; the effect of which is that That which anoints is called man, and makes that which is anointed God." Gregory Nazianzen, *The Fourth Theological Oration* 21 (*NPNF*[2] 7:317).

45. John of Damascus, *An Exact Exposition of the Orthodox Faith* 3.3 (*NPNF*[2] 9:47).

46. A point forcefully made by exegete Potterie, "L'Onction du Christ," 225-52.

change (and not simply reveal or proclaim) his identity as Son in a new way.[47] By actualization, I mean an understanding of the Son's identity in terms of his "being-in-act" or becoming throughout his entire human history. In other words, I am suggesting a more dynamic view of the incarnation—an *incarnating*, as it were—that complements the more static Logos-oriented view in which the term incarnation applies strictly to an event that takes place at a set or absolute point in time (i.e., hypostatic union). The ecstatic, social, or relational dimension of the Spirit's presence in the incarnate Son points to the intrinsic *pro nobis* character of the incarnation, to its soteriological orientation towards all events in Jesus' life and work carried out *in the Spirit*, namely, in loving obedience to the Father and as our Servant.[48] From an ontological angle, pneumatology brings dynamism and relationality to an incarnational Christology.

A Spirit Christology does not have to deny the baptism its proclamatory and exemplary character as an event that leads others to Jesus as the Christ. Neither does our approach to the anointing seek to do away with the import of the Jordan event for the church's administration of Christian baptism. However, a Spirit Christology insists in grounding these aspects of Christ's anointing in the significance of the event for the incarnate Son himself. If the baptism serves as an occasion to deny Christ's preexistence or undermine his full reception of the Spirit from conception, then it is appropriate to say that he does not need the baptism according to his divinity or that he does not only receive the Spirit for the first time at the Jordan. Yet too much stress on these points can make us forget a critical dimension of the narrative (especially in the Synoptics), namely, that the Jordan event is a free, loving, and generous act of the Father towards his incarnate Son through a new descent of his [i.e., the Father's] Spirit in and upon him for mission. It is also, therefore, a free, loving, and new reception of the Spirit of the Father by his incarnate Son in the economy to carry out the work of salvation for us and in view of his giving of the Spirit to us.

Theologians already cited admittedly succeeded in articulating the import of Jesus' anointing for the Christian church, but less so for Jesus himself as the anointed one of the Father in his own right. By proposing a needed corrective in Logos-oriented approaches to the anointing of Christ,

---

47. Congar writes, "God's work takes place in human history. It is achieved in a series of events situated in time, which, once they have happened, contribute something new and bring about changes . . . There were successive events in which the Spirit descended on Jesus as Christ the Saviour." *Holy Spirit*, 3:166.

48. "Christology should not be separated from soteriology . . . The incarnation has an aim and that aim is Easter, the resurrection, and eschatological fulfillment." Ibid., 165.

I do not intend to undermine what church fathers clearly saw, namely, the soteriological significance of Jesus' receiving of the Spirit for the church's receiving of the same. A Spirit Christology can most naturally incorporate this genuine patristic concern in a discussion of Jesus' identity as giver of the Spirit. But such giving of the Spirit will have to assume and be grounded in the Son's prior receiving of the same Spirit for us in his humanity at the Jordan. Whereas the Son has the Spirit for himself already from conception, a Spirit Christology notes that it is only from the moment of his anointing with the Spirit at the Jordan that the Gospels link more directly the presence of the Spirit in the Son with his giving of the same to others in the new creation.

Risen, Ascended, and Seated at the Right Hand of God: The Confirming Character of Jesus' Resurrection and His Exaltation at the Incarnation

As the risen and ascended Christ and Lord, Jesus receives the Spirit of God the Father in order to pour it forth: "Being therefore exalted at the right hand of God, and having received (*labōn*) from the Father the promise (Gk. *epangelian*) of the Holy Spirit, he has poured out this that you both see and hear" (Acts 2:33).[49] What Jesus receives from God the Father after his resurrection is the Spirit as eschatological "promise" (*epangelian*, Luke 24:49, Acts 1:4), namely, as the Spirit whom the Father promises to send unto others through his exalted Son: "for John baptized with water, but you will be baptized with the Holy Spirit not many days from now" (Acts 1:5, cf. Luke 24:49). Admittedly, a strong link exists between Jesus' reception of the Spirit at Jordan and his reception of the Spirit as the risen Messiah and Lord. The former event serves as the condition for the latter, and in the end both are oriented towards the communication of the eschatological Spirit to others. Jesus receives the Spirit from the Father at the Jordan for his eschatological mission to break in God's kingdom in our midst. But only upon his completion of such a redemptive mission does he, as risen and exalted Lord, receive the "promise" of the Spirit from the Father to gather the nations in the apostolic church through the Word and baptism in the name of Jesus.

In a Logos-oriented Christology, Jesus may be said to receive the fullness of grace both in a "personal" manner (i.e., for himself) and in a "capital" manner (i.e., as head of the church) already from the first moment of the

---

49. From an economic perspective, Acts 2:33 points to a new reception of the Spirit by Jesus as exalted Messiah and Lord in view of his giving of the Spirit to all flesh for the sake of bringing the nations under the lordship of Jesus. Cf. Montague, *Holy Spirit*, 286.

hypostatic union. Although personal and capital grace are strictly identical in Christ, the Thomistic system highlights how personal grace is the condition for capital grace just as the grace of union precedes and is the cause of habitual grace.[50] This argument purports to ground Christ's communicable grace to and for others on his personal and unrepeatable reception of grace at the moment of the hypostatic union. A historical relativization of Jesus' reception of the Spirit at the Jordan and then as exalted Lord occurs.

In post-Vatican II circles, Heribert Mühlen sought to amend Thomas on this point. Seeing the church as a continuation of Christ's anointing (not of his incarnation per se) for others, Mühlen rightly sought to give habitual grace its complete historical dimension throughout the whole Christ-event.[51] This is a salutary move, even if Mühlen only saw the baptism as a public declaration of a reality already established at the incarnation.[52] He correctly understands that Jesus' perfect Spirit-led life of obedience to the Father throughout his messianic mission spanning from baptism to glorification is what allows for the extension of his habitual grace to the church.[53] However, Mühlen also seems somewhat hesitant to give the Holy Spirit a proper role in the sanctification of the Logos's assumed humanity, at least in part because of his strong concern for safeguarding the essential unity of God and of the divine operations in the economy of salvation.[54] Like Aquinas, he holds to the notion that Jesus' habitual grace in the Spirit must be the consequence of the Logos's prior sanctification of his assumed humanity.[55]

In a Logos Christology, even if one speaks of the glorification of Christ's humanity as risen Christ and Lord, the exaltation only confirms for or proclaims to others the lordship that the Logos already had *in the flesh* from the time of his incarnation. In classic Lutheran Christology, for instance, one can say that Christ "was elevated to the right hand of majesty" according to the assumed flesh, not merely "through the exaltation

---

50. Congar, *Holy Spirit*, 3:166, 172 (citing *ST* 3a, q. 7 and 8).

51. "El acontecimiento Cristo como acción del Espíritu Santo," 960–84; for a full treatment of the topic, see Mühlen, *Una Mystica Persona*; for a brief study in English, see Congar, *Holy Spirit*, 1:22–25; in Spanish, see Antón, "El Espíritu Santo y la Iglesia," 101–13; for a brief Greek approach to the link between the work of the Spirit in Christ and Christians, see Nissiotis, "Pneumatological Christology," 235–52.

52. See Mühlen, "Acontecimiento Cristo," 974.

53. Ibid., 975ff.

54. Ibid., 963–64.

55. Ibid., 973. Thomas's argument is based on the idea that the Son's procession from the Father logically precedes the Holy Spirit's procession from the Father *and the Son*. Mühlen cites *ST* 1, q. 7, a. 13.

or glorification" but already "through the personal union."[56] Therefore, the exaltation of Jesus as risen and ascended Lord and Messiah has an unveiling or revelatory character *for others*, but not a constitutive one *for Jesus himself* in the flesh. The significance of the Logos's unique reception of the Spirit of God the Father at this particular moment in the economy is transposed to the divine Logos's glorifying of his assumed humanity at the time of the hypostatic union.

If a Logos Christology posits the full communication of the Logos's divine attributes to the assumed humanity from conception, a Spirit-oriented Christology complements this view by attending to the particular actualizations of God's communication of the Spirit to this assumed humanity of the Logos at distinct stages of his human life and history.[57] Although we can affirm that Christ is always Lord according to his divinity just as he is always Lord in his humanity throughout his earthly life because of the personal union, the biblical data still does not allow us to conclude that he has been exalted at God's right hand *as risen Lord* prior to his resurrection. We can say, however, that the preexistent Word's "lordship," communicated to his assumed flesh at conception in a *personal* way, also becomes actualized (in contrast to only revealed or unveiled) for us and thus in a *capital* way (i.e., as head of the church) by means of an act of God through his Spirit in and upon the incarnate Word. These complementary formulations uphold the Logos-oriented concern for avoiding an adoptionist view of the Son's glorification as a mere man's exaltation to godhood, while also giving full weight to the Son's exaltation in the flesh as a new pneumatological event in God's economy of salvation that touches his humanity and thus opens the way for our exaltation in and through him.

---

56. FC, SD 8.13, in *BC*, 618. Consider the immediately preceding statement: "Christ did not only receive this majesty to which he was exalted according to his humanity only after he rose from the dead and ascended into heaven, but he received it already when he was conceived in his mother's womb and became a human being and the divine and human natures were united personally with each other" (Ibid., 8.12).

57. The Lutheran tradition has room for this approach: "Based upon the personal union... the human nature (when it was glorified *after laying aside the form of a servant* and after the humiliation and was exalted to the right hand of the majesty and power of God) *also received, alongside of and in addition to* its natural, essential characteristics (which always remain), special, high, great, supernatural, incomprehensible, indescribable heavenly prerogatives and privileges in majesty, glory, power, and might over all things that can be named, not only in this world but also in the world to come." FC, SD 8.51, in *BC*, 625; italics mine. The question remains as to how the Logos's reception of *the Spirit* for us as glorified Messiah and Lord may be said to effect such additional supernatural "prerogatives and privileges" in his own humanity "after laying aside the form of a servant."

Reading the Story of Jesus as Receiver and Bearer of God's Spirit 49

Following Congar, we may say that a Spirit Christology invigorates Logos-oriented approaches to the exaltation of Jesus by seeing his resurrection as a new *kairos* in which God has actually made him (not simply proclaimed or declared him as) ascended Lord and Messiah (see Acts 2:32–36 and Heb 1:13; cf. Ps 110:1).[58] Significantly, there is a similar concern for expressing such a historically dynamic or economically conscious Christology in the pre-Augustinian Western tradition. Following the New Testament's appropriation of Psalm 2:7 ("You are my son; today I have begotten you") to refer to Jesus' exalted status as ascended Lord (cf. Acts 13:32–33), Hilary of Poitiers (ca. 315–67) interprets God's raising of Jesus from the dead as a new "birth" as Son *in his own humanity*, and because of that, *for us*. Moreover, the doctor applies the psalm's language of begetting to other events in Jesus' life and work. Hilary speaks of Jesus' four births: 1) in eternity as Son of God, begotten of the Father; 2) in Bethlehem as incarnate Son of God, born of Mary according to his humanity; 3) in the Jordan as Son of God, reborn in his humanity for obedience to God for our sake; and 4) at the resurrection as Son of God, fully reborn in his glorified humanity for us.[59] The basis for this christological dynamism is Hilary's view of the influential role of "Spirit" (*spiritus*) in the growth or progress in sanctification of the Son's humanity—a growth in holiness that enters a decisive moment at his anointing at Jordan and comes to fulfillment in his bodily resurrection, securing our participation by grace in his glorified humanity.[60]

Hilary defines "Spirit" substantially as "divinity" and personally (or hypostatically) as the third member of the Trinity who is the Father's "gift"

---

58. Congar, *Holy Spirit*, 3:168–69.

59. See Ladaria, "El bautismo y la unción de Jesús en Hilario de Poitiers," 283, 287–88; and "El Espíritu Santo en San Hilario de Poitiers," esp. 250–51. Both articles follow ideas first developed in his books *El Espíritu Santo en San Hilario de Poitiers*; and *La cristología de Hilario de Poitiers*. Congar outlines an approach similar to Hilary's intention: "Jesus is Son on several accounts. He is Son by eternal generation: 'begotten, not made.' He is therefore the *monogenitus* or *monogenēs*. In a theology of the economy of salvation, however, we must take very seriously the texts in which Ps 2:7—'You are my son, today I have begotten you'—is applied to history. It is so applied in the first place . . . to the annunciation by the angel: 'he will be called the Son of God' (Lk 1:35). Later, it is applied to the theophany at Jesus' baptism (Mt 3:17; Mk 1:10; Lk 3:22) and to the resurrection and exaltation of Christ (Acts 13: 33; Heb 1:5; 5:5)." *Holy Spirit*, 3:170.

60. Ladaria notes that Hilary is aware of the Arian teaching on the deification of the Son *as god*, and against it "insists that this sanctification is a 'rebirth' [Sp. *renacimiento*] that affects the assumed humanity so that it can 'progress' until its full deification at the resurrection, and so that *as man* Jesus too might be the Son of God . . . the full rebirth of the *man* Jesus as Son of God happens at the resurrection, but the baptism at the Jordan constitutes a decisive moment in this process of growth of Christ's humanity." *La cristología de Hilario de Poitiers*, 117–18 (cf. 115–16); translation and italics mine.

for others. The former use is equally applied to the Father or the Son according to the *pneuma/sarx* pattern of ante-Nicene Spirit-oriented Christologies; the latter one applies only to the Holy Spirit as God's personal gift to the church.[61] Since Hilary interprets "Spirit" in substantial terms as the divinity of the Son, then, it follows that the incarnation takes place through the descent of the Holy Spirit (= Son) upon Mary (Luke 1:35).[62] Similarly, the anointing of Jesus for mission occurs at the moment of the Spirit's descent upon him, or in other words, of the Son's descent upon himself with the divine power that he receives from the Father (Luke 3:22, 4:18).[63] Still the action of "Spirit" (= divinity) in Jesus at each of these moments does not cease to point to a growth or process of sanctification or divinization of his own "flesh" (humanity) that only reaches its final glorification at the resurrection.[64] At that time, he is reborn as the glorified or risen Son in his humanity and thus for us.

Undoubtedly, Hilary's dynamic understanding of "Spirit" in the life of Christ allows us to interpret Jesus' anointing and resurrection in non-adoptionist fashion as "births" in the sense of Luke's appropriation of Psalm 2:7 in the Western variant reading (D) of Luke 3:22 (for the baptism) and Acts 13:33 (for the resurrection). Unlike other theologians who lived before, during, and after him (e.g., Justin, Athanasius, and Augustine), Hilary sees no conflict between this dynamic form of early Spirit Christology and his strong orthodox anti-Arian commitment. Hilary gives full weight to the active role of "Spirit" as the divine power of the Father in and upon the humanity of Christ during his life and mission as obedient and faithful Son.

An important question remains: Should Hilary's exegesis be interpreted through the *pneuma/sarx* pattern? At this point, the problem of the precise "identity" of the "Spirit" that comes upon Jesus—so common in many

---

61. Ladaria observes that Hilary thinks of the Spirit's personal essence largely in terms of gift, so that being the third person of the Trinity amounts to being gift. See Ladaria, "El Espíritu Santo en San Hilario de Poitiers," 244. This view seems to be related to the Holy Spirit's being *ex Patre per Filium* (i.e., from the Father through the Son), although Hilary does not speak definitively (or is reserved) on articulating the Spirit's *ad intra* mode of procession. Ibid., 244, 246–48. Hilary appears to be more interested in the Holy Spirit's work *ad extra* in relation to believers. Ibid., 245–48, esp. 247.

62. Ibid., 249.

63. Ibid., 250.

64. Ibid., 250–51; for a summary, see Granado, "El Don del Espíritu de Jesús en san Hilario de Poitiers," 436–45. Granado includes Hilary's view of Jesus' miracles (e.g., exorcisms) as demonstrations of his divinity (= Spirit)—and thus also as a moment of partial glorification of his flesh (= humanity) on the road to its full glorification at the resurrection—and rarely as instances of the Spirit's activity in him as the third one of the Trinity. Granado, "El Don del Espíritu de Jesús en san Hilario de Poitiers," 441–44.

of Hilary's writings—comes to the forefront.[65] Who or what is "Spirit"? We can surely benefit from Hilary's insights into the Spirit-oriented dimensions of Jesus' progress in sanctification and economic identity as "Son" for us, but this would require a revision of his exegetical basis for such a claim so that the Holy Spirit as such (i.e., as a personal agent) and not simply as "divinity" or divine "power" in general is incorporated into the readings of Luke 1:35 (conception) and 3:22 (baptism). Needless to say, in a Niceno-Constantinopolitan Spirit-Christology, the active role assigned by Hilary to Jesus' "divinity" (= Spirit) in the sanctifying and anointing of his own humanity will be assigned instead to the Holy Spirit and not exactly to the Word or the divine power of the Father. It is at this point that Hilary's conception of "the Spirit" in more personal terms as the Father's gift to the church can be used to rehabilitate his more substance-oriented use of the term "Spirit" to refer to the divine power that operates in the Son's human life. The Son must receive the Spirit as gift from the Father too, so that he might anoint us with the gift of the Spirit after his resurrection.

Hillary's theology of the power of Spirit in the Son's humanity is illustrative of the possibility of an orthodox Spirit-Christology that makes room for the place of the Father's Spirit in the growth of the Son's human sanctification and its soteriological implications without doing harm to the church's confession of the divinity and incarnation of the Son. Hilary's theology of the incarnation is historically conscious, allowing for the notion of progress and fulfillment in Christ's humanity as the economic ground for human participation by grace in his salvation. Hilary tells that story in the biblical framework of the Spirit's activity in the Son. Despite the ambiguity of the term "Spirit," Hilary's pneumatic sensibility in his Christology helps us to make sense of biblical passages where something new is said of the Son because of the Spirit's dynamic presence in and upon him. For instance, take Paul's teaching that, upon completing his earthly mission, God "established" his Son as "Son of God in power according to the Spirit of holiness through the resurrection from the dead" (Rom 1:4; cf. 8:11). In non-historical theology, one can state that at the resurrection God only "declared" his Son as Lord, since he has always been Lord and God even before his resurrection. How might Hilary's historically conscious pneumatological hermeneutic help us to make sense of the same text without denying the Son's lordship and divinity? We may say that, at the Son's resurrection, and thus at *this* new time in the economy (and not before), the Son is reborn for us in the flesh so that we might receive his Spirit as the down payment of our future

---

65. For Ladaria, the multivalent character of the term *spiritus* is partly what makes Hilary's theology interesting. See "El Espíritu Santo en San Hilario de Poitiers," 253.

resurrection in Christ. The Son is reborn as man in the Spirit, and thus in the body, for the sake of our bodily resurrection in and through him. The imminent implication of this new event or *kairos* (Hilary: "birth") is that the glorified Son will give the Spirit to the church from Pentecost onwards as eschatological "gift" (Acts 2:16–21, 38–39). The receiver of the Spirit gives the Spirit.

JESUS AS BEARER OF GOD'S SPIRIT: THE DYNAMIC ESCHATOLOGICAL PRESENCE OF THE SPIRIT IN JESUS—MINISTRY IN THE SPIRIT

The Spirit whom Jesus openly receives from his Father is the Spirit whom Jesus fully possesses as his own. In various ways, all moments in Jesus' life and ministry as obedient Son underscore this dynamic bearing or possession of the Spirit of God for mission on our behalf. As eschatological preacher, teacher, exorcist, and healer, Jesus acts in word and deed with authority and in the power of God's Spirit. Even though the Spirit's indwelling in Jesus can be traced to his birth, I have also argued that the Spirit's place in the life of Christ is *dynamic*, oriented towards all events in the course of Christ's human and thus historical existence. In assuming a human nature (hypostatic union, incarnation), the Son also assumes a human history that reaches its fulfillment in the resurrection (incarnating). To this affirmation, I have added that the character of the Spirit's presence in Jesus is *relational* or ecstatic. This is to say that, in the successive events of his eschatological ministry, Jesus bears the Spirit both in obedience to the Father and for the sake of the neighbor. The purpose of the following section is to look briefly at some biblical witnesses to Jesus' identity as the bearer of God's Spirit in the course of his mission and inquire into some key theological issues related to the best ways of describing the nature of the Holy Spirit's presence in the Logos's assumed humanity.

Biblical Contours of Jesus' Ministry As Bearer of the Spirit

At the Jordan, the Spirit descends anew like a dove "in" (Gk. *eis*) him and immediately drives him into the desert to be tempted (Mark 1:10, 12). There his faithfulness as Son is tested: "If you are the Son of God . . ." (Matt 4:3, 6; Luke 4:3, 9). Here Jesus' bearing of the Spirit's fullness points to his complete openness to the constant leading of God's Spirit (Matt 4:1, Luke 4:1, 14),

Reading the Story of Jesus as Receiver and Bearer of God's Spirit 53

which amounts to his openness to doing the Father's will.[66] If at the Jordan the Father says to the Son, "You are my Son, the Beloved," it is in the desert that Jesus (in one of many struggles against Satan; see Luke 4:13) especially reciprocates the Father's complete love for him through unconditional obedience and faithfulness to him alone. In the desert struggle against the devil, the obedient Son is the new Israel, who triumphantly recapitulates Israel's earlier failure and disobedience to the one and only God (see Deut 32).[67] The Spirit takes Jesus on a redemptive mission to proclaim good news to the poor, set captives free, and bring sight to the blind (Luke 4:18; cf. Isa 61:1, Acts 10:38). His mission in the Spirit also involves teaching his disciples with authority (e.g., Acts 1:1–2). It is a tragedy that Jesus' preaching and teaching often encounters opposition and finally leads to his death on the cross, where his faithfulness as obedient Son of the Father is tested to the fullest. God's offer of love in his beloved Son is rejected from the start, as he begins the ministry for which he was anointed with the Spirit. After Jesus preaches in the synagogue of his own hometown that the prophecy of Isaiah 61 is fulfilled in him, and convicts his hearers of their historic rejection of God's prophets, Jesus' fellow Galileans become enraged, drive him out of town, and want to throw him off a cliff (Luke 4:16–30). Bearing the Spirit does not make the Son immune to suffering, but actually bring the cross upon him.

As the anointed Servant who takes upon himself our infirmities, Jesus "cast out the spirits with a word, and cured all who were sick" (Matt 8:16–17; cf. Isa 53:4). By the Spirit of God, Jesus delivers others from the oppression of the devil and his demons: "But if it is by the Spirit of God that I cast out demons, then the kingdom of God has come to you" (Matt 12:28; cf. Luke 11:20). Dunn sees in Jesus' words "not so much a case of Where *Jesus* is there is the kingdom, as Where the *Spirit* is there is the kingdom."[68] While Dunn highlights in the strongest possible terms the role of the eschatological Spirit upon the Son, it is best to see Jesus and the Spirit working together in a *joint mission* to bring God's kingdom on earth. For even if the Spirit is particularly active in, with, and upon Christ, we cannot forget that Jesus is the one who commands demons to leave their victims (e.g., Matt 8:32; Mark 5:8; Luke 8:29a). Jesus is led by the Spirit and acts in the Spirit, but is also the subject of his own acts and personal agent in his own right. With a word, he casts out tormenting spirits. As exorcist, Jesus stands as the mightier man

---

66. "The Son obeys the Father's will. The Spirit drives him forth. The two statements describe the same inward compulsion which could not be denied, which had to find expression in word and deed." Dunn, *Jesus and the Spirit*, 66.

67. See Davies and Allison, *The Gospel according to Saint Matthew*, 1:371–72.

68. Dunn, "Spirit and Kingdom," 140.

who ties up "the strong man" (= Beelzebub) in order to take away from his house (or dominion) those people (property) in bondage to him (Matt 12:29, cf. 3:11). At the same time, Jesus clearly warns his hearers against the blasphemy of attributing to Satan what can only belong to the Spirit of God (Matt 12:29-32). It is, after all, "by the Spirit" that he drives out demons and brings God's gracious kingdom to the oppressed. Nothing less than an eschatological inbreaking of God's kingdom among sinners takes place through the Son who acts in the power of the eschatological Spirit. Where God rules both through his Son and in his Spirit, the rule of sin, death, and the devil comes to an end.

Jesus lives his whole life and does all his work *in the Spirit*, that is to say, as the obedient Son of God and for his neighbor's sake. For Dunn, Jesus' consciousness of "Spirit" in his mission means that he knew himself to be God's appointed end-time exorcist and inspired prophet.[69] While a Spirit-oriented Christology may probe into the growth of "consciousness" in the Son's human appropriation of his divine mission, my proposal focuses ultimately on the soteriological implications of the Son's mission in the Spirit. A Spirit-Christology does have to deal at some point with the issue of continuity between Jesus as bearer of the Spirit and other bearers of the Spirit. Other prophets also possess and are filled with the Spirit to various degrees and even for similar purposes (e.g., Luke 1:15, 41-42, 67, and 2:25-26). Significantly, however, while Jesus drives out demons immediately "by the Spirit of God," his disciples do the same only *mediately* through Jesus' authority or in his name (Luke 10:17). A Spirit Christology has to negotiate the limits of pneumatic continuity and discontinuity between Christ and his saints.

Even though the language of possession or fullness itself does not suffice to place Jesus above the line of Spirit-filled and Spirit-led prophets and evangelists, the ideas of permanency and inexhaustibility, which accompany such language, do.[70] John's Gospel gives us examples of such language. The Father gives his Spirit to the Son in a permanent way: "I saw the Spirit descending from heaven like a dove, and it remained (Gk. *emeinen*) on him" (1:32). The Spirit does not simply come and go for a special task as in the case of the prophets of old and other Spirit-anointed people. The Son is the unique locus of the Spirit. To this note of permanency, John adds the idea of inexhaustibility: God gives the Spirit to his Son "without measure" (Gk. *ek metrou*, 3:34). The gift of the Spirit flows from the Son as living water pouring over a bottomless well, and consequently the same Spirit

---

69. Ibid., 43, 67; cf. Dunn, "Spirit and Holy Spirit in the New Testament," 5-8, and "Rediscovering the Spirit (2)," 75.

70. Porsch, *El Espíritu Santo*, 1.1.2.

Reading the Story of Jesus as Receiver and Bearer of God's Spirit

flows from within those who believe in him (cf. 4:7-15, 7:37-39). In the biblical narratives, Jesus bears the Holy Spirit as God's gift in a permanent and inexhaustible way, but also in view of his sharing of the gift of the Spirit with others. We may say that Jesus' authority as God's eschatological Messiah, obedient Son, and suffering Servant, which is also intrinsically linked to this unique presence of the Spirit in and upon him for our salvation and share in his Spirit, is still an unparalleled and unrepeatable one. In short, an account of Jesus as bearer of God's Spirit must be attentive to the similarity, difference, and relation between the Spirit's presence and activity in Christ and in his saints. Such a consideration is important not only because of ontological considerations concerning Jesus' unique status as Son, but also for articulating a theology of the adopted sons' sharing by grace in Jesus' Spirit.

On the Presence of the Spirit in Jesus: A Preliminary Look at Logos and Spirit-Oriented Concerns

In a Logos-oriented Christology, Jesus' miracles and wonders (e.g., healings and exorcisms) serve mainly as "proofs of his Godhead."[71] For instance, to highlight the divine Son as the personal subject of acts taking place through his assumed humanity and his possession of the Holy Spirit in a substantial way (that is, as God), Cyril of Alexandria interprets the Spirit's glorification of the Son (John 16:14) as the Son's glorification of himself with his own Spirit. The Son glorifies himself with his own Spirit "because he used the Holy Spirit to show forth his own divinity in his mighty works."[72] To distinguish the Spirit's indwelling in Christ from his indwelling in other saints, Cyril directs us to Christ's substantial (as opposed to adventitious) bearing of the Spirit with whom he shares equal divinity, and anchors this view in the Spirit's eternal being from the Son.[73] For this reason, Cyril tends to see miracles as epiphanic instances that point to the incarnate Word's divine

---

71. For the Eastern tradition, see Athanasius, *Incarnation of the Word*, §18.2 (*NPNF*² 4:46); in the West, Leo writes, "For each 'form' does the acts which belong to it, in communion with the other; the Word, that is, performing what belongs to the Word, and the flesh carrying out what belongs to the flesh; the one of these shines out in miracles, the other succumbs to injuries." *The Tome of St. Leo* (*NPNF*² 14:256); cf. Leo's *Letter XXVIII* (to Flavian) 4 (*NPNF*² 12:40-41); early Lutheran theologians follow a similar approach: "On this basis [i.e., of the personal union] he also performed all his miracles, and he revealed his divine nature as he pleased, when and how he wanted to." FC, SD 8.25, in *BC*, 620.

72. *The Epistle of Cyril to Nestorius with the XII. Anathematisms* (*NPNF*² 14:204).

73. See Cyril's ninth anathema against Nestorius (*NPNF*² 14:214-15).

glory more than as events that point to the Holy Spirit's active role in bringing to fulfillment God's redemption through the incarnate Word.

Together with Cyril, we gather that a Spirit Christology in Nicene key must not deny that the Spirit of the Son is "his own" insofar as both are inseparably united with the Father in the one divine substance. A Spirit Christology also seeks a more reciprocal way to describe the relationship between the Son who gives the Spirit *and* the Spirit who rests on him. To say that the Spirit is the Son's "own Spirit" in the economy of salvation, because the Spirit proceeds from the Son in the order of immanent processions, does not give enough attention to the biblical datum that the Spirit also remains on the Son in the economy and thus is not foreign to the Son's own procession (= generation) from the Father at the immanent level. If a Logos-oriented Christology in Alexandrian key focuses on the Spirit's glorification of the Son through the revelation of his divine power to others in his miracles as the economic side of the Spirit's immanent being or proceeding from the Son, a Spirit Christology complements this approach by focusing on the fullness of the Son's bearing of the Spirit in his miracles to establish the kingdom of God in our midst as the economic side of the Son's immanent being in the Spirit (or the Spirit's eternal resting on the Son).

In a Spirit Christology, the unique eschatological character of Jesus' identity as Son and Servant in and by the power of God's Spirit, who leads, fills, and remains in him, points to God the Father as a personal subject of acts through his Spirit towards his incarnate Son. In the biblical narrative, the Son surely works through his own Spirit who proceeds from the Father (most clearly, from his resurrection onwards), but the Spirit of God the Father also works in the Son upon whom it rests from his conception onwards. Both aspects of this *joint mission* of the Son and the Spirit in God's economy of salvation deserve attention. A Logos Christology will focus on the Word as the personal subject of what he does through his humanity in and by the Spirit. A Spirit Christology will highlight what the Father does through his incarnate Son in and by the Spirit. In a full Trinitarian theology, these are complementary aspects of Christ's identity as Son.

Jesus' life as bearer of the Spirit also has implications for one's methodological approach to Christology. Only in light of the resurrection can Jesus' mission of proclamation, teaching, healing, and exorcisms—all events leading to Jesus' ultimate rejection and death—point to his unique, authoritative, permanent, inexhaustible, unparalleled, and unrepeatable possession of God's Spirit. Only in light of Jesus' giving of the Spirit as exalted and glorified Messiah, Servant, Son of God in power, and Lord to the church can we affirm today that the bearer of the Spirit is more than a mere human being. Thus we can state that Jesus has the Spirit not only by degree (like other saints) but also by nature (or kind), and therefore, that this man is God. What a Logos Christology affirms *a priori* by proceeding "from above" (i.e., that the preexistent and divine Logos is Jesus the Christ), a Spirit Christology affirms *a posteriori* by proceeding "from below" (i.e., that Jesus the Christ is the preexistent and divine Logos). In terms of method, either starting point can be employed in the presentation of Christology as long as the one person of the Son is confessed as true God and true man.

In arguments from below, a Spirit Christology that serves as a complement to Logos Christology must also be sensitive to the classic affirmation of the priority of the hypostatic union over the Spirit's sanctification of the Son's assumed humanity. Unlike Mühlen's proposal, which I introduced earlier as a qualified revitalization of Thomas's, Walter Kasper's Spirit Christology seems to reverse this order. He argues *from* Jesus' incarnating in history by his Spirit-led life of obedience to the Father and for us *to* his ontology as the incarnate Logos. To move from the incarnation conceived in terms of the Spirit's action in the life of Christ (dynamic view) to the Logos's incarnation conceived of as a past event of hypostatic union (static view), Kasper argues that Jesus' grace of union follows from or is grounded in his habitual grace.

> By wholly filling Jesus' humanity, the Spirit endows it with the openness by which it can freely and wholly constitute a mould and receptacle for God's self-communication. The sanctification of Jesus by the Spirit and his gifts is, therefore . . . not merely an adventitious consequence of the sanctification by the *Logos* through the hypostatic union, but its presupposition.[74]

Kasper reverses Thomas' argument, by making the Son's *gratia habitualis* the condition for the *gratia unionis*. But is it correct to make the Spirit's sanctification of the human nature of the Logos the logical condition for the Logos's assumption of the same? How does one give full weight to the Spirit's agency in the incarnation without minimizing the Son's proper agency in becoming incarnate, and viceversa? For now, suffice it to say that a solution to the issue of the logical priority of the Logos's assumption over the Spirit's sanctification of the assumed humanity will have to be worked out and reconciled with the distinction between the personal identity of Jesus and the Logos and the non-identity of Jesus and the Holy Spirit, as well as the distinction between the orders of being (with its starting point from above) and the order of knowledge (starting from below). In chapter

---

74. Kasper, *Jesus the Christ*, 251; for a comparative summary of Mühlen's and Kasper's Spirit Christologies, see Badcock, *Light of Truth & Fire of Love*, 145–59.

6, I shall apply such theological distinctions to the questions above. In the meantime, let us offer a few reflections.

A Logos Christology asserts that the Son was one with his Spirit in eternity and then, logically speaking, communicated the same to his humanity in time at the incarnation (hypostatic union) *after* assuming the flesh. Just as the generation of the Son logically precedes the procession of the Holy Spirit in the inner-life of the Trinity, so does the economic mission of the Son (assumption or union) logically precede that of the Holy Spirit (indwelling or sanctification). A Spirit-oriented Christology points out that such conclusions can only follow from Jesus' life and deeds as messianic Son and Servant carried out in the power of Spirit throughout his human history. Here God's raising of his Son according to the Spirit of holiness through the resurrection from the dead holds the central place in the church's confession of the Son's power, lordship, and divinity—attributes that can only be grasped and contemplated in his true humanity through his Spirit-led mission of proclamation, teaching, healings, and exorcisms.

Jesus' receiving and bearing of the Spirit also has implications for ways of approaching the correspondence between the economic and the immanent Trinity. The Spirit of God must not be seen simply as an instrument in the economy that reveals the Son's identity as one from whom the Spirit proceeds, but also as the Spirit who has a part in constituting the incarnate and eternal Son's identity as one on whom the Spirit of the Father rests. Just as the Spirit of the Father never exists without his Son, so the Son of God never exists without the Spirit of the Father. The Spirit of the Father rests on the Son eternally prior to his conception and then also temporally from his conception onwards.

In a reciprocal Trinitarian account of the incarnation, one could argue that logical priority may be given to either the Son's assumption or the Spirit's sanctification of his humanity, depending on the concerns or issues at hand. If the danger of adoptionism or Nestorianism looms in the horizon, and thus the divinity of the Son or the unity of his person are respectively at stake, then priority goes to the Word's assumption of humanity in order to avoid the idea of a human existence of the Son prior to his hypostatic union or an adoption into sonship by the disposition or merit of such a human being. The classic dogmatic notions of *enhypostasis* and *anhypostasis* safeguard respectively the positive existence of the assumed humanity in the person (or hypostasis) of the Logos and its non-existence as a person apart from the hypostasis of the Logos.

However, what if docetic and monophysite tendencies come to the fore and Christ's humanity is merely understood as a mask behind which the preexistent Logos does his real work?[75] Should we then speak of a "reciprocal enhypostasis" of the divine Logos in the man Jesus and of something analogous to this reciprocity for the presence of the Spirit in Jesus?[76] A thorny christological issue arises with the notion of a "reciprocal enhypostasis" of the divine Logos in the man Jesus. Neither a natural nor an accidental difference in grace, Schoonenberg proposes that Jesus' grace uniquely differs from other saints' according to a "gradual" difference (or a difference of degree) between full and "partial sanctity."[77] But if so, then God's holy presence in Jesus still seems to differ from other saints only in degree. Schoonenberg correctly seeks to avoid the idea that Jesus' humanity is unlike ours in a substantial or natural sense. Otherwise, Jesus would not be truly human. While the distinction Schoonenberg proposes between full and partial holiness does distinguish between the Son and the sons at some level, it still does not seem able to reach the level of an incommunicable union of the divine person of the Logos and his flesh that applies only to the Son (and thus not to the adopted sons). The Spirit dwells in the Son and the saints, but the saints are not incarnations of the Logos.

We can speak of a presence of the Holy Spirit in the *incarnate* Son that makes possible its communication to the saints through the Logos. I have spoken in passing of the church's sharing in Jesus' anointing in the Spirit by grace. Nevertheless, this gracious communication still depends on Jesus' prior reception and bearing of the Spirit of God in his humanity in a way unlike others. Indeed, Jesus is a true human being like us (as Schoonenberg stresses), but also one unlike us, in that he is without sin.

The unique presence of the Spirit in Jesus from conception differs from its presence in other saints in that the latter remain sinners (although forgiven ones) in this life and thus need the continual descent of the same Spirit upon them for the forgiveness of sins. In this sense, Jesus as "holy" child has the Spirit from conception (see Luke 1:35) in an unrepeatable way that others can neither participate in nor replicate. This does not mean that the presence of the Spirit in Jesus throughout the course of his life and work prevents him from suffering the attacks of the devil. After all, it is the Spirit of God who drives Jesus into the desert to be tested by Satan. The same Spirit, who makes his humanity holy from conception and anoints him for mission, accompanies him as he withstands Satan's temptations in the

---

75. For Rahner, this is the greater danger among Christians. See Rahner, "Current Problems in Christology," 156n1.

76. Schoonenberg, "Spirit Christology and Logos Christology," 364–65.

77. "The difference at stake could be labeled gradual, but the grade, the measure in which Jesus differs from others is unique. It is the difference of partial sanctity from the fullness which in others was either anticipated or participated." Ibid., 364.

wilderness. The Son's life in the Holy Spirit brings him into conflict with the evil spirit. The evil forces of the anti-kingdom oppose the coming of God's spiritual kingdom in Christ. In a Spirit-oriented Christology, the sanctifying presence of the Spirit in the Logos's assumed humanity will have a place in the reality of his sinlessness, which in turn should be seen in view of the fulfillment of his saving work for sinful humanity through his death and resurrection. Schoonenberg does not seem to touch on how the depth of our sin and Christ's sinlessness fully play into a discussion of Jesus' full possession of the Spirit in distinction from ours and for the sake of our salvation.

In Trinitarian terms, one can also argue that Jesus' reception of the Spirit from birth is the historical side of the Son's eternal openness to God the Father in the Spirit. In this sense, the Son has the Spirit by nature (or more precisely, in his hypostatic uniqueness) as the one person of the Trinity upon whom the Spirit of the Father eternally rests and even as the eternal bearer of the same Spirit. However, such a proposition presupposes a clear ontological distinction between the Son and the Spirit that in turn applies to the economy of salvation. Thus Jesus is the Logos and not the Holy Spirit.

Schoonenberg's concept of "reciprocal enhypostasis" raises some problems for Trinitarian theology. He suggests that prior to the appearance of Jesus' human reality in history, the Logos and the Holy Spirit were active "personal extensions" of God towards the world.[78] Only through Jesus' coming into history can we affirm that the Logos and the Spirit become "persons" enhypostatized in this Jesus respectively from the moment of his incarnation and from his glorification onwards.[79] According to our author, such a view presupposes a certain functional and ontological identity between the Logos and the Spirit that is only partially clarified for us in the New Testament at the moment of Jesus' glorification when the Spirit is given to the church.[80] According to Schoonenberg, only from the moment of the glorification forward can we speak of the Spirit as the fullness of the Logos's self-communication in Jesus flowing to others.[81]

Schoonenberg's reciprocal enhypostasis and Trinitarian synthesis of Logos and Spirit Christologies focus on Jesus' human reality as the final ontological ground for speaking about the Logos and the Spirit, but his

---

78. Ibid. 367–68.

79. Ibid., 368–70. Schoonenberg writes: "My 'modalism,' if one is pleased to label it that way, is confined to the divine existence of the Logos and the Spirit before the Christ event" (ibid., 370).

80. Ibid., 371–74; Ladaria has pointed out that, at least in Paul, there is no passage equivalent to John 1:14 to describe the relationship between Jesus and the Spirit. See "Cristología del Logos y cristología del Espíritu," 356–57nn9–10.

81. Schoonenberg, "Spirit Christology and Logos Christology," 374–75.

proposals seem too close to reducing the mystery of God to the economy of salvation.[82] However, even if we choose not to follow Schoonenberg's post-Trinitarian revisionary project, should we not, in the face of monophysite tendencies in Christology, give priority to the Spirit's sanctification of the flesh that the Word assumes at once (speaking, of course, in temporal terms, since sanctification and union happen simultaneously)? And yet, is Schoonenberg's revisionist move necessary to give full weight to the perfection of Christ's humanity as obedient Son and suffering Servant in the power of God's Spirit throughout his true human existence and, consequently, to show through this existence that he is indeed the divine Word? If not Schoonenberg's, then, what is the proper Trinitarian ground for an approach to Christology that makes room for the Spirit's work in his life and mission? These are difficult and long-standing issues in Christology.[83] While we cannot address them all in this project, it is clear that the dangers of falling into docetic and monophysite tendencies are as real as the dangers of falling into Ebionite and adoptionist ones. For now, let us assert two basic points. First, a Logos Christology affirms that there is a true human nature that subsists in the divine person of the Word. Second, a Spirit Christology affirms that there is no access to the divine Logos apart from the concrete man Jesus of

82. See Schoonenberg, "Trinity—The Consummated Covenant," 111–16. Consider the following theses from the author: "The salvation-economy fatherhood of God is the inner-divine fatherhood, and vice versa./ The salvation-economy filiation is the inner-divine filiation, and vice versa./ The Spirit of God at work in salvation history is the inner-divine Spirit, and vice versa./ The missions are the processions, and vice versa./ The salvation-economy relations are the inner-divine ones, and vice versa" (theses 11–15). Some qualification may be seen in the following statement: "Although trinitarian theology presupposes that God really revealed himself, his own being, to us, it must at the same time recognize the ineffability of that being" (thesis 25); Kasper sees Schoonenberg's theses as an example of a collapse of the immanent into the economic Trinity: "In eternity the distinctions between the three persons would be at best modal, and would become real only in history." Kasper, *The God of Jesus Christ*, 276.

83. Congar ascribes the production (creation) and sanctification of the human nature to the Holy Spirit and the assumption of such nature to the Word. See *Holy Spirit*, 1:25n6; in a review of Del Colle's *Christ and the Spirit*, Weinandy takes to task a reading of David Coffey that Del Colle uses to posit a logical priority of sanctification (habitual grace) over hypostatic union (grace of union) in describing the Spirit's role in the incarnation. Weinandy sees such a move as adoptionistic and Nestorianizing. See "Review of Ralph Del Colle's *Christ and the Spirit*." He states: "[T]he Father, in one and the same act, brings the humanity into existence, unites it to the person of the Son, and sanctifies it, all by the power of the Spirit" (658); on the other hand, Coffey argues that "the Holy Spirit . . . in the one act created the humanity of Jesus from nothing, radically sanctified it in the fullness of grace, and united it hypostatically to the preexistent divine Son." *Deus Trinitas*, 148. In response to Weinandy, Coffey adds: "We cannot conceive a union of divinity and humanity apart from a humanity that already exists, and indeed exists as disposed for union" (183n75).

Nazareth who receives, bears, and gives the Spirit of God. In light of Jesus' resurrection, the eschatological character of his proclamation, teaching, healings, and exorcisms have a defining (even if not exhaustive) role to play in drawing us closer to Jesus as Messiah, Savior, Lord, and finally God the Logos. I will return to the Trinitarian ground and implications of a Spirit Christology in the next two chapters.

Summary

I have argued for the constitutive or defining—in contrast to instrumental or accidental—role of the Holy Spirit in the events of Jesus' life and mission by drawing attention to texts bearing witness to his identity as receiver and bearer of God's Spirit. Admittedly, I have relativized to some degree the concerns of Logos-oriented readings of Jesus' story in order to highlight the partially—or at times, totally—neglected pneumatic and thus economic-Trinitarian dimensions of the incarnation. I have shown how Jesus' identity as receiver and bearer of the Spirit raises a number of issues that must be dealt with if a successful move towards the complementarity of Spirit- and Logos-oriented Christologies will take place. Those issues include: 1) The character of the Holy Spirit's presence in the humanity of the Logos, and its implications for articulating Christology and soteriology, 2) the economic and immanent Trinitarian assumptions and implications of such a pneumatic presence, 3) the continuity and discontinuity between the Spirit's measureless resting on the incarnate Son and its indwelling by grace of the adopted sons, and 4) the methodology that best serves to approach the aforementioned issues without doing harm to the legitimate apologetic concerns of a Logos Christology.

I have shown that the presence of the Spirit in Jesus may be described as dynamic and relational. What does this mean? First of all, the Spirit of God in its own right must be seen as a personal agent of actions in and through the man Jesus, who is the incarnate Logos, through each new special phase or *kairos* of his human existence and history. The pneumatic trajectory of the life of the Son as bearer of the Spirit highlights his becoming in history and his progress in sanctification reaching fulfillment at his bodily resurrection for the sake of human participation by grace in his Spirit. Second, in a Spirit Christology, God the Father is the causal personal agent of actions towards his incarnate Son through his own [i.e., the Father's] Spirit. As receiver of the gift of the Spirit, the incarnate Son receives from the Father the eschatological promise of the Spirit for the church. By the power of the Spirit, the Father makes (and not merely proclaims, declares, reveals, or confirms)

Jesus holy child, anointed Servant, and exalted Lord respectively at his conception (holiness or sanctification), baptism (anointing), and resurrection. In the Spirit, the Son also relates to the Father for us as his obedient Son and suffering Servant.

Otherwise stated, a Spirit Christology invigorates classic Logos-oriented approaches to Christology with a dynamic (actualizing) and relational (ecstatic, social) orientation that places the question of Jesus' identity in its broader soteriological and economic-Trinitarian trajectory. It affirms that the important starting point for approaching soteriology and Trinitarian theology is Jesus of Nazareth, and, more specifically, Jesus in his being and acting as receiver and bearer of God's Spirit. In light of the resurrection, Jesus' eschatological bearing of God's Spirit throughout his mission of proclamation, healings, and exorcisms can point to his power, lordship, and divinity. The presence of the Spirit of God in the incarnate Son throughout his human existence serves as the economic condition for affirming the Logos's assumption unto himself of a humanity that the Spirit sanctifies. The Holy Spirit's eternal resting on the Son stands as a Trinitarian ground for the incarnate Son's reception and possession of the Spirit from conception onwards. Moreover, the Son's reception and bearing of the Spirit serves as the condition in history for the saints' reception of the same Spirit from the risen Lord. We see how a Spirit Christology serves as a lens for Christology, Trinitarian theology, and the Christian life.

At this point, we do not need to concern ourselves at length with yet another Trinitarian problem, namely, whether the Holy Spirit's role in the conception and sanctification of Jesus is proper and exclusive to it (and thus not applicable to the other two persons) or only appropriated to its person even though the other two persons are also involved in the one divine act of conception and sanctification. Suffice it to say that a Spirit Christology highlights the place of the Holy Spirit as the Father's gift and power in the life of his Son, and the Son's human reception of the Father's Spirit, in the Trinitarian plan of salvation. In this framework, the unique personal quality of the Spirit may be described in Eastern terms as his bringing to perfection or fulfillment what the Father does through his Son in order to bring us back to himself through fellowship with his Son. Here the work of the Spirit is located in the Trinitarian movement "from the Father to the Father" (Lat. *a Patre ad Patrem*), and the biblical image of the Spirit's "power" is adequate to describe such activity. In Western terms, we can describe the Spirit as mediating the Father-Son relationship of mutual self-giving for us in the economy of salvation. As Augustine puts it, the Holy Spirit "intimates to us a mutual love, wherewith the Father and the Son reciprocally love one another."[84] Here the biblical language of "gift" and "love" speak more directly to the Spirit's unique role of incorporating the saints into the mystery of filiation by their reception of the Spirit in their hearts. Both Greek and Latin traditions, East and West, can accommodate our proposal, highlighting its ecumenical potential.

---

84. *On the Holy Trinity* 15.17.27 (NPNF[1] 3:215).

3

Reading the Story of Jesus as Giver of God's Spirit

Invigorating Logos-Oriented Approaches to the Paschal Mystery and the Atonement

THE PURPOSE OF THIS chapter is twofold. First, I inquire into the pneumatic dimensions of Jesus' identity as giver of the Spirit through a look at biblical passages bearing witness to his paschal mystery. Second, I show how a Spirit Christology invigorates Logos-oriented approaches to atonement theories. Seen as one theological-liturgical moment, Jesus' suffering and death on the cross (Lent), resurrection (Easter), and pouring out of the Spirit from God the Father upon the church (Pentecost) together constitute the paschal mystery. This series of events directs our minds especially to Jesus' identity as giver, sender, or dispenser of the Spirit unto us in God's economy of salvation. The Spirit whom the Son openly receives from his Father and possesses as his own in inexhaustible fullness throughout his ministry is the same Spirit from the Father whom the Son pours out to others freely and out of love at the end of his earthly mission.

Through the anointing of his beloved Son and Servant with the Spirit at the Jordan, the Father inaugurates God's kingdom among us. The final goal of this eschatological inbreaking of the kingdom in the words and deeds of the Son is nothing less than the universal outpouring of the Spirit of the Father through Jesus to all who call upon his saving name (Acts 2:17–21; cf. Joel 3:1–5). In the new creation, it is from the time of his resurrection, ascension, and session at the right hand of God onwards that this particular receiver and bearer of God's Spirit becomes the universal giver of the Spirit unto others. What the baptism in the Jordan becomes for Jesus, Pentecost becomes for the church. The baptized one becomes the baptizer, the anointed one becomes the anointing one. To use the language of the apostle John: "He on whom you see the Spirit descend and remain is the one who baptizes with the Holy Spirit" (John 1:33). Yet the central moment in the move from Jesus' bearing to his dispensing of the Spirit is the cross. God the Father anointed the Son with the Spirit to be the obedient Son and suffering Servant. The way of the Spirit in, upon, and with Jesus is the way of the cross.[1] At the Jordan, therefore, Jesus was anointed to die on our behalf and thus open for us, through his sacrifice, the way of life in the new creation. Life in the Spirit leads to and flows from his cross.

LENT, EASTER, AND PENTECOST: JESUS' GLORIFICATION AND THE GIFT OF THE SPIRIT

The Father's voice at the Jordan River indicates that the messianic work of his beloved Son will have the characteristics of the mission of Isaiah's suffering and exalted Servant.[2] By willingly receiving the baptism in water from a hesitant John the Baptist, Jesus opens himself up to the fulfillment of Old Testament hopes concerning the promised Messiah's activity: "Let it be so now; for it is proper for us in this way to fulfill all righteousness" (Matt 3:15).[3] As the new Israel, Jesus, God's Son, stands in solidarity with Israel, who is God's firstborn son, thus anticipating that he will take upon himself their sins.[4] Jesus' baptism in water eventually leads to his baptism in blood or death (Luke 12:50). At one point, he asks the sons of Zebedee, who wanted to share in his glory, if they were also willing to "be baptized with the baptism that I am baptized with" (Mark 10:38). Mark relates this event in the context of a pericope that ultimately points to Jesus' giving of his life as the highest act of service (10:45). Jesus' imminent death on the cross is a baptism of blood that he undergoes to fulfill the mission he willingly

---

1. Moltmann speaks of a *pneumatologia crucis*, in which the self-emptying or kenosis of the Spirit as "Shekinah" in Jesus' death (esp. Heb 9:14) is the "cost" for Jesus' giving of the Spirit to his people. See *The Spirit of Life*, 60–71.

2. All the Synoptics quote Isaiah 42:1, "with you I am well pleased," the beginning of the first Servant Song (for the other songs, see Isa 49:1–7, 50:4–11, 52:13—53:12); as far as John's Gospel goes, there are some manuscripts that make an allusion to Isaiah 42:1 through the use of the title "God's chosen one" (1:34).

3. On righteousness in 3:15, see Davies and Allison, *The Gospel according to Saint Matthew*, 325–27.

4. Gibbs, "Israel Standing with Israel," 511–26.

accepted at his baptism in water. The anointing at Jordan marks him for his death on Calvary. John has his own way of highlighting the cruciform trajectory of Christ's life in the Spirit. The incarnate Son on whom the Spirit remains and who will baptize with the Spirit (John 1:33) is none other than "the Lamb of God who takes away the sin of the world" (v. 29).

In John's Gospel, the cross is the entry point into the mystery of Christ's glorification and handing over of the Spirit to his disciples. The apostle highlights the pneumatological link between Jesus' death on the cross, resurrection, and giving of the Spirit. The Son receives the Spirit *from* God "without measure" (John 3:34). Could this affirmation also apply to the reception of the Spirit *from the Son* by those who believe in him (v. 36a)? John writes, "For the one [i.e., the Son] whom God (*ho theos*) sent speaks the words of God, for not by measure does he give (Gk. *didōsin*) the Spirit" (translation mine). The question is: Who gives (*didōsin*) the Spirit? God the Father or his Son? A number of manuscripts state that "God gives the Spirit" (*ho theos didōsin to pneuma*).[5] If God is the Spirit giver, then the Son receives and bears it. This give-and-take is consistent with the statement that immediately follows: "The Father loves the Son and has given (*dedōken*) all things in his hands" (v. 35, translation mine). But what if the Son is also the Spirit *giver* in this passage, the one whom God sent to speak his words and give the Spirit without measure to whoever believes in him? Does the text reveal a case of intentional ambiguity, in which the author points to two complementary aspects of Jesus' pneumatic identity both in relation to his Father and to us? If so, then, John makes a remarkable theological statement that anticipates and is consistent with a reading of his Gospel from a Spirit-oriented angle. In John 3, the apostle intimates that the Father gives to his Son the Spirit whom the Son gives to the church. The Son's identity as bearer and giver of the Spirit is announced at the beginning of the Gospel (1:33), and fulfilled at the end of the story in the glorified Son's breathing of the Spirit whom he received from the Father upon the disciples (20:22).

For John, however, there is no bearing and giving of the Spirit to the church apart from the Son's glorification, which begins with his cross. Although Jesus specifically gives believers in John 3:36a "eternal life" (not exactly "the Spirit"), he later links the notion of "eternal life" to Jesus' giving of "water" to the Samaritan woman and other believers like herself: "The water that I will give will become in them a spring of water gushing up to eternal life" (4:14). John refers to the Spirit, "which believers in him [i.e., Jesus] were to receive" at the time of his glorification, as "rivers of living

---

5. Nestle-Aland cites, among others, A, C2, Θ, Ψ, D, 086, and f3. See *Novum Testamentum Graece*, 27th ed. (Stuttgart: Deustche Bibelgesellschaft, 1993) 255.

water" (vv. 38–39a). From a pneumatic angle, the Gospel acquires an orientation towards Jesus' coming glorification, which in turn is the condition for his giving of the Spirit to the church: "[F]or as yet there was no Spirit, because Jesus was not yet glorified."[6] John brings together Jesus' death, resurrection, and breathing of the Holy Spirit on the disciples under one grand theological conception, that of the glorified Son's identity as giver of the Spirit. In liturgical terms, Lent, Easter, and Pentecost form one reality of salvation and new creation.

Ultimately, Jesus breathes out the Holy Spirit on his disciples as the risen Lord (John 20:22). Prior to Easter, however, John tells us that on the cross Jesus already "gave up his spirit" (Gk. *paredōken to pneuma*, John 19:30), a literal reference to the loss of his life (a handing over of his spirit or life to the Father) but also a symbolic one to his imminent giving of the Holy Spirit to those who believe in him.[7] If this double sense of *pneuma* constitutes a case of intentional ambiguity, then John has brilliantly brought together anthropological and christological notions of *pneuma* under one theological vision. In John 19:30, one can posit such a symbolic sense of the term by extension in light of at least four relevant passages in the Gospel, namely, 4:14, 7:37–39, 20:22, and 19:34. In the first two passages, "water" is used as an image for the Spirit; in particular, the second one tells that the same water (= Spirit) will not be given until Jesus' glorification. In the third passage, Jesus finally gives the Holy Spirit to his disciples, bestowing on them the power to forgive and retain sins. In the fourth passage, we learn that from the pierced side of the crucified, "at once blood and water came out" (19:34), thereby uniting the bloody reality of the rejected Messiah's death with the pneumatic image of water once again.

Between the first two and the last two passages, we find the text where Jesus is said to have "handed over" his *pneuma* from the cross (19:30). At a symbolic level, John can point to the inseparable connection between the cross (blood) and the gift of the Spirit (water).[8] This link is not surprising

---

6. Porsch, *El Espíritu Santo*, 27–34.

7. "Jesus, in the fourth gospel, 'breathes out' over Mary and John, who are, as the Church, at the foot of the cross, and thus hands over the spirit. It is, of course, not possible to say that this is the Holy Spirit. John shows that the Holy Spirit is given on the evening of Easter (20:22). At the symbolic level, however, which is endowed in John's gospel with such intense significance, however, there is clearly a very close connection between the gift of the Spirit and Jesus' self-sacrifice . . . This is, finally, a further example of a term with double intention of the kind that John liked to use. Jesus breathes his last breath and, through his death, which he willingly accepts, hands over the Spirit to his disciples." Congar, *Holy Spirit*, 1:52.

8. For a comparison of this passage with 1 John 5:6–8, see Tábet, "El Testimonio «del Espíritu, y del agua y la sangre» (1 Jn 5,8)," 79–90.

in light of the Gospel's reference to Jesus' coming baptizing with the Spirit (1:33), the promise of Jesus' giving of the Spirit (= water) at his glorification (7:39), and the datum that Jesus' "hour" inaugurates his glorification (e.g., 13:31–32; 17:1, 5). The Son's glorification is part of his return or ascent to the Father, which begins with his being lifted up on the cross (3:13–14). Thus John shows Jesus' death on the cross as the point of entry into his glorification, the climax of God's love for the world (3:16, cf. 1 John 4:9–10), and the fulfillment of the Son's mission (Gk. *tetelestai*, "It is finished," 19:30) on his way back to the Father who sent him. From this angle, the apostle seems especially eager to see the event as a constitutive one for Christ's giving of the Spirit to the church out of his self-sacrificial love, or as the Lamb of God who bears and baptizes with the Spirit to take away the sin of the world.

In an economic sense, the Holy Spirit is the paschal fruit, the gift of the crucified Christ to the church. What follows from the painful cross is Jesus' breathing of the Spirit on the disciples as their risen Lord for the purpose of giving them the authority to forgive sins in the case of the penitent and withhold forgiveness from the impenitent (John 20:23). How can the Son breathe the Spirit upon the church to absolve the sins of others unless he first takes away the sin of the world on the cross? For this reason, the Son "handed over the Spirit" already from the cross. Yet we approach Christ's words, "It is finished," in light of the whole paschal mystery, which includes his resurrection and giving of the Spirit to the church. Without the resurrection and the bestowal of the Holy Spirit, Jesus' death on the cross remains unfulfilled for us and we are left with no hope in the forgiveness of sins or the fulfillment of Christ's comforting promises concerning the Paraclete's teaching and defense of the church in the world.[9]

The Spirit of the Father who remains on the incarnate Son also accompanies him in the midst of rejection all the way to his crucifixion. The sanctification and anointing of Jesus lead him on the way of the cross. If Jesus' whole life in the power of the Spirit is a holy act of loving obedience to his Father for our sake, then his final sacrificial self-giving on the cross is the ultimate unblemished offering to the Father on our behalf made "through the eternal Spirit" (Gk. *dia pneumatos aiōniou*) (9:14). As in all events of the Son's life of holiness and faithfulness, the Spirit drives the Son's highest act of love offered to his Father on the cross for the sins of the world. As victim

---

9. Christ's bestowal of the Holy Spirit has different dimensions to it (e.g., a gift to the disciples to forgive sins, a fulfillment of Farewell discourse promises concerning the Paraclete). Therefore, the reality of Pentecost in John's Gospel must be seen broadly as a "gradual process" rather than as an event that occurs only at "one particular moment." See van Rossum, "The 'Johannine Pentecost,'" 149–67.

and priest, the Son gives up his life for us to the Father through the Holy Spirit.

Vanhoye contests a Logos-oriented interpretation of Hebrews 9:14 that sees "the eternal Spirit" as a reference to Christ's divinity on the grounds that such identification is a later notion often read into the letter.[10] Nor is the identification of "the eternal Spirit" with Jesus' spirit (as separate from his body upon death) acceptable; after all, how can a bodiless spirit offer his blood as a sacrifice?[11] Rather, Vanhoye sees the "eternal Spirit" as the animating agent behind Jesus' self-offering and God as the receiver of his sacrificial oblation.[12] The action of the Holy Spirit in Jesus took place by means of an internal force in Jesus that transformed his death into a covenantal act enacted both in perfect obedience to God and in solidarity with human beings.[13] Montague suggests another option. Along Pauline lines, he interprets the expression "eternal Spirit" more eschatologically as "the sphere of existence in which the exalted Jesus presents his sacrifice eternally to the Father."[14] Both interpretations have merits because Jesus lives both his earthly and glorified existence—as victim and priest, servant and intercessor—in the eschatological Spirit of the new creation. The paschal mystery stands at the center in the transition from one state of existence to the next and, therefore, *from* Jesus' receiving and bearing of the Spirit as suffering Servant from Jordan to Golgotha *to* his giving of the same as exalted Servant and Lord from the time of his resurrection.

Paul and Luke see the gift of the Holy Spirit to the church as the gift of the risen and ascended Christ who rules in power at God's right hand (Eph 4:7–8; Acts 2:33). As risen Lord and Messiah, Jesus pours out the "gift" (Gk. *dōrean*) and promise of the Holy Spirit whom he first received from the Father for the forgiveness of all who call upon his name with a contrite and trusting heart (Acts 2:32–39; cf. 5:30–32). The Holy Spirit is given to the church as the power for missionary witness to Jesus (Acts 1:8), and for this reason it is called "the Spirit of Jesus" (see Acts 16:6–7). The Holy Spirit is the gift and promise of the ascended Jesus to everyone whom the Father calls. From Pentecost onwards, the Spirit of Jesus comes to the church through repentance and baptism in the name of Jesus for the forgiveness of

---

10. Vanhoye, "L'azione dello Spirito Santo nella Passione de Cristo secondo l'Epistola agli Ebrei," 761.

11. Ibid.

12. Ibid., 760.

13. Ibid., 771.

14. "This identification of the risen Lord with the realm of the Spirit is Pauline (1 Cor 15:45; 2 Cor 3:17–18)." Montague, *Holy Spirit*, 317.

sins (Acts 2:38). The Holy Spirit acts in inseparable unity with the Word and baptism to incorporate Jews and Gentiles into the nascent apostolic church.

For Paul, the last Adam takes upon himself the sin of the first Adam in order to give us forgiveness and resurrection life through his Spirit (1 Cor 15:20-23; cf. Rom 5:12-21). As risen Lord, "the last Adam became a life-giving spirit" (1 Cor 15:45). This last title points to a functional identity between the risen Lord and the Spirit from the perspective of the church's experience of salvation, since for God's people living "in Christ" is the same as living "in the Spirit."[15] Similarly, the church experiences in faith and hope both the risen Christ and the eschatological Spirit as "the first fruits" (Gk. *aparchē*) of her coming resurrection (1 Cor 15:20; Rom 8:23; cf. the term *arrabōn*, e.g., 2 Cor 1:22). Thus Schweizer can argue that the risen Christ's identity as *pneuma* is a material one "[i]n so far as Christ is regarded in His significance for the community, in His powerful action upon it. . . ."[16] Without miminizing in the least the functional identity of Christ and the Spirit at the level of the church's faith, and the blessings of Christ's giving of the Spirit to the church (e.g., the forgiveness of sins, empowerment for witness, and our final redemption or resurrection in the flesh), we must still inquire further into the exalted Lord's *own* pneumatic identity as giver of God's Spirit.

God established Jesus, the Son of David "according to the flesh" (Gk. *kata sarx*), as Son of God in power "according to the Spirit of holiness" (Gk. *kata pneuma hagiōsunēs*] through his resurrection from the dead (Rom 1:3-4). In his earthly state of existence, Jesus was manifested and put to death "in the flesh" (Gk. *en sarxi, mēn sarxi*), but God vindicated and made him alive "in the Spirit" [Gk. *en pneumati* or *de pneumati*] (respectively 1 Tim 3:16 and 1 Pet 3:18). Exegetes are in general agreement that the parallelism *pneuma/sarx* in all these passages (as in the case of Rom 1:13-14) refers neither to a distinction between Christ's physical body and soul nor to one between his humanity and divinity.[17] They typically interpret *en pneumati* or *pneumati* impersonally as a dative of reference (instead of one of means)

---

15. Dunn, "Rediscovering the Spirit (2)," 78-79; cf. Congar, *Holy Spirit*, 1:39.

16. Eduard Schweizer, *TNDT*, 6:417-20, 433; Dunn affirms that in passages such as Romans 1:3-4, 1 Peter 3:18, 1 Timothy 3:16, 1 Corinthians 15:45, and Hebrews 9:13-14 the authors appear to use "deliberate ambiguity between Christ's Spirit and the Holy Spirit—precisely because the Spirit which empowered Christ from Jordan onward was now wholly identified with Christ as his Spirit, the Spirit of Christ." See Dunn, "Jesus—Flesh and Spirit: An Exposition of Romans 1:3-4," 152, 165-66. However, Dunn does not interpret 2 Corinthians 3:17-18 in this manner. See Dunn, "2 Corinthians 3:17 'The Lord is the Spirit,'" 115-25.

17. Schweizer, *TDNT*, 6:417n555; Dalton, *Christ's Proclamation to the Spirits*, 136-41; Fee, *God's Empowering Presence*, 482-83, 764-65.

to refer to the realm, sphere, or state of eschatological existence into (or according to) which Jesus enters upon his exaltation (above all, his resurrection) after his life and work on earth.[18] In the case of 1 Peter 3:18, opting for the notion that Jesus was made alive through or by means of the Spirit—in other words, through the use a dative of means—can leave us with the odd idea in the first part of the parallelism that he was put to death by means of the flesh.[19] Indirectly, however, Dalton looks for a link between the more impersonal notion of a realm of spirit and the eschatological Spirit itself as the personal agent of actions so that the ideas of personal being, presence, and activity merge in a description of the new life in Christ.[20]

For Romans 1:4, Fee similarly affirms that "the sphere of spirit life ... in Paul would be another way of referring to the sphere of our final eschatological existence, which will be Spirit life par excellence."[21] His instructive comments on 1 Timothy 3:16 also seek to bring together explicit and implicit senses of the phrase "in the spirit/Spirit":

> '[I]n the spirit' most likely refers to the new 'spiritual,' supernatural realm of existence, entered by Christ through his resurrection. However, this choice of words is scarcely accidental. Whatever else, this new 'sphere' is precisely that of the Spirit. Just as Christ when 'in the flesh' ministered in the power of the Spirit, so now Christ, by virtue of his resurrection, has entered the spiritual/supernatural realm, the realm of the Spirit, which is the final goal of those for whom the present gift of the Spirit is the ... 'down-payment.'[22]

Although Fee sees the link between Jesus' risen status in the realm of the Spirit and our resurrection through his Spirit (cf. Rom 8:11), he sees no explicit scriptural reference to the Spirit as the agent who raises Jesus from the dead and instead reserves this function for God.[23] While favoring the dative

---

18. Schweitzer, *TNDT*, 6:416-17, 433; Montague, *Holy Spirit*, 204, 230, 314, 317; Dalton, *Christ's Proclamation to the Spirits*, 141; Fee, *God's Empowering Presence*, 481-82, 766.

19. Dalton, *Christ's Proclamation to the Spirits*, 141. However, Dalton is open to the idea that 1 Timothy 3:16 may be interpreted through a dative of means.

20. Dalton suggests that *en pneumati* or *pneumati* "designates not so much the action of the Spirit, but the *sphere* of the Spirit. In a number of Pauline passages, it is difficult to know whether 'spirit' should be taken as personal being, or as the new life communicated by the presence and activity of this person. One meaning fuses into the other." Ibid., 139.

21. Fee, *God's Empowering Presence*, 481.

22. Ibid., 766.

23. Ibid., 484, 553, 765.

of reference for *pneuma/sarx* passages, Montague, on the other hand, does not hesitate to ascribe Jesus' resurrection to the Holy Spirit as he comments on Romans 1:4 and 1 Timothy 3:16.[24] Dunn has suggested that the functional identity between the risen Lord and the Spirit in the earliest church's experience of salvation may have impeded the biblical writers from explicitly making the statement that Jesus was raised through or by means of the Spirit.[25] Whether this is the case or not, I do agree with Dunn's argument that such teaching is implicit in the ideas that our resurrection takes place through the Spirit (Rom 8:11) and that Christ is the firstfruits of our future resurrection (1 Cor 15:20).[26] Although Fee rightly wants to speak of God the Father as the ultimate personal agent of Jesus' resurrection—a principle that also applies to the resurrection of Christians—one should note that this concern for preserving the Father's primary agency should not exclude the idea that the Spirit actually mediates this action (i.e., raising the body) in the humanity of the Son and through his in ours.

A Spirit-oriented Christology allows us to affirm that a genuine participation of the saints in the resurrection of Jesus Christ must amount to a full participation in his Spirit-glorified humanity. The affirmation that our bodies will be raised at the last day through the Spirit of God, the Spirit of Christ, cannot stand unless Jesus himself was raised from the dead by God the Father through the same Spirit. A Spirit Christology grounds the future glorification of our bodies in the life-giving work of the eschatological Spirit, whom Christ fully possesses as the last Adam in his glorified body and from the moment of his resurrection forward gives to the members of his mystical body. From this angle, the terms "last Adam" and "life-giving Spirit" (1 Cor 15:45) cannot be seen merely as a functional identification between Christ and the Spirit at the level of the church's faith and knowledge of salvation, but must point to the risen Lord's *own glorified humanity* and thus to his pneumatic identity as bearer and giver of God's Spirit to others.[27]

---

24. Montague, *Holy Spirit*, 204, 314.

25. Dunn, "Jesus—Flesh and Spirit: An Exposition of Romans 1:3–4," 152.

26. Ibid.

27. "It is the Spirit, as the content and the end of the Promise and therefore as eschatological gift, who establishes 'Jesus,' that is, Christ in his crucified humanity, in his condition as the 'Son of God in power' and as Kyrios. The Spirit permeates him and makes him a *Pneuma zōopoioun*, a spiritual being giving life. It is therefore not difficult to understand why Paul attributes activities and consequences in the Christian life to either Christ or to the Spirit, to such an extent that he apparently identifies the two." Congar, *Holy Spirit*, 1:39; Montague writes, "For while Adam came to *have life* as a result of God's inbreathing, Christ became a *life-giving spirit*. This apparently implies that Paul sees the Father's inbreathing into the body of Jesus in the tomb the power of the Holy Spirit . . . and the result was that the risen body of Jesus possessed the Spirit

To invoke Hilary's dynamic "birth" language again, we may say that in an economic sense Jesus is "born" as Son in a *new* way, and thus in the body, through the resurrection from the dead (cf. Acts 13:33). Reborn for us as last Adam according to the Spirit of holiness, Jesus now pours out the Spirit to the members of his body as their head, and the fallen race of Adam is thus restored to the image and likeness of the glorified Christ.

In light of the paschal mystery, we can return to the Jordan and see in the Father's unction of the incarnate Son the condition for the communication of the Spirit to his members as their head and Lord for the purpose of making them adopted sons (and daughters) of the Father in the Spirit (Rom 8:15–16, Gal 4:4–17). Jesus' reception of the Spirit at the Jordan has the character of a *new* presence of the Spirit in him for others, which his being with the Spirit from eternity or his reception of the Spirit from conception per se do not have. I have noted that the evangelists only speak of Jesus' baptizing of others with the Spirit from the moment of his being baptized with the same at the Jordan. Over against an adoptionist interpretation of Jesus' anointing, Justin's answer to Trypho and Athanasius's response to the Arians are correct in the sense that Christ does not need the anointing to be constituted as preexistent Logos, begotten of the Father in eternity, nor to receive the Spirit and its powers for the very first time in history (as if the incarnate Logos did not have the Spirit from the time of conception). However, they are somewhat uncomfortable with the idea that Christ otherwise needs the anointing *in his humanity* to be constituted as Son *for us*, in such a way that he, as head of the church, might make us participants by adoption through baptism in his anointing.[28] In a non-adoptionist sense, then, Jesus' rebirth as obedient Son in his anointed and exalted humanity in and through the Spirit serves as the condition for our adoption as sons (and daughters) of God through baptism (anointing) into Jesus' death and resurrection. Spirit Christology links Christology and ecclesiology.

Let us now review some of the promising patristic reflections on the ecclesiological implications of Jesus' anointing. By descending upon the incarnate Son, Irenaeus tells us, the Spirit of God becomes "accustomed in fellowship with Him to dwell in the human race . . . working the will of the Father in them, and renewing them from their old habits into the newness of Christ."[29] In other words, God "had promised by the prophets that He would anoint Him, so that we, receiving from the abundance of His unc-

---

in a way to give it to whoever contacts the risen Lord through faith and sacrament." Montague, *Holy Spirit*, 142.

28. See Orbe, *La unción*, 635–36.

29. Irenaeus, *Against Heresies* 3.17.1 (*ANF* 1:444).

tion, might be saved."[30] In the same way, Athanasius reminds us that the Son's baptism "did not take place for promotion of the Word, but again for our sanctification, that we might share in His anointing."[31] In his theology of anointing, Justin speaks of Jesus' baptism as a type of birth that turns children of Adam into adopted sons of God. At the Jordan, the voice of the Father reveals (quoting Psalm 2:7) "that His [i.e. Christ's] generation would take place for men, at the time when they would become acquainted with Him."[32]

We can add to these witnesses the work of Gregory Nazianzen, who speaks of Jesus' purification at the Jordan river as a mystery of salvation that takes place "for my Purification, or rather, sanctifying the waters by His purification" in order to accomplish "my perfection and return to the first condition of Adam."[33] Echoing Athanasius's language, Cyril of Alexandria notes that "although Christ was the giver of the Holy Spirit . . . nevertheless as he is man he was called anointed economically, the Holy Spirit resting upon him spiritually . . . in order that he might abide in us."[34] While Cyril avoids giving the Spirit an "active" sanctifying presence or power in the humanity of the Word, he nevertheless does speak of the Holy Spirit's resting on Christ as the second Adam and firstfruits so that we, who are of the fallen race of the first Adam, might be restored unto new life through his sanctifying Spirit.[35] Cyril's narrative of the departure of the Spirit from Adam and its return to the human race through the second Adam shows the lasting influence of Irenaeus in later fathers.[36] A Spirit Christology can assume these salutary ecclesiological perspectives on the anointing of Christ.

30. Ibid., 3.9.3 (*ANF* 1:423).

31. Athanasius, *First Discourse* 12.47 (*NPNF*[2] 4:333).

32. Justin, *Dialogue* 89 (*ANF* 1:244).

33. Gregory Nazianzen, *Oration XXXVIII* 16 ([*NPNF*[2] 7:350-51]; cf. his *Oration XXXIX* 15 [*NPNF*[2] 7:357]); on the patristic theme of the sanctification of the waters as a prefiguration of Christian baptism, see Granado, "Pneumatologia de San Cirilo de Jerusalén," 448-56; Ladaria, "Jesús y el Espíritu Santo según Gregorio de Elvira," 309-29; and McDonnell, *The Baptism of Jesus in the Jordan*, 55, 67-68.

34. *The XII. Anathematisms of St. Cyril against Nestorius* (*NPNF*[2] 14:214).

35. For the narrative of the departure and return of the Spirit, see Cyril's treatment of John 1:32-33 in his *Commentary on John* 182-85 (trans. Maxwell, 81-82; see also Cyril's exegesis of John 7:39 in ibid., 691-97 [trans. Maxwell, 308-312]); for references to other key passages from Cyril, see Bobrinskoy, *The Mystery of the Trinity*, 258-60.

36. In his exegesis of John 1:32-33, Cyril echoes Irenaeus's language: "The Spirit flew away from us because of sin, but the one who knew no sin became one of us so that the Spirit might become *accustomed* to remain in us, since the Spirit finds no reason in him for leaving or shrinking back." *Commentary on John* 184 (trans. Maxwell, 82; italics mine). Like Irenaeus, Cyril also includes the gift of the Spirit on human nature as part of God's work of recapitulating all things in Christ. Ibid., 691-92 (trans. Maxwell, 309).

But it insists that Jesus' giving of the Spirit to the church from the time of his glorification onwards must be grounded clearly in his own constitutive (and not merely proclamatory or confirming) receiving of the same Spirit for us at the Jordan. Generally speaking, church fathers were aware of the pneumatological link between Christ's baptism and Christian baptism, even if at times and to various degrees they were a bit hesitant to link his giving of the Holy Spirit to his receiving and bearing of the same in his humanity.

ANSELM, ABELARD, AND AULÉN ON THE ATONEMENT: REVISITING LOGOS-ORIENTED APPROACHES IN LIGHT OF A SPIRIT-ORIENTED CHRISTOLOGY

Like the paschal mystery, the atonement is a comprehensive reality. It directs us to God's reconciliation of the world through Christ, and thus to the redemptive significance of his *whole* life, death, and resurrection. Because the Spirit is inseparably united to Christ in his work for us, a Spirit-oriented Christology can look critically at traditional Logos-oriented views of the atonement and invigorate them with a broader soteriological, Trinitarian, and ecclesiological trajectory. God the Father reconciles us to himself through his faithful Son in the eschatological power of his Spirit. A Logos-oriented view of the atonement tends to frame the discussion in terms of the divine-human dialectic expressed in Christ's own inner-constitution as God-man and the place of divinity and/or humanity in reconciliation. In Abelard's case, there is a tendency to stress Christ's atoning work as an example of self-sacrificial love for the church. In providing us a broader economic-Trinitarian framework for approaching Anselmian (Latin), Abelardian (exemplary), and Aulénian (classic) views of atonement, I argue that reading the story of Jesus' identity as receiver, bearer, and giver of God's Spirit can assume the strengths of each one of these approaches or theories. These strengths are respectively and comparatively the central place of Christ's *human* obedience unto death in atonement (Anselm), the affirmation that reconciliation is always and exclusively the eschatological work *of God* against his enemies (Aulén on the classic approach), and the non-exclusive stress on the church's subjective appropriation of atonement in self-sacrificial Christ-like works of love (Abelard).

In Anselm's Logos-oriented reading of Jesus' death, the cross becomes the natural outcome of the Word's assumption of humanity unto himself. As

God, Jesus *can* make satisfaction for our sins; as man, he *ought* to do so.[37] So goes Anselm's view of the atonement and the answer to his question "Why the God-man?" To arrive at his view, Anselm (ca. 1033–1109) first defines the nature of "God" by ranking the attribute of justice over that of love. Let us frame Anselm's thought in logical fashion. Since the proposition "God's being is supreme justice" takes priority over "God is love," then God must necessarily maintain his honor and dignity whenever sins are committed against him for his own sake, i.e., for the sake of justice.[38] Otherwise, God is no longer just, and thus not God either, for to be just is God's essence.[39] This argument logically requires an infinite satisfaction for sins that only *God* can pay and only *man* must pay. Incarnation must occur so that, in the God-man, satisfaction is made to God for man on the cross.

If a reversal of priorities occurs and the attribute of love takes precedence over divine justice, then we begin to approach in some measure the thought of Peter Abelard (1079–1142). Because God is ultimately love, God can freely forgive and deliver from punishment precisely because of the forbearance of his infinite mercy (= righteousness or justice) for the sinner in Christ.[40] Should God then necessarily require the death of an innocent man as satisfaction for sins? Even before his passion, Christ forgives the sins of many and delivers them from Satan.[41] Is this not enough for God? Abelard continues:

> Indeed, how cruel and wicked it seems that anyone should demand the blood of an innocent person as the price for anything, or that it should in any way please him that an innocent man should be slain—still less that God should consider the death of his Son so agreeable that by it he should be reconciled to the whole world![42]

Anselm's argument on this point may be more nuanced than Abelard gives him credit for. Indeed, Anselm states that the Father wills or wishes the death of his Son in order to restore to the human race the life and happiness lost in paradise.[43] Yet another crucial statement accompanies this thought. Although Christ obeyed the Father in his humanity, he was not constrained by his obedience to suffer death for sins because—unlike other

---

37. Anselm, *Cur Deus Homo?* 2.6, p. 259.
38. Ibid., 1.12, pp. 219–20.
39. Ibid., 1.13, pp. 220–21.
40. Abelard, *Epistle to the Romans* 2.1 (*LCC* 10:279).
41. Ibid., 2.2 (*LCC* 10:282).
42. Ibid. (*LCC* 10:283).
43. *Cur Deus Homo?* 1.9.

human beings—he had no sin.[44] Admittedly, in his humanity Christ speaks of doing not his own but the Father's will, but in his divinity his will is really one with the Father's.[45] In the end, Anselm asks us to hold two ideas in tension: 1) the Father wills the death of his Son to restore the human race to its prior condition in paradise, and 2) the Son wills his own death without coercion from the Father. Furthermore, Anselm asks us to affirm that the Father is not pleased with the *suffering* of his Son, but with the *choice* of the Son to suffer of his own accord for our sake.[46]

Having given Anselm his credit, Abelard rightly wants to understand God's love for humanity in Christ in terms of his righteousness or unconditional love. Such love is the ultimate predicate for God; not retributive justice, which requires either the punishment of the sinner or satisfaction in the God-man. By biblical standards, the wrath of God and his punishment for sin is to be taken seriously and a conception of love in the form of an unqualified universalism is also out of the question. But our authors do not frame their discussion in this manner. For now, suffice it to say that Abelard sees the ground for our justification by the blood of Christ and reconciliation to God in him in God's own great love for us demonstrated in his Son by his incarnation and perseverance unto death.[47]

Through such an "act of grace"—indeed, an exemplary one, but not exclusively so—God "has more fully bound us to himself by love; with the result that our hearts should be enkindled by such a gift of divine grace, and true charity should not now shrink from enduring anything for him."[48] The theological emphasis falls on the *believer's* internal appropriation of God's grace and love for us shown in Christ's life and death. As Abelard describes it, "our redemption through Christ's suffering is that deeper affection [Lat. *dilectio*] in us which not only frees us from slavery to sin, but also wins for us the true liberty of sons of God, so that we do all things out of love rather than fear...."[49]

Anselm and Abelard respectively stress so-called "objective" and "subjective" views of atonement, but they arrive at their conclusions through the same procedure. They define God by prioritizing divine attributes (i.e.,

---

44. Ibid. Was Christ's humanity inherently mortal, so that if he had not died by crucifixion he should have eventually died anyway? Anselm says no. For mortality is not inherent in human nature essentially, but only as an accident due to corruption from sin. Since Christ had no sin, he lays down his own life freely for us (see ibid., 2.11).

45. *Cur Deus Homo?* 1.9.

46. Ibid., 1.10, p. 213.

47. *Epistle to the Romans*, 2.3 (*LCC* 10:283).

48. Ibid.

49. Ibid., (*LCC* 10:284).

justice or love), which then serve as controlling variables into which Jesus and his work are later situated. A Logos-oriented Christology is not immune from assuming previously ranked divine attributes that in turn interpret all of Jesus' life and mission.[50] For Anselm, God's *justice* requires the Son's incarnation and death. From another angle, Christ's inner-constitution as God-man serves as the logical possibility for reading the cross as a payment or satisfaction for vindicating God's justice. The necessity of the cross follows from the nature of the incarnation, and the necessity of the incarnation follows from the nature of God.

Gustaf Aulén (1879–1978), Swedish Lutheran theologian, fomented a contemporary revival of the classic or *Christus Victor* view or theory of the atonement as a final victory of "God in Christ" over his enemies. His response to Anselm and Abelard seeks to provide a proper account of the divine-human dialectic in the work of atonement on the basis of a theology of grace. In the framework of this divine-human dialectic, he posits a "thoroughly objective" approach that sees atonement as a *"continuous"* divine act, which in terms of grace amounts to *"a movement of God to man."*[51] Seen through Aulén's eyes, we may say that Anselm's approach does not seem as "subjective" (or Pelagian?) as Abelard's but still needs a semi-Pelagian theology of grace as its presupposition. Aulén argues that, in Abelard's thoroughly "subjective" view, "no atonement is needed, and all the emphasis is on *man's movement to God."*[52] The dominant Latin type stands in the middle of the two views. It represents the option "in which the act of Atonement has indeed its origin in God's will, but is in its carrying-out, an offering made to God by Christ as man and on man's behalf, and may therefore be called a *discontinuous* divine work."[53] Aulén concludes that "the essential Christian idea of a way of God to man, which dominates the classic type, is weakened in the Latin type, and lost in the subjective type...."[54]

In terms of method, Aulén conceives of a theology of grace that applies to all human beings and later situates Jesus into this framework. Since human beings cannot move towards God or pay satisfaction for their sins to God, then the same principle must hold for Christ's human nature. Aulén reverses Anselm's theology of grace, which in the broader context of Aulén's

---

50. Scaer, has noted that defining Jesus' identity as the crucified one in terms of *a priori* divine attributes is inevitably susceptible to personal hierarchical classification or philosophical meanings. Scaer, "*Homo Factus Est* as the Revelation of God," 114–15, 122.

51. Aulén, *Christus Victor*, 171.

52. Ibid.

53. Ibid., 21–22.

54. Ibid., 171–72.

analysis, is perceived to be influenced by the medieval Roman theology of penance and merit, and therefore requires in some degree a movement from man towards God in order to settle accounts and make amends with God. In short, Aulén defines human nature and then proceeds to place God's work in Christ into this scheme. While there is a place in a reflection of the kenosis or humiliation of the Son for discussing the passivity of Christ's human nature vis-à-vis his divine nature, or vis-à-vis the priority of the Father who sends him into the world and to whom he returns, Aulén's approach still proceeds with a certain view of "humanity" into which he then lays out Christology and soteriology. Is this not the opposite of defining "God" first according to his attributes (as Anselm and Abelard do)? Is defining "humanity" first another way to begin with questions typically asked of the incarnation, i.e., the *how* of Christ's individual constitution as God-man?

Aulén's procedure and analysis of Anselm and Abelard illustrate how the three types of atonement theories take as their starting point some side of the divine-human dialectic as the dominant theological framework for their discussion of atonement. Historically, pneumatology does not appear to have made any significant contribution in views of the atonement. Logos-oriented readings have dominated. Without denying the possibility or usefulness of looking at Christ's work through the lens of the divine-human dialectic grounded in the incarnation, I propose to look at Jesus' life and work as Son in the Spirit as another vantage point for reflection on atonement. Is there a way to relate the three types of concerns exhibited by the aforementioned atonement theories, which Aulén so strongly placed in opposition to one another, through a Spirit-oriented approach to the Christ-event centered on the paschal mystery? If so, a Spirit Christology can serve to integrate the best biblical insights of these approaches.

Aulén's view of atonement as a victory of God over his enemies (e.g., sin, death, and the devil) clearly favors an eschatological view of Jesus' whole life and work that allows us to see his death within the broader perspective of what went on before and after Calvary. Within this framework, events like Jesus' temptation, exorcisms, descent into hell, and resurrection become special instances of God's vanquishing of his enemies in Christ.[55] Yet Christ's humanity appears to have a merely passive role in God's victories, for Aulén fails to see it as genuinely active in the accomplishment of atonement. He does not take into full consideration that although the humanity of Christ is like ours, it is also *without sin*. For Anselm, since death does

---

55. The *Christus Victor* theme fits particularly well with Christ's descent into hell. See Scaer, *Christology*, 83–88.

not essentially inhere in the human constitution of Christ (as in the case of sinners), he can freely lay down his life of his own accord for us.

The issue is not whether the assumed humanity is that of the person of the Logos, who acts in and through it (as opposed to a humanity independently conceived), but rather whether the incarnate Logos, in his true human kenosis, willingly takes on the path of obedience unto death. In his critique of Anselm, Aulén does not seem to take into proper account Anselm's broader Trinitarian assumption that Christ's uncoerced human will is one (or is in harmony) with his divine will and therefore one with God the Father's will. For Anselm, Christ died "of his own accord" for two reasons: 1) his perfect obedience to God as man, whereby he spoke and lived in truth and justice, made him an object of persecution; and 2) God cannot compel an innocent man to die for the sake of guilty sinners.[56] In both cases, Christ's humanity has an active role in carrying out the work of atonement. Christ's active (and faithful) obedience (*obedientia activa*) to his Father's will finally leads to his passive obedience (*obedientia passiva*) in suffering and death.

Anselm's approach is not without its need for complementarity. Since the cross in and of itself closes the deal that allows for full atonement, the resurrection does not have a place in Anselm's system.[57] At this point, Aulén's broader eschatological perspective helps us to incorporate the resurrection (and other events of Jesus' life and work) into a discussion of atonement as God's work against his enemies. In the case of Abelard, Jesus' cruciform life and work of perseverance unto death for us becomes, by grace, God's love within us. Abelard's approach gives its proper due to the subjective appropriation of God's objective act of grace shown to us and fulfilled in the crucified Christ in a way that Anselm's or Aulén's approaches do not. Can a Spirit Christology bring together the strengths of these three major understandings of the atonement? Let us bring some data already presented in previous sections of this chapter to bear on this particular question.

A pneumatological Christology can incorporate Anselm's emphasis on Jesus' obedience unto death on the cross as a satisfaction to God for sins, Aulén's eschatological view of the whole Christ-event as God's victory over his enemies, and Abelard's concern for the effect of Jesus' death in believers. Freely and out of love for humankind, God sends his Son into the world and anoints him with his Spirit to establish the kingdom of heaven on earth through deliverance from the oppression and bondage of sin, death, and Satan. The Spirit of the Lord empowers Jesus to proclaim good news, teach with authority, heal the sick, drive out demons and, in all these ways,

---

56. *Cur Deus Homo?* 1.9, pp. 206–8.
57. See Jenson, *Systematic Theology*, 1:180.

defeat the enemies of God's kingdom. A Spirit Christology allows us to place Aulén's theocentric view of the atonement in its proper eschatological framework.

From Jordan to Golgotha, from the baptism in water to the baptism in blood, Jesus' sacrificial life of obedience to God for the sake of the neighbor leads to his repeated rejection, persecution, and finally death on the cross. Anselm's concern for preserving Christ's active human obedience on the road that leads to Golgotha can be read from a pneumatological angle. Not only his anointing at Jordan with the Spirit, but also his exorcisms and healings by the Spirit of God, lead to his rejection and point to his role as suffering Servant (e.g., Matt 8:14–17). Without minimizing the guilt of sinners in the Son's death (see Acts 2:23b), we can also assert that Christ's highest sacrificial act is to offer himself as high priest to God "through the eternal Spirit" as an unblemished sacrifice for the sins of the world (Heb 9:11–15). Jesus dies by his own choice (see John 10:18). Indeed, Jesus foresees the consequences of his radical faithfulness to his Father at the hands of his accusers, and yet he openly speaks and lives in truth and justice; moreover, he prays for the strength to fulfill the Father's will to the bitter end, even for sinners like us who killed him (e.g., Luke 18:31–33, 22:42, 23:34). Empowered and led by God's Spirit, the incarnate Son walks the *via dolorosa* leading to Golgotha in the Spirit, namely, in faithfulness to his Father and for us.

Although the biblical witnesses allow us to place the guilt for Jesus' death on all sinners and at the same time to describe his death as his own free act and self-offering for sins, we can also affirm that God alone, not man, was in the end effecting his plan of salvation through his Son's life and innocent death (Acts 2:23a; 1 Pet 1:20; Rev 13:8). Indeed, only God has the power to use his own enemies (e.g., sin, death, the devil, the law) as instruments of his wrath to punish all unrighteousness.[58] These insights help us to give its proper place to Aulén's interest in preserving God's initiative and agency in the work of atonement. But not at the expense of Christ's true human sacrifice for sins. Both ideas can be brought together under a Spirit Christology. In all of the Son's works for us, he ultimately acts through his Spirit-indwelt humanity in order to vanquish God's enemies (above all, Satan and death) by offering himself up as a living sacrifice for our sins.

Along with the metaphor of "baptism," Jesus uses that of the "cup" to speak of his own sacrificial death as a ransom for many (Mark 10:38–39). Significantly, the term cup (Gk. *potērion*) can point to God's wrathful judgment for the sins of the world, thus adding a propitiatory character to

---

58. See Althaus, *The Theology of Martin Luther*, 218–23.

Christ's true human obedience unto death as a ransom for many.[59] On the cross, however, God's wrath also gives way to his love, so that his serious and just demand for righteousness becomes an unmerited gift of love for us precisely on account of Christ's death. God the Father reconciles the world to himself in Christ; it is God who makes the sinless one to be sin for us so that we might become in him the righteousness of God (2 Cor 5:18-21). God is against us in order to be for us. And yet the incarnate Son goes to his death of his own will. Even as Father and Son accomplish what is proper to each, there is no opposition of wills and deeds in their common work of atonement. In a Trinitarian account of the atonement, the action of the Spirit of the Father in the incarnate Son is not in opposition to the Son's willing and humble obedience to the Father in the Spirit. These are two sides of the same coin.

Furthermore, as I have intimated before, what comes before and follows after the cross plays an important part in God's work of reconciliation in Christ. I have already spoken of events prior to the cross: Jesus' temptation, ministry of proclamation, healings, and exorcisms. What about what follows from the cross? When Christ is vindicated by and made alive in the Spirit after the end of his earthly mission on the cross, then, through the descent into hell, he also proclaims his victory over God's spiritual enemies as exalted Lord in the power of the Spirit (see 1 Tim 3:16; 1 Pet 3:18; cf. Rom 1:3-4, 8:11).[60] Here rings the theme of *Christus Victor* once again.

For John, the Son's handing over of the Spirit on the cross already anticipates his giving of the same to the disciples as risen Lord. For Luke, it is as the ascended Lord, seated at God's right hand, that Christ dispenses the promise and gift of the Spirit from the Father to all who call upon his name. In both cases, the special aim or goal of the giving of the Spirit is the forgiveness of sins. The gift of the Spirit of God to the church presupposes Christ's active and passive obedience. Paul makes this dimension of the mystery clear. For God sent his Son into the world to fulfill the law in order to redeem those oppressed under the law (Gal 4:4). And it is by hanging on a tree that Christ becomes a curse for us to redeem us from the curse of the law (Gal 3:13). Those who through Christ's sacrificial life and death are freed from the curse of the law—another one of God's enemies in its function as accusing law—have received "the promise of the Spirit through faith" (Gal 3:14). Into their hearts God has sent the Spirit of sonship and thus the hope of final redemption at the last day (Gal 4:6; Rom. 8:11, 14-24a). To

---

59. See Leonhard Goppelt, *TDNT*, 6:149-53, esp. 153; cf. Scaer, *Christology*, 79.

60. Dalton argues for a victorious proclamation of the ascended Christ to "hostile angelic powers in the heavens." *Christ's Proclamation to the Spirits*, 26.

deliverance from sin and the law, we add deliverance from death because the Spirit of the Son is also the downpayment of our coming resurrection. Furthermore, living in the Spirit of the crucified and risen Christ, the same Spirit in whom Christ lived the course of his entire life and work, God's children are free to serve and be faithful to God and love one another. They are thus shaped by or conformed to the Spirit of Christ to follow the example of the crucified Christ in their dealings with others (Phil 2:4–8; 1 Pet 2:20–21). In the Spirit's shaping of the believer after Christ the Servant, according to the fruit of the Spirit of love, Abelard's concern for the subjective appropriation of the atonement gets its due.

In the move from Jesus' receiving and bearing of the Spirit to his giving of the same to others, a Spirit-oriented Christology can offer a biblical narrative and economic trajectory that affirms the main emphases of atonement theories expressed by Anselm, Aulén, and Abelard. In distinction from a Logos-oriented Christology, our approach does not need to resort to previously established and competing definitions of "God" or "humanity" into which God's work in Christ is situated in a second moment of reflection. Instead, reading the story of Jesus from a pneumatological angle brings together classic, objective, and subjective dimensions of God's work of reconciliation in his Son for sinful humanity without giving up the best of each approach. A Spirit Christology can speak adequately of the Son's identity as *Christus Vicar* (Anselm), *Victor* (Aulén on the classic approach), and *exemplum* (Abelard). The Son receives the Spirit to be our substitute, bears the Spirit to be our victor over God's enemies, and gives the Spirit to shape our lives after the Son's life in the Spirit by making us adopted children of the Father. By the Spirit, the Son delivers us from sin and the power of the devil, raises us from the dead, and conforms us to be servants.

Summary

I have argued for a Spirit-oriented Christology centered on the paschal mystery. Jesus' particular receiving and bearing of the Spirit from the Father as obedient Son, suffering Servant, and exalted Lord is oriented towards his eschatological and universal giving of the Spirit from the Father to others from his glorification forward so that they can be made adopted sons and daughters of God by grace through faith in Christ. We reviewed briefly the contributions of church fathers, who taught the soteriological link between the baptism of Jesus and Christian baptism, as a way of illustrating the basic biblical insight that the Son upon whom the Spirit remains is the one who baptizes with the Holy Spirit. We focused on Christ's life in the Spirit as one that leads him to the cross and one that flows from the cross to the world through his handing over of the Spirit of new life to his disciples.

Moreover, I showed that pneumatology has a significant place in articulating God's gracious work of reconciling the world to himself in Jesus Christ, thereby showing the contribution of a Spirit Christology to reflection on soteriology. Logos-oriented readings of atonement theories work within the framework of Christ's inner-constitution as divine and human. Aulén's claim that Anselm makes too little of atonement as an objective *divine* work and Abelard makes too much of its subjective *human* dimension illustrates this point. An exclusive Logos-oriented approach tends to pit the Latin (Anselm), subjective (Abelard), and classic (Aulén) types of atonement against one another. Their contrast appears too great and an integration hard to conceive. A Spirit Christology provides what is lacking in these approaches, showing how the Holy Spirit is involved in all aspects of the Son's identity and work as vicar, victor, and example. A pneumatic reading helps to integrate various insights of each atonement story.

The last two chapters have shown how Jesus' identity as receiver, bearer, and giver of the Spirit provides an adequate biblical and theological framework for complementing Logos-oriented approaches to the mystery of the incarnation, the paschal mystery, and the atonement. In the next two chapters, I focus on Trinitarian theology, exploring further the productivity of a Spirit-oriented Christology grounded in the economy of salvation for reflection on issues such as ontology, personhood, relation, and immanent models of the Trinity. In chapter six, I return to the question of the complementarity of Logos and Spirit-oriented approaches to Christology and suggest four ways towards a theological synthesis.

4

The Joint Mission of the Son and the Spirit

The Holy Spirit's Proper Work in the Incarnation and the Reciprocity of the Son-Spirit Relationship

IN THIS CHAPTER, I show how a Spirit-oriented Christology places the question of Jesus' identity in the context of his acts and relation to God the Father in the power of the Spirit, and therefore, in a framework conducive for reflection on the economic Trinity. Using Karl Rahner's *Grundaxiom* ("the economic Trinity is the immanent Trinity, and viceversa) as a starting point for recovering the distinct work of each divine person in Trinitarian theology, I show how a Spirit Christology gives us an economic basis for reflection on the proper work (*proprium*) of the Holy Spirit in the humanity of the Son.

Moreover, on the basis of Congar's qualification of the *Grundaxiom* on ontological and eschatological grounds, I explore how the sanctifying indwelling of the Holy Spirit in the Son's whole life and mission (incarnating) relates to the Son's assumption of a human nature (incarnation or hypostatic union). We inquire in what sense the relationship between the Son and the Spirit in the economy can be conceived as a reciprocal one without doing away with the logical priority of the assumption over the sanctification of the Logos's assumed humanity—a priority that prevents the potentially adoptionist notion that, logically speaking, the divine Logos can only assume a humanity that the Spirit has already sanctified. Anticipating the next chapter, I also offer a preliminary look at some models of the Trinity inspired by key narratives that speak to the joint mission of the Son and the Spirit in the history of salvation.

THE MYSTERY OF THE TRINITY AS A MYSTERY OF SALVATION: ON THE SOTERIOLOGICAL IMPORT OF THE CORRESPONDENCE BETWEEN THE ECONOMIC AND THE IMMANENT TRINITY

Like many theologians, I am in basic agreement with the contemporary recovery of the economy of salvation as the ground for reflection on the mystery of the Trinity. The underlying assumption behind this move lies in the conviction that God's threefold self-revelation (Barth) or self-communication (Rahner) in the Son and in the Holy Spirit corresponds in some direct (even if not absolute) manner to God's own triune being as Father, Son, and Holy Spirit. What then are the historical and dogmatic concerns (especially in the Western tradition) behind this renewed stress on the correspondence between the economic and the immanent Trinity? Moreover, in light of God's self-revelation in the incarnate Son, the receiver, bearer, and giver of the Spirit, to what extent or in what way do the economic and immanent aspects of the Trinity correspond to one another? Let us begin with the first question by looking at the critical soteriological concerns behind and enduring significance of Karl Rahner's famous proposal that the economic Trinity is the immanent Trinity and viceversa.

Before Rahner, Karl Barth had reflected on the problem of the doctrine of the Trinity on the basis of his theology of revelation. Only insofar as Scripture, the written form of the Word, attests to Christ as God's own Revealed Word can the church in turn ask of Scripture: "[W]ho is revealing Himself in it . . . and then also and subsequently, what this God does; and thirdly, what he effects, accomplishes, creates, and gives in His revelation."[1] Even if the reality of revelation initially leads us to ask somewhat abstractly about its subject (Revealer), its predicate (Revelation), and its object (Revealedness), the ground or root of the doctrine of the Trinity is ultimately an actual event of revelation. We can approach the mystery of God's triunity in what God does as Lord in his act of revelation, that is to say, in Jesus Christ.[2] From this christological horizon, the church then arrives at the notion of a self-differentiation in God. In other words, God reveals Godself to us in a threefold manner that corresponds to his intradivine antecedent

---

1. Barth, *Church Dogmatics*, I/1, § 8.1, p. 341.
2. Ibid., § 8.2, esp. p. 361.

"modes of existence" as Father, Son, and Holy Spirit.[3] In the end, it is not revelation conceived in abstract terms (as subject, predicate, and object) that grounds the doctrine of the Trinity, but rather God's own revelation in Jesus Christ.

God's threefold self-revelation as Lord points to God's independent freedom to relate to human beings: "Revelation in the Bible means the self-unveiling, imparted to men, of the God who according to His nature cannot be unveiled to man."[4] None other than God in Godself (immanent aspect) comes to us in God's self-revelation as Father, Son, and Holy Spirit (economic aspect): "[T]he Trinity of God is to be found not only in His revelation but, because in His revelation, in God Himself and of itself . . . therefore the Trinity is to be regarded not only as 'economic' but also as 'immanent.'"[5] As to the Holy Spirit, for example, Barth states: "What He is in revelation He is antecedently in Himself. And what He is antecedently in Himself he is in revelation."[6] The same principle applies to the other two persons of the Trinity.[7] Because of the triune God's own freedom as Lord to unveil and impart Godself to us in a threefold way, there is simply no other God behind God for us as Father, Son, and Holy Spirit.

Karl Rahner affirms a correspondence between God's self-communication to creatures through the Son and the Spirit, and the one God's three "distinct manners of subsisting" as Father, Son, and Holy Spirit.[8] He describes such correspondence with the famous axiom "The economic Trinity is the immanent Trinity and viceversa."[9] Positing some identity between both aspects of the mystery of God involves a major shift from the traditional Western (especially neo-scholastic) focus on the Trinity as a formal treatise on God's inner-life to a renewed appropriation of the same as a mystery of salvation.

Rahner's proposal is a corrective to "mere monotheism" in the West,[10] namely, the tendency to think of the one God and its indivisible acts to-

---

3. Ibid., esp. § 9.2. Barth uses the term "modes of existence" to define the three persons of the Trinity while strongly safeguarding their identity as the one God.

4. Ibid., § 8.2, pp. 362, 368, 373.

5. Ibid., p. 382.

6. Ibid., § 12.2, p. 533.

7. Ibid., § 10.2, p. 448ff.; and § 11.2, p. 474ff.

8. Rahner's definition of person seeks to safeguard the unity of God against what he conceives as the modern tritheistic notion of person as an individual or subjective center of consciousness and activity. *The Trinity*, 106–7.

9. Ibid., 21–24. The study that serves as background for this work is Rahner's "Remarks on the Dogmatic Treatise 'De Trinitate,'" 77–102.

10. Thus Rahner's well-known judgment that "despite their orthodox confession

wards the created world as a reality *prior* to the person of the Father and the twofold differentiation of his own self-giving in the economy of salvation through the Son and the Holy Spirit.[11] Rahner is critical of theologies that interpret the "Our Father" as an unqualified address to the entire Trinity or interpret the atoning work of the incarnate Logos as an offering of man in general (or conceived in abstract terms) made to all three persons of the Trinity.[12]

Rahner traces the roots of mere monotheism in the West tentatively to Augustine's stress on God's undivided essence as the starting point for reflecting on the Trinity (in his *De Trinitate*),[13] and more definitely to Thomas's logical conception of the treatise on the one God (*De Deo Uno*) *before* the one on the triune God (*De Deo Trino*). Augustine emphasizes God's essential unity and the divine persons' indivisible manner of relating to creation. At least potentially, such an emphasis on God's undivided causality in relation to the world relativizes the distinctiveness of God's self-communication in the Son and the Spirit in the economy of salvation. As Rahner rightly sees the problem, God's threefold self-giving in the economy no longer has to correspond directly to God's triunity. Trinity and soteriology then become detached from one another, and it becomes difficult to see the relevance of the doctrine of the Trinity for us and for our salvation. Indeed, too much stress on the simplicity or indivisibility of God in relation to creatures can lead not only to mere monotheism—as Rahner put it—but in some cases to formal unitarianism.[14] How do we solve this problem?

In the spirit of Greek-Eastern theology, Rahner prefers to speak of the one self-communicating God as the person of the Father in particular and not as the one divine substance shared by all persons of the Trinity

---

of the Trinity, Christians are, in their practical life, almost mere 'monotheists.' We must be willing to admit that, should the doctrine of the Trinity have to be dropped as false, the major part of religious literature could well remain virtually unchanged." *The Trinity*, 10–11.

11. Ibid., 11–13.

12. Ibid., 12.

13. Ibid., 15–21. Schwöbel's comments summarize general contemporary agreement on Rahner's diagnosis: "It would not be a gross exaggeration to see the mainstream of the history of Western trinitarian reflection as a series of footnotes on Augustine's conception of the Trinity in *De Trinitate*. Augustine's emphasis on the unity of the divine essence of God's triune being, his stress on the undivided mode of God's relating to what is not God and his attempt to trace the intelligibility of the doctrine of the Trinity through the vestigia trinitatis in the human consciousness, mediating unity and differentiation, defined the parameters for the mainstream of Western trinitarian reflection." Schwöbel, *Trinitarian Theology Today*, 4–5.

14. Mere monotheism may be interpreted as practical unitarianism. One may believe in a triune God, but live, act, and speak as if God were not triune.

in general and without distinction.[15] The initial move to identify God (*ho theos*) with a particular person of the Trinity (i.e., the Father) constitutes a genuine shift to biblical and creedal language. The Bible and the creeds in turn point to God's loving self-giving for humanity in his Son and his Spirit. Arguably, one may say that, after Rahner, the tendency in contemporary theology to arrive at conclusions on God's indivisible nature apart from reading Scripture and the Creeds as the narrative of God the Father's self-communication to creatures through his Son and Spirit has (or at least should) come to an end.[16]

Catherine M. LaCugna finds in Augustine's stress on the unity of God and God's Trinitarian acts in the economy a basis for the relegation of the doctrine of the Trinity to the inner-life of God and its separation from the mystery of salvation.[17] For Augustine, strictly speaking, proper distinctions among the persons in the one divine essence only occur in the intradivine life (i.e., in their operations *ad intra*). Accordingly, the axiom *opera ad intra divisa sunt* affirms that the internal processions of the persons in the one divine essence are distinguishable in relation to one another.[18] In the West, each person is affirmed precisely through its relation in opposition to another.[19] The Father is *not* the Son and viceversa. And yet, in their correlative relation in opposition, they at once imply one another. Moreover, since the Holy Spirit is neither the Father of the Son nor the Son of the Father, its only possible relation in opposition is to both the Father and the Son. In the one divine essence, then, the Father begets the Son and the Son is begotten of the Father; furthermore, the Holy Spirit is given or proceeds from the Father and the Son.[20] In any case, note that distinctions among the persons apply to the immanent Trinity.

To safeguard the oneness of God, the external works of the Trinity towards creation are said to be indivisible (Lat. *opera ad extra indivisa sunt*):

15. Rahner, *The Trinity*, 59–60.

16. If the classic distinction between natural and special revelation leads Christians to conceive of "God" and divine attributes as realities logically prior to the person and work of the Father, then treating the former type of revelation and engaging the issues surrounding it as a separate concern from the latter type may be, strictly speaking, a philosophical (in contrast to a theological) problem.

17. LaCugna, *God for Us*, chap. 3.

18. A relative distinction is one made of the persons in relation to one another without doing harm to the one divine essence that they ultimately have (are) in common. Augustine, *On the Holy Trinity* 5.5.6 (*NPNF*[1] 3:89); see also ibid., 5.11.12 (*NPNF*[1] 3:93).

19. Although the axiom *in Deo omnia sunt unum, ubi non obviat relationis oppositio* (Council of Florence, 1442) has its Western roots in Augustine, its conciliar form finds a closer parallel in Anselm's language. See Congar, *Holy Spirit*, 3:98.

20. Ibid., 5.12.13, 93–94; 5.14.15, 94; 5.15.16, 95.

"[T]he Father, Son, and Holy Spirit, of one and the same substance, God the Creator, the Omnipotent Trinity, work indivisibly."[21] Although Augustine held to this anti-subordinationist principle, he also saw the need to posit relative distinctions between these works through a doctrine of appropriations. While the divine persons are said to share equally in all their operations *ad extra*, they are ascribed (or appropriated) certain functions in particular. To give an example, the Father creates, the Son redeems, and the Holy Spirit sanctifies. Yet by virtue of their common divine essence and activity, they may all be equally ascribed these functions—as seen in the quote above, God the Trinity, not God the Father, is "God the Creator." Augustine explains the concept of appropriations as follows: "[T]he operation of the Trinity is also inseparable in each severally of those things which are said to pertain properly to the manifesting of either the Father, or the Son, or the Holy Spirit."[22]

LaCugna sees the idea of appropriations as a "compensating strategy" to attribute a proper work (*propium*) to a particular person of the Trinity—a move demanded by the indivisibility of Trinitarian acts in the economy and the relegation of personal distinctions to the immanent Trinity.[23] It is now a generally accepted thesis that unless a real differentiation among the persons (even in their works *ad extra*) qualifies the theory of appropriations, Augustine's teaching makes it extremely difficult to speak of a *propium* for any of the persons in the economy of salvation. As he begins his work, Augustine himself admits that faith must allow for differentiation lest the data of revelation on each person of the Trinity becomes superfluous. Not the Trinity, but only the Son was born, crucified, died, was buried, and ascended into heaven; not the Trinity, but only the Holy Spirit descended upon Jesus at Jordan and upon the disciples on Pentecost; not the Trinity, but only the Father spoke his word and was heard at Jordan and on the mount of transfiguration.[24] To highlight Trinitarian self-differentiation, LaCugna highlights the following *propia*:

> The mission of the Son to become incarnate belongs properly to the Son as Son. The Spirit is the one sent to make the creature holy. Each of these is a *propium*, an identifying characteristic of a unique person, and as such cannot be appropriated. The

---

21. Ibid., 4.21.30, p. 85.
22. Ibid., p. 86.
23. LaCugna, *God for Us*, 100 (cf. 86, 97–99); "Once the Augustinian axiom that 'works of the Trinity *ad extra* are one' is affirmed, and the economy no longer gives access to the distinction of persons, then the corrective of a doctrine of appropriations is needed in order to restore a *propium* to each divine person." Ibid., 102.
24. Augustine, *On the Holy Trinity* 1.4.7 (*NPNF*[1] 3:20).

Father's role in *sending* the Son and Spirit belongs to the Father alone and cannot indifferently be appropriated either to the Son or Spirit *or* to a generic Godhead.²⁵

In a fully Trinitarian theology, the indivisible unity of God cannot be protected to the detriment of the proper (and not merely appropriated) distinctiveness of the three persons of the Trinity.

Thomas further confirms some of the potential dangers of Western-Augustinian Trinitarianism. Rahner argues that Augustine's emphasis on the one divine essence over the person of the Father prepared the way for Thomas's treatment of the treatise on the one God (*De Deo Uno*) as a topic logically disconnected from the one on the triune God (*De Deo Trino*).²⁶ The former deals with the divine attributes and the proofs for the existence of God; the latter becomes a formal treatment of Trinitarian relations and processions in the intradivine life apart from God's self-communication in the Son and the Spirit in salvation-history.²⁷ When the unity of the divine essence takes priority over the person of God the Father (and the distinctiveness of the divine persons), conclusions on the one God are easily drawn apart from the biblical data on the triune God. It is on this point that Rahner criticizes scholastic theologians like Thomas for claiming that any one of the persons of the Trinity could have become incarnate if God in his will had chosen to do so—admittedly, a conclusion that Augustine does not reach.²⁸

As a response to such a highly speculative approach, Rahner posits the incarnation of the Son as a certain dogmatic instance of a reality proper (*propium*) to the person of the Logos and not merely appropriated to him as any one of the divine persons.

> Jesus is not simply God in general, but the Son. The second divine person, God's Logos, is man, and only he is man. Hence, there is at least *one* 'mission,' *one* presence in the world, *one* reality in salvation history which is not merely appropriated to some divine person, but which is proper to him.²⁹

---

25. LaCugna, *God for Us*, 100.

26. Rahner, *The Trinity*, 16–17. I say "logically disconnected" because, in Thomas's thought, the one God is really none other than the triune God.

27. Ibid., 17–18.

28. Ibid., 11; for Thomas's position, see *ST* 3, q. 23, a. 2; in contrast, Augustine states that "not God the Father, not the Holy Spirit, not the Trinity itself, but the Son only, which is the Word of God, was made flesh; although the Trinity was the maker." *On the Holy Trinity* 15.11.20 (*NPNF*¹ 3:210).

29. Rahner, *The Trinity*, 23.

The incarnation of the Son in salvation-history constitutes something distinctively unique to the second person of the Trinity (i.e., only the Logos became flesh) and does not just tell us something about God's "efficient causality" operating as indivisible essence in the world.[30] Thus God's self-communication in the Son's proper assumption of creaturely humanity (hypostatic union) proves Rahner's axiom. In terms of his *Grundaxiom*, then, the economic Logos is the immanent Logos and viceversa. None other than the Logos himself, the second person of the Trinity, is the incarnate Logos.

If we speak in particular of the creature's sanctification, then, Rahner arguably appears to ascribe this as a work proper (and not merely appropriated) to the Holy Spirit.[31] As in the case of God's self-communication to the Son's assumed humanity in the incarnation, God's self-communication in the Spirit to the graced creature allows us to posit self-differentiation in God and thus proves Rahner's axiom. Following its logic, we may say that the economic Spirit is the immanent Spirit and viceversa. None other than the Spirit itself—i.e., the third person of the Trinity, not just God in general—in the Spirit's own indwelling of the creature, which allows for his/her reception of God's grace "in faith, hope, and love."[32]

What then can we learn from the contemporary move to the correspondence between the economic Trinity and the immanent Trinity? Barth and Rahner remind us that, in the economy of salvation, God does not

---

30. Ibid.

31. Ibid., 86n9; Coffey notes that Rahner ultimately ascribes formal causality to all persons of the Trinity, and not only to the Holy Spirit, in what concerns the indwelling of the graced person. Coffey sees this move as a step backwards in Rahner's proposal, and moves to recover the bestowal of grace to the human person as a *proprium* for the Holy Spirit that is unique to his person. For his critique of Rahner, see Coffey, *Did You Receive the Holy Spirit When You Believed?*, 19–20.

32. *The Trinity*, 86n9; Rahner is aware of the danger of positing a full self-communication of God to the creature in the order of grace. On the one hand, he does not want to speak of God's self-giving to the creature in terms of "efficient" causality because then his twofold self-communication in the Son at the incarnation and in the Spirit in sanctification as *uncreated* grace (and not merely in created grace) is jeopardized. On the other hand, if God's self-communication is understood in terms of "formal" causality, the distinction between Creator and creature no longer stands. See *The Trinity*, 36; in her introduction to Rahner's work, LaCugna explains that he uses the language of "quasi-formal" causality to define God's self-communication to the creature in a way that "the indwelling of the divine persons in grace makes the graced person as close to God as possible without erasing the ontological distinction between God and creature." *The Trinity*, xiii; in a Lutheran response, God's gracious self-giving to the creature in the Spirit of Christ will have to be studied further in terms of its justifying and sanctifying aspects, since Rahner's theology assumes an affinity between the human spirit and the Holy Spirit that Lutheran dogmatics would be suspicious of due to its teaching of justification by grace alone and the corruption of sin in humans.

simply reveal or communicate something *other* than or *less* than Godself, but rather Godself as Father, Son, and Holy Spirit. God never fools or deceives us, for God is always faithful and trustworthy. Moreover, as Moltmann puts it so well, "There can be no question of half a revelation, let alone a merely fragmentary revelation. This is the main point behind modern talk about God's self-revelation."[33] Salvation depends on the condition that the triune God—again, not someone other than or less than God in three distinct or differentiated persons—relates to humanity as the Father's free self-giving to the creature in his Son and Spirit.[34] Jesus' identity as God's incarnate Son and the receiver, bearer, and giver of God's Spirit, gives us access to this Trinitarian reality in its economic and immanent aspects.

QUALIFYING THE EXTENT OF CORRESPONDENCE: EXPLORING THE IMMANENT TRINITARIAN IMPLICATIONS OF THE JOINT MISSION OF THE SON AND THE SPIRIT IN THE INCARNATION

Rahner's axiom posits the incarnation (hypostatic union) as the proper mission of the Son and thus as an instance of the self-communication of the Logos (not God in general), the second person of the Trinity, to his human nature. But given the biblical witness to the conception of Jesus by the Holy Spirit and its subsequent participation in all events of his life and work, what is the proper mission of the third person in the hypostatic union (incarnation) and in Christ's entire life and mission (incarnating)?[35] And what does the answer to this question on the joint mission of the Son and the Spirit in God's economy of salvation allow us to say about their intradivine relations?

---

33. Moltmann, *The Spirit of Life*, 302.

34. To preserve the distinction between Creator and creation, we may say that God the Father communicates himself to the creature freely and out of love through the missions of his Son and Spirit and, therefore, not out of necessity or dependence on the world (as in process thought). God may not be essentially related to creation (a concern in classical theism), but God is not detached from it either for God comes and relates to us in a concrete way in the life and mission of Jesus of Nazareth. See O'Donnell, *The Mystery of the Triune God*, 2–7; and a fuller treatment in O'Donnell, *Trinity and Temporality*, esp. chap. 5.

35. The reader should note that the dynamic term "incarnating" denotes the incarnate Son's identity in terms of his "being-in-act" throughout the whole Christ-event. By comparison, "incarnation" denotes the Son's inner-constitution as God-man "from-the-beginning" at a set point in time (hypostatic union). For lack of a better term, I include both static and dynamic senses under the general rubric of "incarnation." Karl Rahner only dealt with the static aspect of the incarnation in the christological application of his axiom.

What is the extent of the correspondence between the economic Trinity and the immanent Trinity?

A Preliminary Look at the Immanent Trinitarian Implications of the Incarnation

The point of departure for reflecting on God's self-revelation, self-communication, or self-giving through the missions of the Son and the Holy Spirit is Jesus of Nazareth. Otherwise stated, Jesus' identity as incarnate Son of the Father and as receiver, bearer, and giver of the Father's Spirit reveals the mystery of the Trinity. If we begin with the creedal presentation of the mysteries of Jesus' life, his conception by the Holy Spirit appears as the first moment that leads us to ask what it means for God to communicate his Spirit to his Son's humanity. On the basis of Luke 1:35, I have already ascribed the sanctification of Mary's unborn child to the Holy Spirit under the rubric of Jesus as the receiver of God's Spirit. Even if the coming upon of the Holy Spirit first touches the virgin Mary, the end result (Luke uses the conjunction *dio*) of this overshadowing of the power of the Most High upon her is to make the fruit of her womb "holy" from conception.[36] From that moment on, the Holy Spirit who has always been with the Son and the Father *ad intra* begins to dwell in the incarnate Son *ad extra*.

If we add to Luke 1:35 the witness of John 1:14 to the mission of the Son, then we can state that God the Father's self-giving at the moment of incarnation and conception takes place respectively in the preexistent Son's (= Logos's) union to human nature (i.e., hypostatic union) and in the Holy Spirit's perfection of this humanity in holiness from conception.[37] Of course,

---

36. See Ladaria, "La unción de Jesús y el don del Espíritu," 553n17.

37. For our purposes in this chapter, it is sufficient to assume the traditional interpretation of John 1:14 as the Word's assumption of a creaturely reality (= flesh) unto himself. In his *Deus Trinitas*, Coffey has disputed this interpretation (12–14). He argues that the phrase "to become flesh" does not explicitly mean "to become human" because flesh refers to weakness, "its vulnerability to decay and to sin, and particularly its predestination to death" (13). In John's Gospel, Son of Man passages also point to Jesus as a preexistent heavenly man in the realm of God's eternity (13). While one could argue the possible merits (by no means indisputable) of these exegetical insights, I do question Coffey's conclusion that they do not attain the level of an ontological view of the incarnation (i.e., that the divine Word becomes a human being) and thus only point to a more functional embodiment of the Word in Jesus. Even if the designation "flesh" denotes—and especially, I would add, in a non-pejorative way—the weakness constitutive of every human reality in contrast to God, it is still the case (as Coffey himself suggests) that flesh cannot exist apart from a true human being. And even if, from the perspective of God's foreknowledge, we were to speculate that the Word has always existed as man, I would clarify that the divine Word exists only in view of his incarnation

union and sanctification (indwelling) occur at once, so that no temporal distinction severs these differentiated operations or proper works. As a particular event in God's economy of salvation, the joint mission of the Son and the Holy Spirit in conception already shows that none other than these two persons freely cooperate with one another in distinct ways in God's self-communication to the humanity of Christ. To sum up, the Holy Spirit, the power of the Most High, descends upon the virgin and makes the fruit of her womb "holy" (Luke 1:35) even as the Word and only-begotten Son of God "becomes flesh" (John 1:14). Here, at the incarnation, a twofold differentiated and unrepeatable communication of God the Father to Christ's humanity takes place in time and history. The Son who is from the Father's substance ("God *of God*," or "begotten *of the Father*") is sent by the Father to assume our flesh in order to redeem it. The Holy Spirit who with the Son is also from the Father's substance ("who proceeds *from* the Father") is sent by the Father to rest on or indwell the flesh that the Son unites to himself. If the Son's proper work is the incarnation (hypostatic union), the Spirit's proper work is to make human nature holy by its indwelling. The Holy Spirit's *proprium* applies to the sanctification of the human nature of the Son, and then to the holiness of God's adopted sons who receive the same Spirit by grace through the Son.

Coffey offers a helpful way to distinguish further the Son's self-communication to his assumed humanity from the Holy Spirit's self-communication to a human person.[38] Using philosophical language, he distinguishes between a "substantial" and an "accidental union." The former is a type of union that only applies to the hypostatic union. The divine Logos comes into union with the assumed humanity in such a way that it enhypostasizes it, or makes it the person's own. The latter is a type of union in which the person of the Holy Spirit indwells and sanctifies a human being without making it its own person, or without taking away from the personhood of the indwelt humanity. While Coffey uses this language to distinguish between the hypostatic union and the Spirit's dwelling in the saints, the same distinction may be applied to the humanity of the person of the Logos.

The correspondence between the economic and the immanent aspects of the Trinity helps us to affirm that God as such is fully involved in salvation history through the incarnate Son in whom the Holy Spirit dwells. To bring out the non-negotiable soteriological significance of the incarnation

---

on the basis of John's own witness to the identity of this Word as one through whom God creates all things (1:3). If it is as the creative Word of God that the Logos becomes its creaturely counterpart or flesh, then the term flesh must ultimately be interpreted within the framework of the uncreated-created dialectic.

38. Coffey, *Did You Receive the Holy Spirit When You Believed?*, 40–41.

in its pneumatological trajectory, let us now rephrase Rahner's axiom while keeping in mind the proper missions of the Son and the Holy Spirit already mentioned. Starting with the first half of the axiom, we can say: If the economic Logos in whom the Spirit dwells is the immanent Logos, then the incarnate and sanctified Logos is none other than the preexistent Logos on whom the Spirit of the Father rests. The presence of the Spirit in the incarnate Son does not make him less than or other than the divine Logos, but reveals his being from the Father in the same Spirit.

Regarding the reciprocity or second half of the axiom, we can say: The immanent Logos on whom the Spirit of the Father rests is the economic Logos who freely assumed a true humanity like ours that participates in the Holy Spirit's indwelling, so that through him we might have access to his Spirit. Otherwise stated, the Logos receives and bears the Spirit so that he might give the Spirit to us along with all its benefits and gifts. Rahner's axiom illuminates the salvific import and Trinitarian ground of the proper missions of the Son and the Holy Spirit in the incarnation for our sake.

The Son's *propium* is to unite humanity unto himself and the Holy Spirit's *propium* is to indwell and sanctify that humanity. We can bring the Father into the picture as well. As the origin (*archē*), source (*pēgē*), and cause (*aitia*) of Trinitarian self-giving to the creature, the Father sends his only-begotten Son into the world to assume a human nature (incarnation) and thus a human history (incarnating). At the same time, the Father sends his Holy Spirit to sanctify the Son's humanity from the first moment of incarnation/conception and to dwell in it throughout all moments of his life and mission. This sending of the Son and the Holy Spirit is the *propium* of the Father in the economy. Rahner's axiom helps us in turn to ground this proper mission of the Father in the economy in the Father's own immanent personal identity as the unoriginate origin of the Son and the Holy Spirit.

Having established the Father's proper work, we can argue about the appropriate way to think in logical terms about the relationship between the differentiated missions of the Son and the Holy Spirit. Although union and sanctification take place simultaneously, the former mission *logically* precedes the latter in the economy. In other words, the Spirit sanctifies what the Son has united to himself. Otherwise, the idea of a fully sanctified human being who logically exists prior to its assumption by the Son could lead to the charge of adoptionism or Nestorianism.[39]

---

39. Cyril of Alexandria, for example, states that Jesus Christ "was not first born a common man of the holy Virgin, and then the Word came down and entered into him . . ." *The [Third] Epistle of Cyril to Nestorius* (NPNF[2] 14:198); similarly, in the Lutheran tradition, Martin Chemnitz writes, "For the flesh of Christ was not first formed and animated separately in the womb of Mary in such a way that afterwards the person of

In our introductory study of Irenaeus's response to the Gnostics, I pointed out that his move to place the union of Jesus and Christ at the incarnation (in contrast to the baptism, as the Gnostics often did) paved the way for the priority of the mission of the Word at the incarnation over that of the Spirit at the anointing. At the Jordan, the Spirit descended upon the *already* incarnate Word and anointed him for mission. Later on, others argued for the same priority from the moment of conception. In this regard, I showed that Athanasius and Cyril of Alexandria went further than Irenaeus by making two crucial moves. First, they viewed the chrism or anointing of Jesus by the Spirit at his baptism as a revelatory instance of the Son's prior sanctification of himself with his own Spirit from conception. Second, they grounded the Son's glorification of himself with his own Spirit in the processional priority of the Son over the Holy Spirit at the intradivine level. As Athanasius intimates on one occasion, the Spirit takes from the Son (not viceversa). The economic side of this argument is that the Son gives the Spirit. In the Western tradition, Thomas argued in a similar way. He asserted that the mission of the Son in the incarnation logically precedes that of the Holy Spirit and grounded this reality in the logical priority of the Son's procession (= generation) from the Father over the procession (= spiration) of the Holy Spirit from the Father and the Son.[40] For the same reason, Thomas thought of Christ's habitual grace and capital grace as effects following respectively from the grace of union and personal grace.

At the Council of Nicea, the church fathers grounded the Son's free and gracious descent from the Father "for us and for our salvation" in his being "begotten" of the "substance" of the Father. The terms "begetting" and "being begotten" describe the relationship of origin *ad intra* between the Father and the Son, and form the basis for positing a logical priority *ad extra* of the Father's "sending" over the Son's "being sent" in the economy of salvation. At the level of dogma, however, Constantinople I did not actually offer a pronouncement on the *how* of the immanent relationship between the Son and the Holy Spirit. The Council only pointed to the Holy Spirit's procession from the Father (a hypostatic statement) and his equal glory with the Father and the Son (a substantial statement). Does this conciliar silence mean there is room to consider a *reciprocal* priority of the Son's mission (incarnation) over the Holy Spirit's mission (sanctification) in the mystery

---

the Logos was united with this preformed and animated flesh. For this would mean that the human nature of Christ at some time would have had its own proper and peculiar subsistence before and outside the hypostatic union with the Logos." Chemnitz, *The Two Natures in Christ*, 101 (cf. 30–31).

40. *ST* 1, q. 7, a. 13.

of the incarnation that points to a similar reciprocity of processions in the immanent Trinity?

I raised the question of a possible logical priority for the Holy Spirit's sanctification of the humanity as a corrective to monophysite tendencies in Christology. First, if the missions of the Son and the Holy Spirit in the incarnation are differentiated and yet "reciprocal" at the same time, must not their immanent Trinitarian relations to one another allow for a more flexible perichoretic way of understanding their intradivine processions? I hinted that union and sanctification in the economy must point to and thus find their immanent ground not only in the procession of the Holy Spirit from the Father "and the Son" (Western *filioque*) or the Father "through the Son" (Eastern *per filium*), but also in the generation of the Son from the Father "in the Spirit" (*in spiritu*). The basic Trinitarian assumption behind this argument is straightforward: Just as there is no procession of the Holy Spirit from the Father in which the Son does not participate, so also there is no generation of the Son from the Father in which the Holy Spirit does not participate. Second, and more importantly, in the face of a monophysitism that might deny Christ's humanity its sanctification by the Spirit throughout his life and work, can such a perichoretic view of Trinitarian relations in turn support a logical priority of the Holy Spirit's mission in sanctifying the humanity of the Son over the Son's mission to assume this humanity? Do we want to say that the Son unites to himself what the Holy Spirit has not sanctified? Clearly not.[41] Let us first look at the economic-Trinitarian aspect of the problem, leaving aside for a moment its implications for Trinitarian models of intradivine relations—a point to which I shall return in the next chapter.

Does the Son's assumption of a human nature prior to its indwelling by the Holy Spirit necessarily compromise a full appreciation of the *true* or *full* humanity of Christ? Here I must answer in the negative. Undoubtedly, the history of dogma has shown us in more than a few occasions that the dynamic presence of the Spirit in the Son's humanity has been neglected. We have seen how a number of theologians in the East and the West have posited the logical priority of the incarnation of the Son over his sanctification by the Spirit in ways that made the pneumatic aspects of Jesus' identity merely revelatory of his prior status as God or exemplary for the church. I have already suggested ways to address this partial eclipse of pneumatology in Christology.

---

41. Chemnitz can assert that "the Son of God assumed that individual unit (*massa*) [body] from the flesh and blood of Mary, which the Holy Spirit in the act of conception so sanctified and purified from the whole ruin of sin that that which was born of Mary was holy." *The Two Natures in Christ*, 57 (cf. 75).

On the other hand, we must also learn from theologians like Irenaeus, Basil, and Hilary of Poitiers that the move to prioritize the mission of the Son (union) over that of the Spirit (sanctification at conception, anointing at the Jordan) does not have to take away from the active role of the Spirit of the Father in the human life and mission of the incarnate Son. Irenaeus can presuppose a real union of Word and flesh at conception as a condition for his anointing with the Spirit of the Father at the Jordan without losing sight of the significance of the event for constituting the incarnate Word as "Jesus Christ" or the link between his anointing and our unction in baptism. While Basil affirms the *homoousios* of the Son with the Father and the Lord's coming in the flesh, he does not hesitate to place the Christ-event in a pneumatological framework. Hilary can speak of the birth of the Son from the Father in eternity (generation) and from the virgin Mary at Bethlehem (conception) and still speak in a non-adoptionist way of his births for us in the waters of the Jordan and at his resurrection. In each case, we find a Christology that gives full weight to the dynamic place of the Spirit of the Father in the human history of the Son. At the same time, these views assume the priority of the Son's mission to become flesh over the Spirit's mission to indwell his humanity at conception, anoint it at the Jordan, and glorify it at the resurrection. Recovering the constitutive (and not merely accidental) character of the Spirit's mission throughout the entire life of Christ—as important as this project is—does not finally necessitate a logical inversion of the traditional Trinitarian order. In the incarnation, the Trinitarian taxis *Father-Son-Spirit* avoids the idea of an already existing humanity disposed for union (a logical form of adoptionism).[42] To avoid the danger of a logically opposite monophysitism, however, the order *Father-Spirit-Son* is not necessary, for the active and sanctifying presence of the Spirit in the Son takes place precisely in the assumed humanity of the Son.[43] To what extent the entire life and work of Jesus confirms our preliminary judgment on the issue of priority, and in what way such logical priority of the Son over the

---

42. Coffey, for example, sees the taxis *Father-Spirit-Son* as a biblical/economic-Trinitarian "mission" model that must be clearly distinguished from the classic taxis *Father-Son-Spirit* as an immanent Trinitarian "procession" model. Coffey finds the ground for such a distinction in "the fact that the Spirit who rests on the Son in the immanent Trinity draws into union with him in the economic Trinity." *Deus Trinitas*, 164n7; however, the economic order also allows him to say that the Word cannot assume a humanity that has not been already sanctified and disposed for union by the Holy Spirit. Ibid., 183n75.

43. For a similar judgment on this matter, especially in dialogue with Hans Urs von Balthasar's proposal for an economic "Trinitarian inversion" of the classical taxis, see Ladaria, *La Trinidad*, 189–201.

Spirit at the incarnation touches on their immanent Trinitarian relations, will be discussed in more detail later.

Qualifying the Correspondence between the Economic and the Immanent Trinity

To what extent can Rahner's axiom justify the transition from the differentiated missions of the Son and the Holy Spirit in the incarnation to their immanent relations? The issue at hand is the *extent* of the correspondence between the economic and the immanent Trinity.[44] Rahner does not really touch on this question. Although none other than Trinity reveals itself to us in the Father's economy of salvation through the missions of his Son and Holy Spirit, Rahner still sees the immanent Trinity as the ontological ground for the economic Trinity.[45] Admittedly, even this conclusion follows from God's self-giving for us in the economy. But even though God for us (economic Trinity) is neither less nor another than God in Godself (immanent Trinity), God in Godself still precedes God for us ontologically in the order of being. To speak *a posteriori* of the immanent Trinity as the *a priori* ontological ground of the economic Trinity is to affirm the element of freedom and graciousness in God the Father's twofold manner of self-giving to the creature in the Son and the Spirit—respectively, through incarnation and indwelling.[46] For Rahner, the usefulness of his axiom lies mainly in its capacity to recover the basis for God's own triunity at the intradivine level in God's self-communication in the Son and the Holy Spirit in salvation history, making it possible to reaffirm the salvific import of the doctrine of the Trinity.

In light of Rahner's main soteriological concern, one can hardly charge him with reducing the mystery of God to a functional or economic trinitarianism. Like Rahner, LaCugna's concern is also from first to last soteriological. There can no longer be in Trinitarian theology an unbridgeable separation between God for us and God in Godself, between the mystery of salvation and the mystery of the Trinity. But unlike Rahner, LaCugna, interprets his axiom by arguing for its unqualified identity: "Since our only point of access

---

44. Of course, the idea is not to ascertain an exact degree of correspondence, but simply to acknowledge that such correspondence is not an absolute one and thus requires some qualification.

45. *The Trinity*, 101–3; LaCugna criticizes Rahner for grounding the missions in the processions and, by doing so, moves in the direction of collapsing the immanent into the economic Trinity or identifying too closely *oikonomia* and *theologia*. *God for Us*, 221–23.

46. See *The Trinity*, 83.

to *theologia* is through *oikonomia*, then *an 'immanent' Trinitarian theology of God is nothing more than a theology of the economy of salvation.*"⁴⁷ Is this description of the correspondence between the economic and the immanent Trinity too drastic? Nothing more? Is the mystery of the triune God exhausted in God's gracious self-giving for us? Does the immanent aspect collapse into the economic one? In other words, is the immanent Trinity *always* the economic Trinity without qualification?

There is today much agreement on the first half of Rahner's axiom. Yet a question arises in regard to the reciprocity (or "viceversa") of the axiom. Does the "viceversa" point to an *absolute* or a *qualified* reciprocity of the axiom? And how does the answer to this question affect our preliminary view of the correspondence between the *propia* of the persons in the incarnation and their self-differentiation in God? Walter Kasper, for example, reminds us that the copula "is" in the axiom "must be understood as meaning not an identification but rather a non-deducible, free, gracious, historical presence of the immanent Trinity in the economic Trinity."⁴⁸

In one of the clearest and most articulate presentations of the problem, Congar offers ontological and eschatological reasons for a qualified reciprocity of the *Grundaxiom*. First, he desires to safeguard the existence of the triune God prior to that of created reality and the priority of God's freedom to act towards creation.⁴⁹ Second, he wants to affirm that God's self-communication to the creature takes place "in accordance with a rule of 'condescendence,' humiliation, ministry, and 'kenosis'" that in turn points to the fact that God's fullest self-communication has yet to take place in the beatific vision at the end of the eschatological era.⁵⁰ In these two ways, Congar warns against an absolute identity or correspondence between the economic Trinity and the immanent Trinity.

LaCugna fully recognizes that the distinction between God in Godself (Lat. *ad intra*) and God for us (Lat. *ad extra*) functions as a strategy "(a) to

---

47. *God for Us*, 223.

48. Kasper, *The God of Jesus Christ*, 276; Ladaria argues that the second half of Rahner's axiom "prevents us from too much of a univocal interpretation of the first *is*" (translation mine). Why? In the order of being, the economic Trinity cannot constitute in any way the immanent Trinity that precedes it. Ladaria prefers the use of the term "correspondence" only for the first half of the axiom. *La Trinidad*, 63n133.

49. "The first half of this statement by Rahner is beyond dispute, but the second half has to be clarified. Can the free mystery of the economy and the necessary mystery of the Tri-unity of God be identified? As the Fathers who combated Arianism said, even if God's creatures did not exist, God would still be a Trinity of Father, Son and Spirit, since creation is an act of free will, whereas the procession of the Persons takes place, *kata phusin*." Congar, *Holy Spirit*, 3:13.

50. Ibid., 15.

uphold divine freedom, b) to avoid equating God with the world, and (c) to avoid the agnostic or nominalist perspectives which despair of any real knowledge of God on our part."[51] Still, LaCugna opts for a reverent negative theology in regard to the immanent Trinity for epistemological reasons. Since we only have access to God's self-differentiation as Father, Son, and Holy Spirit through our *a posteriori* reality as already created and redeemed humans, we speculate too much when we speak of God in Godself apart from God's threefold operations in creation and redemption.[52] Like LaCugna, I acknowledge the limits of our knowledge of God and the apophatic principle that warns against reading the economic into the immanent Trinity "by a kind of extrapolation."[53] However, I also want to allow for the idea that, in the order of knowledge and faith, the church's Spirit-led confession of Jesus as her risen Lord (1 Cor 12:3) leads to her full acknowledgment of Jesus' unity with God the Father and thus his preexistence and divinity. Standing in awe before the inexhaustible mystery of God in Christ, the church can fully engage in modest reflection on the immanent Trinitarian ground of her own creation and salvation.

From a pneumatological space, the church can affirm the distinction between God who precedes her as Creator and herself as part of his creation. The distinction prevents the church from reducing or collapsing the mystery of the Trinity to its self-giving in the economy. Congar's first qualification of the reciprocity of Rahner's axiom involves the distinction between Creator and creature. He assumes the uncreated-created dialectic and the concomitant notion of God's freedom to relate to what is not God, namely, the divine freedom to create and redeem creation. Only from a pneumatological horizon can the church affirm God's essential triunity as a reality that does not ultimately depend on God's self-giving in history—even if the former assumes the latter in some manner.[54]

---

51. LaCugna, "Re-conceiving the Trinity as the Mystery of Salvation," 13.

52. LaCugna agrees that asking whether God would be a Trinity apart from his threefold self-revelation (and by implication, his real relation to the world) is purely speculative "because we stand already within the *fact* of creation." *God for Us*, 326 (n21), cf. 227, 230. In her argumentation, she follows Schoonenberg's "Trinity—The Consummated Covenant," 112 (esp. thesis 8). LaCugna also disputes Thomas's idea that only humans have a real relation to God (not viceversa)—a move Thomas made to preserve God's freedom in relation to the world. For Thomas's position, see *ST* 1a, q. 13, a. 7.

53. "To highlight the gracious freedom and the kenotic aspect of the economic Trinity is at the same time to emphasize the apophatic character of the immanent Trinity, that is, the fact that it eludes all language and thought . . . we cannot deduce the immanent Trinity by a kind of extrapolation from the economic Trinity." Kasper, *The God of Jesus Christ*, 276.

54. Kasper observes that we must hold to the freedom, love, and grace of the

Congar's second qualification of Rahner's axiom is eschatologically-oriented. God's self-communication to the creature cannot be complete until the creature's eschatological experience of the beatific vision of God in the state of glorification.[55] We may say that God's self-giving to the creature in the Son and the Spirit in salvation history has a goal that awaits fulfillment in the final resurrection and the life everlasting. At that time, what the Son of God accomplished for us in his Spirit-indwelt flesh will be accomplished in us too in the resurrection of the flesh as the goal of our sanctification in the Spirit. As Bruno Forte has put it so well, "[t]he amount already given in the economy is a pledge of what will be fully revealed in the time of glory."[56] In light of our present hope in what is yet to come, a qualification of the "viceversa" in Rahner's axiom calls us to distinguish without separating the element of eschatological promise in the revealed Trinity from its fulfillment in the glorious presence of the immanent Trinity.

A Look at the Immanent Trinitarian Implications of Christ's Life in the Spirit (Incarnating) in Light of Congar's Qualified Reciprocity of Rahner's Axiom

We can now apply Congar's two insights on the qualification of the second half of Rahner's axiom to God's self-giving in the Son and the Spirit to the assumed human nature at the incarnation, and apply it to the question of the correspondence between the economic Trinity and the immanent Trinity. We may pose the question as follows: How can Congar's two qualifications apply to the move from the proper works of the Son and the Spirit in God's self-giving for us (economic Trinity) to statements regarding their self-differentiation in God (immanent Trinity)? There is a correspondence between God's self-communication to creaturely reality both in the Son's uniting of human nature to himself and in the Spirit's indwelling of the same at conception (economic aspect) and God's own triunity (immanent

---

immanent Trinity "in," not "behind," the economic Trinity: "The need is to maintain not only the kenotic aspect of the economic Trinity but also its character of graciousness and freedom in relation to the immanent Trinity and thus to do justice to the immanent mystery of God in (not: behind!) his self-revelation." *The God of Jesus Christ*, 276.

55. Similarly, Moltmann has argued that in our present life "the Trinitarian doxology" anticipates the eschatological "seeing face to face" of God; but in the end, the immanent Trinity will be worshipped in its own essence and for its own sake and not merely for its saving acts among us in history. *The Spirit of Life*, 301–3.

56. Forte, *The Trinity As History*, 13.

aspect). But in what way? What can we say regarding the triune God's immanence on the basis of its free economic manifestation?

As previously stated, we can affirm that the incarnate Son in whom the Spirit dwells in history is none other than the preexistent Son in whom the Spirit rests or remains in eternity and viceversa. I have also noted that the reciprocity of Rahner's axiom requires qualification because the incarnation constitutes a gracious novelty in the economy of salvation and therefore not an absolute reflection of the immanent Trinity. If the immanent Trinity is always the economic Trinity in an absolute sense, the incarnation also has to be seen as an immanent reality in God. Then we would have to transfer crassly the virgin birth, the anointing, and the crucifixion of Christ to the immanent Trinity, effectively doing away with the basic theological distinction between God and creation.

Indeed, one may speak of God's eternal disposition to send his Son into the world in the flesh to be sanctified, anointed, crucified, and raised for us in the Spirit. Without denying this truth, however, one must also affirm that the dynamic presence of the Spirit of God in the incarnate Son from birth, at the Jordan, unto death, and at the resurrection takes place under the conditions of time and history. Otherwise stated, the Son is always the only-begotten of the Father in the Spirit, but only in the case of the economy can we speak of the incarnate Son's "births," *kairoi*, "incarnating," or becoming in his sanctified humanity as Son in obedience to the Father and for us at his conception, baptism unto death, and resurrection. Only in the case of the economy can we refer to the Spirit's creating, indwelling, leading, sanctifying, perfecting, and vivifying of the incarnate Son in the flesh at special and *new* moments of his life and mission.

These are some examples of provisos that we must keep in mind as we go through other instances of God's self-communication in the Son and the Spirit to the humanity of Christ *after* conception. By drawing attention to these provisos, I have briefly applied Congar's first qualification of the axiom's reciprocity to the incarnation (hypostatic union). The general lesson is this: We must avoid a strict, absolute, or unqualified identity between the economic and the immanent Trinity. The preliminary immanent Trinitarian models I proposed earlier on (i.e., *in spiritu* and *per filium/filioque*) do not violate Congar's ontological qualification. I will say more about this in the next chapter.

We can now also apply Congar's second qualification of the axiom's "viceversa" to the incarnation. Congar sees Thomas's view of the hypostatic union as an example of "non-historical theology" in which Christ's humanity receives everything from conception (including the beatific vision).⁵⁷ In his eschatological qualification of the axiom, Congar recognizes that we cannot ascribe the vision of God to Christ's assumed humanity at the moment of conception. God's self-communication in this case is not exhausted in the Son's descent to unite a human nature unto his person, but has a dynamic eschatological orientation or goal towards its fulfillment in the resurrection of his sanctified humanity. Since the Spirit has a constitutive place in indwelling the human nature that the Son unites to his person, the Spirit must also be seen as an active agent in the actualization or perfecting of the Son's humanity from its conception to exaltation at the right hand of God at his resurrection and ascension.

God's self-communication to the assumed humanity in the Spirit's indwelling of the same cannot be seen merely in static terms but rather in its dynamic actualization until its culmination in Jesus' glorification. After God raises his Son in the power of the Spirit, we can also speak of a fulfilled self-communication of God in the Spirit to the assumed humanity of the Son.⁵⁸ We can then affirm the full glorification of the Son's exalted humanity in the presence of the Father upon completion of his mission, without erasing the ontological distinction between the divine and human natures in Christ—i.e., without collapsing the immanent Logos into the economic Logos. After conception, what then are the subsequent events in the joint mission of the Son and the Spirit in God's economy of salvation? What do they tell us about the relationship between the Son and the Spirit at the immanent level? Do these events support *in spiritu* and *per filium* (or even *filioque*) models of the immanent Trinity on the basis of the hypostatic union? Do they support the Father's unique hypostatic property as origin of the Son and the Spirit?

The Father's self-communication in the Spirit throughout the human life of the Son is a dynamic one and therefore acquires an orientation from the Spirit's sanctification or indwelling of the Son's human nature to its anointing and glorification of the same. In Mark's Gospel, the anointing of Jesus at the Jordan explicitly points to the Spirit's descent "*in him*" (Gk. *eis auton*, 1:10), thus confirming the notion of an actual indwelling already anticipated in Luke 1:35. In the account of the temptation, Luke alludes to the same reality by telling us that Jesus returned from the Jordan "full of the Holy Spirit" (Gk. *plērēs pneumatos hagiou*) and was led "*in/by* the Spirit"

---

57. Congar, *The Word and the Spirit*, 85. Congar cites ST 3a, q. 34, a. 4 (see 97n2).

58. In a Logos Christology, the assumed humanity receives the divine Logos's communication of his divine majesty and power already at the hypostatic union. But is it not too speculative to ascribe the beatific vision to Christ at that time? Here the Father's self-communication in the Spirit to Christ's humanity complements a Logos Christology with a much needed historically-oriented trajectory.

(Gk. *en tō pneumati*) into the desert (4:1). In economic terms, the fullness of the Spirit in Jesus means he is led by the Spirit. The sanctification of the child from conception (Luke 1:35) does not prevent the evangelist from giving the Spirit's indwelling in Jesus its economic dynamism throughout his life and mission.

In John's Gospel, the language of permanency best describes the anointing of the Son, upon whom the Spirit remains, rests, or dwells (Gk. *emeinen*, 1:32; cf. v. 33). God gives his Spirit to the Son "not by measure" (Gk. *ou . . . ek metrou*, John 3:34). After his anointing at the Jordan, Jesus begins his ministry "in/by the power of the Holy Spirit" (Gk. *en tē dynamei tou pneumatos*, Luke 4:14). He drives out demons "in/by the Spirit of God" (Gk. *en pneumati theou*, Matt 12:28; cf. Luke 12:28). He rejoices "in/by the Holy Spirit" (Gk. *en tō pneumati tō hagiō*, Luke 10:21). Prior to his ascension, Jesus also instructed the apostles "through the Holy Spirit" (Gk. *dia pneumatos hagiou*, Acts 1:2). As high priest, Jesus sacrificially offers his unblemished life "through the eternal Spirit" (*dia pneumatos aiōniou*) to God (Heb 9:14). As risen Lord, Christ is vindicated "in/by the Spirit" (*en pneumati*, 1 Tim 3:16).

Since the incarnate Son does all his life and work in or by the Spirit, the Spirit has an unquestionable role in God the Father's self-communicating to the Son's humanity. To some extent, such a role is an instrumental one in the sense that the Spirit is the means through or by which God empowers the Son to carry out his redemptive mission for us. We can ground this economic reality in the Son's generation from the Father in the Spirit (*in spiritu*). The dynamic indwelling of the Holy Spirit in the incarnate Son can also be understood as being mediated unto others through the Son. Upon healing the woman with hemorrhage, for example, Jesus knew that "power" —a term that Luke associates with the Holy Spirit (cf. Luke 24:49; Acts 1:8, 10:38)—had come out *"from* him" (Gk. *ap' emou*, Luke 8:46). The Son lives in or by the Spirit and the Spirit comes from or through the Son.

The clearest instances of the Son's mediation of the Spirit of the Father unto others are associated with his glorification in the paschal mystery. On the cross, Jesus "handed over the Spirit" (*paredōken to pneuma*, John 19:30). Soon thereafter, blood and "water"—the latter is, of course, a Johannine symbol for the Spirit (cf. 7:38-39, 4:14, and 3:5)—at once "came out from" (Gk. *exēlthen*, 3:34) the pierced side of the crucified. In John's Gospel, the cross anticipates Jesus' breathing of the Spirit on the disciples as the risen Lord: "[H]e breathed on them (Gk. *enephysēsen . . . autois*) and said to them, 'Receive [*labete*] the Holy Spirit. . . .'" (20:22). In the West, the verb "to breathe" in Latin was rendered "*spirare*" and served to describe the procession of the Holy Spirit from the Father and the Son in terms of "spiration." The Greeks, on the other hand, have typically pointed to the Johannine passage giving witness to the Spirit of truth, "who *proceeds from the Father*" [Gk. *ho para tou patros ekporeuetai*] in a way that is unique to the Father (15:26). In the same passage, the Son clearly has a mediating role in the procession of the Paraclete from the Father unto the disciples. Jesus refers to the Paraclete "whom I will *send* to you from the Father" (Gk. *hon egō pempsō hymin para tou patros*). Finally, the role of the Son as mediator of the sending or breathing of the Spirit from the Father also appears in Luke's account of Pentecost and the exaltation of Christ at the right hand of God. As risen Lord and Messiah, Jesus "pours out" [*execheen*] the promise of the Spirit "*from* the Father" [*para tou patros*] to all believers (Acts 2:33).

In light of the paschal mystery's witness to the Son's role as mediator in God's self-giving to humanity in the Spirit, we can once again posit a logical priority of union over sanctification at the incarnation (against adoptionism). This economic reality corresponds to a logical priority of the Son's procession from the Father by generation over the Holy Spirit's procession from the same by spiration. We can ground the Father's economic giving of the Spirit through the Son in the Spirit's immanent procession from the Father through the Son (*per filium*), or from the Father and the Son (*filioque*). Otherwise stated, the Holy Spirit proceeds or is breathed forth from the Father through (or and) the Son.

In the economy, we are also reminded of the Spirit's role in the resurrection of Christ. It is "in" or "by" the Spirit that God vindicates his Son (1 Tim 3:16). It is "according to the Spirit of holiness" that God declares and constitutes his Jesus as "Son of God in power" (Rom 1:4). I also suggested that God raised his Son "through" the Spirit on the grounds that our genuine participation in Christ's resurrection (see Rom 8:11 and 1 Cor 15:20) must amount to a full participation in his Spirit-glorified humanity. God the Father's self-communication in the incarnate Son has attained its goal in his resurrection, ascension, and session at the right hand of the Father in or by the power of the Spirit. In this respect, God's self-communication in the Spirit to the Son's humanity has reached a fulfillment that no other graced creature, including those who have gone before us, can receive until the final resurrection at the parousia. The final redemption of our bodies at the last day takes place because of the Son's filial relationship to God the Father. The adopted sons participate in this Father-Son relationship by the life-giving Spirit who sanctifies, anoints, and raises the Son's humanity—and through his, ours. The Son's giving of his Spirit to the flesh is grounded in the Son's own bearing of the Spirit in his flesh.

Since the Spirit plays a perfecting role in the incarnation of the Son throughout his life and mission, should we not speak of a *per spiritum* or even a *spirituque* model of the immanent Trinity instead of an *in spiritu* one? Or do these models amount to the same thing? We have said that in the immanent Trinity the Son is begotten from the Father in the Spirit, or that the Son in whom the Spirit rests is begotten of the Father. But can we also affirm that in the immanent Trinity the Son is begotten of the Father *by* or *through* the Spirit? Or from the Father *and* the Spirit? Would these proposals not amount to an immanent-Trinitarian inversion of the traditional taxis *Father–Son–Spirit*? I shall take up the question of the viability of these other models of the Trinity in the next chapter.

Summary

I have inquired into Rahner's famous axiom concerning the non-absolute identity of the economic and the immanent Trinity in the context of his criticism of "mere monotheism" in Western theology. I did so as a way to recover what is proper (*proprium*) to the person the Holy Spirit. The Father's *proprium* is the sending of the Son and the Holy Spirit, the Son's is the assumption of a human nature unto his person (hypostatic union), and the Holy Spirit's is its sanctifying indwelling in the humanity of the Son and the adopted sons. Accounting for Congar's qualified reciprocity of Rahner's axiom, and noting the care theologians took to avoid the potentially adoptionist idea of a Spirit-indwelt humanity as the cause of the hypostatic union, I thus highlighted what is proper to the Son and the Spirit in the incarnation, while preserving the God-creation distinction and the priority of the hypostatic union over the sanctification of the Son's humanity.

Furthermore, I engaged Congar's qualification of Rahner's axiom as a way to suggest preliminary ways to speak about immanent models of the Trinity that might reflect the Son-Holy Spirit relation and interaction in those biblical narratives that shape our thinking on the economic Trinity. On the basis of the incarnation—in its static (hypostatic union) and dynamic (incarnating) dimensions—as an instance of God's self-giving to the creature in the Son's assumption of a human nature and a historic existence and in the Holy Spirit's logically subsequent sanctification, anointing, and raising of the Son's humanity for us, I proposed *in spiritu* and *per filium* (or *filioque*) immanent models of the Trinity. The latter model affirms that the Holy Spirit proceeds from God the Father *through* the Son (or, *and* the Son). The former model states that the Son is begotten of the Father *in the Spirit*, namely, as one in whom the Holy Spirit eternally rests or remains.

5

The Son's Eternal Life in the Spirit
Person, Relation, and Models of the Immanent Trinity

THIS CHAPTER FOCUSES ON the contribution of a Spirit Christology to discourse on the immanent Trinity. A Logos-oriented Christology stresses the *processional* aspect of relations among the divine persons, according to the Trinitarian taxis or order *Father-Son-Spirit*. The processional model highlights the logical priority of the Son over the Holy Spirit in the order of intradivine processions, a priority that corresponds in the economy of the incarnation to the logical priority of the hypostatic union over the sanctification of the Logos's assumed humanity.

Nowadays we hear much about social, relational, or perichoretic models of the Trinity that stress the mutual indwelling of the divine persons in one another. Can a Spirit Christology help us to complement the Logos-oriented processional aspect with a social or perichoretic one? Otherwise stated, is there a more reciprocal way of seeing the Son-Spirit relation in an account of the immanent Trinity? How can a Spirit-oriented Christology contribute to this discussion without neglecting the Logos-oriented concern for preserving the traditional taxis in the processional model of Trinitarian relations?

In this chapter, I will argue that processional and reciprocal models of the Trinity are complementary and not contradictory aspects of the mystery of the immanent Trinity. Otherwise stated, I will inquire about the usefulness of a Spirit Christology for strengthening the processional character of intradivine relations represented by the traditional order *Father-Son-Spirit* with a more community-oriented or social notion of Trinitarian fellowship. But before we enter this discussion, we have to arrive at some understanding of the Trinitarian ideas of "person" and "relation." Such a study will lead us into a clearer understanding of the relationship between the ideas of procession and reciprocity in Trinitarian theology.

A Logos-oriented Christology directs us to Jesus' origin as the incarnate Son sent by the Father from the first moment of his conception (economic aspect), and as preexistent Son in his eternal begetting in the bosom of the Father (immanent aspect). What matters most in this perspective, ontologically speaking, is the Son's "being-from-before." A Spirit Christology complements this reading of Christ's identity by showing how God the Father also acts in his incarnate Son through his Spirit in new ways and thus at special times (*kairoi*) in the economy of salvation. What matters most is the Son's "being-in-act." What immanent-Trinitarian ground does such a complementary Spirit-oriented *dynamic* view of the incarnation (or "incarnating") of the Son reflect?

Moreover, a Logos Christology tends to focus on Christ's *individual* identity or personal inner-constitution as the God-man from the first moment of the hypostatic union (economic aspect), and thus tends to stress his personal self-subsistence in distinction from the Father and the Spirit (immanent aspect). Under this individual dimension of Logos Christology, what matters most, ontologically speaking, is the Son's "being-in-himself." The incarnate Son also does all his life and mission *relationally*, that is to say, in loving obedience to his Father and for us in the power of the Holy Spirit. What immanent-Trinitarian ground might such a Spirit-oriented *relational*, social, or ecstatic understanding of the person of the Son reflect?

Before finding in a Spirit Christology an economic-Trinitarian basis for the Son's "being-in-act" and "being-in-relation" in the immanent Trinity, a look into some of the historico-theological reasons for the Logos-oriented *static* and *individual* approaches or emphases concerning the Trinitarian concepts of "person" and "relation" will be helpful. I only wish to point to a few key normative influences for the Logos-oriented emphases in the history of dogma. Then I will look to the East and the West for insights into the dynamic and relational aspects of the Trinitarian person. Our investigation will conclude with an assessment of immanent models of the Trinity, arguing for the complementarity of Logos-oriented *per filium* and *filioque* models and the Spirit-oriented in *spiritu* model. In short, I will argue that even as the Holy Spirit proceeds from the Father *through* (or *and*) the Son in the traditional Trinitarian taxis, we may also say that the Son is begotten of the Father "in the Spirit" (*in spiritu*) in whom both the Father and Son exist for and in each other.

CLASSIC MOVES TOWARDS ONTOLOGIZATION, ITS STATIC AND INDIVIDUAL DIMENSIONS

Raniero Cantalamesa argues that an external (cultural) factor contributing to a partial weakening of the pneumatic dimensions of Christology was the move towards Greek "ontologization" as a philosophical tool employed by theologians to define Jesus' identity in their historical context.[1] For the Greek mind, "what matters, in everything, is 'what it was at the beginning,' the *arché* of things, that is to say their metaphysical constitution, not their becoming and their history; what matters is the essence, not the existence."[2] The ecumenical Councils of the church provide examples of this move in the history of dogma.

A Look at Councils: Nicea I, Ephesus, Chalcedon, and Constantinople II

The church's historic struggle against and response to Arianism is illustrative of the move towards ontologization. Church theologians turned to the philosophical language of *ousia* to affirm the basic biblical truth that the Son's generation from the Father did not begin in time and history, but belonged to the eternal substance of God. Through the use of the term *homoousios*, theologians intended to accord the Son his divine dignity with God the Father in their cultural context through the reappropriation of a Greek philosophical category in light of the biblical witness to the Logos's identity as Creator. Thus the Logos is not merely a human being belonging to the created order—not even one greater than the rest of God's creatures. Of the same substance with the Father, the Logos stands in contrast to the world as its Creator and thus as the one "through whom all things were made." Concerning the church's appropriation of *homoousios* language, Zizioulas concludes:

> Its employment by Athanasius and Nicea was not intended to create a speculative or metaphysical theology . . . but to express the *utter* dialectic between God and the world. The *homoousios* is not to be understood so much as a positive statement, telling us something about God's being, but rather as a negative one, indicating what the Logos is *not*, namely a creature.[3]

---

1. Cantalamessa, *The Holy Spirit in the Life of Jesus*, 8.
2. Ibid.
3. Zizioulas, "The Teaching of the 2nd Ecumenical Council on the Holy Spirit," 32.

In light of Zizioulas's comments, we note that at first the formal move towards "ontologization" at Nicea did not necessarily foster a positive metaphysics of substance, but rather intended to formulate a kind of apophatic statement on the Son's identity in terms of the scriptural distinction between Creator and creation.

At Nicea, there is a shift made from an emphasis on language concerning Jesus' relationship to the Father in history and for us (*oikonomia*) to language about the Son's relationship to the Father at the level of the intradivine life (*theologia*)—a move necessitated by Arius's ontological subordination of the Son to the Father.[4] Thus the church has to answer the question of Jesus' being as a concern in itself, as a reality prior to and relatively distinct from—though not unrelated to—the question of his deeds and acts for us in the economy of salvation. There was a legitimate reason to ground *oikonomia* in *theologia*. How could the flesh be redeemed unless the divine Word had assumed it? The church begins to define Jesus' identity in terms of who he is "at the beginning" (or better yet, "from before") in eternity—or to use our ontological categories, the weight of discourse begins to fall on the "static" dimension of Jesus' identity.

After Nicea, the move towards ontologization eventually comes to stress the "individual" dimension of Jesus' identity, namely, his inner-constitution as the God-man from the time of the incarnation. Jesus Christ is consubstantial with God the Father according to his divinity, and consubstantial with us according to his humanity. Given the focus on the nature of the hypostatic union, Cantalamesa argues that "we see attention being transferred, little by little, from the events and concrete mysteries of Jesus' life (he was born, was baptized, died, rose again) to the moment of the incarnation."[5] In the aftermath of Nicea, we begin to see that the ontological emphasis for defining Jesus' identity as Son—whether in eternity as preexistent Logos or in time as incarnate Logos—centers on his "being-from-before" and "being-in-himself."

Several stages of christological reflection in the history of dogma lead to important ontological conclusions on the question of Jesus' relationship to God the Father. But all of them center on the proper manner of understanding the divine-human dialectic (or the incarnation as hypostatic union) in the person of the Son in and of himself. At the Council of Ephesus (A.D. 431), the fathers conceive the person of the Word as the one subject in his divine and human operations, especially in reaction to Nestorius's inability to anchor what he defined as the "conjunction" of natures in the

---

4. LaCugna, *God for Us*, chap. 1.
5. Cantalamessa, *The Holy Spirit in the Life of Jesus*, 8.

one subject.⁶ Efforts at Ephesus led to a more formal dogmatic formulation twenty years later at the Council of Chalcedon (A.D. 451) and its witness to Jesus Christ as one person and subsistence in two natures.

By then Eutyches, a sympathizer of Cyril and Apollinaris, had entered the picture, arguing for the post-incarnational existence of one divine nature alone in Christ — a move that the Council interpreted as a confusion of natures in the one person of the Son.⁷ In a single stroke reaction to Apollinarianism, Eutychianism, and Nestorianism, the Definition of Faith at Chalcedon makes an explicit distinction for the first time in Christological dogma between the terms nature and person or subsistent being.⁸

> This one and the same Jesus Christ, the only-begotten Son [of God] must be confessed to be in two natures, unconfusedly, immutably, indivisibly, inseparably [united] . . . without the distinction of natures taken away by such union, but rather the peculiar nature of each property being preserved and being united in one Person and subsistence.⁹

As Zizioulas argued in regard to the use of the *homoousios* at Nicea, one could say that the use of negative adverbs in the Definition safeguards the unity in duality and viceversa of Christ's person against heresies more than it provides a definitive positive theology of the union as such.¹⁰ On the other hand, the Definition's use of the post-biblical or auxiliary rubrics of nature (Gk. *physis*), person (Gk. *prosōpon*), and subsistent being (*hypostasis*) opens the door for reconceptualizing positively the scriptural witness to Jesus' identity as Son of the Father in terms of his individual inner-constitution at the hypostatic union. To the static dimension of Jesus' ontology (first considered at Nicea) we can now add a formal shift towards the question of the

---

6. On Theodore of Mopsuestia and Nestorius, see Davis, *The First Seven Ecumenical Councils*, 142–48. For Cyril, Nestorius's position inevitably led to the idea of the Word "taking to himself a person," or "into the error of speaking of two sons" or "two persons." See *The [Third] Epistle of Cyril to Nestorius* (NPNF² 14:198), and cf. *The Epistle of Cyril to Nestorius with the XII. Anathematisms* (NPNF² 14:202–3).

7. According to Davis, Eutyches "hated the idea of two natures in Christ after the Incarnation because he understood nature to mean concrete existence. To affirm two natures was for him to affirm two concrete existences, two *hypostases*, two persons in Christ." *The First Seven Ecumenical Councils*, 171 (cf. 186); Leo criticizes Eutyches for doing away with the existence of Christ's true humanity in the only-begotten Son of God, and in particular, for his famous statement "I confess that our Lord was of two natures before the union, but after the union I confess one nature." See *The Tome of St. Leo* (NPNF² 14:257–58).

8. Davis, *The First Seven Ecumenical Councils*, 186–87.

9. For Chalcedon's Definition of Faith (NPNF² 14:264–65).

10. See Kasper, *Jesus the Christ*, 238.

incarnate Logos's *individual* ontological make-up or personal constitution. With the anti-Nestorianizing focus on the Logos as the hypostatic subject of his own human actions, the ontological interest does not fall only on Jesus' "being-from-before," but also on his "being-in-himself."

At Constantinople II (A.D. 553), Apollinaris and Eutyches were anathemized for mixing or confounding the two natures in Christ, and theologians such as Theodorus and Nestorius were condemned for dividing or relativizing the union of both natures in the one person of Christ.[11] In the aftermath of Chalcedon, however, monophysites were particularly adamant against the language of its Definition and insisted in identifying the concrete hypostatic existence of the incarnate Word with his divine nature (*physis*).[12] In this case, at least logically speaking, the identity of hypostasis and physis could lead to a confusion concerning the existence of two natures in the one person of Christ, to the particular detriment of the Word's assumption of a true humanity. This concern leads to further reflection on the *how* of the unity of two unmixed (and also undivided) natures in the person of Christ. At every turn, the ontology at work reflects the legitimate concerns of the Logos-oriented defense of the Son's identity against heterodox views.

Leontius of Byzantium introduced the notion of a humanity that exists or subsists in the eternal person of the Word (enhypostasis) and thus has no concrete existence apart from this person (anhypostasis).[13] Significantly, this crucial move is predicated on the "individuality" of the hypostasis of the Son, and thus the emphasis of his formulation falls on the individual self-subsistence of the preexistent person of the Logos as the concrete subject of his divine and human actions. Although this argument legitimately anchors the incarnation in the initiative of the divine Logos to bring into existence and assume a human nature, its understanding of the hypostasis as an individually constituted reality in eternity does not pay attention to the ecstatic, relational, or social dimension of the same. Leontius operates within an established ontological framework that focuses on what I have characterized as static and individual Christology. That Jesus' human reality is that of the divine Logos is not predicated on the basis of the Son's relation to God the Father in the economy of salvation.[14] How might a Spirit Christology, with

---

11. For the fourth sentence or anathema of the Council, see *The Capitula of the Council* (NPNF² 14:312).

12. For an account of the development of monophysitism after Chalcedon, see Davis, *The First Seven Ecumenical Councils*, 207–20.

13. See "Extracts from Leontius of Byzantium" (*LCC* 3:376–77).

14. Pannenberg notes that Leontius's position is not incorrect because of what it says as much as for what it leaves unsaid, namely, that the ground for the identification of Jesus' human reality with the eternal Son is Jesus' own relation of obedience

its focus on the Son's relation to God the Father in the Spirit, complement the aforementioned and legitimate Logos-oriented ontological declarations of the church Councils?

A Look at Some Key Influences in the West: Hippolytus, Tertullian, and Augustine

In the West, the origin of the notion of person has deep roots in the church's rejection of modalism, that is, the idea that Father, Son, and Holy Spirit are mere manifestations, modalities, names, or masks of the one absolute monad-God. Such a strong view of the unity of God does not allow for a threefold self-differentiation of the one God. Already in Hippolytus (ca. 170–ca. 236), we see a refutation of Noetus's belief that Father and Son are interchangeable names for the one who is born, suffers, and dies.[15] In reaction to a certain Callistus, Hippolytus criticizes the use of the term person as a nominal concept that refers without differentiation to the one Father and God (= Spirit or Deity).[16] "Person" is not a synonym for "substance" (or more generally, for the one undifferentiated Deity). Although Hippolytus regularly speaks of the unity of God in terms of power, and of the threefold manifestation of the one God in the economy, he still wants to refer to Father, Son, and Holy Spirit as three distinct persons.[17]

In a pre-Augustinian context, Tertullian offers a more precise and articulate answer to Hippolytus's anti-modalist concern. Tertullian argues that the Unity (*unitas*) of God is distributed in a Trinity (*trinitas*) of persons according to an economic (or monarchic) order or manifestation,[18] and that

---

to the Father during his life and mission. Pannenberg argues that Jesus' dedication to the Father in history is the ground that allows for a relational notion of his person—an insight that, I would argue, does not play a part in Leontius's argumentation because of his starting point in the eternal Logos and his emphasis on the individuality of the hypostasis of the Logos. See Pannenberg, *Jesus—God and Man*, 338–39.

15. Hippolytus, *The Refutation of All Heresies* 10.23 (*ANF* 5:148), and his *Against the Heresy of One Noetus* (*ANF* 5:223) [hereafter *Against Noetus*].

16. "[H]e acknowledges that there is one Father and God ... spoken of, and called by the name of Son, yet that in substance He is one Spirit. For Spirit, *as* the Deity, is, he says, not any *being* different from the Logos, or the Logos from the Deity; therefore this one person ... is divided nominally, but substantially not so." *Refutation of All Heresies* 10.23 (*ANF* 5:148).

17. *Against Noetus* 8 (*ANF* 5:226), and ibid., 14 (*ANF* 5:228).

18. Tertullian, *Against Praxeas* 1–2 (*ANF* 3:597–98). For now, I leave aside the question of whether Tertullian understands the notion of person in a metaphysical or juridical sense. For the former view, see Fortman, *The Triune God*, 113, 115; for the latter view, see González, *A History of Christian Thought*, 178–79.

such an economic Trinity has its ground in a threefold self-differentiation *in God*. For example, Tertullian confesses the Holy Spirit as "the third degree *in the Godhead*, because I believe the Spirit *to proceed* from no other source than from the Father through the Son."[19] As to the existence of the Son before creation, Tertullian, inspired in the language of earlier Greek apologists, writes that God "had within Himself both Reason, and, inherently in Reason, His Word, which He made second to Himself by agitating it *within Himself*" (italics mine).[20]

Prior to the ecumenical Councils, "person" in the pre-Augustinian West points above all to individual distinctiveness in the economy and at times in the Godhead. In terms of the Son's identity, the stress naturally falls on his "being-in-himself"—either from before the incarnation or from the incarnation forward—in distinction from the Father and the Holy Spirit.[21] That one individual person is not another is a necessary point to make in the face of modalism, but this legitimate turn also pays little attention to how the persons *relate* to one another in their mutual Trinitarian interdependence. Modalists could interpret the idea of relation in such a way that the persons "simply become so related to themselves, that the Father can make Himself a Son to Himself, and the Son render Himself a Father to Himself."[22] Any notion of the person as self-subsisting, or as existing in its own right, finally gets lost in the modalist approach to relation. At the same time, we observe that relation in the positive sense does not denote at this point in the history of dogma the contemporary sense social interdependence, but rather distinction among equals in the one divine substance and thus in history.

Tertullian argues that a person may relate to another but is not constituted as such by his relations: "A father must needs have a son; so likewise a son, to be a son, must needs have a father. It is, however, one thing to *have*, and another thing to *be*" (italics mine).[23] This priority of being-in-itself over being-in-relation (of being over having a relation), as well as the move to anchor the latter in the former, shows that "person" denotes individuality. According to the modalists, God is only *trinitas* in the world (*ad extra*) and thus only *unitas* in Godself (*ad intra*). In an anti-modalistic

---

19. *Against Praxeas* 3 (*ANF* 3:599).

20. Ibid., 5 (*ANF* 3:601).

21. Admittedly, the place of the Spirit in Hippolytus's and Tertullian's formulations is not the clearest in every case. Prior to the fourth century, Spirit can refer to God or Deity in general, the divine principle in Christ (or the preexistent Word), the economic manifestation of God's power in history, or a third person distinct from the Father and the Son in the economy of salvation and even at the intradivine level.

22. Tertullian, *Against Praxeas* 10 (*ANF* 3:604).

23. Ibid.

polemic, therefore, the person is not first constituted in relation to another at the immanent level, but in distinction from another. This move helps to establish that God is not only a Trinity of persons *ad extra*, but also a Trinity in itself (*ad intra*). While legitimate, it is clear that the anti-modalistic discourse gives little to no attention to the mutual openness to the other among the divine persons. At this early stage of the history of dogma, and in light of the modalist threat, we simply observe how difficult it might have been to bring individuality and relationality together into one synthesis of the person.

After the church's struggle with Arianism in the East, Augustine arises as the most influential figure in the West for centuries to come. Of particular significance is his anti-subordinationist turn to the indivisible unity of God as the highest ontological principle for Trinitarian reflection and discourse. Since I have already discussed some of the basic highlights of Augustine's Trinitarian theology, I will only briefly review some of them to show how his view of relation, because of his overriding emphasis on God's undivided essence, tends to eclipse the uniqueness of the person in its relationship to another. For Augustine, relation functions more as a way to distinguish among the persons of the Trinity while preserving divine simplicity, than as a way to stress the radical uniqueness of the person as such or its social character vis-à-vis other divine or human persons.

Augustine's definition of the person is set in the context of his anti-Arian commitment to the unity of the divine essence, which makes it impossible for the person to be conceived as either an accidental or substantial reality.[24] An accidental definition of person would make the persons less than God, for in the one God there can be no accidents, parts, or divisions. A substantial definition of person logically leads to Arian subordinationism by making the Father's personal property of being unbegotten into an attribute of the divine essence. Such subordinationism would make only the Father "God," but not the Son who is begotten of the Father or the Holy Spirit who proceeds from the Father.

To distinguish the persons in God without compromising the simplicity of the one divine essence, Augustine speaks of the persons *relatively* or in "relative" terms (as opposed to accidental or substantial categories)—that is to say, in terms of an "opposition in relation" (Lat. *oppositio relationis*) to one another. In other words, each person is defined in terms of the person from whom it is distinguished as its opposite. The Father is *not* the Son and viceversa. By *not* being the other, they affirm each other. Relation serves to

---

24. What follows is a summary of Augustine's classic anti-Arian theological rationale for his Trinitarian approach as developed in Book V of his *On the Holy Trinity* (*NPNF*[1] 3:87–96).

distinguish between the three persons of the Trinity without doing harm to the one divine essence. In this approach, persons are identical with relations and both are in turn identical with the one divine essence. In the Western tradition, the notion of person is eventually defined according to the principle—with roots in Augustine and seen more formally in Anselm—that all in the one God is common except for what can be distinguished in the one essence by a logical opposition in relation. In Augustine's vision, we see a turn towards a notion of the person that is subsumed under the higher principle of divine unity. Persons are constituted in terms of an opposition (although of an affirming kind) in relation to another *in the one divine essence*. Given the strong focus on the unity of God as the highest ontological principle in Augustine's approach, persons and relations are logically subsumed and equated with the divine essence.

To be sure, the Augustinian idea of a relative—yet non-accidental (for in God there can be no accidents)—differentiation between the persons in the one divine essence has a major strength. By strongly safeguarding God's unity, this concept does not allow for a subordinationist or tritheistic interpretation of person. But at what expense? What is relativized in the process is a more ecstatic view of relation that gives due weight to the openness of each person of the Trinity to exist for, in, and with one another in triadic communion. This intimate trinitarian fellowship is often best described with the term *perichoresis* (Gk. *perichōrēsis*), signifying a mutual dwelling in or permeating of each other (Lat. *circumincessio, circuminsessio*). This requires that person, and not essence, be the logical point of departure and highest ontological principle for Trinitarian discourse. Moreover, it requires that the idea of person include within itself the biblical notion that God is love. For the idea of openness to exist with another, or relationality in and of itself is merely philosophical unless it finds its meaning in God's own character as a loving Father, who does not live for himself but rather for others through his Son and in others through his Holy Spirit. As we shall see, Augustine's theology is never one-dimensional. He also contributes to the Trinitarian theme of love, speaking about the Holy Spirit as the mutual bond of love between the Father and the Son. Without doing away with his greater focus on the Holy Spirit as a certain bond of unity in the intradivine life, Augustine's related theme of love also allows for a more social, relational, or ecstatic conception of the Holy Spirit as the person in whom the Father and the Son relate to one another. A Spirit Christology can speak to the economic basis and immanent implications of this pneumatological image.

REVITALIZING LOGOS-ORIENTED ONTOLOGIZATION: PROPOSED MOVES IN TRINITARIAN PNEUMATOLOGY, ITS DYNAMIC AND RELATIONAL DIMENSIONS

Are there any building blocks in the Eastern and Western traditions that can help us to bring a social dynamic into Logos-oriented approaches to person and relation? To answer this question, I will first review and assess the significance of the Eastern-Cappadocian contributions to the notion of person (especially Basil) in light of John Zizioulas's contemporary interpretation of the Greek tradition on this point. Second, I consider two Western insights into a more relational ontology, namely Augustine's and Richard of St. Victor's Trinitarian reflections under the theme of love. Finally, I look at Walter Kasper's thoughts on the contributions that a Spirit-oriented Christology in particular can make to revitalize Logos-oriented approaches to the interrelated ideas of person and relation.

Person and Relation in the Eastern-Cappadocian Tradition

In the Greek tradition, the three persons are the concrete mode of existence of the one God. There is no access to the divine essence apart from the persons. Congar cites T. de Régnon as an authority on the difference between Latin and Greek approaches: "The Latins regarded the personality as the way in which nature was expressed, while the Greeks thought of nature as the content of the person."[25] Since person is the ultimate principle in Eastern Trinitarian discourse, the Greeks define the concept according to relations of origin from the one God who is Father. In other words, the person (i.e., the Son, or the Holy Spirit) is defined in terms of the person (i.e., the Father) from whom it originates. The Son is the only-begotten *of* the Father and the Holy Spirit proceeds *from* the Father. In both cases, the Father is the source of communion (or divine unity) among the persons. As Basil puts it, divine communion (Gr. *koinonia*) is derived "from the fact that He [i.e., the Holy Spirit] moreover is said to be 'of God' . . . in the sense of proceeding out of God [= Father], not by generation, like the Son, but as Breath of His mouth."[26]

Basil's understanding of divine unity as *koinonia* at once highlights the activity and relationality of the persons towards one another in their own right, while protecting their differentiation from each other and the personal uniqueness of God the Father as the source and cause of such

---

25. Congar, *Holy Spirit*, 3:xvi.
26. Basil, *On the Spirit* 18.46 (*NPNF*² 8:29).

communion. From divine unity as intradivine communion, Basil moves to unified divine outreach to the world from the Father, through the Son, and in the Spirit.[27] There is a unified operation of the divine persons towards creation, but according to a descending taxis or order among them that highlights what is unique or proper to each. Regarding the economy of creation, Basil states: "For the first principle of existing things is One [= the Father], creating through the Son and perfecting through the Spirit."[28] What is true of creation is true of the incarnation and the church.

God's plan of salvation in Jesus Christ was "accomplished through the grace of the Spirit."[29] According to the plan of salvation, God sends his Spirit upon the incarnate Son to perfect or bring to fulfillment his humanity in the fullness of grace, accompanying him in his mission until its completion. Through baptism, the church is made "spiritual by fellowship (*koinonia*) with Himself."[30] In the Spirit, the church confesses Christ as Lord and, through the only-begotten Son, is able to call upon the Father in the Spirit of adoption.[31] At this point, we can speak of an ascending taxis in the order of grace from the Holy Spirit, through the Son, to the Father. The Holy Spirit brings to completion the Father's plan of salvation through Christ by bringing us back to the Father through baptism into Christ. The role of the Spirit in Christ and his church is set in the Trinitarian movement of love that comes from the Father (Lat. *a Patre*) and returns to the Father (Lat. *ad Patrem*).

To speak of divine unity in terms of persons in communion leads away from the notion of a static and self-enclosed intradivine reality. Instead, the notion of *koinonia* points to God the Father's open and gracious outreach to the world through the Son and in the Spirit (*a Patre*) and to the Spirit's gracious bringing of sinners into the fellowship of the Father through the Son (*ad Patrem*). In Basil's account of the economy, divine unity is placed in the context of an ontology of divine persons in communion with each other. What are the deeper roots behind this Eastern-Cappadocian notion of personhood? How do they support the idea of relation as determinative for the person?

Zizioulas has shown that, in classical Greek culture, philosophers held to the substantial and non-personal affinity or unity of God with all things

---

27. Ibid., 7.16 (*NPNF*² 8:10–11); ibid., 26.63 (*NPNF*² 8:39–40); and ibid., 27.68 (*NPNF*² 8:43).

28. Ibid., 16.38 (*NPNF*² 8:23).

29. Ibid., 19.39 (*NPNF*² 8:25).

30. Ibid., 9.23 (*NPNF*² 8:15).

31. Ibid., 11.27 (*NPNF*² 8:17–18).

in the cosmos (ontological monism).³² In the classical mind, therefore, the world exists from the substance and not from the will of God; otherwise stated, the world exists out of an ontological necessity in God and not out of God's own free will.³³ In reaction to monism, Zizioulas argues that the Cappadocians identified for the first time in the history of dogma the classical Greco-Roman terms person (Gk. *prosōpon*, signifying relation) and substance (*ousia, hypostasis*, signifying being itself) to affirm God's being-in-relation to the world by an act of personal freedom and love.³⁴ Because hypostasis is the concrete mode of being, then person becomes the basic and ultimate ontological category for defining God's being-in-relation to what is not God (i.e., the created world). To be is "to be for another" in freedom and love.

After the Cappadocians, person (*prosōpon*) is no longer secondary to being (*ousia*) but its hypostasis; therefore, hypostasis (being) is essentially relational (being-in-relation).³⁵ Since the real existence of substance (*ousia*) is to be found in the person (= hypostasis), then the cause (Gk. *aitia*) of the divine existence must also be found in a particular person (not in the common divine essence).³⁶ Thus God the Father (not God in general) is the personal cause of the generation of the Son and the procession of the Holy Spirit.

Person cannot be defined solely in terms of its individual self-subsistence, for the notion of person carries with it the idea of relating to another in freedom and love. Such personal freedom and love in turn points to a dynamic perichoresis or mutual dwelling of persons in each other. Unlike Tertullian's anti-modalist priority of being over relation, person cannot precede relation in the Eastern-Cappadocian system. Unlike Augustine's anti-Arian priority of essence over person, *ousia* cannot precede *hypostasis* among the Greek fathers. Now, if persons are *a priori* the concrete mode of existence of the one divine substance and there is no access to the unity of God apart from the communion of persons whose source is the Father, then relation for the Greeks does not point so much to that which *distinguishes* in the divine essence (as in Augustine) as much as to that which *unites* the Son and the Holy Spirit to the person of the Father. In short, person cannot be seen only in terms of its "being-from-before" and "being-in-itself."

---

32. Zizioulas, *Being as Communion*, 29–30.

33. Ibid.

34. Ibid., 31–46.

35. Ibid., 39; the reader should note the difference with Tertullian's position, according to which the person first *is* and then *has* relations.

36. Ibid., 39–41.

From an Eastern-Cappadocian Trinitarian perspective, "being-in-act" and "being-in-relation" are actually constitutive dimensions of the person that complement the ideas of self-subsistence and self-differentiation.

Two Western Insights on the Theme of Love: Augustine and Richard of St. Victor on the Persons of the Trinity

Are there building blocks in the Western Trinitarian tradition that allow us to conceive of the person in a more relational manner? A productive area of inquiry is the theme of love. If God is love, this predicate must give us insight into what it means for God to be triune and therefore a tripersonal community of love. Based on the analogy of the human mind and its internal faculties of knowledge (intellect) and love (will), Augustine attempted to see the relative distinctions (relations) among the persons of the Trinity in terms of love.[37] He speaks of the one divine essence as an indivisible self-presence who internally knows itself and, in knowing itself, loves itself.[38]

> But love is *of* some one that loves, and *with* love something *is* loved. Behold, then, there are three things: he that loves, and that which is loved, and love. What, then, is love, except a certain life which couples or seeks to couple together some two things, namely him that loves, and that which is loved?"[39]

In the one divine essence or consubstantial communion of the three persons, the Holy Spirit is said to be "something common both to the Father and the Son.... And therefore they are not more than three: One who loves Him who is from Himself, and One who loves Him from whom He is, and Love itself."[40] The Father utters the Son in an internal act of knowledge and the Father and the Son give the Holy Spirit in a common act of love through which the immanent Trinitarian circle of love is closed. In addition to safeguarding the unity of God in the strongest possible way, Augustine's approach shows how there are only three persons and two processions in the one God by highlighting the Son's and the Holy Spirit's relatively distinct manners of proceeding from the Father.[41]

In his proceeding from the Father (principally) and the Son, the Holy Spirit "intimates to us a mutual love, wherewith the Father and the Son

---

37. Augustine, *On the Holy Trinity*, bk. 9 (*NPNF*¹ 3:125–33).
38. Ibid., 9.2–4 (*NPNF*¹ 3:126–28).
39. Ibid., 8.10.14 (*NPNF*¹ 3:124).
40. Ibid., 6.5.7 (*NPNF*¹ 3:100).
41. See O'Donnell, "The Trinity as Divine Community," 6–7.

reciprocally love one another."[42] Since love is especially appropriated to the Holy Spirit, Augustine can also speak of the Holy Spirit as gift of love to others in the economy of salvation.[43] From intradivine love, there is a move to divine love towards creatures. As the immanent bond of love between the Father and the Son, the Holy Spirit directs us to a kind of interiority in God. But Augustine's pneumatology also directs us to a certain exteriority from God to the world in that, as gift of love, the Spirit of the Father and the Son indwells the saints and binds them to each other.

> Love ... which is of God and is God, is specially the Holy Spirit, by whom the love of God is shed abroad in our hearts, by which love the whole Trinity dwells in us.... love, which brings to God...."[44]

Augustine's analogy of love applies more directly to his concern for confessing the one divine essence and the three persons in their relative distinctions in such essence. The language of love also applies indirectly to the theologian's reflection on the Holy Spirit as the bond of love in the order of immanent processions and, by an appropriation in the economy, as the gift of love unto others. Yet Augustine's use of the love analogy also introduces a certain intra-Trinitarian dynamism in the divine essence, even if the relational character of divine love among three distinct persons of the Trinity in their perichoretic plurality is eclipsed to some extent by the stronger emphasis on preserving the unity of God. Significantly, the immanent-Trinitarian ground for appropriating love to the Holy Spirit in the indwelling of the saints (and in inflaming their love for God and for each other) is his intradivine identity as the bond of love between the Father and the Son. There is a pneumatological correspondence between the economic and immanent Trinity.

Assuming the unity of the divine substance, Richard of St. Victor (d. 1173) wants to show that divine love requires a plurality of persons in communion with one another.[45] God is the supreme fullness and perfection of goodness, which necessarily implies that God is "true and supreme charity" (Lat. *vera et summa caritas*). At the same time, charity is never private, selfish, or self-enclosed. It is necessarily "a love that tends to another" (Lat. *amor in alterum tendat*) and, therefore, it requires a divine person who is fully deserving of this love. Such a worthy person, the *condignus*, is the di-

---

42. Augustine, *On the Holy Trinity* 15.17.27 (*NPNF*¹ 3:215).
43. Ibid., 15.17.29 (*NPNF1* 3:216), and ibid., 15.18.32 (*NPNF*¹ 3:216–17).
44. Ibid., 15.18.32 (*NPNF*¹ 3:217).
45. I have consulted Richard de Saint-Victor, *La Trinité*, esp. 3.2–3, 11; 5.16; 6.14.

vine Son. True and supreme charity, however, does not end with the mutual love between the one who loves and the one who is loved, but rather with their sharing of their mutual love with a third. This third one is the Holy Spirit, the *condilectus*, who is the overflow of the mutual love between the Father and the Son. From duality in God, Richard arrives at a Trinity.

Richard defines person in terms of its individual, rational, and incommunicable dimensions, but he does so within a "personalistic perspective."[46] These aspects of the divine persons must be seen within his broader interpersonal approach to their relations (and immanent processions) under the theme of charity, which points to the divine love that is given (Lat. *gratuitus*), is both received and given (Lat. *debitus et gratuitus*), and is received (Lat. *debitus*).[47] Similar to Augustine, Richard notes that it is through the Spirit of the Father and the Son as their gift that intradivine love is communicated to and received by creatures.[48] One of Richard's strengths is to take the language of charity as the driving principle for his reflections on the self-differentiation of the persons in the divine substance. It is a helpful vantage point to articulate the ecstatic character of divine love among the persons of the Trinity and in the economy of salvation, although the economic aspect per se does not receive much attention in this approach.

In Augustine, we find a certain interiority in the image of the Holy Spirit as the *ad intra* bond of love between the Father and the Son, and as the *ad extra* gift of both the Father and the Son to the saints. In both cases, love brings life and being to completion, closing the Trinitarian circle of life. In Richard, we find a complementary emphasis on the interpersonal nature of this interiority among a plurality of persons in their own right. Augustine's note of interiority is invigorated by Richard's stress on the ecstatic overflow of divine love from the Father and the Son to the Holy Spirit and from the Holy Spirit as the *ad extra* gift of the Father and the Son to the saints. We begin to see the significant place that the Holy Spirit plays in the notions of person and relation in these Western approaches to the mystery of God. In the Western-Augustinian tradition, there is room for a theology of the person that effectively moves from self-constitution to self-giving.

In post-Vatican II Roman Catholic theology, Heribert Mühlen provided a synthesis of these Western approaches. He expresses the relationship between the Father and the Son not so much in terms of their consubstantiality (Augustine's starting point) as much as their interrelatedness (closer to Richard's intuitions) as the "I-Thou-Agreement" (Ger.

---

46. Congar, *Holy Spirit*, 3:104; for Richard's definition of person, see *La Trinité*, 4.24.
47. *La Trinité*, 5.16.
48. Ibid., 6.14.

Ich-Du-Begegnung).[49] In proceeding from the Father and the Son, the Holy Spirit is seen as the bond of love between the "I" and the "Thou," namely, the "We-union" (Ger. Wir-Vereiningung).[50] The closest human analogy to the mystery is that of the child who, being the fruit of the common marital love between his father and mother, does not cease to be distinct from his/her progenitors.[51] As the "We-union," the Holy Spirit is neither the mathematical sum nor the merely external manifestation of the other two, but rather the overflowing and yet distinct fruit of the love between the "I" and the "Thou" who can thus be described as being a person in two other persons.[52]

What the person of the Holy Spirit is eternally in the intradivine life, the Holy Spirit is also at the economic level in the sense that he is oriented towards a plurality of persons. Using the image of the church as the mystical body of Christ, and attaching the greatest importance to Jesus' anointing at his baptism in view of others, Mühlen defines the church as one person (i.e., the Holy Spirit) in many persons (i.e., Christ and Christians).[53] While strongly maintaining the unity of God in accordance with the spirit of Western Augustinianism, our author still wants to find in the interpersonal character of the Holy Spirit's personhood the link between Trinity, Christology, and ecclesiology.

Walter Kasper: Person and Relation in Light of a Spirit-Oriented Christology

Neither the Eastern-Cappadocian nor the Western-Augustinian approaches thus far examined take as their starting point and material basis for Trinitarian reflection the life and mission of Jesus in his actions and relation to the Father and for us in the power of the Spirit. Kasper recognizes the Councils' contributions to the definition of Jesus' ontology in terms of his inner-constitution from the moment of the incarnation, but also desires to

---

49. Mühlen, *Der Heilige Geist als Person*, 82.
50. Ibid., 195–97 (cf. 157, 164).
51. Ibid., 76.
52. Coffey does not think that Mühlen's use of terms like "We in person" or "We-relation" accurately affirms the distinctiveness of the Holy Spirit "over against" the Father and the Son [i.e., the actual 'We']. He writes, "the Holy Spirit is not the 'We,' but the one who stands *over against* the 'We' (therefore in a relationship of opposition to it [them]), as the *objectivization* of its (their) notional (i.e., person-producing) activity . . . the fuller and more exact expression would have to be that the Holy Spirit is the objectivization, or hypostasization, or personalization, of this mutual love [between the Father and the Son], and hence in this sense its product or outcome." *Deus Trinitas*, 134–35.
53. Mühlen, *Una Mystica Persona*, 196–200.

complement the static and individual ontology of a Logos-oriented Christology with a more dynamic and ecstatic view of the incarnation. In this basic intention and point of departure, my own approach shares much with Kasper's work.

> If the divine-human person Jesus is constituted through the Incarnation once and for all, the history and activity of Jesus, and above all the cross and the Resurrection, no longer have any constitutive meaning whatsoever . . . God assumed not only a human nature but a human history.[54]

Kasper finds ontological dynamism and relationality in a Spirit-oriented Christology, which places Jesus' identity in the soteriological and Trinitarian context of his acts and relation to the Father and us—in other words, a way of being and living "in the Spirit."

Because the Spirit mediates the relationship between the Father and the Son in eternity and then also for us in salvation history, Kasper speaks of the Spirit as "freedom in person, the superabundance of God's love."[55] The Holy Spirit is both overflowing freedom and love. Only in the Spirit does God's free self-giving in love to the Son takes place. And only in the Spirit does the Son freely open himself back to the Father's love. At the immanent level, this points us to the Western-Augustinian teaching on the Holy Spirit as the mutual love between the Father and the Son that itself closes the Trinitarian circle of communion among the divine persons in the one divine essence. In the Latin view, Kasper argues that "the Spirit is, as it were, what is innermost and most hidden in God," or, in somewhat less precise terms, that the Spirit is "God's innermost essence."[56]

The Western emphasis on interiority is mainly intra-Trinitarian and does not yet touch on God's self-giving in freedom and love (i.e., in the Spirit) to the Son in the history of salvation. For this, Kasper draws on the Eastern Trinitarian tradition, in which "the Spirit is, as it were, the excess, the overflow of the love [of God the Father] manifest in the Son."[57] The Spirit is the "surplus and effusion of freedom" in history of the mutual love between the Father and the Son in the inner-divine life.[58] Otherwise stated, as "God's outermost and uttermost,"[59] the Spirit is "the theological transcen-

---

54. Kasper, *Jesus the Christ*, 37.
55. Ibid., 259.
56. Ibid., 250, 257.
57. Ibid., 258.
58. Ibid., 250.
59. Ibid., 258.

dental condition of the very possibility of a free self-communication of God in history."[60] Here Kasper brings together Latin and Greek theologies of the Trinity in order to argue for the dynamic and social (or ecstatic) character of the Holy Spirit's personhood in the inner-life of God and in history.

How does Kasper see the incarnation in light of a Spirit Christology? First of all, he assumes Rahner's view of the hypostatic union as the definitive expression of God's self-communication to the creature and the creature's self-transcendence to God. Second, Kasper interprets Rahner from a pneumatic angle, arguing that the Holy Spirit mediates the incarnation by bringing God's loving self-communication to fruition in a creaturely reality (= Jesus), which at the same time is endowed by the Spirit to respond in reciprocal love and obedience to God's self-communication in him. He concludes that "the Spirit is thus in person God's love as freedom, and the creative principle which sanctifies the man Jesus in such a way as to enable him, by free obedience and dedication, to be the incarnate response to God's self-communication."[61] For Kasper, this amounts to a logical priority of the *gratia habitualis* over the *gratia unionis* and, therefore, to an implied economic order *Father–Spirit–Son*—a move that has been both praised and criticized.[62] It is on the basis of Jesus' relation to God in the Spirit that Kasper argues for the personal identity of Jesus and the Logos and, by implication, for the consubstantiality of the Logos with the Father and the Spirit. I have already pointed out that, in the order of being, an economic inversion of the traditional order of processions *Father–Son–Spirit* is not necessary to give full and adequate weight to the Holy Spirit's constitutive (although often relativized) role in the sanctification of the humanity of Jesus Christ throughout his life and mission. Kasper's contribution lies in his use of Spirit Christology as a basis for thinking through a more ontologically dynamic and relational Trinitarian theology than the traditional ontology of the church Councils.

---

60. Ibid., 250.

61. Ibid., 251.

62. Ladaria has criticized Kasper on this point. See Ladaria, "Cristología del Logos y del Espíritu," 357, and *La Trinidad*, 198n73; Kasper's position finds support and a more detailed Trinitarian articulation in Coffey's ascending or return economic model of the Trinity in which the Spirit creates and sanctifies or disposes for union the humanity of the Son. Coffey, *Deus Trinitas*, 164n7; however, Coffey places what he calls "mission" (descending order *Father–Son–Spirit*) and "return" (ascending taxis *Father–Spirit–Son–Spirit–Father*) biblical/economic models of the Trinity under the wider umbrella of their respective correlative "procession" (*Father–Son–Spirit*) and "return" immanent models (*Father–Son–Spirit–Son–Father*). *Deus Trinitas*, 33–65.

A Preliminary Synthesis on the Person of the Son in Light of Logos and Spirit Christologies

The incarnate Son's free obedience and faithfulness to the Father in the Spirit in some way points to an immanent reality in God, namely, the only-begotten Son's eternal openness to his Father in the Spirit. Openness is the eternal side of the Son's freedom in history. If openness and freedom to be for another serve to describe the Son's love for the Father, then a look at Trinitarian theology under the Western-Augustinian theme of love—with its prominent place given to the Holy Spirit—can help us find an economic basis and an immanent-Trinitarian ground for the biblical affirmation that "God is love." My previous categorization of Spirit Christology under the rubrics of Jesus as receiver, bearer, and giver of God's Spirit hinted at the theme of love, but I did not develop these insights for the sake of reflection on the immanent Trinity.

The Father loves and gives his Son all things—above all, his Spirit. In the same Spirit, the Son reciprocates the Father's love for him by carrying out his mission in faithfulness to the Father even unto death on the cross. At Golgotha, God's greatest love for us is manifested in his Son, and the Son offers his unblemished life to the Father through the Spirit. From the cross, the Spirit of the Father and the Son is then given to the church as their common gift of love. In the case of the Father and the Son, their mutual love for one another is the same as their coexisting in the Holy Spirit. Yet the Holy Spirit is distinct from the Father and the Son. One can speak of a Spirit-led mission of the Son in obedience to the Father and at the same time speak of the Son's love for the Father in the Spirit. These two propositions amount to the same thing, even though the first one emphasizes the Spirit's distinct activity *over against* that of the Son and the Father, and the latter stresses the personal space or horizon *in whom* the Son acts in relation to his Father and viceversa. There is, in the language of the Spirit as the personal horizon or space in whom the Father and Son love one another, a certain elusiveness concerning the Holy Spirit's personhood in the sense that the Spirit (though a distinct person) remains to some extent anonymous. If we follow Augustine, under the pneumatology of love, there is a similar anonymity in the idea that the Spirit is a certain communion or bond between the Father and the Son; and yet this view does not take away from his intuition that the Holy Spirit is in some way the ground and completion of the reciprocal relation between Father and Son in the intradivine circle of love.

David Coffey has argued from a Spirit Christology grounded in the economy of salvation that the Holy Spirit is "the objectivization of the mutual love between the Father and the Son."⁶³ This is another way of referring to what I have called the Son's existence "in the Spirit." Coffey even speaks of the love of Jesus for the Father and for us as an "'incarnation' of the Holy Spirit" in the Son: "[I]n an analogous way to the Incarnation of the divine being in human being in the person of Jesus, there is an incarnation of divine love in human love in the love of Jesus, this latter incarnation being the Holy Spirit."⁶⁴ Whether or not "incarnation" language is appropriate to refer to the Spirit's presence in Jesus, I resonate with Coffey's pneumatological reading of the biblical data under the Western theme of love.⁶⁵ He goes on to develop in depth the Trinitarian implications of this approach.

For instance, Coffey proposes that, as the "objectivization," "hypostasization," or "personalization" of the mutual love between the Father and the Son in the economy, the Holy Spirit remains "a distinct person" without having "a personality distinct from the Father or the Son."⁶⁶ To put the same thought in my own language, there is a certain anonymity or hiddenness of the Holy Spirit that does not threaten its personhood. As far as the immanent Trinity goes, Coffey concludes that the mutual love theory "alone explains exactly what it is that the Holy Spirit receives from the Son, namely, the quality of being the Son's love for the Father, which, completing that of the Father for the Son, constitutes in its objectivization the person of the Holy Spirit."⁶⁷ To affirm that the Son exists in the Spirit does not take away from the Son's individuality (or the Spirit's), but it places the same in the context of his relation to the Father both in the economy of salvation and at the immanent level.

To assert that the Spirit is the ground and completion of the inner-divine circle of love (Augustinian focus) does not mean that the Spirit is the personal origin, source, and cause of such Trinitarian communion. In the economy of salvation it is the Father who sends his beloved Son into the world to unite a human nature unto himself. It is also the Father who sends his Spirit into the world to dwell in the Son's humanity throughout his human history. In light of economy, we can gather from the Eastern-Cappadocian tradition that the Father is the personal cause of love and

---

63. Coffey, *Deus Trinitas*, 4.

64. Ibid., 39.

65. Ibid. 41. Strictly speaking, incarnation typically refers either to the hypostatic union or to the whole human existence of the incarnate Son (incarnating). However, notice that Coffey distinguishes between the incarnation of divine "being" in the humanity of Christ (a mission proper to the second person or Logos) and the incarnation of divine "love" in the same (a mission proper to the third person or Holy Spirit).

66. Ibid., 41.

67. Ibid., 155.

communion among all divine persons. A Western-Augustinian approach to social Trinitarianism will have to take into full account the Greek-Cappadocian concern for the hypostatic priority of the Father.

In a Spirit-oriented Christology, the incarnate Son's particular reception and bearing of the Spirit from the Father prior to his death is oriented towards his giving of the same Spirit unto others from the moment of his paschal mystery. To use Kasper's language, we may say that the Spirit now clearly appears as the overflowing surplus of the divine love and freedom that finds its personal cause in the Father (not in the divine essence in general) and is manifested in his Son and mediated to others through him. Here we can also bring in Richard's idea that the fullness of charity implies a plurality of persons in which the mutual love of the Father and the Son for one another must perfect itself by going beyond its own duality to a third, and from this third (= Spirit) to others.

What a Spirit-oriented Christology adds to the Logos-oriented one—in terms of its immanent-Trinitarian implications—amounts to the basic idea that the immanent Logos's personal response to the Father's love as his only-begotten Son always happens in the Spirit (*in spiritu*) or is mediated by the Spirit who proceeds from the Father. Otherwise stated, the immanent Logos's individual existence as the Father's only-begotten Son from before time is an existence in the Spirit of the Father. The other side of this statement is that the Father's own existence towards the Son is also an existence in the Spirit. If we follow Coffey, insofar as this mutual love between the Father and the Son is in its "objectivization" the person of the Holy Spirit, then the Spirit is common to both the Father and the Son. To account for the East's interest in safeguarding the personal identity of the Father as the unoriginate source of the Son and the Spirit, the Holy Spirit may be said to proceed from the Father *principally*—a phrase Augustine uses. For the same reason, the Holy Spirit may be said to proceed from the Son in some mediated form (say, *through* the Son, as some Eastern fathers suggest) as long as such an approach can account for the West's strong sense of consubstantiality in its approach to Trinitarian relations.

Seeking to bring Spirit- and Logos-oriented dimensions of the mystery of Jesus Christ into a single ontological conception of the *person* of the Son, we propose the following christological-Trinitarian synthesis:

> The deepest truth regarding the Logos's distinct self-subsistence (individual aspect) and being from before (static aspect), whether in the intradivine life as God the Son or in the economy of salvation as incarnate Son (God-man), is that he exists in openness towards (dynamic aspect) and thus in relation to

(ecstatic aspect) God the Father and us freely and out of love. In the Spirit, the Son exists before his Father and in his mission lives out that life before the Father for our sake without ceasing to be himself.

ESSENCE, PERSON, AND *PERICHORESIS*: ON THE PROCESSIONAL AND SOCIAL CHARACTER OF TRINITARIAN RELATIONS IN LIGHT OF A SPIRIT-ORIENTED CHRISTOLOGY

Our study of Logos-oriented static and individual approaches to person and relation in the Councils and in the West led to a proposal for their invigoration with respective dynamic and relational dimensions in light of a Spirit Christology. I wanted to see how we might speak of the person of the Son not simply as a self-subsistent and self-enclosed individual from eternity, but also as one who from eternity actively opens himself to exist in a free and thus loving relation to the Father in the Spirit. Following Kasper, I argued that such reflections ultimately find their economic basis in Jesus' own life and mission of obedience to the Father and for us in the power of the Spirit.

Moreover, I briefly attempted to ground in a Spirit Christology other moves towards revitalizing dynamic and ecstatic views of person and relation already developed in the Eastern-Cappadocian tradition and in two significant Western reflections on the Trinity under the theme of love (i.e., Augustine and Richard of St. Victor). In the spirit of Greek theology, we found the source of divine love in the Father, its manifestation in the Son, and its perfection in the Spirit. In the spirit of Latin theology, we found the source of divine charity in the mutual love between the Father and the Son and its completion in the Holy Spirit as their bond of love that brings to full circle the interior life of the Trinity. Following Coffey, we also looked into the economic basis for this Augustinian mutual love theory of processions, which he grounds in the Father's sending of the Son with the Spirit and finally in the Son's return to the Father in the Spirit. We also noted Richard of St. Victor's reflections on the Holy Spirit as the ecstatic overflow of the mutual love between two other persons of the Trinity in a third. We showed that this insight brings an interpersonal complement (not replacement) to Augustine's emphasis on interiority.

Our study of the joint mission of Jesus and the Spirit in God's economy of salvation has served so far to support a dynamic and ecstatic understanding intradivine processions. It reminds us to bring to our reflections on the immanent Trinity the defining note of reciprocity whereby the three divine persons exist with and in one another—either through the Eastern language of *koinonia* (fellowship) or the Western language of *caritas* (love). These complementary ways of approaching Trinitarian theology assume a corresponding complementarity of pneumatologies. Whether the Holy Spirit is seen as the personal power and sanctifying grace of the Father who brings us to himself through baptism into his Son, or as the gift and bond of love of the Father and the Son who brings the saints into their mutual love for one another, it is clear that a robust pneumatologically-oriented account the Father-Son relation has shaped discourse on the Trinity in the East and the West. A question remains: How should we understand more precisely the relationship between the processional and community-oriented (social, ecstatic, or perichoretic) character of Trinitarian relations?

My thesis is that a Spirit-oriented Christology yields models of intradivine processions that do not contradict the equally important notion of intradivine perichoresis among the persons of the Trinity. Another way to put the argument is that the idea of Trinitarian reciprocity requires some qualification to safeguard the unique personal properties of the divine persons in the order of processions. In the rest of the chapter, I will assess some immanent-Trinitarian models (i.e., *per filium, filioque, per spiritum, spirituque,* and *in spiritu*) in terms of their usefulness for safeguarding: 1) the Greek concern for the identity of the Father as ultimate cause (*aitia*) of the Son and the Holy Spirit, 2) the Latin concern for the consubstantiality of the Son with God the Father and the Son's role in the procession of the Holy Spirit from the Father, and 3) the contemporary Western concern for other immanent models of the Trinity that reflect on the constitutive role of the Holy Spirit in the generation of the Son from the Father.

Essence, Person, or *Perichoresis*?: Starting Points and Their Implications for Defining Intradivine Processions (*Filioque, Per Filium,* and Other Models)

What should be the point of departure and the highest ontological principle for Trinitarian reflection and discourse? Should the Western-Augustinian stress on the indivisible divine *essence* frame the issues and discussion? If so, then the ultimate referents in the system are the unity of God, the indivisible (but also appropriated) operations of the one God towards creation, and the idea of relation as that which relatively distinguishes the persons in the one divine essence. Here all forms of tritheism and subordinationism are rightly avoided, but the radicality of the person as a unique instance of the one divine essence in its own right logically takes second place. Such a strong emphasis on the priority of the one divine essence has led at times to a conception of "God" as a reality prior to any particular person of the Trinity—a problem Rahner identified as "mere monotheism." The danger of a unitarian view of God, whether formal or practical modalism, looms in the horizon.

On the other hand, should the Eastern-Cappadocian emphasis on the *person* or hypostasis drive our Trinitarian thinking and language? If so, then the ultimate referents are the divine hypostases as concrete instances of the one divine essence, the proper (not merely appropriated) acts of each divine hypostasis in the economy, and the idea of relation as that which unites the hypostases to each other and particularly the Son and the Holy Spirit to the one God and Father of us all. In this system, the genuine plurality of the hypostases and the hypostatic uniqueness of the Father as cause (*aitia*) of the Son and the Holy Spirit are given proper due, but the closer identity between the hypostases and the one divine essence does not receive the stress it does in the Western-Augustinian tradition. Since the Son and the Holy Spirit receive the divine essence from the one God who is Father, there is a logical danger of subordinationism. This danger is a logical one, of course, since the Nicene fathers and Athanasius in particular actually fought against an Arian subordinationist conception of the Son's origination from the Father. They did so by confessing that the Son was not begotten out of the creative will of the Father as the rest of the creatures and saints, but rather is begotten of the very *ousia* of the Father so that the Son is "very God *of* very God."

In contrast to the Greek and Latin points of departure, what if we made communion (*koinonia*) or mutual indwelling (*perichoresis*) the ultimate ontological principle for reflection on the mystery of God? In contemporary theology, perichoresis (in contrast to substance or person) has been proposed as the highest category for Trinitarian discourse. The idea of community serves as the primary human analogy for the mystery of God, seeing in the mutual dependence of three equal and unique persons and their indwelling in one another the Trinitarian ground for a social project in which human relations can reflect the full communitarian character of Trinitarian relations.[68] Due to the stress on the correlative triadic communion between

---

68. See, for example, Boff, *Trinity and Society*, esp. chap. 7; and Moltmann, *The Trinity and the Kingdom*; "The Fellowship of the Holy Spirit—Trinitarian Pneumatology," 287–300; and "The Unity of the Triune God," 157–88; see also Silanes, *La santísima Trinidad*.

all persons, this option at times gives occasion to the danger of tritheism by its relativization of the unity of essence among the persons.[69]

Western Filioque *and Eastern* Per Filium *Models*

Each corresponding starting point has implications for understanding the processional character of intradivine relations. The Western-Augustinian approach to the Trinity can support a *filioque* model, the Eastern tradition a *per filium* one, and the contemporary move towards perichoresis seeks any number of complementary models such as the *spirituque* and *per spiritum*. I have already argued in a preliminary way for the *in spiritu* model of the Trinity as the best complement to the Western *filioque* and Eastern *per filium*. Briefly put, my proposal brings out more explicitly the role of the Holy Spirit in the intradivine life without inverting the classic order of processions *Father-Son-Spirit*. Let us look more closely at the theological systems behind each particular approach to immanent Trinitarian models.

In the Latin tradition, the one God is the Holy Trinity. In the divine essence, the Father begets the Son and the Son is begotten of the Father in one act of knowledge. In a common act of will, the Father and the Son together breathe forth the Holy Spirit who proceeds from them so that the circle of love in the intradivine life of communion is closed. The Son is begotten of the Father (generation) and the Holy Spirit proceeds from the Father and the Son (spiration). Persons are differentiated from each other by their opposition in relation (*oppositio relationis*) in the undivided divine essence, thus safeguarding the oneness of God in the strongest possible way. Father affirms Son and viceversa as logical opposites (e.g., in begetting and being begotten), but in the case of the Holy Spirit, its only logical opposition is to the Father "and the Son" in common (i.e., in the Father and the Son spirating it and in the Holy Spirit being spirated by both). A basic biblical insight that inspires Augustine to make this move is, quite simply, that the Scriptures themselves speak of the Holy Spirit neither as the Father of the Son nor as the Son of the Father, but rather as the Spirit of the Father and/or the Spirit of the Son.

---

69. For example, Moltmann's eschatological ontology, in which the future determines the past and the present, understands the essential unity of God as something yet to be achieved by the Holy Spirit in "the total unification of the world with God and in God." Moltmann, "The Trinitarian History of God," 643. Eschatological unification relativizes essential unity. Although superabundant love (and not a deficiency of being) is what makes God leave room within Godself for the whole world (see pp. 643–45), the charge can still be made that such a panentheistic view makes the unity of the triune God depend on world history and thus compromises divine transcendence.

What are the advantages of the Latin framework? First of all, since the Holy Spirit proceeds from the Father "and the Son" (*filioque*), a clear distinction emerges between the processions of the Son and the Holy Spirit from the Father.[70] Second, the Latin approach highlights the consubstantiality of the Son with the Father, dealing satisfactorily with the anti-Arian concern that originally led to the inclusion of the *filioque* clause in the West.[71] There is a sense in which the *filioque* tells us more about the Son—namely, that he is *homoousios* with the Father—than about the Holy Spirit. Third, and closely related to the first point, the Western approach shows that there can only be three persons and two divine processions in the immanent divine circle of life.[72] Yet the question still remains as to whether this view adequately addresses the Greek concern to preserve the hypostatic uniqueness of God the Father as the ultimate origin, source, and cause of the procession of the Holy Spirit.

In the Greek tradition, the one God (*ho theos*) is, first of all, a reference to God the Father. From the unoriginate God and Father, the Son is begotten and the Holy Spirit proceeds. Because the Eastern view anchors the cause of the divine substance in a concrete hypostatic mode of existence (i.e., the Father), from whom such substance is then logically given to the other two hypostases (i.e., the Son and the Holy Spirit), it tends to be more linear and causal than the Latin approach to the processions in which the

---

70. "In the community and unity of substance, the hypostases are distinguished by the mutual relationship which opposes them by affirming them. That relationship is and can only be a relationship of origin, or of principle or beginning and end. On the one hand, spiration of the Spirit does not bring about any opposition in relationship between the Father and the Son and, on the other hand, the Spirit proceeding from the Father and the Son can be distinguished hypostatically from the Son only if he has a relationship of procession or origin with that Son. He is, in many scriptural texts, Spirit of the Father and Spirit of the Son and for this reason he must be confessed as proceeding from the two by a single common act of active spiration." Congar, *Holy Spirit*, 3:73.

71. Against Arianism, the *filioque* functions primarily as a *substantial* statement regarding the unity of the Father and the Son. Jenson is correct in saying that "[t]he West's initial motive for the creed's insertion was not so much to say something about the Spirit as to say something about the Son." *The Triune God*, 150; Congar argued the same: "Historically, the *Filioque* was introduced as a measure against Arianism, by Augustine and by the Hispano-Visigothic councils" (thesis 7, *Holy Spirit*, 3:213). Congar adds: "In the West . . . we have always been conscious of the principle that, in God, everything is common, apart from what is distinguished by an opposition in relationship. . . . [T]his principle is not a defined article of faith. It does, however, express a very acute sense of consubstantiality within the Trinity." Ibid., 202. Congar traces the aforementioned axiom (*in Deo omnia sunt unum, ubi non obviat relationis oppositio*) to Anselm (cf. ibid., 98).

72. O'Donnell, "The Trinity as Divine Community," 7.

persons are identical with the divine essence.[73] No less significant is the fact that, as Congar has noted, the Latins use the verb *procedere* (to proceed) to refer *both* to the generation of the Son from the Father and the procession of the Holy Spirit from the Father and the Son. This is not permissible for the Greeks, since for them the somewhat equivalent verb *ekporeusthai* conveys a relation of origin between the Holy Spirit and the Father as cause that is not transferable to the Son. Although the Greeks affirm the generation of the Son and the procession of the Holy Spirit from the Father, they do not reflect on the manner of distinguishing the former from the latter as Western theologians do. The closest model in the East that could account for the West's concern for distinguishing between the generation and the procession is a *per filium*, which allows the Son a mediating role in the procession of the Holy Spirit from the Father.[74] Thus the Holy Spirit proceeds from the Father uniquely, but also "through the Son."

A solution to the *filioque* problem requires the West to take seriously the unique hypostatic identity of the Father as the principal cause of the procession of the Holy Spirit. This could be achieved by saying, with Augustine's *principaliter*, that the Holy Spirit from proceeds from the Father and the Son, but "principally" from the Father.[75] It also requires the East to recognize that the Son who is begotten of the Father is not foreign to the

---

73. Congar summarizes the differences between East and West as follows: 1) In the East, the divine hypostases are seen as relatively autonomous or independent principles of existence in that they can be spoken of either in terms of their relation to the divine essence or as divine hypostases as such; and 2) In the West, the divine hypostases are seen as identical (in the strongest possible sense) with the divine essence. *Holy Spirit*, 3:72, 200, 202.

74. On the Son as mediator, but not the source of the Spirit's procession, see Zizioulas, "The Teaching of the 2nd Ecumenical Council on the Holy Spirit," 42–45.

75. Significantly, Augustine approaches the Greek teaching by arguing that, although the Holy Spirit proceeds from the Father and the Son, he proceeds from the Father "principally" (*principaliter*). *On the Holy Trinity* 15.26.47 (*NPNF*[1] 3:225); cf. ibid., 15.17.29 (*NPNF*[1] 3:216).

procession of the Holy Spirit from the Father.[76] Congar believes that Latin and Greek theologies share these basic concerns.[77]

The *per filium* differs from the *filioque* in that the latter sees the Father *and* the Son as the single principle of the Holy Spirit's procession by spiration. The *per filium*, on the other hand, is identified with a number of proposals that, while safeguarding the identity of the Father as the ultimate principle of the Holy Spirit, point in the direction of either a non-subordinationist mediation of the Son in the procession of the Spirit or, more generally, a resting of the Spirit on the Son.[78] I prefer to call the latter

---

76. Jean Garrigues's ecumenical formula attempts to bridge East and West: "I believe in the Holy Spirit, the Lord and giver of life, who, issued from the Father (*ek tou Patros ekporeumenon*), proceeds from the Father and the Son (*ex Patre Filioque procedit; ek tou Patros kai tou Huiou proïon*)." Cited in Congar, *Holy Spirit*, 3:200. As Congar notes, Garrigues's formula uses the verb *ekporeusthai* exclusively for the Father and the verb *proïenai* for the Father and the Son: "[T]he Father is the original source and the Son is associated or a participant . . . The Latin only has the verb *procedere* to cover the meanings of both Greek verbs. The aspect of the Son that is recognized in the procession of the Spirit is his eternal being." Ibid., 201. Thus, one could interpret Garrigues's formula to mean that the Spirit is issued from the Father *hypostatically* and proceeds from the Father and the Son *essentially*. Garrigues discusses his proposal in "A Roman Catholic view of the position now reached in the question of the *filioque*," 149–63; on the Orthodox side, however, Staniloae does not see this proposal as acceptable on the grounds that whatever the Holy Spirit receives from the Son must be better distinguished from what the Holy Spirit receives from the Father in order to safeguard the monarchy of the latter. Instead of the *filioque*, it would be better to use patristic expressions such as the Holy Spirit proceeds from the Father and "goes out from," "shines out from," or "is manifested by" the Son. See Staniloae's "The Procession of the Holy Spirit," esp. 174–78; on the Protestant side, Moltmann proposes that the Spirit receives his hypostatic existence from the Father and his relational (interpersonal) form (Gestalt) from the Son. See "Theological proposals toward the resolution of the *filioque* controversy," esp. 169–71. Since in the East the intra-Trinitarian (interpersonal) relations are dependent upon the existence of the hypostases, it is not difficult to grasp Staniloae's further criticism (in his article quoted above) of Moltmann's proposal: "The personal character of anyone cannot be separated from his/her existence," 184; on the Catholic side, Congar notes that in Latin Trinitarian theology the strong identity between hypostases and essence that arises from defining persons in terms of their opposition in relation within the one undivided divine essence does not make Garrigues's proposal acceptable to the Western position either. *Holy Spirit*, 3:201.

77. Congar summarizes the basic points of historical agreement: "For both, 'the Spirit is confessed as the third Person-hypostasis of the one divine nature-essence and consubstantial with the Father and the Son.' Both confess the Father as the Principle without principle or beginning of the whole divinity. Both profess the Son as not unrelated to the Father in the production of the Holy Spirit." *Holy Spirit*, 3:201.

78. Consider the following expressions: the Spirit proceeds from the Father "through (by means of) the Son" (Maximus the Confessor, Gregory Palamas), "and receives from the Son" (Epiphanius), "and rests (reposes) on the Son" (Pseudo-Cyril, John of Damascus, Pope Zacharias), and "shines out through the Son" (Athanasius),

option the *in spiritu* model of the immanent Trinity. Both Western *filioque* and Eastern *per filium* immanent Trinitarian models follow the classic taxis of processions *Father–Son–Spirit*, this showing sensitivity to the Logos-oriented concern for preserving the logical priority of the mission of the Son (incarnation) over the mission of the Holy Spirit who dwells in him and is also sent by him to the saints (indwelling).

Spirituque, Per spiritum, *and* In Spiritu *Models*

In the contemporary scene, theologians have proposed other ways to describe the relations between the Son and the Holy Spirit at the intradivine level of processions. The reality of Trinitarian perichoresis, in which the unity of the Godhead is expressed by the reciprocal permeating and dwelling of the persons in one another, serves as a major justification for this consideration. From this perspective, relations in the Trinity are seen as fully triadic in that all three hypostases always act towards each other in a correlative fashion. There is no procession of the Holy Spirit in which the Son does not participate (*per filium, filioque*) but also—and this is where the stress falls—no begetting of the Son in which the Holy Spirit does not participate.

Paul Evdokimov was among the first Orthodox theologians who proposed a *spirituque* model complementary to the *filioque*.[79] He argued that the "causal" approach to Trinitarian relations had only served to foster the "filioquism" of the West and the "monopatrism" of the East (represented by Photius) to such an extent that it was necessary to return to a more perichoretic view in which all relations between the persons are seen as fully triadic.[80] Just as the Holy Spirit proceeds from the Father "and the Son" (*fil-*

---

or the variation "conjointly with the Son on whom he rests." Breck offers a sort of *per filium* synthesis of East and West by affirming that "while the Spirit '*proceeds*' from the Father alone, he is *communicated* by the Father and the Son together, both within the immanent Trinity itself as the expression of their mutual love, and from the Trinity to creation in the divine *economia*." Breck, "The Two Hands of God," 241–42; Congar notes that the Greek fathers' variety of images for speaking of the Son's place in the eternal (not only economic) procession of the Holy Spirit from the Father suggests that the Son's share in the production of the Spirit has not been defined precisely in the East (thesis 4). *Holy Spirit*, 3:213.

79. Another one is Sergius Bulgakov, who argues only in passing for the inseparability of the Son-Spirit relations along the lines of complementing the *filioque* with a *spirituque*. See Bulgakov, *Le Paraclet*, 140–43.

80. Evdokimov, *L'Esprit Saint dans la tradition orthodoxe*, 49–78, esp. 59–60, 70–72, 75. The ecumenical impulse from the Orthodox side for a reconsideration of the *filioque* problem came from Bolotov's famous twenty-seven theses, in which he concluded that

ioque) or "through the Son" (*per filium*), so does the Son may be said to be begotten from the Father "and the Spirit" (*spirituque*)[81] or perhaps "through the Spirit" (*per spiritum*). However, the latter two models unveil an inversion of the taxis of immanent processions (*Father–Spirit–Son*), which as we have seen remains a problem for a Logos-oriented approach to Trinitarian theology.

Some theologians have followed Evdokimov's argument. In addition to the *per filium* and *filioque*, Boff, for example, arrives at a *spirituque* and even a "patreque":

> So the Son through his begetting receives the Holy Spirit from the Father and is then, in his being, eternally inseparable from the Holy Spirit; the Son is then begotten *ex Patre Spirituque*. . . . Even the Father's unbornness involves the participation of the Son and the Holy Spirit, who witness to it by the fact of deriving from the Father as their only source."[82]

Boff does not attempt to reach his conclusions on the basis of the life and mission of Jesus Christ, but simply wishes to describe in a general way the

---

the Western *filioque* was not an impediment for reestablishing communion between the Eastern Orthodox and the Old Catholic Churches. For a discussion of these theses, see Congar, *Holy Spirit*, 3:194–95; for Photius's thesis that the Holy Spirit proceeds "from the Father alone" (monopatrism), see Photios, *The Mystagogy of the Holy Spirit*.

81. Congar first argued that a *spirituque* necessarily implied a transposing of the incarnation to eternity. See *Holy Spirit*, 3:16, 75; Karl Barth showed the same concern earlier in his *Church Dogmatics*, 1/1:554–56; but Congar later reconsiders and instead builds on Barth's idea that the Son of God as the first object of God's election is eternally *destined* to be the Son of Man and thus the preexistent God-man Jesus Christ who is in turn the ground of our election (*Church Dogmatics*, 2/2:94–194, esp. 110)—in order to arrive at the preliminary idea that "the Word was conceived *incarnandum* and even *crucifigendum, glorificandum, caput multorum Dei filiorum* . . . in such a way that the Word proceeds *a Patre Spirituque*, from the Father and the Spirit, since the latter intervenes in all the acts or moments in the history of the Word *incarnate*. If all the *acta* and *passa* of the divine economy are traced back to the eternal begetting of the Word, then the Spirit has to be situated at that point." Congar, *The Word and the Spirit*, 93; Congar considers Cullmann's exegetical insights on a Son of Man Christology, which seeks to identify Jesus as a preexistent heavenly man in perfect likeness to God and in this way also to bypass the eternity-time dialectic in a two-natures Christology [Cullmann, *The Christology of the New Testament*, 137–92], but settles the issue brought up by Benoît as to whether the incarnation should be thought of as an "absolute beginning" [see Benoît, "Préexistence et Incarnation," 5–29] by approvingly quoting Bouyer's judgment: "It is in time that God makes Himself man, i.e., it is in a definite moment of time that our humanity is assumed. But as far as He is concerned, He assumes it eternally. Then the Father eternally generates the Son, not only as before His incarnation but also as the Word made flesh" [See Bouyer, *The Eternal Son*, 401]; on the *spirituque*, see Congar, *The Word and the Spirit*, 93–97.

82. Boff, *Trinity and Society*, 205 (cf. 145–47, 236)

The Son's Eternal Life in the Spirit   141

mutual interdependence or communion of the persons in and with one another. An *a priori* immanent concept of perichoresis per se serves as the ultimate ontological principle for Trinitarian discourse.

Xabier Pikaza, on the other hand, provides the basic direction and programmatic challenge for finding the economic basis of a *spirituque* in the Christ-event:

> It seems to me that the decision to complement the Filioque with the Spirituque is absolutely defensible. But I am convinced that the Filioque and the Spirituque must arise precisely from the economy of salvation (conception of Jesus by the spirit, effusion of the spirit by the risen Jesus), thus revealing in this same economy the root and reality of the immanence. I believe that this vision, of biblico-theological character, has not been sufficiently accentuated.[83]

In response to these proposals, I resonate to some extent with Thomas Weinandy's basic thesis that "within the Trinity the Father begets the Son in or by the Holy Spirit, who proceeds from the Father as the one in whom the Son is begotten."[84] Unlike Boff, Weinandy finds support for his reciprocal view of Trinitarian relations in the economy of salvation, seeing events like the birth of Jesus as an icon of an immanent reality: "The depiction of the Father begetting his Son in the womb of Mary by the Holy Spirit becomes, I believe, a temporal icon of his eternally begetting the Son by the Holy Spirit."[85] Although I hold to an *in spiritu* model of the Trinity and support it on the basis of a Spirit Christology, I am not in agreement with Weinandy's presuppositions for making the same move—particularly, with his assessment of the inadequacies of the Greek and Western views of Trinitarian relations.

Weinandy argues, for instance, that neither the Greek nor the Latin view of processions give the Holy Spirit an active personhood.[86] In the Greek view, the Spirit is third in the order of processions; in the Latin view, the Spirit is the bond of the other two persons. Weinandy finds the philosophical basis for this problem in the remaining influence of "Neo-Platonic emanationist sequentialism" in the Eastern view and "Aristotelian epistemology" in the Western one.[87] Are these criticisms justified and necessary to give the Spirit its due?

83. Pikaza, *El Espíritu Santo y Jesús*, 17; translation mine.
84. Weinandy, *The Father's Spirit of Sonship*, ix (cf. 17).
85. Ibid., 42.
86. Ibid., 7–9.
87. Ibid., 10–15.

In regards to the Greek view, Weinandy follows the same thinking as Evdokimov in his criticism of a linear or causal view of the processions. But Weinandy has not taken into account Zizioulas's argument (precisely in reaction to Evdokimov) that the idea of cause (*aitia*) among the Cappadocians pointed above all to personal freedom and love (contra Greek monism), and not to an ontological priority of the Father over the Son and the Holy Spirit.[88] Zizioulas's comments on the basic concern behind the Nicene-Constantinopolitan teaching that the Spirit proceeds from the Father are illuminating:

> The concern . . . is not simply to keep the traditional idea of the *Monarchia*, since that could be done by simply keeping the notion of « Source » to describe the one « Principle » or *archē*. It is rather to safeguard the faith that the *person precedes substance and « causes » it to be*. The Spirit, therefore, is not simply a power issuing from divine substance; he is another personal identity standing *vis-à-vis* the Father. He is a product of love and freedom and not of substantial necessity.[89]

In the Eastern view, the Father shares the monarchy with the other two persons of the Trinity without ceasing to be the cause of intradivine communion. The Father gives himself to the Son and the Holy Spirit without remainder. Significantly, the argument for the non-subordinationist view of processions that the Cappadocians apply in the midst of the pneumatomachian controversy also applies to the Arians at Nicea. Both of these heterodox groups shared precisely what Weinandy calls a Neo-Platonic emanationist or sequentialist view of the divine processions, one that actually implied ontological subordinationism. Does the generation of the Son from the Father imply such subordinationism? Is the Son no longer a divine person because he is said to proceed from the Father by being begotten? Why, then, if the procession of the Son from the Father does not imply subordination, should we argue that the Holy Spirit's procession from the Father through the Son does? Why should an argument no one makes in the East or the West against the *genitus* now apply to the Holy Spirit's proceeding from the Father *per filium* (or the *filioque* for that matter)?

To borrow Durrwell's terms, if the Spirit is third in the order of processions, this does not mean that it is "last" in the order of being,[90] just

---

88. Zizioulas, "The Teaching of the 2nd Ecumenical Council on the Holy Spirit," 42 (cf. 37).

89. Ibid., 37–38.

90. Durrwell, *Jesús Hijo de Dios en el Espíritu Santo*, 100, cited in Ladaria, *La Trinidad*, 215.

as the Son is not second-to-last in the order of being because he is second in the order of processions. It is too easily assumed (rather than proved) that a processional view of Trinitarian relations necessarily amounts to some imagined or real ontological subordination among the persons that impedes their true reciprocity in or with each other. In the Eastern view, the Holy Spirit actually brings to perfection the love of the Father manifested in the Son, thereby allowing for creatures in the economy to participate by grace in the intradivine communion of love between the persons. In the ascending order of grace, the Spirit is actually the one who brings creatures to the Son and through him to the Father. If the Spirit is first and the Father third in the order of grace, does this mean that the Father (or the Son) is in the end subordinated to the Holy Spirit? Not at all. In short, one does not need to affirm an inversion of the taxis, as part of an approach to perichoresis, to show the reciprocity between the persons.[91]

Weinandy also sees the Western analogical view of relations as a by-product of Aristotelian epistemology in which a person's intellect (knowledge) logically precedes his/her will (love). While this is true of human persons, Weinandy argues that the analogy does not apply in the same way to the immanent Trinity:

> While in human beings something must first be known before it is loved, in God the knowing and loving are simultaneous — the begetting and spirating come forth from the Father as distinct, but concurrent, acts. The Father does not, *even logically*, first beget the Son and then love the Son in the Spirit. The begetting of the Son and the proceeding of the Spirit are simultaneous and, while distinct, mutually inhere in one another. The Father is the Father because, in the one act by which he is eternally constituted as the Father, the Spirit proceeds as the Love . . . in whom the Son is begotten of the Father.[92]

While I agree that analogies do not provide an absolute correspondence between temporal reality and the mystery of God *ad intra*, I still want to affirm that they provide a *direct* correspondence. I have argued for a

---

91. This point became clear to me after a conversation with Luis F. Ladaria. He argues that reciprocity does not imply a rupture of the traditional taxis of processions. If the Father gives to the Son everything he has and is according to essence, should we compensate for the fact that the Son is begotten of the Father? Is this necessary? No. Why not? Because the Son's procession from the Father by generation does not imply subordination. According to Ladaria, the move towards complementary models that invert the Trinitarian order of processions often assumes that this order constitutes a degeneration or a diminution.

92. Weinandy, *The Father's Spirit of Sonship*, 71-72; italics mine.

logical priority of the mission of the Son over that of the Spirit on the basis of the hypostatic union (incarnation) and the entire Christ-event (incarnating) that does not take away from the constitutive role of the Holy Spirit in the humanity of the Son. If the economic Trinity is the immanent Trinity, then this logical priority must find its ground in a similar immanent reality. Of course, as Weinandy points out, this does not mean that the missions or the processions cease to be simultaneous realities. Union and indwelling happen at once; so do begetting and spiration. We do not deny this. However, given the historic problem of adoptionism, it is difficult not to argue on logical grounds when it comes to the distinction between the Logos's *proprium* of assuming a human nature unto his person and the Holy Spirit's sanctifying indwelling in the Logos's human life and history. Weinandy's hesitation about the place of logical priority discourse in Trinitarian theology is not ultimately necessary to protect the person of the Spirit from being subordinated to the other two.

An *in spiritu* model of the Trinity does not necessitate a revisionist approach to the classic taxis of processions *Father–Son–Spirit*, which is supported in distinct ways by both the Eastern and Western Trinitarian traditions. A *per spiritum* immanent model, which Weinandy alludes to in speaking of the Son's generation from the Father "by" the Spirit, more readily implies an inversion of this taxis (i.e., *Father–Spirit–Son*) that does not seem necessary to speak of the Holy Spirit's participation in the Father-Son relationship. Though more tentatively, the *in spiritu* model gives the Holy Spirit an active mediating (although somewhat anonymous) role in the Father's begetting of the Son. I spoke of a coexistence of the Father and the Son in the Holy Spirit that can be expressed as their reciprocal love for one another. Here the Spirit is, as it were, the hypostatic space or horizon *in whom* the Son openly acts in a reciprocal relation of love towards his Father and viceversa. Is the Holy Spirit who grounds and brings to completion this intradivine communion of love between the Father and the Son less of an active person because in the order of processions the same Spirit proceeds from them as their mutual love? An *in spiritu* model does not require that the Western *filioque* be compensated with a *spirituque* or a *per spiritum* to reach a triadic symmetry. As in the Eastern *per filium*, the *in spiritu* simply brings out in a more explicit manner the dynamic and ecstatic role of the Spirit in the intra-Trinitarian life without doing away with the traditional taxis ecumenically attested to in the Eastern *per filium* and Western *filioque*. The *filioque* itself does not have to imply a subordination of the Holy Spirit to the Father and the Son in the Western approach to Trinitarian relations for two reasons. First, the *filioque* arises out of a notion of relation that works within the framework of the anti-Arian concern for safeguarding the unity of the divine essence. Second, the *filioque* can accommodate the Augustinian theme of love, so that the Holy Spirit who proceeds from the Father and the Son is none other than the Spirit in whom the Father and the Son mutually love another. Augustine is working with two interrelated models of the Trinity, two sides of the same coin, that make it difficult to think of the Holy Spirit merely in a passive sense vis-à-vis the Father and the Son.

Some final considerations on Trinitarian models are in order. It seems to me that the *spirituque* runs into the same problems as the *filioque* does because it is open to the Eastern criticism that the begetting of the Son from the Father and the Spirit as from a *single* principle ultimately destroys the begetting of the Son from the *Father* as the only source of this generation. In this sense, the *per spiritum* may then serve as a more viable model because of its acknowledgment of the Father's unique hypostatic identity as the only source of the Son's generation. Its use, however, would imply a Trinitarian inversion of the taxis of processions that the Eastern fathers have not traditionally endorsed. Basil, for example, maintains a descending order of processions, even though he affirmed the divine unity in communion (*koinonia*) of all the persons and found its ultimate source in the person of the Father (in contrast to an impersonal divine substance).

A *spirituque* or a *per spiritum* cannot stand in the West. In differentiating the persons according to an opposition in relation, both models can logically allow for *two* Fathers of the Son—as if the only-begotten of the Father could also be related to the Holy Spirit as its Son. There is only one Father and one Son who are correlative to one another. Both *spirituque* and *per spiritum* models do not seem to take into full account the biblical datum that whereas the Spirit is referred to in the Scriptures as the Spirit of the Father (or God) and the Spirit of the Son (or of Jesus, Jesus Christ, or Christ), nowhere do the Scriptures actually refer to the Son as the Son of the Spirit but only as the Son of the Father (or of God). This is the case even if the Son exists in the Spirit (*in spiritu*) before the Father and for our sake, even if the Spirit mediates sonship in some sense.

Among some fathers and in some contemporary literature, the Eastern *per filium* often appears to include within itself the *in spiritu* model.[93] How-

---

93. Staniloae's discussion of the active repose of the Holy Spirit in the Son is described as a *per filium* model, and therefore, as supporting the order of processions Father-Son-Spirit. See "The Procession of the Holy Spirit," esp. 180–82; in contrast to Staniloae's treatment of the patristic idea of the Spirit's repose in the Son, Bobrinskoy seems to see the Spirit's resting on the Son as a separate model than the *per filium*, but in doing so posits the taxis Father-Spirit-Son. See Bobrinskoy, "The filioque yesterday and today," esp. 143–45. Bobrinskoy comments: "The descent of the Spirit on Jesus at the Jordan . . . appears in the Orthodox Trinitarian vision as an icon, a manifestation in history of the eternal resting of the Spirit of the Father on the Son" (144).

ever, I am inclined to argue that the *per filium* has more affinity with the idea that the Holy Spirit proceeds from the Father "through the Son." Therefore, the idea that the Spirit proceeds from the Father and *rests* or *remains* in the Son seems better fit as another manner of expressing that the Son is begotten of the Father "in the Spirit." Most important, however, these models are complementary since the Spirit's procession from the Father through the Son (*per filium*) is inseparable from the Son's generation from the Father as the one in whom the Spirit rests (*in spiritu*). The Spirit who rests in or remains on the Son (*in spiritu*) also shines forth from the Son (*per filium*).[94] In other words, the *in spiritu* brings out more clearly the role of the Holy Spirit in the Son's generation from the Father within the traditional taxis or order of processions supported by the *per filium*.[95]

In conclusion, the *per filium* and *in spiritu* models best satisfy: 1) the Eastern concern for preserving the hypostatic uniqueness of the Father as the cause of divine communion and perichoresis in contrast to the principle of a single spiration inclusive of the Son (as in the *filioque*); 2) the Western requirement of the East for a more precise description of the place of the Son in the procession of the Holy Spirit besides the *filioque*; and 3) more

---

94. Breck notes that Gregory of Cyprus speaks of the "shining forth" of the Spirit through the Son, even though Gregory's reference is to the shining forth of "the uncreated energies (but not the hypostasis) of the Spirit, precisely by the *Son*." Breck, however, acknowledges that (1) the West would not distinguish between the hypostasis and the energies of the Spirit in discussing the Spirit's eternal being from the Son, (2) the East still has room for speaking of the Spirit's being from the Son in the immanent Trinity, and (3) recent Orthodox theology makes room for the implications of a biblical narrative of "double sending" (i.e., the Son sends the Spirit, and the Spirit sends the Son) in its Trinitarian approach (citing Bobrinskoy's work). See Breck, "The Two Hands of God," 235, 240–241.

95. Coffey argues, against Weinandy, that the *in spiritu* is the same as the *spirituque*, and thus inverses the Trinitarian taxis by making the Holy Spirit a source (or principle) of the Son. This would in turn go against the *filioque*. I argue against Weinandy's synonymous use of *in spiritu* and *per spiritum* language. However, in response to Coffey's critique of Weinandy, I do not think that the Son's begetting from the Father "in" the Spirit has to be interpreted as a *spirituque*. In our usage, the *in spiritu* simply highlights that the Spirit is never separated from but rests on the Son, who is begotten of the Father. To avoid the Trinitarian inversion, perhaps it is better to say that the Spirit is present (rather than "participates") in the Son's begetting. Coffey proposes the following: "I hold that in the immanent Trinity the Son returns to the Father 'in' the Spirit, but that is possible only because the Son is co-principle of the Spirit." I find Coffey's proposal intriguing. And yet, in the immanent Trinity, the Son's return to the Father is not subsequent to the Son's begetting from the Father anyway. Both aspects of filiation (begetting, return) assume the priority of the Father vis-à-vis the Son (preserving the taxis Father-Son), as well as the Spirit's presence in the Son's being from the Father and the Son's return to the Father. I see the *in spiritu* more generally as encompassing both aspects of filiation. See Coffey, "Spirit Christology and the Trinity," 334–35.

recent calls for other models of Trinitarian communion that allow for a description of the Holy Spirit's own place in the Father's begetting of the Son. Having said that, I agree with Congar's conclusion that the Western *filioque* expresses the consubstantiality of the Father with the Son and distinguishes the processions of the Son and the Holy Spirit from the Father in the one divine essence in a way that the *per filium* does not. In this case, theological differences are not an impediment to unity, for neither approach to the mystery of God is ultimately antithetical to Scripture or the Christian Trinitarian tradition represented by the East and the West.

Summary

I have inquired into the productivity of a Spirit Christology for reflection on the mystery of the Trinity. In the previous chapter, I argued that God's self-giving in the person of the Son to the assumed humanity at the hypostatic union (incarnation) and his self-giving to the incarnate Son in the indwelling Spirit throughout his entire life and mission (incarnating) yields *per filium* (or a qualified *filioque*) and *in spiritu* economic and immanent models of the Trinity. In this chapter, I showed further that a Spirit Christology complements Logos-oriented static (being-from-before) and individual (being-in-itself) approaches to person and relation with corresponding dynamic (being-in-act) and relational (being-with-another) elements. Thus the Son exists in a reciprocal relation of love and communion with his Father "in the Spirit."

Finally, I proposed that the idea of Trinitarian reciprocity supported by a Spirit Christology, and its concomitant *in spiritu* model of the Trinity, does not necessitate the inversion of the classic order of processions in the economic or the immanent Trinity—an order that is historically required by a Logos Christology's concern for preserving the integrity of the hypostatic union against adoptionism. Briefly put, the *in spiritu* model of the Trinity serves to bring out more clearly the dynamic and ecstatic role of the Holy Spirit in the framework of either *per filium* or *filioque* views of intradivine relations. Thus the Father begets the Son and the Son is begotten of the Father in the Spirit. They coexist in the Spirit. To say that the Holy Spirit is the surplus of the Father's love manifested in the Son (Eastern view) or the communion of the mutual love between the Father and the Son (Western view) does not take away from the Spirit's constitutive place respectively in the *perfection* of the Father's love for the Son (or the Son's love for the Father) and in the *completion* of their reciprocal love for each other.

6

The Holy Spirit in the Incarnate Logos
Toward the Complementarity of Logos and Spirit Christologies

TO RECOVER THE SPIRIT-ORIENTED trajectory of the life and mission of Christ partially eclipsed in the history of dogma, I relativized its otherwise legitimate Logos-oriented dimensions. Yet true complementarity calls for a systematic synthesis that honors the basic concerns of each approach. In this chapter, I propose four ways to bring together these approaches to the mystery of Christ under four categories. These categories are: 1) the Trinitarian distinction between the personal "identity" of Jesus *and* the Logos and the "non-identity" of Jesus and the Holy Spirit, 2) the philosophico-theological distinction and relation between the order of knowledge (Lat. *ordo cognoscendi*) and the order of being (Lat. *ordo essendi*), 3) the conciliar distinction and relation between the human and divine wills and operations in Jesus Christ, and 4) a contemporary Lutheran appropriation of the Eastern doctrine of the communication of attributes in the person of Christ, and the Western scholastic distinction between the incarnation (grace of union) and the holiness of Christ (habitual grace). The fourth category, and its proposal for a way of highlighting the Holy Spirit's role *in* Christ's human nature—namely, the *genus habitualis* or *genus pneumatikon*—brings together Greek and Latin accents in Lutheran Christology in the service of a fuller Trinitarian account of the mystery of Christ.

Due to the intrinsic emphases and demands of Logos and Spirit Christologies, a measure of tension is likely to remain in any attempt to bring them together.[1] In the case of a Logos Christology, for example, what is constitutive is the immanent ground for the Son's free action in the world, but in upholding this legitimate concern there remains a tendency to undervalue the Son's economic actions per se as fully constitutive (even for his humanity). If a Spirit Christology is incorporated under a Logos-oriented framework, care must be taken so that an account of the incarnation and person of the Son can retain its dynamic and relational trajectory. On the other hand, if a Logos Christology is set in the context of a Spirit Christology, care must be taken so that the static and individual dimensions of the incarnation and the person of the Son also remain. Without attempting to be exhaustive or remove tensions completely, I present four ways of approaching the complementarity of Logos and Spirit Christologies.

IDENTITY AND NON-IDENTITY: JESUS IS THE LOGOS, NOT THE HOLY SPIRIT

As Manlio Simonetti reminds us, early orthodox Spirit Christology often identified Spirit (*pneuma, spiritus*)—and even "Holy Spirit" in the case of Luke 1:35—as the divine element of Christ and, more specifically, as the name of the preexistent Logos.[2] I argued that such identification ultimately weakened the particular agency of the Spirit in all events of Jesus' life and mission, since its activities were now ascribed to the Logos. It seems quite remarkable, however, that in spite of this relativization and even confusion between Spirit and Logos in interpreting various biblical passages, pre-Augustinian theologians like Tertullian and Hilary of Poitiers can still leave room for the notion that the Holy Spirit is a person distinct from the Father and the Son.[3] Early orthodox Spirit Christology is thus not necessarily detrimental to the church's Trinitarian faith, because as Simonetti puts it, it did not lead to a binitarian concept of God.[4] The story is another in contemporary attempts at a Spirit Christology as a substitute for the classical Logos Christology of the church formally consolidated at Chalcedon.

In biblical studies, for instance, Dunn has spoken of Jesus' self-consciousness of his unparalleled eschatological role in history and uniquely intimate relation to his Father (*Abba*) during his mission as an experience

---

1. See González de Cardedal, "Un problema teológico fundamental: la preexistencia de Cristo," 179–211.

2. Simonetti, "Note di cristologia pneumatica," esp. 203–17.

3. For Tertullian and Hilary, see ibid., 227, 229; for Hilary, see also Ladaria's article "El Espíritu Santo en San Hilario de Poitiers," 245–46.

4. Simonetti, "Note di cristología pneumatica," 226–32.

of the Spirit's presence in him. Initially, Dunn concluded "that Jesus' possession and experience of the Spirit is that which later dogma has called his divinity. The 'deity' of the Jesus of history is a function of the Spirit — is, in fact, no more and no less than the Spirit."[5] In order to recover the "dynamic" pneumatological character of Jesus' human experiences, Dunn felt compelled to reinterpret the two-natures Chalcedonian approach to Jesus' identity under the *pneuma/sarx* pattern typically used in early Spirit Christologies: "[I]t would be better to express the theory of the two natures in the Pauline terms of flesh and Spirit . . . and recognize that what we call the deity of Jesus was no more and no less than the Spirit of God in him."[6]

Later on, Dunn moved away from identifying "the Spirit with experience [i.e., of Christ] quite so crudely"[7] and preferred to speak of its presence in Jesus under the category of prophecy or, more specifically, in terms "of empowering for exorcism, of inspiration for proclamation."[8] One cannot, as some early church fathers did, use the *pneuma/sarx* pattern of Romans 1:3-4 to support exegetically "an incarnational Spirit Christology," that is, the "concept of Christ as the incarnation of the Spirit."[9] In the end, Dunn suggested that a Spirit Christology that sees Jesus as pre-Easter prophet and then functionally identifies him with the life-giving Spirit (1 Cor 15:45) in the church's post-Easter experience can help us to bring together incarnational Logos/Wisdom and Adam/Lord NT Christologies.[10] Significantly, Dunn moved away from substituting the presence of the Spirit in Jesus for that of the Logos and instead moved towards recognizing that a complementarity of approaches is the best option. Others have not done the same.

G. W. H. Lampe exemplifies the shift towards replacement in two ways. First, he does not consider the Spirit as an agent distinct from God in the biblical sense or as a divine person in the conciliar sense. Consider the author's definition of God as Spirit:

---

5. Dunn, "Rediscovering the Spirit (1)," 50.
6. Ibid., 51.
7. Ibid., Preface, ix.
8. Dunn, "Rediscovering the Spirit (2)," 75; earlier in "Spirit and Holy Spirit in the New Testament," 5-8; see also *Jesus and the Spirit*, where Dunn adds to Jesus' self-consciousness as end-time exorcist and inspired prophet his unique "Abba" experience of sonship: "*Jesus thought of himself as God's son and as anointed by the eschatological Spirit, because in prayer he experienced God as Father and in ministry he experienced a power to heal which he could only understand as the gospel of the end-time*" (67).
9. "Rediscovering the Spirit (2)," 74-76.
10. Ibid., 76-80.

> In speaking now of God as Spirit we are not referring to an impersonal influence, an energy transmitted by God but distinct from himself. Nor are we indicating a divine entity or hypostasis which is a third person of the Godhead. We are speaking of God himself, his personal presence, as active and related.[11]

Neither a divine power nor a concrete hypostatic expression of the divine substance, the designation "Spirit," to our author, is a way of describing "God" in terms of his dynamic and ecstatic "presence" in the world. Thus "Spirit" is at once God's transcendent (other-worldly) and yet active immanent (worldly) presence in and towards creation.[12]

Second, it follows that Lampe does not speak of Christ's divinity in terms of the Logos's presence in and activity through his assumed humanity, opting instead for a definition of his divinity according to what the human being Jesus does in cooperation with God's Spirit. In his development of a Spirit Christology, he distinguishes between substantival, adjectival, and adverbial definitions of Jesus' divinity:

> Spirit christology must be content to acknowledge that the personal subject of the experience of Jesus Christ is a man. The

---

11. Lampe, *God as Spirit*, 208; in *The Doctrine of the Holy Spirit*, Berkhof had argued that the Holy Spirit "is not an autonomous substance, but a predicate to the substance God and to the substance Christ . . . the way of functioning of both" (28). He writes, "In creation he [the Spirit] is the acting Person of God, in re-creation he is the acting Person of Christ, who is no other than the acting Person of God . . . The Spirit is Person because he is God acting as Person. However, we cannot say that the Spirit is a Person distinct from God the Father" (116). Berkhof robs the Spirit of its personhood, but Christ suffers the same fate: "Jesus Christ is not a Person beside the Person of God; in him the Person of God becomes the shape of a human person" (ibid).

12. Similarly, Haight conceives of Spirit as a biblical symbol qualitatively equal to other biblical metaphors (such as Logos and Wisdom) for describing God's *ad extra* energy at work in creation: "[A]ll these symbols are basically the same insofar as they point to the same generalized experience of God outside of God's self and immanent in the world in presence and active power . . . When the metaphorical character of personification is not respected, when it becomes hypostasized, i.e., conceived as objective and individual, in the same measure the power of the symbol tends to be undermined." Haight, "The Case for Spirit Christology," 267–68; in a recorded interview, John O'Donnell interprets Haight's proposal as a "kind of *either/or*" approach because of the leveling of metaphors to the same function, so that one can choose *either* one model *or* the other depending on the demands of one's historical context. Although Haight at first seems to allow for both approaches to stand *alongside each other*, I think that in the end no true synthesis occurs and in fact a Spirit Christology only stands *in place of* a Logos Christology. One approach replaces the other. See Haight, "The Case for Spirit Christology," 259, 266 (n16); for criticisms of Haight's article above, see Wright, "Roger Haight's Spirit Christology," 729–35; and Weinandy, "The Case for Spirit Christology," 173–88.

> hypostasis is not the Logos incarnate but a human being. Spirit christology cannot affirm that Jesus is 'substantivally' God.... It does not follow that Jesus is only 'adjectivally' God, that is to say, God-*like* or 'divine' in the sense of being a man who possessed to an excellent degree the qualities that we attribute to God. An interpretation of the union of Jesus with God in terms of his total possession by God's Spirit makes it possible, rather, to acknowledge him to be God 'adverbially.' By the mutual interaction of the Spirit's influence and the free response of the human spirit such a unity of will and operation was established that in all his actions the human Jesus acted divinely.[13]

To make the human being Jesus a legitimate subject of experiences and actions, Lampe feels compelled to leave behind the possibility of speaking of his divinity in terms of the Logos's self-communication to his assumed humanity. It is enough for Lampe to speak of the Spirit's presence in Jesus, but then in the authors's way of speaking "Logos" and "Spirit" are nothing more than interchangeable terms or metaphors for God's general presence as experienced in his works in creation.[14] Is this enough to posit the unity of the divine and the human in Jesus Christ? In Lampe's system, it is unclear how saying that the man Jesus is God because he acts "divinely" in cooperation with Spirit (adverbial sense) is finally any different from saying that he is divine because he has Spirit in a most excellent manner (adjectival sense).[15] In either case, Jesus' being and acts as one in whom God as Spirit dwells fully makes him significantly and even uniquely distinct from other saints, but still only in intensity or degree.[16] Neither the adverbial nor the adjectival sense reaches the level of an ontological union grounded in the *person* of the Logos.

---

13. Lampe, "The Holy Spirit and the Person of Christ," 124.

14. See Lampe, *God as Spirit*, 37, 115–16; similarly, Haight can define his approach as follows: "By a Spirit Christology I mean one that 'explains' how God is present and active in Jesus, and thus Jesus' divinity, by using the biblical symbol of God as Spirit, and not the symbol Logos." Haight, "The Case for Spirit Christology," 257 (see also 274–77).

15. Hansen finds the same lack of clarity in his discussion of Lampe. See Hansen, "Spirit Christology," 193–95; for a critique of Spirit Christology in the style of Lampe's proposal, see Hunter, "Spirit Christology . . . (1)," 127–40, and "Spirit Christology . . . (2)," 266–77.

16. For a short proposal similar to Lampe's, see Hook, "A Spirit Christology," 226–32; for a more extensive proposal that, like Lampe, posits the need to move beyond the traditional "Christocentric trinitarianism" of the ecumenical Councils and toward a "theocentric Spirit Christology," see Newman, *A Spirit Christology*.

Dunn and Lampe share a basic concern for understanding the divinity of Jesus in such a way that his true humanity—e.g., its self-consciousness, experiences, historical deeds, relationships, and will—does not lose its character in the process. To the extent that the classical Chalcedonian Christology allowed for the Logos's full communication of divine attributes to his assumed humanity at the hypostatic union, subsequent events in Jesus' life and mission naturally became more epiphanic of his prior identity as God than constitutive for his own humanity as Christ (= anointed one), suffering Servant, Savior, and risen Lord. It is this lack of historical dynamism that Dunn and Lampe seek to recover in their revisionist studies of the place of "Spirit" in Jesus' human experiences.

In Lampe's case, however, the recovery of pneumatology leads to a denial of the classical approach's *static* view of the incarnation as hypostatic union and *individual* conception of the incarnate Word as a self-constituted person (subject) distinct from the Father and the Holy Spirit. In fact, Lampe turns early orthodox Spirit Christology on its head by using the reality of Spirit to relativize (instead of affirm) the Logos's unique presence in Jesus— or more accurately, in his assumed human nature. If some of the early patristic writers weakened the pneumatic aspects of Christology by subsuming the "Spirit" under the divine element of Christ, Lampe does the opposite by subsuming the "Logos" under the general idea of Spirit as God (or divinity). Unlike early orthodox Spirit Christology, however, Lampe does away with a Trinitarian framework that supports a distinction between the persons of the Logos and the Spirit and thus their proper character (*proprium*) vis-à-vis the humanity of Christ.

Scripture gives us a basic witness to what theologians have formally referred to as a differentiated unity of Father (God), Son (Word), and Holy Spirit in their works for us in history and in their relations to one another. Ladaria correctly points out that no passage in the New Testament says of the Spirit what John 1:14 says of the Logos.[17] On the one hand, assigning to the Spirit what belongs to the Logos is the basic danger of a Spirit Christology that describes the divinity of Jesus exclusively in terms of his possession of Spirit, or his acting divinely because of his cooperation with Spirit, thus leaving aside the issue of the identity of Jesus as the Logos made flesh. On the other hand, one must fully account for the pneumatological element and trajectory in Jesus' life and mission. A post-Trinitarian move is not necessary to do so. One can readily acknowledge that the active presence of the Spirit as a distinct person in Jesus is not merely something "accidental

---

17. Ladaria, "Cristología del Logos y cristología del Espíritu," 356n9.

or secondary" to his identity.[18] I have argued that the partial eclipse of the pneumatological element is a basic danger of a Logos Christology that does not give full weight to the special times (*kairoi*) of Jesus' life and work in which God's Spirit descends in and works through and with Jesus. How does one bring together the aforementioned Logos- and Spirit-oriented concerns into a more holistic account of the mystery of Christ?

Ladaria is hesitant to speak of Logos and Spirit Christologies as two discrete "models" because such terminology could lead to the misconception that either approach can carry the whole weight of Jesus' identity on its own. An exchange with Ladaria on this point gives us a basic Trinitarian starting point and framework towards complementarity.[19]

> Sánchez: Well, here we have two models, alongside one another. These are complementary in the sense that one is next to the other. But where is...
>
> Ladaria: ... the integration?
>
> Sánchez: ... the integration, the cohesiveness. You see? What would you say?
>
> Ladaria: These are not two models. The aspects must be integrated.
>
> Sánchez: The aspects...
>
> Ladaria: And the point of departure is the personal identity of Jesus. Jesus is not the Holy Spirit. Jesus is the Son of God. Jesus is the Logos. He is the Son. This is his personal identity. And on him descends the Spirit.
>
> Sánchez: The non-identity of Jesus [and the Spirit]...
>
> Ladaria: That they are not the same.
>
> Sánchez: Yes. In that sense, these are not simply two models. I see.
>
> Ladaria: These are two aspects of one reality for bringing us close to Jesus who personally is the Son, not the Spirit.

What seems like such a basic distinction between the "personal identity" of Jesus and the Logos (Son) and the "non-identity" of Jesus and the Spirit can never be appreciated in its fullness unless one understands both the historic relativization of the pneumatological aspects of Jesus' identity

---

18. Ibid., 354.

19. Ladaria, interview by Sánchez; translation mine. For a short example of the use of two models without proper integration, see Thomsen, "A Christology of the Spirit and the Nicene Creed," 135–38.

The Holy Spirit in the Incarnate Logos 155

in early orthodox Spirit Christology and, conversely, the more recent relativization of the Logos-oriented dimensions of Jesus' identity in what may be described as "post-Chalcedonian" (or post-Trinitarian) Spirit-oriented Christologies.[20] By identifying "Spirit" with the divine element or name of the preexistent Logos, early orthodox Spirit Christology tended to deny the person of the Holy Spirit its active place in the Christ-event (incarnating). By replacing the metaphor of Logos with that of Spirit, the post-Chalcedonian type of Spirit Christology denies the Logos its unique assumption of a human nature or his becoming flesh at the hypostatic union (incarnation).

In light of these shortcomings past and present, the issue of personal identity and non-identity provides a framework or prepares the way for distinguishing what is proper to the Logos and to the Holy Spirit in the humanity of Christ in such a way that both dynamic and static, as well as ecstatic and individual, views of the incarnation are preserved. This is how I interpret the function of Spanish theologian Luis Ladaria's distinction. Let us hear Ladaria himself:

> If we cannot speak of an identity between Jesus and the Holy Spirit, we must on the other hand affirm that the Holy Spirit is the one who acts in Jesus during all the stages of his life, and not precisely the Logos or the Son. Nowhere in the New Testament are we told that the Son descended upon Jesus at Jordan or raised him from the dead. Therefore, upon this Jesus, personally identical with the Logos, the Holy Spirit acts in distinct moments of his existence towards the realization of his life as Son, for the perfecting of his filiation, already certainly possessed from the beginning (cf. *Heb* 5:9). If Jesus' divine filiation has its foundation in the fact that he is the Logos of God, the historical realization of his filial life for the salvation of humankind appears to have to be ascribed according to the New Testament to the action of the Spirit of God in him. . . . What a Logos Christology sees realized once and for all in the incarnation is seen from the perspective of a Spirit Christology as a historical process that finds its goal in the resurrection.[21]

We can now assess the import of Ladaria's proposal for complementarity in its historical and theological context. First, since Ladaria assumes a logical priority of the incarnation over the anointing that still gives the Jordan event its proper weight, his words echo Irenaeus's statement that

---

20. I first came upon the term "post-Chalcedonian" for describing Lampe's approach in Del Colle, *Christ and the Spirit*, 161–64.

21. Ladaria, "Cristología del Logos y cristología del Espíritu," 355–56; translation mine.

"inasmuch as the Word of God was man . . . in this respect did the Spirit of God rest upon him, and anoint him to preach the Gospel to the lowly."[22] Second, Ladaria wants to stress the Trinitarian picture of events in Jesus' life from a pneumatic angle as a complement to, for example, an Alexandrian interpretation of his anointing and exaltation as glorifying instances of the Logos's prior sanctification of himself with his own Spirit at conception.[23] Athanasius and Cyril of Alexandria advocate the latter move, which does not take full account of the Father as personal cause of acts in and through Jesus by the power of the Spirit, or of the distinction between the Spirit's sanctification and indwelling of Jesus from conception and the Father's anointing of Jesus with the Spirit at the Jordan.[24] Finally, one can note the underlying Western pre-Augustinian influence of Hilary of Poitiers. In particular, Ladaria finds useful Hilary's view of the incarnation, anointing, and resurrection of the Son as economic "births" because such language points to a process of sanctification of the Son's humanity that reaches its goal in his bodily glorification upon his return to the Father's glory.[25]

Briefly put, we can affirm both the incarnate Logos's individual inner-constitution as God-man at an absolute point in time and the Spirit's dynamic and ecstatic presence in the incarnate Logos throughout his life and mission in obedience to the Father and also for us and for our salvation. In the economy of salvation, then, a Spirit Christology's dynamic and relational dimensions complement, without replacing, Logos-oriented static and individual aspects of the identity of Jesus. This is the basic truth that I have conveyed at various times in my proposal for a Spirit-oriented Christology as an aspect of the mystery of Christ that invigorates its Logos-oriented dimensions.

The distinction between identity and non-identity applies both to the economic Trinity and the immanent Trinity. The Logos is not the Holy

---

22. Irenaeus, *Against Heresies* 3.18.1 (*ANF* 1:446); also Ladaria, interview by Sánchez.

23. Ladaria develops this insight in "La unción de Jesús y el don del Espíritu," 562-64.

24. Cyril uses anointing not so much as a reference to the Father's anointing of his Son at the baptism, but as a reference to the Holy Spirit, whom the Son has preserved holy in his flesh from the moment of his incarnation for the sake of humanity. See his exegesis of John 7:39 (citing Ps 45:7), in *Commentary on John* 694 (trans. Maxwell, 310).

25. For Hilary, the glorified humanity retains its properties and thus is not divinized in the sense that it is swallowed up in divinity. What is left aside after Jesus' resurrection is the corruptible nature of the body in death. In an economic sense, the resurrection is a rebirth unto immortality or participation in the glory of the Father, a glory that Jesus always had from eternity as the Logos, but now fully receives as incarnate Logos at the resurrection. For a fuller treatment, see Ladaria, *La cristología de Hilario de Poitiers*, chap. 7.

Spirit, and viceversa. And yet the Logos can be said to exist as one in whom the Spirit of the Father rests, just as the Holy Spirit can be said to exist as one who proceeds from the Father through (or and) the Son. Following Barth and Rahner, I inquired into the immanent implications of God's twofold self-differentiated givenness or communication in the Son and in the Holy Spirit to the humanity of Christ. This move did not prevent me from giving the person of the Son its proper due in the definition of the person of the Holy Spirit (either through a *per filium* or a qualified *filioque* model of processions). Neither did the same move prevent me from giving the person of the Holy Spirit its proper due in the definition of the person of the Son and his relation to the Father. Building particularly on the themes of communion (*koinonia*) and love (*caritas*) in Greek and Latin pneumatology respectively, I did so through an *in spiritu* model that did not overturn either a *per filium* or a qualified *filioque*. In regards to the person of the Logos, I provided a christological-Trinitarian synthesis, which I can now present once again as an affirmation in agreement not only with the correspondence between the economic Trinity and the immanent Trinity, but also with the distinction between identity and non-identity introduced in this essay.

> The deepest truth regarding the Logos's distinct self-subsistence (individual aspect) from before (static aspect), whether in the intradivine life as God the Son or in the economy of salvation as incarnate Son (God-man), is that he exists in an open (dynamic aspect) and ecstatic (relational aspect) to God the Father and to us freely and out of love in the Spirit (*in spiritu*) without ceasing to be himself.

ORDERS OF KNOWLEDGE AND BEING: JESUS THE CHRIST IS THE LOGOS AND THE LOGOS IS JESUS THE CHRIST

Another way to approach the issue of complementarity is by means of the distinction and relationship between Christologies "from above" and "from below."[26] The classical starting point for the mystery of Christ ("from above") begins with the preexistent divine Logos whose assumption of hu-

---

26. For a description of the two approaches, see Fitzmyer, *Scripture and Christology*, 90; cf. Pannenberg, *Jesus—God and Man*, 33; Illanes Maestre offers five aspects marking the distinction between both methodologies. See Illanes Maestre, "Cristología «desde arriba» y cristología «desde abajo»," 144–46; for a proposal to bring together ontological and functional concerns in Logos- and Spirit-oriented Christologies respectively, see Habets, *The Anointed Son*, 10–52.

manity unto himself constitutes him as God-man from the first moment of the incarnation. A Spirit Christology ("from below") follows the man Jesus of Nazareth in the economic *kairoi* of his earthly life and ministry as the incarnate Son relates to his Father and to us in the Spirit, and then moves to confess him as Servant, Savior, Lord, and ultimately God. One may formulate a Christology from either starting point as long as neither approach ends by denying the church's basic confession of Jesus' humanity and divinity (more generally, the Chalcedonian formula) and, in more material terms, as long as Jesus of Nazareth (in his life, words, and deeds)—and not preconceived philosophico-theological systems—is the "norming norm" (Lat. *norma normans*) for Christology.[27]

The classical approach "from above" looks at Jesus Christ in *ontological-immanent* terms according to the categories of preexistence and incarnation (= hypostatic union); conversely, one "from below" looks at Jesus' identity in *soteriological-economic* terms according to a dynamic series of successive events spanning from his birth to his baptism, and from his baptism to his death and resurrection.[28] A Christology purely "from below" ends by denying Jesus' full divinity; a Christology purely "from above," Jesus' full humanity. A Spirit Christology exclusively "from below" leads to Ebionite, adoptionist, and Nestorian views. A Logos Christology exclusively "from above" leads to docetic, Apollinarian, monophysite, and monothelite views. If we cannot speak of an *either/or*, but rather of a *both/and*[29] approach to Christology, we must also try to provide some synthesis.[30]

---

27. Moltmann objects to the distinction between Christologies "from above" and "from below" when it assumes either a general metaphysical or anthropological framework into which Jesus is later situated. The danger is to "end up with a theological christology without Jesus, or with an anthropological Jesuology without God." Moltmann, *The Way of Jesus Christ*, 69.

28. The terms "ontological-immanent" and "soteriological-economic" describe orientations and not absolute conditions, as if a fundamental choice had to be made between either an ontological (metaphysical) or a soteriological (functional) Christology. Both approaches should have both types of concerns in mind.

29. Rahner, for example, delineates characteristics of "saving history" and "metaphysical" types, but not without the proviso that these two categories are strictly abstract, since both approaches have often appeared together in mixed varieties. Rahner, "The Two Basic Types of Christology," 213–24.

30. Even a Christology "from below" must proceed "from above" in that the former must assume that God as such freely saves us in Jesus Christ. At the same time, we must also illuminate this truth with the fact that God cannot save what God has not assumed (although freely so). In the latter case, the soteriological-economic concern of a Christology "from below" that looks at the actualization and relationality of the Son's humanity in a wider Trinitarian framework complements the move "from above."

Let us begin with a question: "Does Jesus help me because he is the Son of God, or is he the Son of God because he helps me?"[31] Moltmann asks this question in the context of a discussion on the classical philosophical distinction between the order of knowing (Lat. *ratio cognoscendi*) and the order of being (Lat. *ratio essendi*): "Whereas Jesus is not recognizable as the Son of God until his death and his resurrection, in the order of being he is the Son of God before this history takes place."[32] Whereas our knowledge of Jesus' divinity always comes afterwards (Lat. *a posteriori*), the divinity of Jesus is always a reality that exists beforehand (Lat. *a priori*) in the order of being. As Pannenberg has pointed out, this principle does not assume that humans arrive at this knowledge on their own, for even "in the order of knowledge the movement "from above" proceeds only by means of divine revelation."[33] Moltmann exemplifies that approach "from below" to the question of Jesus' divinity, which places the paschal mystery at the center of reflection.[34] According to Moltmann's eschatological ontology, the end in history reveals the origin in eternity. The same applies to our knowledge of Jesus' divine origin. Christ's exaltation to God reveals his sending and origin from God, and his glorious resurrection reveals his descent to become incarnate.

> The early Christian community evidently deduced Christ's original sending *by* and *from* the Father from his eschatological exaltation *to* the Father. . . . [T]he future reveals the origin. . . . Jesus' resurrection from the dead was not understood as merely happening in time to the dead Jesus. It was simultaneously seen as the beginning of the eschatological era, when the dead will be raised. It therefore also meant the immediate presence of God's eternity. In time, Jesus is raised 'on the third day' after his death, but as the immediate presence of eternity his raising is simultaneous to all moments of his life. To adopt this standpoint is already to assume the perspective which looks from Jesus'

---

31. Moltmann, *The Crucified God*, 91.

32. Ibid.; Moltmann finds in Aristotle the basis for the underlying thought behind the distinction, namely, that "what is last in perception is always first in being." See Moltmann, *The Way of Jesus Christ*, 49; cf. Pannenberg's discussion in his *Systematic Theology*, 1:264–66, and 2:363–72.

33. Pannenberg, *Jesus—God and Man*, 405.

34. See ibid., chap. 3; "That Jesus Christ is the Logos, God's Word incarnate, may have been abstractly and essentially true at the moment of his conception. But its full human realization and historical revelation is Paschal . . . We discern the *Logos*, the 'logic' of the human life of God, from its end, its *eschatos*." Imbelli, "The New Adam," 246.

divine to his human nature, and it is then possible to talk about his incarnation."[35]

We can affirm the centrality of the resurrection appearances of Jesus to his disciples and the Spirit's descent upon the church from Pentecost onwards for witnessing to this Easter reality (e.g., Luke 24:26, 46-49; Acts 1:3-4, 8, and 2:32-33, 36-39) as the epistemological basis for our subsequent identification of Jesus as Lord and God (e.g., 1 Cor 12:3; John 20:28). Let us make the same point in terms of a Spirit Christology.[36] In the order of knowledge (*ordo cognoscendi*), Jesus is a man who is fully recognized and confessed as Lord, Son of God in power, and finally God only upon the completion of his life and mission in the Spirit at the moment of his exaltation. In light of the resurrection, the presence of the Spirit in Jesus—his identity as receiver, bearer, and giver of the same—points us to his divinity, to the fact that Jesus is none other than the Logos upon whom the Spirit remains. We can speak of a Logos Christology operating *within* a Spirit-oriented Christology.

In our reality as post-Easter/post-Pentecost Christians, in our being and living in the Spirit of the risen Lord and Messiah, we can read the biblical story of Jesus as receiver, bearer, and giver of the Spirit of the Father for us and then confess that this concrete man is God, the divine Logos. To read the Christ-event from a pneumatological horizon means that the story of this man becomes for us the narrative of the Father's love for us through his Son in the Spirit and of the Son's love to the Father for us in the same Spirit.[37] Only from the perspective of the order of knowledge can we interpret

---

35. Moltmann, *The Way of Jesus Christ*, 49.

36. Following Kasper and Pannenberg, Rosato preserves both the uniqueness and universal significance of Jesus Christ as bearer and giver of the Spirit in intrinsically related functional and ontological terms. He argues, for example, that a paschally-rooted Spirit Christology is advantageous because "it corrects the ontological and Trinitarian deficiencies of Ebionite Christology by not merely dwelling on the functional significance of Jesus, but insisting that Jesus' universal function is unavoidably rooted in his unique being which pre-exists with the being of the triune God . . . It has as its starting point in the historical event of the paschal mystery and, in retroactive fashion, guarantees Jesus' uniqueness even before the beginning of his existence; in eschatological fashion, however, it opens up the universal significance of his being for all mankind and for the whole cosmos." Rosato, "Spirit Christology," 447.

37. In a sermon for Trinity Sunday, Luther writes: "The Scriptures gradually and beautifully lead us to Christ; first revealing him to us as a man, then as the Lord of all creatures, and finally as God. Thus we are successfully led to the true knowledge of God. But the philosophers and the wise men of this world would begin at the top and so they have become fools. We must begin at the bottom and gradually advance in knowledge." Luther, "Sunday after Pentecost, or Trinity Sunday," 409-10. Here I have simply pointed out the pneumatological horizon from which such reading of the Scriptures is possible

Kasper's proposal that the *gratia habitualis* is the basis for the *gratia unionis*, or that Jesus' sanctification in the Spirit and endowment with its gifts is the ground for affirming the hypostatic union or the identity of Jesus and the Logos.[38] In the order of knowledge, therefore, Jesus the Christ is the Son of God *because* he helps us. Jesus of Nazareth, the one anointed by the Father with the Spirit, is the Logos.

In the order of being (*ordo essendi*), however, Jesus is not only a man who is or becomes divine because of the perfect fulfillment of his life and mission in the Spirit. Herein lies a danger of post-Chalcedonian attempts to make the presence of "Spirit" (in contrast to that of the Logos) in Jesus' human reality the ontological (in contrast to epistemological) ground for affirming his divinity. Although the Holy Spirit has a constitutive (and not accidental) ontological role in defining the identity of the *incarnate* Logos, the principle of non-identity still prevents us from concluding that this communication of the Spirit in him is identical with the Logos's communication to his assumed humanity. We cannot speak of a hypostasization or incarnation of the Holy Spirit in the humanity that only the Logos has assumed unto himself. The Spirit is not the Logos, and viceversa.

To speak of the Holy Spirit's disposition of a human nature for its assumption by or union with the Logos, of a logical priority of the sanctification over the union (in reaction to monophysite tendencies), cannot ultimately point to Jesus' divinity or his personal identity with the Logos in an ontological sense. Why? Because the proper mission of the Holy Spirit is to sanctify, not a human nature in general, but precisely the humanity of the Logos. Otherwise, in a legitimate attempt to avoid monophysitism and give the Spirit's dynamic presence in the various events of Jesus' life and mission its proper weight, we may simply overdo it and fall into adoptionism or Nestorianism—not the best remedy against monophysitism.[39] The theological pendulum must not swing in the direction of the opposite danger.

---

and the Trinitarian framework of the identity of Christ to whom the Scriptures ultimately point.

38. A point that Ladaria and I share concerning Kasper's pneumatological application of Rahner's axiom. See Ladaria, interview by Sánchez; for Ladaria's critique of Kasper, see Ladaria, "Cristología del Logos y cristología del Espíritu," 357.

39. "In the case of Jesus, it is important to avoid Adoptianism [*sic*]. He is ontologically the Son of God because of the hypostatic union from the moment of his conception. Because of that too, he is the Temple of the Holy Spirit and is made holy by that Spirit in his humanity. We have, however, as believers, to respect the successive moments or stages in the history of salvation and to accord the New Testament texts their full realism. Because of this, I would suggest that there were two moments when the *virtus* or effectiveness of the Spirit in Jesus was actuated in a new way. The first was at his baptism, when he was constituted (and not simply proclaimed as) Messiah and Servant

From the perspective of the order of being, Spirit Christology must be seen *within* the matrix of a Logos-oriented Christology. To use scholastic categories, the *gratia unionis* remains the basis and presupposition for the *gratia habitualis*. In other words, the incarnation (hypostatic union) remains the ground and presupposition for the Spirit's ongoing historical presence in the life and mission of the incarnate Son (incarnating). As the church has argued against adoptionism, God's self-giving to the humanity of Christ in the personal union is the logical priority for God's self-giving in the Holy Spirit to the same humanity in indwelling and sanctification. In the order of being, Jesus the Christ, the Spirit-anointed Son, helps me precisely *because* he is first the Son of God who in time became flesh for us and for our salvation. The Logos is Jesus the Christ.

To sum up, in the classical move "from above" which follows the order of being, the identity of Jesus as divine Logos is affirmed and then we move to speak of him as the receiver and bearer of the Spirit in the flesh. The strength of this approach lies in preserving the personal identity of Jesus and the Logos while avoiding the idea that the Holy Spirit disposes or prepares a human nature for its assumption by the Logos (an adoptionist tendency). From a Trinitarian perspective, the move "from above" preserves the order of Trinitarian processions *Father–Son–Spirit*, which gives logical priority to the Father's *generation* of the Son over the *spiration* of the Holy Spirit from the Father through/and the Son. In the order of being, we affirm that this processional priority is the ontological-immanent ground for the same priority in the historical missions of the Son and the Holy Spirit.

In the move "from below," which follows the order of knowledge, we affirm, on the basis of Jesus' works, that his bearing and giving of the Spirit reveals him to be none other than the divine Logos. The strength of this approach lies in preserving the non-identity of Jesus and the person of the Holy Spirit, while allowing the latter a defining role in the economic actualization or fulfillment of the humanity of the Logos in his mission of love before the Father and for us (contra monophysite tendencies). From a Trinitarian angle and in the order of knowledge, the move "from below" also allows us to speak of Jesus' dynamic and ecstatic existence in the Spirit of the Father throughout the economy of salvation as the basis for assigning the Spirit a participation in the Son's procession from the Father. We have called this form of participation an *in spiritu* Trinitarian model that does not invert the classic order of processions, but also gives the Holy Spirit its constitutive role in the perfection or completion of the Father's love for

---

by God. The second moment was at the time of his resurrection and exaltation, when he was made Lord." Congar, *Holy Spirit*, 3:171; cf. Congar, *The Word and the Spirit*, 92.

the Son and in the Son's reciprocal love for the Father in the mystery of the incarnation.

A synthesis of the orders of knowledge and being in our present reality as post-Easter/post-Pentecost Christians may proceed as follows. We can approach the mystery of Christ "from below," beginning with the man Jesus of Nazareth in his life and mission of faithfulness to the Father and for us in the power of the Spirit. A Spirit Christology looks at the man Jesus in the context of his "being-in-act" and "being-in-relation," of his dynamic and ecstatic existence lived precisely "in the Spirit." We can speak of Jesus' identity as receiver, bearer, and giver of the Spirit of the Father and look at the mysteries of Jesus' life from this pneumatic angle. In light of the paschal mystery, we can then confess in the Spirit of the risen Lord that this particular Spirit-constituted man whom we call Jesus of Nazareth is not a *mere* man but our Lord, Son of God in power, and God. The bearer and giver of the Spirit *is* the Logos.

In the move from the order of knowledge to the order of being, it is then possible to begin "from above"—the classic Christological approach—and assume beforehand that the divine Logos is Jesus the Christ. We can then speak of Jesus' identity in terms of his "being-from-before" and "being-in-himself," both from eternity as the individual self-subsistent person of the Logos and then in time according to his individual inner-constitution as incarnate Logos. We can also look at events in Jesus' life as revelatory, epiphanic, confirming, or declarative of his divinity. Yet these static and individual dimensions of Jesus' identity have to be invigorated with the dynamic and relational aspects of a Spirit Christology arrived at in our initial approach "from below."

Admittedly, my initial approach "from below" already assumes that God as such saves us in Christ and, indeed, that the man Jesus is none other than the divine Logos. In light of the long history of dogma that precedes us, even a Spirit-oriented Christology looks at the order of knowledge in light of the Logos-oriented order of being. This is our present reality as people who already confess Jesus as Lord and God, and who, in addition, have learned from Scripture and the creeds of the church to identify this Jesus as the Word (= Logos) made flesh. A Spirit Christology presupposes a Logos Christology, just as the order of knowledge presupposes the order of being.

From a methodological point of view, however, I felt it necessary to relativize the Logos-oriented approach in order to complement it. Otherwise, as my investigation has shown extensively, one loses sight of the significance of events like the baptism and the resurrection for the incarnate Son himself, as well as the broader Trinitarian dimensions of his life and mission as the one who comes from and goes to the Father in the Spirit.

Once such dimensions have been restored, and the place of the Holy Spirit has been given its due in God's self-giving to the humanity of the Son, both at the economic and immanent levels, then we can again see a Spirit Christology *within* the matrix of a Logos Christology. Only after we affirm the Son's (and, for that matter, the Father's) existence "in the Spirit," can we reconcile this partially neglected pneumatic trajectory of the story of Jesus with the confession that the same Spirit, in the order of being, proceeds from the Father through/and the Son (immanent Trinity) and sanctifies the humanity that the Son has already assumed unto himself (economic Trinity). A strong Spirit Christology in Trinitarian key does not have to set itself against the logical priority of the Son over the Spirit, either in the immanent processions or in the economic missions.

HUMAN AND DIVINE WILLS AND OPERATIONS: CONSTANTINOPLE III AND THE COMPLEMENTARITY OF APPROACHES

Congar has suggested that the crisis of monotheletism and the church's response to it at Constantinople III (A.D. 680–81) opened the door for a full study of "the fact that Christ had been called in the truth of his human nature to fulfil himself and his mission as Messiah and Saviour through conscious and free activity in which the movement of the Spirit was present."[40] Historically, the struggle against Arianism already demanded the acknowledgement that Jesus' obedience to the Father did not make him ontologically subordinate to the Father. Basil solved the apparent contradiction between Christ's human obedience to the Father's will and his divine equality with the Father by affirming the essential unity of will between the Father and the Son manifested historically in their common works.[41] The unity of will in their works outside of themselves or towards the world (Lat. *ad extra*) pointed to their unity of will among themselves (Lat. *ad intra*) in the Godhead. Such an articulation of the issue at hand did not take away from the proper differentiation of the persons in their common works *ad extra* or in their relations *ad intra*. Just as the divine persons express their common unity of essence in their own distinct way (i.e., as Father, Son, and Holy Spirit), so too do the divine persons express their unity of will in their own distinct ways.

---

40. Congar, *The Word and the Spirit*, 86.
41. Basil, *On the Spirit* 8.20–21 (*NPNF*[2] 8:14–15).

The Holy Spirit in the Incarnate Logos

What this implied for the incarnate Son, however, was not quite clear until the rise of Apollinarianism, monophysitism, and ultimately monotheletism engaged the church in a struggle to safeguard the Son's true humanity against attempts to strip it of a rational soul or human mind, subsume it under the one and only divine nature, or strip it of a will.[42] In these cases, strong affirmations of the divinity of the Logos turned heterodox and his full humanity suffered in the process. Monothelites held to the unity of will and operation among the persons of the Trinity, but did not admit that the incarnation of the Logos demanded the notion of two natural wills and operations in the one person. Yet the Council's Definition of Faith also avoided a lapse into Nestorianism by affirming that, in the person of Christ, divine and human wills are not in opposition to one another.

> We likewise declare that in him are two natural wills and two natural operations indivisibly, inconvertibly, inseparably, inconfusedly.... And these two natural wills are not contrary the one to the other (God forbid!) ... but his human will follows and that not as resisting and reluctant, but rather as subject to his divine and omnipotent will.... [F]or although joined together each nature wills and does the things proper to it and that indivisibly and inconfusedly. Wherefore we confess two wills and two operations, concurring most fitly in him for the salvation of the human race.[43]

In our earlier discussion of atonement theories, we came upon Anselm's thesis that, on the one hand, the Father wills the death of his Son to restore humanity to paradise, and, on the other hand, the Son wills his own death without coercion from the Father. Abelard has serious difficulties with the notion that the Father wills the death of an innocent man. Yet Anselm affirms that the Father does not actually rejoice in his Son's suffering, but in his Son's own choice to suffer for us. Anselm's broader Trinitarian assumption is that Jesus' uncoerced human will is one with his divine will,

---

42. Significantly, the Definition of Faith drawn at Constantinople III understands Apollinaris and Severus (a monophysite) as "endeavouring craftily to destroy the perfection of the incarnation of the same our Lord Jesus Christ, our God, by blasphemously representing his flesh endowed with a rational soul as devoid of will and operation." *Definition of Faith* (NPNF² 14:344); on Severus's theology, see Davis, *The First Seven Ecumenical Councils*, 212–25.

43. *Definition of Faith* (NPNF² 14:345); cf. Pope Agathos's letter read at the fourth session of the Council, where he writes, "[W]e say that as the same our Lord Jesus Christ has two natures so also he has two natural wills and operations, to wit, the divine and the human: the divine will and operation he has in common with the coessential Father from all eternity: the human, he has received from us, taken with our nature in time." Agathos's *Letter* (NPNF² 14:331).

and therefore, one with the will of the Father. Since there is no opposition between Christ's human and divine wills and operations, there is none between the Son's will and the Father's will either. From this Trinitarian framework, Aulén's criticism of Anselm's view as a "discontinuous divine work"—i.e., one involving both God's will and man's will—actually fails to give proper weight to Christ's active human will and work in the accomplishment of atonement. Unlike Anselm, Aulén does not see that in Christ human and divine wills are in complete harmony, "concurring most fitly in him for the salvation of the human race"—as the Definition of Faith puts it.

A Logos-oriented Christology places the union of human and divine wills in the person of Christ at the moment of the hypostatic union. An influential voice (through letters) in the deliberations at Constantinople III, Pope Agathos at one point appeals to Gregory Nazianzen on this point:

> [H]e shews that the human will of the Saviour was deified through its union with the Word, and therefore it is not contrary to God. So likewise he proves that he had a human, although deified will, and this same he had . . . as well as his divine will, which was one and the same with that of the Father.[44]

The unity of divine and human wills in the one person of the incarnate Word is predicated upon the unity of divine and human natures in him from the moment of the hypostatic union. A Spirit-oriented Christology complements the Logos-oriented one by taking full account of the concrete and distinct moments (*kairoi*) of the incarnate Word's life and work in which the Spirit indwells and empowers him to accomplish the will of God the Father. A synthesis will have to point to the fact that, just as there is no opposition in the person of the Son between his human will and operations (in which the Spirit fully participates) and his divine will and operations, so also there is none between the divine Son's will and those of the Father and the Spirit as they work together for us and for our salvation.

In the Christ-event, the unity of wills *ad extra* points to the unity of wills *ad intra* but without neglecting the differentiation among the persons. The identity of Jesus and the Logos and the non-identity of Jesus and the Holy Spirit remain. The Logos becomes flesh, the Spirit indwells the incarnate Logos, and the Father sends them into the world. In their differentiated unity of will and operation, we may say that the Father loves the Son in the Spirit and the Son reciprocates this love in the Spirit. There is, as it were, a harmony of wills and works founded in their common love for us that finds its immanent ground in their love for one another.

---

44. Agathos's *Letter* (*NPNF*² 14:335).

In begetting his Son, the Father gives everything he is and has to the Son in complete openness. In his being begotten from the Father, the Son is and receives the Father's self-givenness in total openness as well. As Ladaria puts it, the Son is "the total response to the Father's self-communication, the total openness without possible closure, pure relation to the Father of whom he is the original Thou, complete reflection of his glory."[45] The Holy Spirit is the one in whom the Father and the Son are open to and for each other. The Holy Spirit is the hypostasized love, in whom God the Father and the Son mutually love one another and in whom their common love finds its perfection and reaches its fulfillment. If the Son always exists in relation to the Father in the Spirit, then the incarnate Son "neither puts nor is able to put any obstacle to the action of the Holy Spirit in him . . . [T]herefore, in the man Jesus the Holy Spirit finds no opposition in its sanctifying action."[46] To sum up, the dynamic and ecstatic presence of the Spirit of the Father in the incarnate Son's human actions for us has its eternal ground in the divine Son's loving response in the Spirit to the Father's inexhaustible love for him in the Spirit.

THE HOLY SPIRIT IN THE INCARNATE CHRIST: A LUTHERAN CONTRIBUTION TOWARDS THE COMPLEMENTARITY OF LOGOS AND SPIRIT CHRISTOLOGIES

In this section, I argue that Lutheran theology contributes towards the complementarity of Logos and Spirit Christologies by bringing its strong Logos-oriented Eastern-Alexandrian approach to Christology into dialogue with its less developed Western scholastic heritage. I will show how Lutheran Christology provides building blocks, in its appropriation of Western scholastic categories, for reflecting on the Holy Spirit in the humanity of Christ and what such presence and activity means for Christ, salvation in him, and the life of the saints. In this effort towards constructing a Spirit Christology from the Western scholastic side of Lutheran Christology, I will argue for a *genus pneumatikon* or *genus habitualis*, namely, a way of speaking about the presence of the Spirit in Christ that complements his identity as the incarnate Logos. In the framework of the *genus habitualis*, the Holy Spirit will surface as the link between the life of Christ and the life of Christians, providing a bridge between Christology and ecclesiology. I will suggest ways

---

45. Ladaria, "Cristología del Logos y cristología del Espíritu," 358; translation mine.
46. Ibid.

Christians can speak of the Holy Spirit in their lives in a Christ-shaped way, namely, in terms of how the Holy Spirit shapes their lives after Christ's own life. Our proposal will prepare the way for the next three chapters, where I explore more in depth the productivity of a Spirit Christology for reflection on the Christian practices of proclamation, prayer, and sanctification.

The Spirit after Christ, the Spirit in Christ

When we speak about the Holy Spirit, our first inclination is to speak of him as the one who leads us to faith in Christ through the preaching of the gospel. When we make that confession, the Holy Spirit is placed *after* Christ, so that only after the work of Christ is finished, we proceed to speak of the Spirit's proclamation and application to us of Christ's redeeming work.[47] This is the movement of the Creed and the Catechism that begins with God the Father who creates us, then speaks of the Son who redeems us, and ends with the Holy Spirit who sanctifies us. It is at this point, as the third person in the order of the divine missions, of Trinitarian self-giving and salvation, that the Holy Spirit descends and comes to us freely and out of love through the Word and baptism in order to bring to us the benefits of Christ's redeeming work.

What immediately follows, logically speaking, is the order of faith and its fruits, of prayer and works. Here the Holy Spirit is first in the order of salvation history, making us sons of God by creating and sustaining faith in Christ, who in turn brings us to know God as our gracious Father. In the same Spirit, we have access to God the Father in prayer through his Son, in whose name we are bold to pray "Abba" and "Our Father, who art in heaven." The same Spirit showers us with gifts for service in church and world. The Holy Spirit who comes to us from the Father through the Son in baptism and the Word brings us through the Son to the Father by faith and in prayer. The same Spirit shapes Christ in us to serve our neighbor in thanksgiving to God for his gifts in Christ. The descending pattern of the Trinitarian missions and the eucharistic pattern of our Trinitarian adoption has served the church well, highlighting the mercy of God in his giving to us without any merit on our part as well as the church's reception of these

---

47. "The work is finished and completed; Christ has acquired and won the treasure for us by his sufferings, death, and resurrection, etc. But if the work remained hidden so that no one knew it, it would have been all in vain, all lost. In order that this treasure might not remain buried but be put to use and enjoyed, God has caused the Word to be published and proclaimed, in which he has given the Holy Spirit to offer and apply to us this treasure, this redemption." LC, Third Article, 38–39, in *BC*, 436; cf. 61–62, 64, p. 439.

gifts by faith and her response to the same in prayer, praise, thanksgiving, and good works.[48]

Oddly enough, placing the Spirit *after* Christ in order for the Spirit to bring us *to* Christ does have the tendency to disconnect the Spirit from the life of Christ. We speak of the Spirit after Christ, but do not see the Spirit already *in* Christ, in Christ's own human life and history. The church fathers represent a bit of a mixed bag when it comes to reflection on the active role of the Spirit *in* Christ. As we have shown before, Athanasius sees both ambiguity and promise in the teaching of the pneumatological dimensions of the life of Christ. On the one hand, he is against reducing Christ to a *mere* man in whom the Spirit dwells. He is aware of the adoptionist danger, prominently displayed in the Arian argument that the anointing of the Son is an instance of the elevation of his humanity to godhood on the basis of his works, virtue, or obedience. The Arian adoptionist principle is the other side of its ontological subordinationism. For the Arians, Jesus is a son adopted by grace (or by the Spirit) at the Jordan in order to be exalted or deified as a creature at the resurrection. Perhaps it should not surprise us, therefore, that no reference is made to the baptism of Jesus in the Nicene Creed, written in the historical context of the Arian controversy. The place of the Spirit *in* Christ had become a hot potato.

On the other hand, Athanasius can link Christian baptism to the anointing of the Son at the Jordan. Against the Arians, Athanasius prefers to speak of the Son, considered as God, as the giver of the Spirit.[49] Considered as man, the Son does have the Spirit from the first moment of the incarnation. While Athanasius does not reflect on the nature of the distinction between the Son's possession of the Spirit from the incarnation and the Father's later anointing of the Son with the same Spirit at the baptism, he does want to show the ecclesiological trajectory of the Jordan event. The significance of the baptism at Jordan is not ultimately about what the event means for the one who is Son by nature, but rather what it means for those who are made sons by grace or adoption through the waters of Christian baptism.[50] In making the move towards an ecclesial anointing grounded in Christ's

---

48. Reflecting on Romans 12, the Lutheran confessors speak of eucharistic sacrifices as "the work of the Holy Spirit within us" or "spiritual worship," defining it as follows: "In summary, the worship of the New Testament is spiritual, that is, it is the righteousness of faith in the heart and the fruits of faith." Ap, XXIV, 26-27, in *BC*, 262-63; more specifically, eucharistic sacrifices (or "sacrifices or praise") include "the preaching of the gospel, faith, prayer, thanksgiving, confession, the afflictions of the saints, and indeed, all the good works of the saints." Ap XXIV, 25, p. 262.

49. Athanasius, *First Discourse* 5.15 (*NPNF*² 4:315); cf. ibid., 12.46 (*NPNF*² 4:333).

50. Ibid., 12.47-48 (*NPNF*² 4:334-35).

anointing, Athanasius appeals not only to the soteriological significance of the incarnation of the Word as such (that is to say, seeing the incarnation as the divine *Word's* glorification or deification of his own flesh). He also appeals to the Holy Spirit's presence and activity in the incarnate Word in view of the Word's giving of the Holy Spirit to us. Similarly, for Athanasius, it is not enough to affirm that the Son was exalted according to his humanity so that humanity might be exalted (deified) in or through the Son. The Holy Spirit has yet to be located in the life of Christ, in the mystery of the incarnation broadly conceived as the whole life of Christ, so that we might be exalted in and through Christ. How then is man exalted through Christ? How is man incorporated into the mystery of Christ's salvation? The Holy Spirit plays a critical role in salvation history. The answer, for Athanasius, is that the Son is anointed with the Holy Spirit as man so that man might be anointed with the same Holy Spirit in baptism.[51] There is a pneumatological trajectory in Athanasius's teaching on the Logos's deification of his flesh and all flesh. The incarnate Logos receives the Spirit in order to give us the Spirit.

Towards a *Genus Habitualis* or *Genus Pneumatikon*: A Contemporary Lutheran Contribution Towards Complementarity

Does Lutheran theology have a place for speaking about the Holy Spirit in the life of Christ? That may not appear to be the case at first, given the strong Alexandrian Logos-oriented approach to Lutheran Christology. For instance, Martin Chemnitz's (1522–1586) classic Lutheran treatment of Christology speaks of the person of Christ in terms of the communication of attributes (*communicatio idiomatum*). The framework of Chemnitz's presentation is that of a creedal Logos Christology, which asks how the divine and human natures relate to one another and to the one person of the Logos. Three types or kinds (*genera*) of relations are posited.[52] The *genus idiomaticum* and the *genus apotelesmaticum* point out that divine and human attributes can be ascribed to the whole person of the Son and thus applied to what the Son does in all his works. We are allowed to say things like, "the divine Logos was born and died for us," or "the man Jesus, who was born and crucified, is our Lord and God." Furthermore, chief among the Lutheran *genera* is the

---

51. "And when were we enabled to receive It [i.e., the Holy Spirit], except when the Word became man? . . . We had not been redeemed and highly exalted, had not He who exists in the form of God taken a servant's form . . . no otherwise should we have partaken the Spirit and been sanctified, but that the Giver of the Spirit, the Word Himself, had spoken of Himself as anointed with the Spirit for us." Ibid., 12.50 (*NPNF*² 4:336).

52. Chemnitz, *The Two Natures in Christ*, 157–69.

genus maiestaticum, which teaches that the divine Logos communicates his divine majesty, power, and glory to and through his assumed human nature. We are allowed to say things like, "the Son of God gives us life and salvation through his flesh, through his body and blood, in his Supper." For such statements, Lutheran Christology draws from the Alexandrian tradition represented by Cyril of Alexandria (d. 444) in his teaching against Nestorius (d. c. 451). All these christological statements or *genera* are ultimately meant to assure Christians that, in accordance with God's promises, none other than the divine Son has taken upon himself our humanity, and even now works in and through the same, in order to save us.[53]

It is difficult at first to see how the Holy Spirit may be located in an account that focuses on the two natures (and communication of attributes) in the one person of the Son. Where does another person of the Trinity fit into this system? We may recall how Athanasius, in the framework of what we now call a Nicene Christology, can speak of the divine Word who becomes man so that man might be deified (saved). And yet, as we saw earlier, Athanasius can be read as allowing for the Holy Spirit's mediation in our salvation by making our adoption as sons of God dependent upon our reception in baptism of the same Spirit with whom Word was anointed from the time of his incarnation. A foundation is laid out for us in the Alexandrian tradition, which Athanasius and Cyril represent, for developing what may be called the pneumatological dimensions of a Logos Christology.

While acknowledging the Alexandrian heritage of Lutheran Christology and the potential of such tradition for reflecting on the place of the Spirit in Christ, Chemnitz's most promising framework for situating the Holy Spirit in his christological presentation comes from another source, namely, the Western scholastic tradition and its category of habitual gifts.[54] Chemnitz speaks of "supernatural gifts" (*hyperphysica*) that inhere in the as-

---

53. For our purposes, we need not go into the well-known historical and theological link between Lutheran Christology and its doctrine of the Lord's Supper. For a brief historical account, see FC, SD VIII, 1–5, in *BC*, 616. "Through his divine omnipotence Christ can be present in his body, which he has placed at the right hand of the majesty and power of God, wherever he wishes, especially where he has promised his presence in his Word, such as in the Holy Supper." FC, SD VIII, 92 in *BC*, 633–34.

54. One can argue that there is a pneumatic element in Alexandrian Christology that is underdeveloped in Lutheran Christology, along the lines of Athanasius's (and later on, Cyril of Alexandria's) reflection on the soteriological significance of the baptism of Christ. For the purposes of this chapter, however, we will only focus on the underdeveloped Western side of Lutheran Christology. For a discussion of the functions of the Eastern (Alexandrian) and Western (scholastic) paradigms in Lutheran Christology vis-à-vis Reformed approaches to Christology and the question of Christ's presence in the Supper, see Sánchez, "More Promise Than Ambiguity: Pneumatological Christology as a Model for Ecumenical Engagement," 198–207.

sumed humanity of Christ.[55] These supernatural gifts are neither the proper human attributes Christ shares with the rest of humanity (e.g., being born, dying) nor the essential attributes of his divine nature (e.g., omnipotence, omnipresence). Therefore, strictly speaking, these supernatural gifts fit neither in a discussion of the *genus idiomaticum* or *apotelesmaticum* (since these *genera* refer to human attributes proper, not to supernatural gifts that inhere in the human nature), nor in a discussion of the *genus maiestaticum* proper (since this *genus* speaks ultimately of divine or essential attributes, not only supernatural gifts, communicated to the assumed human nature).[56]

At times, Chemnitz speaks of these supernatural gifts as the created effects of the Logos's divine majesty—instead of uncreated attributes of his divine majesty as such—that inhere in or shine through his assumed humanity. The category of "created and finite gifts" (Lat. *gratuita dona & finita*) functions as a way to distinguish qualities in Christ's human nature that he shares with the saints from those "essential, uncreated, and infinite attributes of the Deity" (Lat. *essentialia increata & infinita Divinitatis Idiomata*) that are communicated only to his human nature.[57] At times, and most significantly, instead of using the language of the created "effects of the Deity" (Lat. *effectus Deitatis*) on display in Christ's assumed human nature, Chemnitz speaks of these supernatural gifts by referring to scriptural texts that point to the Holy Spirit's activity in Christ's life.[58] While Chemnitz does not do so explicitly,

---

55. For this section, I have also consulted the 1653 edition of *De Duabis Naturis in Christo*.

56. Chemnitz distinguishes the discussion of supernatural gifts inherent in Christ's humanity from the *genus apotelesmaticum*: "But under this third category [i.e., the *genus maiestaticum*] the human nature shares with the divine in the works of Christ, or cooperates with it, not only with its own natural powers and activities, as in the second *genus* [i.e., the *genus apotelesmaticum*], but also with those supernatural gifts which it has received from the hypostatic union and possesses because they have been communicated to it." Chemnitz, *The Two Natures in Christ*, 246; but Chemnitz also distinguishes the discussion of supernatural (infused) gifts from the communication of Christ's divine majesty to his assumed humanity (the *genus maiestaticum* proper), arguing that "these infused gifts are not actually the essential attributes of the divine nature. Rather, they are His workings outside the divine nature which are infused into the human nature of Christ in such a way that they inhere in it, as they say in the schools, formally, habitually, and subjectively." Ibid., 248.

57. Ibid., 247.

58. Texts include Luke 2:40: "The boy grew and gained in strength in the Spirit and was filled with wisdom, and the grace of God was upon Him" (cf. Luke 2:52), and Isaiah 11:1-2: "The Spirit of the Lord rests on the Branch of Jesse, the Spirit of wisdom and understanding, the Spirit of council and strength, or power, the Spirit of knowledge and the fear of the Lord." Chemnitz, *The Two Natures in Christ*, 249; "The other things which are said, wherein the Messiah is described as being anointed above His fellows (Ps. 45:7), anointed with the Spirit (Is. 61:1), giver of the Spirit (John 3:34), also may

his use of the distinction between uncreated (essential) divine properties and created (finite) gifts may be used, in a broader Trinitarian framework, to hold a corresponding distinction between the Logos's own presence and activity in and through his assumed humanity (Logos Christology) *and* the Holy Spirit's presence and activity in the same humanity (Spirit Christology).

On the one hand, a proper distinction between the Logos and the Holy Spirit in a discussion of Christology serves to maintain the integrity of the personal union. Only the Logos becomes incarnate. There is no incarnation of the Holy Spirit in Christ. Moreover, and more importantly, because the incarnation or hypostatic union is unique to the Logos and thus unrepeatable (the Son alone is the *unigenitus*, the only-begotten), his essential divine attributes are not communicated or transferable to the saints who are sons by adoption or grace. On the other hand, the scholastic category of created grace or gift, if complemented with the uncreated Holy Spirit's presence and activity in Christ, has the potential to unpack the pneumatological aspects of the mystery of the incarnation by referring to the indwelling and gifts of the Spirit in Christ's humanity.

The scholastic distinction between the Logos's unique communication of essential divine attributes to his humanity over against the created effects that follow from such union remains useful to distinguish between Christ and the rest of the saints who also have gifts. Yet the same distinction does not seem to account adequately for those biblical texts about the Holy Spirit that Chemnitz presents as narratives for describing the supernatural gifts that inhere in the Logos's human nature. How these Spirit-oriented texts may fit or not in Chemnitz's scholastic system requires some thought. In a broader Trinitarian perspective, for instance, the notion of created grace or finite gifts has its limitations because the presence of the Holy Spirit in Christ cannot be spoken ultimately in terms of the Logos's created effects in his human nature. There are at least two reasons for this contention. First, the Holy Spirit is a divine person, not the created effect of the Logos's divine majesty in his assumed humanity. Second, created effects are in any case common to all three persons of the Trinity, whose works in creation are indivisible (Lat. *opera ad extra indivisa sunt*). Therefore, the scholastic category of created and finite effects does not yet allow for an account that distinguishes and relates the persons of the Trinity according to what is proper to each (*proprium*) in the mystery of the incarnation. Because of these two special considerations, the scholastic language concerning the Logos's created effects in his assumed humanity must give room to the biblical reality

---

be correctly understood of both the whole fullness of the Deity and of all His power ... These statements also apply to the powers, characteristics, or gifts which have been conferred upon Christ's human nature." Ibid., 250.

of the indwelling of the uncreated person of the Holy Spirit itself in Christ's own humanity. The gifts of the Spirit may still be seen as created and finite, but not the Spirit himself. When the Scriptures speak of the place of the Spirit in the life of Christ, we should reduce our discussion neither to a general effective causality of the one God in the assumed humanity of the Logos that makes no personal distinctions between the Logos and the Spirit, nor to a discussion of created gifts that does not explicitly assume the presence of the uncreated Spirit in the humanity of the Son. Instead, we must take into full account the weight Scripture gives to the work of the Holy Spirit in the life of the incarnate Logos.

Our move to rehabilitate slightly Chemnitz's use of the concept of supernatural gifts as created effects of the Logos in his human nature in order to allow for the place of the Holy Spirit as a person in its own right in the humanity of the person of the Logos does not in any way take away from Chemnitz's work. Rather, our critical and constructive appropriation of his work shows how he offers us a useful framework and building blocks to situate the Holy Spirit *in* Christ, his life and work. We learn that a Spirit Christology in the Lutheran dogmatic tradition ought to function within the framework of a creedal Logos Christology, and thus hold to the ontological identity of Jesus and the Logos and by extension to the non-identity of Jesus and the Holy Spirit. We also learn that Lutheran Christology, even if Alexandrian in its inspiration and main themes and development, can also be approached from a Western angle. In particular, Chemnitz assumes and appropriates the Western scholastic distinction between the grace of union (*gratia unionis*), a synonym for the personal union, and habitual grace (*gratia habitualis*), which in turn deals with the special holiness of the Logos in his assumed humanity.[59] Such a Lutheran appropriation of the Western tradition allows room for speaking of the created or finite gifts that inhere in Christ's human nature "habitually" (*habitualiter*) more specifically in terms of the Holy Spirit's work in the sanctification of the assumed humanity.[60] The

---

59. For Thomas's position, see *ST* 3a, q. 6, a. 6; similarly, Chemnitz locates the Logos's communication of supernatural gifts to his assumed humanity as an effect of the hypostatic union, in much the same manner that the scholastics see the *gratia habitualis* as logically following the *gratia unionis*, In order to get at this causative relation, Chemnitz places the teaching of habitual gifts under the *genus maeistaticum*, even though the Logos's communication of created gifts to his humanity is not the same as the communication his uncreated, essential, or divine attributes to the same. See Chemnitz, *The Two Natures in Christ*, 246.

60. "And the Son of God assumed that individual unit (*massa*) [body] from the flesh and blood of Mary, which the Holy Spirit in the act of conception so sanctified and purified from the whole ruin of sin that that which was born of Mary was holy (Luke 1:35); for He did not know sin (2 Cor 5:21); He was separated from sinners (Heb. 7:26);

Alexandrian side of Lutheran Christology, under the *genus maeistaticum*, in principle highlights the Logos's sanctification, exaltation, or glorification of his own humanity through his divine majesty and power.[61] The Western scholastic side of Lutheran Christology is especially conducive to portraying the incarnate Logos as the receiver of the Spirit's holiness for our sake.[62]

If, according to our argument thus far, Chemnitz's comments on the habitual grace or supernatural gifts that inhere in Christ's humanity can be read through a pneumatological lens, one is still left with some questions concerning the usefulness of such a claim. What do we gain by drawing out a pneumatological path in an already complex, Logos-oriented christological matrix? Other than the productivity of the category for distinguishing ontologically between the personal union and the presence of the uncreated Spirit and its created gifts in Christ's humanity, there are at least two other arguably weightier reasons that are discernible in Chemnitz's use of scholastic categories. One is Chemnitz's soteriological interest. Ultimately, the habitual grace or holiness of Christ properly disposes the assumed humanity for the divine Logos to do his work in and through the same. There is a sense in which the *gratia habitualis* serves all the other *genera*, especially the *genus maiestaticum*, by making the assumed human nature a proper "instrument" for the Logos's work of salvation on our behalf.[63] To put the same argument in pneumatological terms, we may say that, for us and for our salvation, the divine Logos allows the Holy Spirit to sanctify and perfect his humanity, to make it holy, so that it may be the Logos's instrument of salvation for all

---

and He is like His brothers in all things but without sin (Heb. 2:17)." Chemnitz, *The Two Natures in Christ*, 57 (cf. 52–53, 56).

61. "Christ did not receive this majesty to which he was exalted according to his humanity only after he rose from the dead and ascended into heaven, but he received it already when he was conceived in his mother's womb and became a human being and the divine and human natures were united personally with each other." FC, SD VIII, 13, in *BC*, 618; "This is the most comforting and salutary exchange, that the Son of God has received from us a human nature and sanctified and blessed and exalted and glorified it in His own person." Chemnitz, *The Two Natures in Christ*, 55.

62. "But He [i.e., the Son of God] willed to be conceived, to be developed in the womb, to leave the womb by being born, just as is the case with our natural conception and birth, with the exception that He was kept from sin by the supervention of the Holy Ghost." *The Two Natures in Christ*, 56.

63. Chemnitz asserts that "these infused gifts are not actually the essential attributes of the divine nature. Rather, they are His workings outside the divine nature which are infused into the human nature of Christ in such a way that they inhere in it, as they say in the schools, formally, habitually, and subjectively, by which the very humanity of Christ in itself and according to itself is formed and perfected, so that it can be an instrument characteristic of, suitable for, and properly disposed for the deity, through which and in communion with and in cooperation with which the divine power of the Logos can exercise and carry out the workings of His divine majesty." Ibid., 248.

humanity. In biblical terms, we may say that the Son's sanctification by the Spirit from conception, as well as his anointing with the Spirit at the Jordan, are completely oriented towards the Servant's obedience unto death and exaltation for us. At this point, the ontological argument about whether the Logos needs the Holy Spirit for his work becomes secondary. The greater issue is the soteriological point, namely, that the divine Logos has chosen to do his work of salvation in, with, and through his humanity in which the Holy Spirit dwells and is active.[64] That is how the Logos chooses to be God for us. From a Trinitarian angle, the Son and the Holy Spirit appear as inseparable companions in the Father's saving work.

Christ and His Saints

There is a second benefit in our appropriating of Chemnitz's exploration of Christ's habitual gifts. Chemnitz wants to distinguish not only between the divine Logos's self-giving to us through his humanity, but also between the presence of supernatural gifts in Christ and the presence of such gifts in Christians. Otherwise stated, the category of habitual gifts deals with the special and unique holiness of Christ in distinction from the holiness of the saints.[65] Chemnitz speaks of supernatural created gifts that inhere in the Logos's humanity, and thus are not the common or proper attributes of human nature (those shared typically by all humans). Since the Fall into

---

64. In my proposal, a *genus habitualis* or *pneumatikon* functions within the *genus maiestaticum* and will stress the soteriological function of the Holy Spirit's role in the humanity of the Logos. In Reformed theology, the mediating role of the Spirit in the humanity of Christ is posited, but typically in such a way that the Lutheran *genus maiestaticum* is rejected because it is perceived to deny Christ's full humanity. The Lutherans stress the soteriological point of the *genera* more than the anthropological one. For Reformed studies, see Owen, *The Holy Spirit*, 160–62; Spence, "Christ's Humanity and Ours," 74–97; Gunton, "Two Dogmas Revisited," 359–76; and McCormack, *For Us and For Our Salvation*, 19 (cf. 36).

65. "But the Scholastics were correct and Scriptural when they said that when Christ according to His human nature was anointed above His fellows [Ps. 45:7] . . . then the divine nature of the Logos by His divine power . . . bestowed and poured out upon His assumed human nature, to which He was hypostatically united, special, spiritual, heavenly, and divine gifts, not only particular gifts with definite measure in certain number and in measured degrees, and limited as in the case of the saints, but rather all divine gifts, in total fullness, in superabundant supply, in the highest and most absolute perfection which can be bestowed upon a created substance in itself, beyond every name, number, and measure." Chemnitz, *The Two Natures in Christ*, 248; see also FC, SD VIII, 72–74, in *BC*, 630 (esp. where the Lutheran confessors note that "God the Father has given his Spirit to Christ, his beloved Son, according to his assumed humanity . . . in such a way that he has not, like other saints, received the gifts of the Spirit with limits").

sin, holiness or sanctification is not a proper attribute that humans share. Christ is distinct from the rest of the saints, not only in that he is God, but also in that the Holy Spirit sanctified his humanity and made it holy from the moment of the personal union, making it not only "a" but "the" suitable instrument for our salvation.

Christ may be seen as having a special holiness not only because he is the divine Logos but also because he bears the Holy Spirit in his humanity like no other saint.[66] Whereas the distinction between the presence of the Spirit in Christ and the saints may be seen as a distinction in degree, the Logos's communication of his divine majesty to his assumed humanity makes him ontologically distinct from the saints in whom the Spirit dwells.[67] A Logos Christology that highlights the *genus maestaticum* is more useful to speak of an ontological difference between the one who is Son by nature and the sons who are adopted by grace (or by the Spirit). In pneumatological terms, however, it is enough to show that Christ is not only the definitive bearer of the Spirit but also the giver of the Spirit—along with the Spirit's holiness and gifts—to the saints.[68]

We now arrive at another soteriological benefit of exploring the place of the Spirit in Christ under the category of habitual gifts. In short, the Logos receives and bears the Spirit for us in a unique manner in order to give the Spirit to us by grace. Christ is the *unigenitus*, the only-begotten Son of God, but also the *primogenitus* (the firstborn among many) as the unique eschatological bearer and giver of the Spirit of God. The Spirit who comes to us *after* Christ is ours because Christ first received that Spirit *in* his human life and history for our sake. This ecclesiological trajectory of the mystery

---

66. "Therefore, Christ, according to His human nature and insofar as this nature is personally united with the Logos, differs from the other saints not only by reason of His gifts, which by comparison excel the others in number and degree, but also by reason of the union He differs totally from the saints." Chemnitz, *The Two Natures in Christ*, 263.

67. Chemnitz argues that "in the human nature of Christ because of the union there are not only natural attributes which result from the constitution of human nature, nor are there only particular and finite gifts which inhere formally in the humanity and are more numerous and more excellent in degree than those which come from the indwelling of the Holy Spirit in the saints, but also because of this union the human nature in Christ not only has the whole fullness of the deity dwelling in it personally, but at the same time, according to the Scripture, it receives the divine majesty which has been given and communicated to it along with divine power, wisdom, life, and other divine qualities." Ibid., 83–84.

68. Chemnitz does not develop Christ's identity as the giver of the Spirit to the saints, even though in various places he acknowledges that the saints also receive from God habitual gifts. As an example, Chemnitz writes: "Although gifts are conferred upon the other saints as God distributes to each the measure of faith (Rom. 12:6), yet to Christ alone is the Spirit not given by measure (John 3:34)." Ibid., 247–50.

of the presence of the Spirit in Christ is not fully developed in Chemnitz's presentation, but the building blocks are available. If the Spirit whom Christ gives to us is none other than the Spirit whom he bears, then, the saints have no other way to speak of the Spirit in their lives except in terms of the mystery of Christ's own life and work in the same Spirit. The implications of this thesis can be worked out in a number of directions.

One is the sacramental trajectory that we have shown already in Athanasius's discourse against the Arians, in which the Son is said to receive the sanctification and anointing of the Spirit in his humanity in order to sanctify us through the same Spirit in the waters of our baptism. One could also show how the same Spirit who is inseparably united to Christ in his flesh is given to us with its gifts through Christ's own body and blood in the Supper.[69] Another fruitful trajectory is the kerygmatic one. Under the rubric of Christ as the bearer and giver of the Spirit, one could show that the Son who receives the Holy Spirit without measure from the Father in order to proclaim words of eternal life also hands over the same Spirit to the disciples so that they might absolve people of their sins.[70] Yet another trajectory deals with the sanctification of the Christian. In a view of sanctification that sees the Christian life in terms of faithfulness and service, the same Spirit with whom Christ was anointed by the Father to be the obedient Son and suffering Servant is also given to the disciples of Christ so that their lives in the Spirit might reflect their Lord's faithfulness to the Father and service to the neighbor. In all these trajectories mentioned above, the same operative principle is at work, namely, the Spirit in whom Christ lived forms Christ in his saints. While a Logos Christology lends itself to focusing on the discontinuity between the Son and the sons (natural sonship in contrast to adoptive sonship), a Spirit Christology lends itself to highlighting the continuity between the presence of the Spirit in the Son and the sons.[71]

69. According to the distinction between the presence of the Logos *and* of the Holy Spirit in the Logos's assumed humanity, Lutheran Christology can speak both to the communication of the Logos's own saving power through his body and blood in his Supper (under the *genus maiestaticum*), as well as to the Logos's communication of the Holy Spirit to us in his Supper (under the category of habitual or supernatural gifts). Lutherans are not against the reception of the Holy Spirit through the Supper (spiritual eating), but against the denial of the oral reception of Christ's own body and blood in the Supper. For a discussion of the twofold eating of Christ's body in the Supper, see FC, SD VII, 61–72, in *BC*, 604–6.

70. Although briefly, the Lutheran confessors suggestively place the teaching of law and gospel in the context of Christ's bearing and sending of the Spirit through the Word. See FC, SD V, 11, in *BC*, 583.

71. The issue of discontinuity-continuity between Christ's humanity and ours is an area of Lutheran-Reformed dialogue that deserves attention. Contemporary Reformed revivals of Owen's and Irving's theology focus on the usefulness of their Spirit

Gathering the benefits of a full recovery of the place of the Holy Spirit *in Christ*, a Lutheran Christology in ecumenical perspective can bridge contributions in the East and the West for the sake of the church at large. I have shown that a Lutheran Christology holds promising building blocks that make room for such a proposal. In particular, Chemnitz's use of the scholastic category of habitual, finite, or created gifts and its relation to pneumatological references in his presentation of Christology suggests that there is an underdeveloped Western side to Lutheran Christology that can serve to complement its classic Alexandrian approach to the person and work of Christ.

In the Lutheran dogmatic tradition, the pneumatological dimensions of the mystery of Christ and their significance for the church's life in the Spirit of Christ will have to be explored further in the framework of a Logos (two-natures) Christology. I contend that such an investigation will benefit from a consideration of what I call a fourth *genus*, which we may aptly label the *genus habitualis* or *genus pneumatikon*.[72] While such *genus* of the Spirit in Christ may be categorized under the *genus maiestaticum* because it assumes the hypostatic union, it may also function in its own right to explore person of the Holy Spirit's presence and activity in and through the Logos's human life and history in the economy of God's salvation. At a time when pneumatology has moved more in the ambiguous direction of the Spirit's general presence in the world and thus away from its center in Christ and its ecclesial trajectory, a *genus habitualis* or *genus pneumatikon* can give Christians a firmer christological framework and ground to speak of the movement of the person and work of the Holy Spirit in and from Christ for the sake of the world. A fourth *genus* will also give us a firmer conceptual christological ground for looking into the implications of Christ's identity as receiver, bearer, and giver of the Spirit for Trinitarian theology, Christology and soteriology, ecclesiology and sacramentology, and the Christian life or sanctification.[73] We have already explored the contributions of a Spirit

---

Christologies for framing a christological anthropology. See Spence, "Christ's Humanity and Ours," 74–97, and Gunton, "Two Dogmas Revisited," 359–76.

72. For my initial proposal of a fourth *genus*, see Sánchez, "Pneumatology," 137–39.

73. I have explored the implications of a Spirit Christology in various areas. For an early attempt at the productivity of the model to foster the task of missions, see Sánchez, "A Missionary Theology of the Holy Spirit," 28–40; for the usefulness of the model for engaging ecumenical questions concerning the *filioque* controversy (between the Orthodox East and the Catholic West), the mode of Christ's presence in the Lord's Supper (Lutheran-Reformed controversy), and the question of authority in the church (among various confessions), see Sánchez, "More Promise Than Ambiguity"; for a monograph that deals with the implications of a Spirit Christology for Trinitarian theology, anthropology, creation, Christology, and ecclesiology, see my book *Pneumatología*; for a work that explores the implications of a Spirit Christology for models of the Christian life or

Christology in some of these areas, and now we have laid yet a stronger foundation to complete our investigation by asking how our model shapes our view of the Christian life in the Spirit. Sketching a fruitful Christ-centered pneumatology for the church will benefit from the wells of a robust Spirit-oriented or pneumatological Christology. In this effort, not only will we find the Holy Spirit in the mission of Christ, but also Christ in the mission of the Holy Spirit.

Summary

A synthesis of Logos and Spirit Christologies must look at the distinctions and relations operative in the Father's twofold self-communication in the persons of the Son and the Holy Spirit to Christ's humanity. I have attempted to accomplish this goal by appealing to the complementarity of aspects under four categories. These are the distinction and relation between 1) the identity of Jesus and the Logos and the non-identity of Jesus and the Holy Spirit, 2) the orders of knowledge and being, 3) the human and divine wills in the one person of Christ, and 4) the incarnation of Christ and the indwelling of the Spirit *in* Christ. My proposal gives full weight to the defining role of the Holy Spirit in the identity of the Son (in his being and acts), in the economy of salvation and at the level of the immanent Trinity, but without identifying the Logos's presence in the assumed humanity with the Holy Spirit's, or inverting the missional and processional logical priority of the Son over the Holy Spirit.

Our proposal highlights the place of the Holy Spirit in the incarnate Logos without overlooking the harmony of natural wills in the person of Jesus Christ with the unity of will among the divine persons. There is, therefore, no opposition of wills between what the Son accomplishes in and through his humanity, and what the Father accomplishes by the power of the Holy Spirit in and through his incarnate Son. Finally, I offered a contemporary Lutheran ecumenical proposal that brings together the concerns of Logos- and Spirit-oriented Christologies, grounded respectively in the Eastern-Alexandrian and Western scholastic traditions, arguing particularly for the productivity of a *genus habitualis* or *genus pneumatikon* for exploring the ontological, soteriological, and ecclesiological trajectories of the incarnate Logos' life in the Spirit. The next three chapters explore three of these ecclesiological trajectories, showing how a recovery of the Spirit in Christ shapes how we view and engage in proclamation, prayer, and holiness.

---

sanctification, see my book *Teología de la santificación*.

7

Preaching Jesus in the Spirit
Pneumatological Christology as a Lens for Proclamation

THUS FAR I HAVE argued for a full rediscovery and appropriation of the role of the Spirit of God in the life and work of Jesus as a theological complement to classic Logos-oriented approaches to Christology, atonement theories, and Trinitarian theology. In the next three chapters, I look at the implications of a Spirit Christology for three practices in the Christian life—namely, proclamation, prayer, and sanctification. In this chapter, I focus on proclamation and its function in the life of the church. I argue that the story of Jesus' life in the Spirit advances preaching in the Spirit that leads sinners to conviction and liberation in Christ. Otherwise stated, I will show how a Spirit Christology offers an economic basis and trajectory that fosters cruciform proclamation—that is to say, the type of speaking that leads hearers to die and be raised with Christ. I shall preface my argument with a personal story.

Growing up in the dark about the things of God never stopped me from wearing as many eighteen-carat gold crucifixes as dear mom every so often brought home to her son. In those days, the cross served as a sort of amulet to protect the child from all harm and danger. Then, after a soccer afternoon in Panama, came that life-changing encounter with a street preacher: *¡Arrepiéntete!* (Repent!) *¡Cristo murió por tus pecados!* (Christ died for/because of your sins!)[1] *¡Pero Dios lo ha resucitado!* (But God has

---

1. The Spanish preposition "por" can point to Christ's death *in place of* sinners,

raised him from the dead!). A few straightforward messages to get across. Such words carried a higher authority than the man speaking them. I was hooked, ready to hear more. Years later, I came to realize that, for the evangelist, his mission was a matter of death and life—mine! From that moment on, the image on the crucifix became the crucified Christ against me and for me; an object around my neck had become a convicting and liberating cross in my life. The crucifix ceased to be a lifeless and static object that I wore to preserve my life from the threat of fate. Instead, the cross became a sign of a deeper and dynamic reality God had brought me into as a participant.

Christian formation took me on a journey from Pentecostalism to Roman Catholicism to Lutheranism. Yet in spite of their distinctive theological expressions and ecclesial forms of life, I realized that no tradition could claim immunity from missing the force of the cross for hearers of the word in the here-and-now. Some preached the cross as the highest model of Christian discipleship. Go and do likewise! Others portrayed the event as the greatest instance of God's identification with all who suffer. God knows your pain! In a homiletics class, a fellow seminarian eloquently explained the cross to us in the spirit of Anselm: As God, Jesus can pay the infinite price owed to the Father for our debts; as man, Jesus must take our place as debtors. Still some were hesitant to ponder on the crucified for too long and moved right on to Christ's lordship. The cross turned into an uneasy step on the path to real victory. Apart from their arguable merits as reflections on aspects of the story of Christ, none of these theological moves made me face the cross as *my* own death and way to new life in Christ—like that first time in Panama.

Gerhard Forde called for a rethinking of the function of systematic theology in relation to the task of church proclamation. He argued that theology must move beyond its usual contentment with explaining God's past deeds and advance the type of thinking that aims at the direct speaking of God's promises to people today. Using the analogy of lovers to speak of God's dealings with human beings through word and sacrament, Forde reminds us that talking about love falls short of its goal unless it leads the lover (God) and the beloved (us) to tell each other, "I love you!"[2] But how do theologians—professional or not—make the transition from explanation to proclamation? That's a lifelong task in itself. It entails an ongoing Spirit-led move, from being read (or spoken to) through Jesus' story, to being killed and made alive with the crucified and risen Christ of the story, to being self-critical of one's detached readings (or hearings) of the same. The final

---

but also to his death *because of* sinners.

2. Forde, *Theology Is for Proclamation*, 3.

self-critical stage should in turn lead to proposals for reading Jesus' story that aim at its proclamation (especially in the form of preaching) as a transforming death-and-life event.

This chapter represents in part the fruit of my personal journey to come to grips with the relevance of a Spirit Christology for the ministry of proclamation in the world. My thesis is that reading the story of "Jesus in the Spirit" facilitates "preaching in the Spirit" that aims at our being crucified and raised with Christ. First, I place my thesis in the context of a broader pastoral concern for advocating the function and use of the biblical narrative as a living spoken word from God against us and for us in the here-and-now. Second, I review some basic assumptions of classic Logos Christology and two contemporary Spirit Christologies to unmask ways in which both approaches to the life of Christ can hinder proclamation. Finally, I show that a Spirit Christology oriented towards and centered in the paschal mystery (i.e., Lent, Easter, and Pentecost), and thus leading to our own Spirit-initiated participation by grace in the mystery of Jesus' baptism (above all, through Christian baptism into Christ's death and resurrection), fosters our preaching and hearing of Jesus' story as our own present death and way to new life in him.

BEING READ BY THE STORY OF JESUS: GOD ADDRESSES AND SHAPES US THROUGH THE BIBLICAL NARRATIVE

With the arrival of modernity, Scripture increasingly became a tool to uncover past historical events and unveil universal truths rather than a living word through which God addresses human beings in their current situations to change their lives. Hans Frei's turn to the world-creating function of the biblical stories in their own right for their readers or hearers stands as a classic critique and corrective to the modern fascination with looking behind the text mainly for its historical and religious references.[3] Reading Scripture as the record or word *about* God's past deeds and eternal truths and letting Scripture read us (or speak to us) as the authoritative word *from* God today are two different ways of understanding the function and use of Scripture.

The written word informs about the past, the spoken word transforms in the present. Yet this insight seems difficult enough to get through the mind of an educated middle-class Westerner. I myself did not get it until

---

3. Frei, *The Eclipse of Biblical Narrative*.

that Sunday I invited a group of elderly Cuban immigrants to open their Bibles and join me in a study—often a synonym for an explanation—of the Gospel for the day. Not one of them did. For various reasons, not many of them could read. But they seemed so eager to listen to God's word in Jesus' story. They taught me a valuable lesson. God had brought them to church to hear the word proclaimed to them in their present situation. For Luther, both the written and spoken forms of the word are ultimately authoritative because through them the Spirit points to Jesus Christ, the enfleshed Word; but the reformer also teaches that the written word exists for the sake of the spoken one.[4] How difficult it is for the children of modernity to recall the words of Paul: "So faith comes from what is heard" (Rom 10:17).

Behind the turn to the narrative lies the assumption that the Spirit addresses human beings in every age through the biblical texts by appropriating what their authors said in the past with the goal of creating in the present a new community of people whose identity is shaped after Jesus' story.[5] How then are preachers in the church formed or shaped by their hearing of the spoken word that points to Jesus? This is a question of *being* a particular kind of theologian or hearer of the story.

How we see ourselves influences how we read or hear God's story of Jesus spoken to us in the Spirit. Following Luther, Forde distinguished theologians by the two stories that define their lives: the glory story and the cross story.[6] At any point in time, we are likely to see ourselves in the light of either story. While theologians of glory see themselves as sinners who have fallen to some degree from God's scale of perfection, theologians of the cross see themselves as sinners who in rebellion against their Creator want to reach upwards and take God's place.[7] Since the former tend to focus on their partially lost goodness and innate freedom to receive God's favor, they will not hear Jesus' story if that implies their complicity in his death and their irreversible rejection of God's mercy through him. To avoid the death of the old Adam and Eve in them, theologians of glory design strategies (theologies, readings of Jesus' story) that will make them immune to their need for repentance and forgiveness. Forde calls this self-preserving move "a defense mechanism against the cross."[8] At a passion play, they are most likely to lament and protest the fact that Jews and Romans killed their Lord.

---

4. Lotz, "Sola Scriptura: *Luther on Biblical Authority*," 262–64; on the Holy Spirit's work as preacher of Christ, see LC, Creed 37–38, in *BC*, 435–36.

5. Grenz, "The Spirit and the Word: The World-Creating Function of the Text," 362–69.

6. Forde, *On Being a Theologian of the Cross*, 4–19.

7. Forde speaks of an "upward fall." See *Theology Is for Proclamation*, 48–49.

8. Forde, *On Being a Theologian of the Cross*, 12.

From a safe distance, they judge others without becoming a part of the story themselves. How many of us have fallen into this trap?

Theologians of the cross first hear the Gospels as God's judgment upon them for rejecting his Son as the way of salvation, but finally as God's word of forgiveness and resurrection hope in Christ for all who repent of their sins against him. The language of "killing" and "making alive" expresses this convicting and liberating Spirit-orchestrated plunging of the theologian into Jesus' story.[9] Before looking for ways to foster proclamation, theologians of the cross recognize that they—along with their best works and attempts at self-preservation[10]—must first die with the crucified in the story to be made alive with the risen one of the story. At a passion play, they see that sinners like them killed their Lord, and they ask God to forgive them for oppressing his Son.

Shaped by the cross, how then do theologian-preachers use Scripture to advance the telling of Jesus' story as a death-and-life event *for others*? This is a question of *doing* theology. Gunton argues that a Spirit-mediated "logical space" exists between the biblical text and our present times, one in which "are to be found both [the theologian's] obedience of true Christian theology to the authoritative word and freedom which is the form of that obedience."[11] Theologians of the church are read or shaped by Scripture in such a way that their Spirit-given freedom to articulate God's truth in a particular context is guided by criteria, norms, or boundaries placed on them by the scriptural content.[12] The Spirit is the mediating agent that allows for the ongoing and dynamic movement from God to us through the word that points to Jesus and from us to God in response for such a gift through its faithful, articulate, and timely appropriation for our congregations.

Gunton offers an example. Although the church's confession of the scriptural witness to Jesus as true God and true man remains an authoritative norm for Christian theology, the expression of this truth in the Nicene language of *homoousios* is a free conceptual response for a particular time and place.[13] The Spirit guides the faithful reception of this norm, but also its fresh appropriation for each generation in which the church seeks to

---

9. See Ap 12.53, in *BC*, 195; cf. FC, SD 5.11, in *BC*, 583, and LC, Creed 58, in *BC*, 438; the early Lutheran theologians also show that the Holy Spirit's continuous plunging of the sinner into Jesus' story occurs through the spoken word and the sacraments (the visible word). See Ap 13.4–5, in *BC*, 219.

10. Forde notes that a theology of the cross attacks the best, not the worst, we have to offer. See Forde, *On Being a Theologian of the Cross*, 1–4, 23ff.

11. Gunton, "Using and Being Used: Scripture and Systematic Theology," 253.

12. Ibid., 255, 258–59.

13. Ibid., 253–54.

crucify and raise sinners with Christ. Otherwise stated, in every new age, theologians have to face Jesus' question, "But who do you say that I am?" (Matt 16:15). The classic answer has been "the incarnate Word." I have proposed a complementary one that points to the incarnate Son as receiver, bearer, and giver of God's Spirit. But will any of these Christological affirmations actually lead to cruciform proclamation?

BEING SELF-CRITICAL: LOGOS AND SPIRIT CHRISTOLOGIES AS HINDRANCES TO PROCLAMATION

If the written and spoken forms of the word ultimately point to the enfleshed Word, then we must at once identify this Word (Logos) with the man Jesus of Nazareth. But how? Assuming that the theologian confesses Jesus Christ as true God and true man, he/she may proceed to answer Jesus' question "from above" or "from below." As an approach "from above," the classic Logos Christology of the ecumenical Councils proceeds from the divine Logos's eternal preexistence to his assumption of a human nature at a point in time (hypostatic or personal union). What matters most in this methodology is explaining the *how* of Jesus Christ's individual inner-constitution as the God-man. In Cantalamesa's words, "the problem of the foundation of salvation (that is, how the Savior is *made*) becomes more important than the problem of the unfolding of salvation (that is, what the Savior *does*)."[14]

In classic Logos Christology, events in Jesus' life and work are interpreted through the lens of the hypostatic union and within the framework of the exchange of divine and human attributes in the one person of Christ. Oddly enough, the cross and the resurrection do not play the central role in defining Christ's identity. For instance, the crucifixion may be explained as a logical necessity to satisfy God's justice—Anselm's highest-ranked divine attribute—and on the basis of the personal union: "[Since] none but God can make and none but man ought to make [satisfaction], it is necessary for the God-man to make it."[15] Logos Christology can also speak of Jesus' glorification as a reality established at the incarnation; consequently, his glorification at and after the resurrection only confirms for (or reveals to) others the divine power he already fully possesses in his humanity through the hypostatic union.[16] In this theological framework, questions on Christ's

14. Cantalamessa, *The Holy Spirit in the Life of Jesus*, 8.

15. *Cur Deus Homo?* 2.6, 259; on the priority of God's justice over his sole compassion, see 1.12–13.

16. FC, SD 8.12–13, 23, in *BC*, 618, 620 (but see FC, SD 8.51, in *BC*, 625, for a possible qualification of this analysis).

death and resurrection are referred back to the moment of his ontological make-up as the God-man. The language of divine preexistence and incarnation frame what is said about the cross.

In the history of dogma, Logos Christology stands mainly as an apologetic approach to Jesus' question driven by a legitimate concern to protect his divine equality with God and the unity of his person against Arian and Nestorian teachings respectively. Yet it remains an ideal theology for explanation, not proclamation. By placing the weight of discourse on prior conditions that define the Word's individual identity before a discussion of his successive works for us leading to his death and resurrection, Logos Christology can give theologians of glory an excuse to avoid the cross.[17] Even such an honorable theology can become a hindrance to having the old sinner in us killed and made alive with Christ.

We can be critical of how a Logos Christology can partially eclipse the function of the cross in hearers of the word. But would a Spirit Christology do any better? A Spirit Christology that begins "from below" with the man Jesus and attempts to arrive at his divinity through a consideration of the Spirit's indwelling in him cannot claim immunity from falling into comfortable explanation. As in early Ebionite (adoptionist) Christologies, Jesus could be reduced to our greatest example of piety "in order to enhance the sanctification of man himself."[18]

Earlier on, I discussed Lampe's post-Chalcedonian Spirit Christology. Against notions of the Holy Spirit as a personal agent or divine hypostasis equal to and distinct from God, Lampe represents the liberal move to define "Spirit" more generally (or along modalist lines) as God's other-worldly (transcendent) and worldly (immanent) presence in all creatures. Without a Trinitarian commitment, Lampe argues for Jesus' divinity solely in terms of his unique possession of "Spirit" as man, leaving aside the question of Jesus' personal identity as the person of the Logos. Jesus' identity as Son is thus reduced to a consideration of the *degree* to which his bearing of Spirit makes him unique from other humans, without consideration of the contrast

---

17. In this section, I have applied Forde's critique of Christologies in which "continuity is established by going back to a Jesus either prior to or at least relatively untouched by the cross." See Forde, *Theology Is for Proclamation*, 69; Luther believed that our knowing of Christ's eternal deity apart from our knowing of the Son as the Father's revelation for us would not bother the devil. Althaus, *The Theology of Martin Luther*, 190.

18. Rosato, "Spirit Christology," 435; Luther believed that our imitation of Jesus' human piety detached from faith in him as the Father's revelation for us would not bother the devil. Althaus, *The Theology of Martin Luther*, 190; Imbelli has noted, in his critique of Haight, that a Spirit Christology centered in the Paschal mystery is critical to prevent Christianity from being "reduced to morality." Imbelli, "The New Adam," 244.

between his *substantial* sonship and our *adoptive* sonship. There is also an anthropological assumption in Lampe's proposal. Since Jesus is seen as the fullest expression of the cooperative interaction between God's Spirit and the spirit in humans, he has "such a unity of will and operation with God" that he can be called God himself in an adverbial sense, namely, in "that in all his actions the human Jesus acted divinely."[19] Jesus' being and human acts as one possessed by Spirit makes him a model or paradigm of divine self-giving and human self-transcendence that other humans can replicate. Because Jesus is truly human, Lampe argues that he must be distinct from other saints only in degree, and yet (paradoxically) in a significant manner.

A conservative Spirit Christology defines the Spirit as one person of the triune God distinct from creation but open to reaching out to creatures in freedom and love. The conservative (neo-Chalcedonian) approach distinguishes between the Logos's and the Holy Spirit's presence in Jesus, but seeks to bring them together in some Trinitarian fashion. Kasper suggests a synthesis, which we have previously presented and discussed: "By wholly filling Jesus' humanity, the Spirit endows it with the openness by which it can freely and wholly constitute a mould for God's self-communication."[20] Here the Holy Spirit's sanctification of Jesus in his life of obedience to God and service for us stands as the historical presupposition or condition for affirming this openness and the fact that he is not simply a mere man but God the Logos.[21]

Kasper rightly sees the incarnation as the whole history of Christ in the Spirit (not just a past event, or hypostatic union). Kasper assumes Rahner's view of the hypostatic union, but gives it a pneumatological spin. Assuming the openness of the human spirit to God on the basis of God's own immanent presence with his creatures, Rahner sees the Word's incarnation as the highest and definitive expression of human (created) potentiality for reaching out to God and for receiving God's own (uncreated) grace or self-communication.[22] Despite their differences, Lampe and Kasper share a common anthropology. Jesus' openness in the Spirit to God's presence in him (as seen in his life and mission) serves as the paradigm for our openness to God in that we (like Jesus) have an innate, grace-given role

---

19. Lampe, "The Holy Spirit and the Person of Christ," 124.

20. Kasper, *Jesus the Christ*, 251. This thesis in itself is susceptible to the charge that it conceives of a logical existence of a humanity endowed with the Spirit prior to and for union with the Logos.

21. Ibid. I see no problem if Kasper's argument refers to our knowledge of Christ's lordship and deity (*ordo cognoscendi*).

22. See Rahner, "Current Problems in Christology," 163–65; cf. Kasper, *Jesus the Christ*, 266–67.

(self-transcendence)—even if a little one—to play in making God's gracious presence in us possible.

If a Spirit Christology will lead to proclamation, a few correctives are needed. Although Jesus is like one of us, we cannot forget that he is also "without sin" (Heb 4:15). The Holy Spirit makes the child in Mary's womb "holy" and the incarnate "Son of God" from conception (Luke 1:35). This unrepeatable indwelling of the Spirit in Jesus surpasses God's presence in humans not merely in degree but in nature. The Son's incarnation by the Spirit of God stands as the historical side of the eternal Son's unique hypostatic or personal openness to the Father in the same Spirit. It is not merely the culmination in history of the Spirit's general work in creation whereby all human creatures are given a partial disposition or affinity towards God.[23] Theologians of the cross acknowledge that since Eden they have lost all inclination to live in the Spirit and thus according to God's will. What we need is not the Spirit's partial help or assistance, but his radical intervention and work of new creation in our lives. We recall the early church fathers' striking image of the Spirit's departure from the race of Adam, which is also and finally the story of the Spirit who graciously returns to the human race. Such return is made possible through Jesus alone, the new Adam who bears the Spirit in the flesh without measure in order to send the same Spirit anew upon all flesh. Jesus' unique reception of the Spirit of God from conception allows for the fulfillment of the Father's original plan for his creatures frustrated by their rebellion, for it serves as the unparalleled condition for the Holy Spirit's gracious indwelling of the saints as gift from the Father through his anointed, crucified, and risen Son. By placing the weight of discourse on our human potential for receiving God's Spirit, liberal and conservative Spirit Christologies can give theologians of glory an excuse to dodge the cross, and therefore avoid their own dying to self and being raised to new life by the Spirit.

BEING CRUCIFIED AND RAISED WITH CHRIST: PNEUMATOLOGICAL CHRISTOLOGY AS A GROUND FOR CONVICTING AND LIBERATING PROCLAMATION

Due to its legitimate interest in the problem of Christ's once-for-all innerconstitution as the God-man, Logos Christology tends to explain the incarnation as a static event in the past and define the person of Christ in terms of his individual subsistence. A Spirit Christology seeks to complement this

---

23. "The cry, 'Abba! Father!' is not a universal cry, but that created in us by the Spirit of Jesus Christ." Hansen, "Spirit Christology," 200.

approach with a dynamic view of the incarnation inclusive of the successive mysteries of Jesus' life (e.g., baptism, death, and resurrection) and an ecstatic understanding of his person that places the Son in the context of his acts and relation before the Father and for us in the Spirit. Because the Son is most deeply himself in his being and acting for others freely and out of love, then a shift from Christ's being-in-himself to his being-for-us in the power of God's Spirit can foster the preaching and hearing of the Gospels as an unfolding soteriological drama where God gets to have his way with us. However, for God's killing and making alive to take place in such a drama, the proposed ontological framework of a Spirit Christology would have to be placed in the context of a theology of the Spirit-breathed word that points to the cross.[24] Such a cruciform trajectory will incorporate hearers into the life of the Son, who was anointed with the Spirit to go to the cross for us and for our salvation.

Admittedly, Jesus' exorcisms, healings, and preaching are all events in which the Spirit plays a defining role. As theologians of glory, we could focus only on one of these awesome facets of Jesus' ministry and forget the tragic result of these very deeds and sayings in the Spirit, namely, his innocent death at the hands of sinners like us. For this reason, a Spirit Christology that aims at the crucifying and raising of sinners with Christ must first lead hearers of the story to Jesus' suffering and death on the cross, but then also to his being raised from the dead and his giving of the Spirit of new life to us. Is calling for the centrality of the paschal mystery an imposition on the Gospels? Or does the story of Jesus in the Spirit at once point the hearer to Lent, Easter, and Pentecost? The latter is the case. The Gospels (especially Luke and John) have an inner-dynamic that flows from Jesus' receiving and bearing of the Spirit of God to his dispensing of the same to others.[25]

The key to placing hearers into the paschal mystery begins with their incorporation into Jesus' anointing or baptism at the Jordan—not into his incarnation as such. Unlike Jesus' non-transferable possession of the Holy Spirit from the moment of his conception (incarnation), the Holy Spirit's new descent on and presence in him at the Jordan can be communicated to us: "He on whom you see the Spirit descend and remain is the one who baptizes with the Holy Spirit" (John 1:33, cf. Luke 3:16 and parallels). Jesus' reception of the Spirit of the Father at the Jordan is the presupposition for the church's reception of the same Spirit through the crucified and risen Christ from Pentecost onwards (Luke 24:46–49, Acts 1:3–5). Logos Christology

24. For a recent proposal toward a cruciform theology of the word, see Nafzger, "There Are Written."

25. For the link between Spirit and sonship in Luke-Acts, see Dunn, "Spirit and Holy Spirit in the New Testament," 8–9; for John, see Porsch, *El Espíritu Santo*, 27–34.

can point hearers to Christ's divinity as the ground for the possibility of their forgiveness and to his exalted humanity (already from the time of the personal union) as the ground for their deification, glorification, or exaltation at the resurrection. Yet such a move tends to be more explanatory than kerygmatic. A Spirit Christology suggests that anointing/baptism—as opposed to preexistence/incarnation—language is more conducive to grasping and advancing the Spirit-initiated plunging of sinners into a present-day reenactment and appropriation of Jesus' anointing with the Father's Spirit. When the pastor says to us, "I baptize you . . . " such a Spirit-led reenactment occurs, and we are thereby initiated into the mysteries of Jesus' life.

Jesus' baptism in water takes him on a mission that leads to his baptism in blood at Golgotha. Upon his anointing, Jesus enters this mission "to fulfill all righteousness" for us as obedient Son and Servant (Matt 3:13–15, and 8:16–17, quoting Isa 53:4; Luke 3:22 and parallels, quoting Isa 42:1; Luke 4:18–19 and Acts 10:38). He is led or driven by the same Spirit into the desert, where Satan puts his faithfulness as Son to the test: "If you are the Son of God. . . ." (Luke 4:1–13 and parallels). Jesus' deeds in obedience to God leads to his death on the cross (cf. Phil 2:8). The term baptism no longer applies only to Jesus' anointing for mission at the Jordan, but serves also as a metaphor for the end of his mission at Golgotha—his highest act of service as a ransom for many (Luke 12:50; Mark 10:38, 45).

Significantly, in John's Gospel, Jesus' giving of the Spirit—"rivers of living water"—to those who believe in him must await his glorification (7:38–39), which does not come until the end of the Gospel narrative. It is as the risen Lord that Jesus breathes the Holy Spirit on his disciples, bestowing on them the power to forgive the sins of the penitent and bind those of the impenitent (20:22–23). Since the Son's obedience unto death already points to his glorification, which begins with his being lifted up on the pole (cf. 3:13–15; 13:31–32; 17:1–5), Jesus' handing over of his *pneuma* (literally, his life) from the cross (19:30) points at a symbolic level to his imminent giving of the Spirit as risen Lord.[26] The blood and the water flowing from Jesus' pierced side (19:34) also points to this indissoluble link between Jesus' death and his dispensing of the Spirit to the church.[27] In 1 John 5:6–8, the Spirit of truth does not only testify to the baptism and death of Jesus "who came by water and blood," but also makes possible the church's participation in

---

26. See Porsch, *El Espíritu Santo*, 103–4; for John, the Son's giving of the Spirit to those who believe in him presupposes his receiving and bearing of the Spirit from God "without measure" (3:34).

27. Ibid., 104–6; on a *pneumatologia crucis*, in which the Spirit's coming depends on Christ's passion, see Moltmann, *The Spirit of Life*, 60–71.

such mysteries through the sacraments of baptism and the Lord's Supper.[28] One recalls the famous scene of the crucifixion depicted by Lucas Cranach the Younger (1515–1586) in the center panel of the altarpiece in the City Church of Saints Peter and Paul in Weimar, Germany. There the blood that flows from Christ's pierced side falls on the head of Cranach, the painter himself, who as a representative of all believers is touched by the blood of the one who hangs on the pole. Like Cranach in the image, believers who came to the altar to receive the Lord's blood in his Supper, were brought into the story of the cross anew and made participants of the benefits of Christ's sacrifice. Today, when the pastor says to us at the altar, "Take and eat. This is the body of Christ . . . take and drink, this is the blood of Christ . . . ," the Spirit incorporates us into Jesus' own death as we partake of his true body (Lat. *corpus verum*) and are made one with our brothers and sisters in his mystical body (Lat. *corpus mysticum*), the church (cf. 1 Cor 10:16–17, cf. 11:27–29).

Being raised from the dead "according to the Spirit of holiness" (Rom. 1:4; cf. 1 Tim 3:16, and 1 Pet 3:18), Jesus enters his final stage of sonship in the history of salvation as "Lord" (Acts 13.33). Seated at God's right hand, he is the end-time giver of the promised Spirit whom he receives from the Father to pour out for the forgiveness of sins on all who call on the Lord's name with a contrite and trusting heart (Acts 2:17–21, quoting Joel 2:28–32; Acts 2:33, 38–39). As last Adam and life-giving Spirit, he becomes the first fruits of our final adoption as God's children through the Spirit of life in the coming resurrection (1 Cor 15:20–23, 45; Rom 8:11, 22–23).

In our case, sharing in Jesus' death and resurrection happens already when we share and are initiated into his anointing through Christian baptism, through which the sinful flesh is crucified and the new creature is raised in the hope of a new life (Rom. 6:3–11). We can speak of a Spirit-orchestrated participation in Jesus' anointing or baptism, which happens in that eschatological time when the old and new ages overlap into the present, and where the old creature in us is drowned in the waters so that a new creature might arise from the waters to live in righteousness and the hope of the resurrection. A Spirit Christology shows that Jesus' giving of the Spirit to the church since Pentecost through word and sacrament depends on his prior reception and bearing of the Spirit in his mission as faithful Son and suffering Servant. I have linked our participation in Jesus' mysteries to the sacraments (visible Word), but the same must be done for preaching. From Romans 6:4, Luther gathers that baptism is not only a past event but a way of life characterized by the daily drowning of the old sinner in us "through

---

28. Tábet, "El Testimonio «del Espíritu, y del agua y la sangre» (1 Jn 5,8)," 71–90.

daily contrition and repentance" and his/her daily rising anew "to live before God in righteousness and purity forever."[29] Preaching brings about this life of daily repentance in us.

If Jesus' story has an orientation that guides hearers into his paschal mystery, then preachers must face and act on what precedes and follows from that center. What does this mean? First, preachers must draw hearers into the story of the cross by pointing out that everything Jesus claims to do and does *in the Spirit*, and, therefore, in obedience to his Father and for the sake of the neighbor, gets him in trouble and leads to his suffering and death at the hands of sinners like us.[30] If preachers are to convict their hearers of their complicity in Jesus' death, they will want to address them in a way similar to the following: "Jesus is God's anointed Son, the one who delivers you from the oppression of sin, death, and the devil. But you will not have God's mercy. You are like the ones who want to throw him off a cliff" (Luke 4:14–30). Another example: "The kingdom of God comes upon you every time Jesus drives out Satan from your lives. But you reject God's Son. You are like the ones who make him out to be Satan" (Luke 11:14–23; cf. Matt 12:22–30). Preachers of the cross convict hearers as sinners by showing them that they are oppressors of the Son. If hearers see themselves as such oppressors, then they have been crucified with Christ. They are then more likely to acknowledge how they might also be complicit, knowingly or unknowingly, in the oppression of other neighbors. Such conviction is not yet proclamation in the ultimate sense unless it also leads to liberation.

If our complicity in Jesus' eventual death precedes the paschal mystery, what follows from this center? Simply stated, the church's preaching of Jesus' story. Peter seeks to bring sinners to face their guilt in Jesus' death (Acts 2:23, 36) and I have applied this insight to the stories that precede the paschal mystery. Yet the goal of this killing word is to deliver the forgiveness of sins and the gift of the Holy Spirit to all who repent of their rejection of God's mercy in Jesus and receive baptism in his name (Acts 2:37–39). God is against us in order to be for us. Going back to Luke 4 and 11, preachers may then address hearers as follows: "You are the poor to whom God's anointed Son brings good news, the captives whom he sets free, the blind whom he heals, the oppressed whom he liberates." In Jesus' name and in his stead,

---

29. SC, Baptism 11–14, in *BC*, 360.

30. A recognition of our oppression and killing of God's Son complements the dimension of the atonement that sees Jesus himself as freely going to the cross to reconcile us with the Father (e.g., John 10:18; Heb 9:14) and that sees in the cross the fulfillment of God's foreknown purposes (e.g., 1 Pet 1:20; Rev 13:8). But if proclamation is to occur, these aspects cannot minimize our own guilt in Jesus' death (esp. Acts 2:23). On actual atonement, see Forde, *Theology Is for Proclamation*, 121–27.

preachers are likewise given the Spirit to proclaim release from the evil one: "I release you from the bondage of Satan. God's gracious kingdom in Christ has come upon you!" Having experienced the promise of deliverance from sin, death, and the devil, hearers of the story are more likely to ask how they might bring such deliverance to other neighbors in the name of Jesus. The aforementioned examples of proclamation illustrate the basic movement or rhythm of a Spirit-oriented reading of the story of Jesus that is centered in the mystery of the cross, namely, one that moves from convicting hearers of the story to their renewal in Christ.

Summary

Ever since Pentecost, each time we are convicted of and liberated from our sins against God's anointed Son and Servant through word and sacrament, we undergo a Spirit-led reenactment or actualization of Jesus' baptism, death, and resurrection in our lives. We are read or spoken to by the living word of God that points to Jesus and in turn are shaped into theologians of the cross who are crucified and raised with him each day until our resurrection from the dead unto everlasting life. In this chapter, I have shown that reading the story of Jesus from a pneumatic angle can serve to pave the way for theologian-preachers to make the transition from their reflections on Jesus' story to its proclamation as a death-and-life event for others.

The church's participation in Jesus' mysteries also involves her sharing in his life of prayer to God and service to the neighbor who is Christ in her midst. In the next chapter, I will focus on the implications of a Spirit Christology for the theology of prayer, entering into conversation with open and classical forms of theism, which espouse Logos-oriented approaches to the function of prayer in Jesus' life. In the final chapter, I will explore the fruitfulness of a Spirit Christology as a model for laying out a theology of the Christian life or sanctification. Such a view of the Christian life flows from a sacramental approach to pneumatology, grounded in the presence and activity of the Spirit in the incarnate Son.

8

Praying to the Father in the Spirit

Reclaiming the Church's Participation in the Son's Prayer Life

DURING HIS LIFE AND mission, does not Jesus himself (above all, as his death becomes imminent) wrestle with God's will in a tragic world—that is, a world hostile to the Father's love, a world where the innocent suffer? At the Garden of Gethsemane, Jesus prays to his Father, "Not what I want, but what you want," but before that he also prayed, "Abba, Father . . . remove this cup from me" (Mark 14:36). The Son leaves his fate in the Father's hands, but that ultimate self-giving and entrusting to God does not come without intense struggle and distress.[1]

We do not speak of the struggle and distress of one who has no hope or trust in God, but rather of the suffering Son who, as the psalmist does, brings up his lament to the Father in heaven when he seems to have abandoned us on earth: "My God, my God, why have you forsaken me?" (Mark 15:34; Ps 22:1). The evangelist speaks honestly about the distress, agitation, and grief that the Son experiences on his way to the cross—human experiences we can identity with. Does not Jesus call us to see prayer in terms of a certain participation in his life? If so, how should we see Christian prayer in light of Christ's paschal mystery, his filiation and mission, his life and death?

---

1. The Gospels highlight the intensity of Jesus' struggle at Gethsemane: "He took with him Peter and James and John, and began to be distressed and agitated. And he said to them, 'I am deeply grieved, even to death; remain here and keep awake.' And going a little farther, he threw himself on the ground and prayed that, if it were possible, the hour might pass from him" (Mark 14:33–35; cf. Matt 26:37–39, Luke 22:43–44).

If Jesus struggled with God's will in a tragic world, should not the church find in him—specifically, in his prayer life—what it means to wrestle with God's will in a world that is surrounded by pain and death? After all, Jesus does teach the church to pray as he himself ultimately prayed to his Father in dark Gethsemane: "Your will be done" (Matt 6:10).

These questions have led me to reflect on the relationship between Christology and ecclesiology and, more concretely, on what it means for the church to participate in the prayer life of Jesus, in that central dimension of his sonship. What does it mean to share in the prayer life of the Son, who was no stranger to suffering a tragic fate in this world even as he sought to be faithful to his Father's will unto death? Like the incarnate Son in Gethsemane, the adopted sons pray to their Abba Father in and by the Spirit: "And because you are children, God has sent the Spirit of his Son into our hearts, crying, Abba! Father!" (Gal 4:6). We begin to see our prayer as an intricate aspect of the mystery of sonship, of filiation, which is grounded in Jesus' own life in the Spirit, in the Son's own intimate relationship to his Abba Father. The world in which the church lives and moves is none other than the world of the Son in the Garden of Gethsemane, dark place where the Son and the sons raise petitions to the Abba they have in common. The adopted sons share with the only-begotten Son that Garden where prayer is a must, that place where, as Luther would say, prayer (Lat. *oratio*) takes place in the midst of spiritual attack and affliction (Lat. *tentatio*, Ger. *Anfechtung*). Prayer is not an add-on to the Christian life, but a defining dimension of our Spirit-created identity as children of God.

As the struggle at Gethsemane indicates, the Son's prayer life in the Spirit unfolds in the broader context of a life marked by suffering and the cross. Therefore, sharing in the Son's prayer life in the Spirit goes hand in hand with sharing in his sufferings, but then also in his glory: "When we cry, 'Abba! Father!' it is that very Spirit bearing witness with our spirit that we are children, and if children, then heirs, heirs of God and joint heirs with Christ—if, in fact, we suffer with him so that we may also be glorified with him" (Rom 8:16–17). Because our prayers in the Spirit of adoption find their meaning in the mystery of sonship, in the identity of the faithful Son who cries out to his Abba and entrusts his life to him in the agony of the Garden, the church's prayer life is linked inextricably to the mystery of suffering and final trust in God's deliverance.

One commends his life to God in prayer in the way of the psalmist, whose words the Son cries out from the cross: "Father, into your hands, I commend my spirit" (Luke 23:46, Ps 31:5). In the lament psalms, the church, the spiritual Israel, learns to pray as sons, who like the Son, the new Israel, experience God's forsakenness as they bear the cross (Ps 22:1). In the final analysis, such laments are not irreverent protests against God, but protests done by faith in the God who has promised to save his people as he did in the exodus of old. Nor are these laments therapeutic strategies that seek to heal the heart by directing people to some prosperous, golden era. Instead, these cries are expressions of hope in God's promises. They are to be seen in the context of the resurrection hope of that eschatological exodus of God's people from death into the promised land: "To you they cried, and were saved; in you they trusted, and were not put to shame" (Ps 22:5).

SEARCHING FOR A DIFFERENT FRAMEWORK: THE GOD OF THEISM(S) OR THE TRIUNE GOD?

In this chapter, I argue that Jesus' prayer life must be seen as an expression in the economy of salvation of his being Son, of his filial trust in the Father. As a result, the church must also see her prayer life as a Trinitarian event in which she—as the Son once did—entrusts herself to the Father's will in a world where struggle, suffering, and death are inescapable realities. However, to accomplish our goal, to ground prayer in the Trinitarian mystery of sonship, we must move beyond the theological bipolarity that in contemporary Evangelicalism has shaped the current debate between classical and open theism. If seen in part but not exclusively as a Calvinist (pro-divine sovereignty) versus Arminian (pro-human freedom) bipolarity, we may better understand how each side thinks about prayer (specifically, prayer of petition). Whereas classical theists want to speak of prayer in ways that do not compromise God's absolute sovereignty, open theists want to present prayer in such a way that it does not become a threat to human freedom.

This bipolar way of framing what prayer is assumes a view of the relationship between God and humanity which, in the end, posits that the most real or definitive statement one can make about God is a substantial (or essential) one. In short, substantial statements refer us to the divine essence (in contrast to the divine persons) as the primary category for speaking about God. Traditionally, substantial affirmations function mainly to direct us to God in Godself in distinction from—and thus not in relation to—what is not God (i.e., creation). As a corollary to this role, substantial statements serve to safeguard divine attributes such as immutability, omniscience, and omnipotence over against moves to collapse the Trinity into creation or make it dependent on the same. However, when a substantial statement becomes the ultimate ontological category for talking about the God-world dialectic, we have a form of "substantialism." Both classical and open theists operate within this subtantialist framework, although in distinct ways, to the detriment of a fully Trinitarian theology of prayer.

Classical theists defend divine attributes like the ones mentioned above to safeguard God's transcendence over against the world. We may call this traditional approach a transcendent substantialism. Open theists do not necessarily deny but rather modify or reinterpret classical divine attributes under the notion of divine self-limitation, which then becomes a more adequate description of God's character or identity in relation to the world.[2] If I am correct in my assessment of open theism, its substantialism does not serve to distinguish radically between God and the world (as in classical theism) but to relate God radically to the world. Paradoxically, therefore, God may be said to show his unchanging nature as a loving God precisely in his self-limitation or openness to change.[3] We may call this approach an immanent (or this-worldly) substantialism.

In either type of theism, a substantialist scheme to the God-world relation remains. Because this move privileges divine substance over divine persons, it works on the basis of a hierarchization of divine attributes, which favors either transcendence (classical theism) or immanence (open theism). What do these options say about God? Either we have an immutable God who cannot change his mind in relation to us and, therefore, a God who looks suspiciously apathetic to our needs and sufferings (a criticism leveled against classical theism). Or we have a self-limiting God who can be influenced by us most of the time in order to change his mind, and thus a God who looks suspiciously vulnerable to our desires and persuasions (a

---

2. In order to safeguard human freedom, open theism elevates divine self-limitation to an ontological level, the truest and ultimate statement one can make about God. Consider the following axioms of open theism: "2. God chose to create us with incompatibilistic (libertarian) freedom—freedom over which he cannot exercise total control." "3. God so values our freedom—the moral integrity of free creatures and a world in which such integrity is possible—that he does not normally override such freedom, even if he sees that it is producing undesirable results." "5. God does not possess exhaustive knowledge of exactly how we will utilize our freedom, although he may well at times be able to predict with great accuracy the choices we will freely make." Basinger, "Practical Implications," 156.

3. "So while proponents of divine openness emphasize the biblical evidence that God is affected by what happens in the world (suffers) and that he changes his mind (repents), they fully accept the biblical affirmations of divine changelessness. They apply the 'changeless' statements to God's existence and character, to his love and reliability. They apply the 'changing' statements to God's actions and experience . . . It is God's nature to love . . . And precisely because this is God's essential nature, he must be sentitive and responsive to the creaturely world. Everything that happens has an effect on him. Because God's love never changes, God's experience must change. In other words, it is part of God's unchanging nature to change." Rice, "Biblical Support for a New Perspective," 48.

criticism leveled against open theism). Either we have an omniscient and omnipotent God, who already knows and has determined our future and, therefore, a God who looks suspiciously indifferent to our present hopes. Or we have a self-limiting God who lets his creatures determine a yet-to-exist future that is unknown perhaps even to himself and, therefore, a God who looks suspiciously helpless. In the end, the options available leave us with an "either/or" God.

Within the substantialist scheme, prayer also loses. What classical theists want to defend is God's unchanging will, foreknowledge, and determination of the future, and thus attributes such as divine immutability, omniscience, and omnipotence. But if an omniscient and omnipotent God has already ordained all things in the future by his immutable will—everything that will happen to us—what are our prayers truly worth anyway? Can such a God really be moved to change his predetermined course of action in history in order to reach out to us and act on our behalf through our prayers? Is this God in his innermost self untouched by our struggles, somewhat detached, self-enclosed, or apathetic and indifferent to our plight? Amidst pain and death, can we trust that this God will hear and respond to our cries for help? The God of classical theism seems too far from us to come near us.

What open theists want to defend is human freedom and therefore God's openness to let the future be what it will be in conjunction with the will and actions of his creatures in the historical process, either because a loving God has chosen to do so himself through self-limitation and/or because the future as such does not really exist (it is a non-entity). But if God is so open so as to let the future be what it will, perhaps with an occasional intervention to change the course of events, but mostly waiting on us to ask him to change his mind about something or waiting for us to cooperate with him to build the future, can we trust that this God is able to deliver us in the end from our own shortcomings, not to mention sins? Amidst pain and death, can we trust that a vulnerable God, whose self-limitation appears to compromise his perfect will, foreknowledge, and determination of our future, still remains powerful enough to hear and respond to our cries for help? The God of open theism seems too close to us to be other than us.[4]

---

4. It is possible to hold neither "theistic" position. It is possible to avoid giving up one's life for a God whose attributes seem somewhat suspicious and, therefore, open to questioning. In such a case, you are left with protest atheism or practical atheism. The first kind of atheism is philosophical because the idea of God and prayer to God must die altogether to let humanity be free to fulfill its historical projects. The second kind is existential ("of the heart") because one can presumably believe in and confess formally God's existence but live as if God did not exist and thus as if one no longer must pray to God. I first came across the distinction between philosophical and practical atheism in Mühlen, *Espíritu. Carisma. Liberación*.

The God of "theisms" either makes prayer seem superfluous and insignificant in the face of God's transcendent sovereignty (the classical sort). or makes God seem weak and susceptible before the power of our prayers (the open sort). One hopes it is possible to leave the God of "theisms" behind and move towards the "triune" God of the biblical narratives and their witness to God's threefold self-revelation in the economy of salvation, particularly as this pattern becomes evident in the Son's life of prayer to God the Father in and by the Spirit. Would the theology and practice of prayer fare better if seen as a Trinitarian event that is shaped after the incarnate Son's own prayer life?

My proposal requires that we proceed in three stages and therefore ask three major questions. First, has there been a partial dogmatic eclipse of the Trinitarian basis of Jesus' prayer in the Western dogmatic tradition? Second, if there has been such a partial eclipse, can the biblical narrative and some elements in the church's theological tradition help us to recover the significance of Jesus' prayer life (and by participation, of the church's prayer life) as a historical expression of sonship? In other words, can we see Jesus' prayer life and ours as a Trinitarian event grounded in the mystery of filial communion between the Son and the Father in the Spirit, instead of finding such ground ultimately in the category of divine substance? Third, what are some theological and practical implications of a Trinitarian theology of prayer for the church in response to both classical and open views of prayer?

THOMAS AQUINAS ON PRAYER AND CHRIST'S PRAYER LIFE: ANATOMY AND CONSEQUENCES OF A CLASSICAL APPROACH

Let us begin with our first question: Has there been a partial eclipse of the Trinitarian basis of Jesus' prayer in the Western dogmatic tradition? Since this question is too broad, I will focus my efforts on an influential theologian in the Latin West, Thomas Aquinas (d. 1274), and see what he has to say on Jesus' prayer in his *Summa Theologiae*. Our choice of Thomas is warranted for at least three reasons.

First, Thomas's affirmation that the world changes in relation to God but not God in relation to the world—that is, that humans have a real relation (Lat. *relatio realis*) to God but God only has a rational (in the mind) relation (Lat. *relatio rationis*) to them—has been the target of theists who argue for God's openness to human influence or persuasion.[5] If Thomas's

---

5. *ST* I, q. 13, a. 7; Evangelical theologian Pinnock notes that open and process theism "contend that God has real, and not merely rational, relationships with the world."

use of "relation" to speak of the distinction between God and the world is representative of classical theism, and thus illustrative of a substantialist theological framework, it makes sense to explore how his approach shapes his theology of prayer.

Second, and most importantly, Thomas approaches the hypostatic union in the context of the philosophical notion of relation, arguing that the divine Logos does not change in relation to his assumed humanity but rather that the assumed humanity changes in relation to the divine Logos.[6] In other words, the assumed human nature has a real relation (*relatio realis*) to the Logos, but the Logos only has a rational relation (*relatio rationis*) to his assumed human nature. Although this substantial framework distinguishes between the divine and the human in Christ, and thus fulfills one of the main concerns of a Logos-oriented approach to Christology, it does not speak adequately of the incarnation as intrinsic (and thus not merely as external) to the *person* of the Logos. This creates problems for seeing aspects of Christ's life, such as his prayer, as historical expressions of his being Son.

Third, our choice of Thomas is defensible on the grounds that his presentation of the treatise on the one God and his divine attributes (*De Deo Uno*) logically precedes his treatment of the triune God (*De Deo Trino*).[7] This logical priority has been criticized as an example of the Western-Augustinian tendency to begin discourse on God in terms of his indivisible divine essence, attributes, and works in creation before speaking of God in personal terms or according to what is proper to each person of the Trinity in relation to creation.[8] To be sure, Thomas speaks of the triune God in his treatise, but he does so more in terms of real relations in the one divine essence (immanent Trinity) than in terms of persons who relate to us in the economy of salvation (economic Trinity).[9] In addition to giving the

---

Most Moved Mover, 142 (cf. 68–74); for Roman Catholic theologian O'Donnell, process theism and atheism are important critical responses to classical theism but unsatisfying answers to the same. Although sympathetic to Thomas, O'Donnell sees the limitations of classical theism for thinking God in relation to time and history. O'Donnell, *The Mystery of the Triune God*, 1–16.

6. *ST* III, q. 2, a. 7.

7. *ST* I, qq. 1–26 (*De Deo Uno*) and 27–43 (*De Deo Trino*).

8. Rahner, *The Trinity*, 15–21; and LaCugna, *God for Us*, chap. 5.

9. In the Augustinian tradition of using "relation" to distinguish in/within God without doing harm to the unity of the divine essence (e.g., Augustine, *On the Holy Trinity* 5.5.6 [*NPNF*[1] 3:89]), Thomas speaks of the three divine persons in terms of four real (subsistent) relations in God, namely, fatherhood, sonship, spiration, and procession. *ST* I, q. 28, a. 4; Thomas's theology of missions follows from a discussion of intradivine relations: "The fact that there are missions follows from suitability: from there being two processions *in divinis*, not from the twofoldness of the events in the

impression that one can conceive of the divine essence as a reality prior to any particular person of the Trinity, Aquinas exhibits a discrete separation of the doctrine of the Trinity from the mystery of salvation. These elements of Thomas's theology make it difficult for him to articulate a robust Trinitarian account of Christ's prayer life that is grounded in his *personal* identity as the incarnate and eternal Son who acts before his Father in the Spirit.

Given these three reasons for choosing Thomas, I will show how he presents us with a classic approach to the relationship between God and the world that privileges divine substance over divine persons. By looking at the anatomy of an illustrative substantialist (in contrast to a personalist) approach to Christ's prayer life, we will be better able to assess any potential weaknesses or advantages in the Western position represented by Thomas.

If we were to ask how God relates to the world, the following illustration should help explain Thomas's position on the question. Imagine the cross above the church's altar. One Sunday morning you decide to take some pictures of the cross to send to your relatives. You move from left to right, from front to back, looking for those picture perfect angles. In the process, you, the photographer, have changed positions in relation to the cross. But the cross has never moved, changed, or acquired a new reality in relation to you. To use Thomas's language, the relation between the cross and you is only real for you, the one member of the relation who is subject to change. Likewise, God can move others to do something or be someone, but as the first cause of all things—the unmoved mover—God cannot be moved by others. For Thomas, God is pure act (Lat. *actus purus*) and as such God cannot be anything else than he already is. As pure act, there is in God no possibility of a move from potency to act and, therefore, no possibility in him for change.

Where does prayer fit in this ontological scheme of things? For Thomas, the usefulness of prayer belongs to the category of secondary causes. Although God is the first efficient cause of the universe, the prime mover of every cause-effect in the world, Thomas does not go as far as concluding from this that we must "attribute necessity to human actions subject to divine providence."[10] Instead, God acts upon the world *indirectly* through our human acts. From this angle, some form of causality can be ascribed to our actions and prayers while preserving divine providence and immutability.

---

economy." LaCugna, *God for Us*, 157. This is LaCugna's way of saying that Thomas argues "from above," namely, from the begetting of the Son and spiration of the Holy Spirit (intradivine processions) to the sending of the Son and the sending of the Holy Spirit (historical missions).

10. *ST* II, q. 83, a. 2.

> Human acts are true causes, and therefore men must perform certain actions, not in order to change divine providence, but in order to obtain certain effects in the manner determined by God. What is true of natural causes is true also of prayer, for we do not pray in order to change the decree of divine providence, rather we pray in order to impetrate [or indirectly effect] those things which God has determined would be obtained only through prayers.[11]

Prayers are means that God uses to effect what he has determined in an eternal now to accomplish in the course of history. Prayer affects us, but not God or what God has already set in stone. Now, seen as a negative affirmation—that is, one that tells us something about who God is *not* (i.e., not mutable)—then, Thomas's move does help us to say that God is not a creature and therefore divine transcendence is safeguarded. Herein lies the relative strength of a substantialist approach: It makes clear that God is distinct from his creation.

But at what expense? If the idea that prayer affects us, but not God, is taken as a definitive ontological, positive affirmation about God, then the logical conclusion is that God literally and strictly speaking cannot be moved to act on our behalf. To be fair, Thomas at times appears to speak of prayer in ways that could potentially allow for a more mutual form of relationality between God and us. Thomas says, for example, that prayer helps to "remind ourselves that ... we need divine assistance,"[12] or "gain confidence in God and acknowledge him as the source of all our blessings."[13] He also refers to prayer as reverent submission to God,[14] and points to the Spirit's role who "by inspiring us with holy desires ... makes us ask for what is right."[15] Thomas concludes the section on prayer by pointing out the reason for supplication—namely, that "from a consideration of divine goodness we dare to approach him [i.e., God]."[16] These statements on prayer present the possibility of positing some form of mutual relation between God and us, but such a move does not appear to be available to Thomas in the Aristotelian substantial category and framework of "relation" he employs.[17]

11. Ibid.; bracketed statement is mine.
12. *ST* II, a. 2, ad. 1.
13. Ibid.; cf. ibid., a. 3, and a. 4, ad. 1 on seeing God as the source of blessings; "Prayer is not offered to God in order to change his mind, but in order to excite confidence in us." Ibid., a. 9, ad. 5.
14. Ibid., a. 3, ad. 3.
15. Ibid., a. 5, ad. 1; cf. a. 10, ad. 1.
16. Ibid., a. 17, ad. 3.
17. The reader is reminded that the idea of relation functions as a substantial

For now, let us move from our prayer to Christ's prayer. As noted before, Thomas applies the notion of real relation to the incarnation. The assumed human (creaturely) nature has a real relation to the divine Logos, but the divine Logos only has a rational or conceptual relation to his assumed human nature. A clear distinction is made between the Logos as Creator and his human nature as creaturely. Again, this approach to the God-world relation tells us more about who the Logos is *not* ontologically—i.e., the Logos is not a creature—than about who the Logos *is* as the unique person or hypostasis of the Son in relation to his Abba Father and us in the economy of salvation.

Where does Christ's prayer life fit in this way of looking at things? The starting point for Thomas is whether Christ needs to pray *for himself*. The language of "need" forces him at once to come to the defense of God's omnipotence is distinction from the created order. Thomas writes, "It is not that he [i.e., Christ as God], as a person [i.e., the divine Logos], lacked any power, he [i.e., Christ] did this [as a man] for our instruction."[18] Having framed the issue in terms of ontological need in God, Thomas has to see Christ's prayer as *revelatory* of his divine dignity and thus as *exemplary* for others. His approach bears the characteristics of a Logos-oriented presentation of prayer in the life of Christ, one that sees the Son's prayer either as a window into his consubtantiality (*homoousios*) with the Father or from the lens of his two natures and what is proper to each. Thomas sums up his position as follows:

> Christ elected to pray to his Father so that he might give us an example of prayer and also in order to reveal his Father as the principle from whom he proceeds eternally according to the divine nature."[19]

Thomas's argument concerns Christ's "vocal" (or audible) prayer before others so that those around him might know "that he was [the divine Son] from the Father" (revelatory view), but also so that we might learn obedience by his supplication to the Father (exemplary view).[20] These views

---

category because its primary role is to radically distinguish God from the world. The relation is real on the creaturely side, but not for God. However, in God (apart from creation), we can speak of the divine persons (Father-Son-Holy Spirit) in terms of real relations. Even in this latter sense, however, one should note that the idea of relation serves primarily to distinguish within the one divine essence.

18. *ST* III, q. 21, a. 1, ad. 1; bracketed statements are mine.

19. *ST* III, q. 21, a. 3.

20. Ibid., a. 1, ad. 1 (citing John 11.42, Hilary, Ambrose, and Augustine); "Hilary is speaking of vocal prayer; as far as Christ himself was concerned, this was unnecessary; he prayed in words purely to help us. Thus it is with intent that Hilary says that it was the *words of petition* that *won no benefit for Christ himself*." Ibid., a. 3, ad. 1.

of Christ's prayer assume and highlight that he prays *as man*: "Christ as man and as possessing a human will needs to pray."[21] This is indisputable. However, we must add at once that the purpose of Christ's prayer as man is instrumental, that is, its ultimate purpose is to reveal his divinity to us or teach us to imitate him by being obedient to the Father. In particular, under the exemplary move, Christ, as a man who prays (and even needs to pray), is above all our "instructor."

We may say that the argumentation for the revelatory and exemplary views works at a substantial level because it refers us to how Christ's prayer life ultimately concerns one of his *natures*, and not what is proper to his *person*. As said before, this emphasis on Christ's praying as man can serve well to preserve his divinity from becoming prey to creaturely necessity.[22] Christ as God and as possessing a divine will does not need to pray. Nevertheless, what is not clear in this move is whether Christ's prayer means anything *for himself*. Does Christ's prayer (even as man) define him? Does prayer mean anything for the person of the Son, not only to teach others something *about* himself, but *for* himself as the incarnate Son who prays to the Father in the Spirit? In other words, does the Son's prayer life expresses anything about what it means for him to be the *person* of the Son? In Trinitarian terms, is there a correspondence between the incarnate Son who prays to the Father in the Spirit in the economy of salvation and the eternal Son who exists always in relation to the Father in the Spirit?

Reflecting on Christ's prayer as a man at Gethsemane ("Let this chalice pass from me. Yet not as I will, but as thou wilt."), Thomas speaks of "a three-fold teaching" we can gather from Christ's prayer life:

> First he wished to reveal to us that he had assumed a true human nature together with all its natural urges. Second, he wished to show that it is permissible for a man to entertain an instinctive affection for something which God does not will. Third, he wished to show that man must submit his own impulses to the divine will.[23]

Since this "three-fold teaching" tells us something about Christ as man, it also tells us something about our own humanity. This is quite evident from

---

21. Ibid., a. 1.

22. "The divine persons are said to receive by reason of their nature [i.e., by reason of their intradivine processions (and real subsistent relations)]; but prayer is an act of one who receives through grace. The Son is said to ask or to pray according to his human nature." *ST* II, q. 82, a. 10, ad. 1; bracketed statements are mine.

23. *ST* III, q. 21, a. 2; cf. ibid., a. 3. We may also speak of the instructional or pedagogical view of prayer.

the philosophical structure that Thomas uses to speak of Christ's prayer at Gethsemane—a framework that speaks to the self-transcending nature of rational man in relation to God. For Thomas, prayer constitutes "an act of reason" because its possibility implies "a certain [logical] ordering since . . . a man proposes that something be done by someone else."[24] As a religious act of reason, prayer transcends sensible phenomena insofar as "the will moves reason to its goal . . . to union with God which is the goal of charity."[25] Here the Holy Spirit "moves the just to desire . . . [to pray] in conformity with the divine will."[26]

Since rational creatures can express their sensuous desires, impulses, or natural urges through prayer, Thomas affirms that Christ as man instinctively shrinks from having to die and, therefore, can and does will something other than what God ultimately wills (thus "let this cup pass from me").[27] In this case, Christ's prayer is "for the sake of our enlightenment to make known to us the instinctive reaction of his will and the sensuous impulses which were his as a man."[28] In the end, however, the spiritual (Spirit-moved) man also wills deliberately in conformity with the divine will. This allows Thomas to say that Christ finally and always wills the same as God ("not as I will, but as thou wilt").[29] Yet Christ does so primarily to give us an example of submission to the Father's will.

At Gethsemane, Christ is our pedagogue in the ways of humanity. Christ assumed a true humanity with its natural urges, expressed an inclination for something not willed by God, but ultimately and deliberately submitted himself to the will of God. Christ's prayer fits easily into the category of secondary causes because it functions indirectly, through his human nature and deliberate will, as a means to an end already determined by God in his providence.[30] That end is to lead us by example in the way

24. *ST* II, q. 83, a. 1.

25. Ibid., a. 1, ad. 1; it is interesting to note that, for Thomas, even non-rational creatures such as animals can be said "to call upon God because of the natural desire whereby all things, each in its own way, seek to attain the divine goodness . . . because of the natural instinct by which God moves them." Ibid., a. 10, ad. 3.

26. *ST* III, q. 21, a. 4; cf. *ST* II, q. 83, a. 5, ad. 1.

27. Cf. *ST* III, q. 18, a. 5.

28. Ibid., q. 21, a. 4, ad. 1.

29. Cf. ibid., q. 18, a. 1, ad. 4.

30. "The very fact that by certain acts of his human will Christ desired something at variance with his divine will had its origin in this same divine will . . . it was by divine decree that Christ's human nature acted in the manner natural to it." *ST* III, q. 18, a. 6, ad. 1; "He judged it to be better, taking all circumstances into account, that through his passion the divine will for mankind's salvation should be fulfilled." Ibid., q. 18, a. 6, ad. 3; on Christ's prayer for glorification (John 17.1), Thomas writes: "The very glory which

of union with God, in the way of salvation, which is the divinely ordained goal for creation.

That Christ's prayer tells us more about us than about his identity as Son can also be illustrated in light of Thomas's application of his distinction between real and rational relations to the hypostatic union. Logically speaking, since the assumed humanity alone has a real relation to the divine Logos, one could conclude that Christ's prayer as man cannot tell us anything about him as God—notwithstanding the substantial and important statement that as God Christ does not *need* to pray. But is that all we can say? At this point, the substantialist argument has not reached the level of a statement concerning the *person* of the Son. This leaves us with a sort of disjunction between the human and the divine natures in Christ, which results inevitably in an interpretation of the incarnate Logos's prayer as a reality seemingly accidental and external to his *person*.

In contemporary Trinitarian theology, Rahner criticized the Thomistic tradition on this point, arguing that unless we are willing to say that the relation of the assumed human nature to the Logos must be reduced to a purely mental relation, then, we must state that "the Logos as such has a real relation to His human nature."[31] Otherwise, we must conclude mistakenly that "nothing referring to salvation history must be stated as such which concerns him [i.e, the Logos]."[32] Rahner recognizes Thomas's concern to preserve the substantial distinction between the divine and the human in Christ, which Thomas's use of relation attempts to do. But Rahner finds that, for the same reason, Thomas does not yet reach the level of a personal or hypostatic statement that speaks of and places Christ's unrepeatable identity as Son in the broader Trinitarian framework of the economy, where the Son prays to his Father in the Spirit.

For Thomas, Christ's vocal prayer reveals to others his sonship, namely, that he is the divine Son from the Father. Thomas speaks of Christ's prayer as an aspect of his sonship, but this is done more as a way of letting others know that he is God with the Father (substantial or natural sonship).

Christ sought for himself in prayer was relevant to the salvation of others, *He rose again for our justification*. Consequently, even the prayer which he uttered in his own name was in some degree for the benefit of others." Ibid., q. 21, a. 3, ad. 3. It is important to note, however, that for Thomas Christ's prayer for glorification was necessary for Him as man (not only for others): "He also made petition in prayer to the Father for those gifts which in his human nature he still lacked, such as glorification of his body." But then Thomas also places the prayer for glorification ultimately within the exemplary perspective: "In this he also set us an example . . . of asking in prayer what still remains to be granted us." Ibid., q. 21, a. 3.

31. Rahner, *The Trinity*, 15n11.

32. Ibid., 24n19.

What is affirmed is the unity of substance between the Son and the Father (a legitimate anti-Arian move), but not their reciprocity as distinct persons. Therefore, prayer does not really tell us what is proper (*proprium*) to Christ, what applies to him alone as the person of the Son in relation to his Father (relational or hypostatic dimension of sonship). There is, in other words, a sort of divide between the mystery of the eternal Son who is one *with God* and the mystery of salvation to which the incarnate Son's prayer *to God* belongs.

One of the most telling examples of this discrete separation between the mystery of the eternal Son and the mystery of salvation is Thomas's well-known statement that if God would have wanted to do otherwise, any of the persons of the Trinity could have become incarnate.[33] Yet in Scripture and the creeds the person of the Logos alone becomes flesh. Thomas's assumption is that one can ultimately talk about the incarnation in substantial terms, namely, as an effect in the world of the one God, the First Cause. Against this move, Rahner notes the following:

> Jesus is not simply God in general, but the Son. The second divine person, God's Logos, is man, and only he is man. . . . Here something occurs 'outside' the intra-divine life in the world itself, something which is not a mere effect of the efficient causality of the triune God acting as one in the world, but something which belongs to the Logos alone, which is the history of one divine person, in contrast to the other divine persons.[34]

If Thomas's statement that any of the divine persons could have become incarnate were true, this would mean that the economy of the Son—including his prayer life—cannot tell us anything *proper* about the person of the Son. Thomas actually arrives at this notion with his rare statement that "when we address God as our Father, this . . . refers to the whole Trinity."[35] Does this mean that when Christ prays to his Father, he is also praying to himself? Such anachronistic statements are examples of an overworked substantialist approach that relativizes God's threefold self-revelation in the events of the economy of salvation for the sake of preserving the unity of God's essence and, in this particular example, an undifferentiated unity of God's acts in relation to the world.

If Thomas qualifies as a classical theist, do we want to follow him all the way? For Thomas, prayer—both Christ's and ours—does not change God's mind but indirectly effect what God has foreordained in eternity.

33. *ST* III, q. 23, a. 2.
34. Rahner, *The Trinity*, 23.
35. *ST* III, q. 23, 1.2.

Christ needs to pray (to God the Father and/or the Trinity?) as man, but this happens primarily to reveal his divinity (or essential sonship) or serve as an example to us of conformity to God's will. Underlying all these arguments we have a substantialist approach to the relation between the one God and his creation that highlights distinction between Creator and creature, but also—and this is key—relativizes what is proper to each person of the Trinity in the economy of salvation. None of these moves allows us to speak of the church's participation in Christ's prayer as an aspect of life in the Spirit that is firmly rooted in his identity as Son. The exemplary view of Christ's prayer comes somewhat close, but there participation in Christ's life happens more by way of imitating his submission to God's will than by being made a trusting child who shares by grace in the identity of the Son who prays and entrusts himself to the Father.

To sum up, Thomas exhibits a partial dogmatic eclipse of the Trinitarian basis of Christ's prayer in the Western tradition because of his substantialist approach to the God-world relation. As a result, it is not clear that Christ's prayer life tells us anything proper to himself as the person of the Son and thus about us as sharers in his sonship.

PRAYER AS AN EXPRESSION OF AND PARTICIPATION IN CHRIST'S SONSHIP: TOWARDS A PERSONALIST-RELATIONAL APPROACH TO JESUS' AND THE CHURCH'S PRAYER LIFE

Our inquiry now leads us to our second question. If there has been a partial eclipse of the Trinitarian basis of Christ's prayer in the Western dogmatic tradition, can the biblical narrative and some of the best of the church's tradition help us to recover the significance of Christ's prayer as an expression of his being Son? Can such sources also help us reclaim prayer as the church's participation in Christ's sonship and, therefore, as a sharing by grace in the Son's life, death, and resurrection, and thus in his relationship to the Father in the Spirit?

To answer these questions, I will look briefly at some of the highlights of the biblical witness to the mystery of prayer in the economy of salvation, first in Christ and then in the body of Christ, first in the incarnate Son of God and then in the adopted sons of God. Then, I will gather some contemporary insights from the Eastern-Cappadocian tradition that can help us ground the biblical witness to the mystery of prayer in a personalist account of God, namely, one that sees prayer as a historical reality grounded in the mystery of divine persons in communion with one another and with us.

Prayer is an instance, a historical expression, of filial life (the life of sonship) both for Jesus and for the followers of Jesus. Both pray to the same Father in and by the same Spirit. Earlier on, we highlighted two realities concerning Christ's prayer life. First, Jesus' prayer to his Abba Father is central to the mystery of sonship, in which the adopted sons of God also participate by grace. Paul speaks of the church as adopted sons who pray in the Spirit *of the Son*. The reference is not only to the Spirit whom the Son sends to them, but also the Spirit in and by whom the Son himself prays to his Father throughout his life and mission. Like the Son, the sons cry out Abba in and by the Spirit. The preposition "in" points to the *indwelling* of the Spirit of the Son in the heart, in the graced creature. The preposition "by" highlights the *leading* of the indwelling Spirit in the believer.

Second, we have noted that Jesus' prayer to his Abba Father is central to the mystery of suffering. For the Son cries out to his Abba most intensely in the agony at Gethsemane, where he struggles with God's will even as he entrusts his life to God unto death. Paul speaks of the Abba prayer of the adopted sons of God as a sharing in the sufferings of the Son, but also and finally as a participation in his glory.

To tie the mystery of prayer to the mystery of suffering and, moreover, to speak of these as one central dimension of Christ's sonship, in which the church also participates by grace, we should look more closely to the Holy Spirit as the one in and by whom both Christ and Christians, the Son and the sons, pray to the Father. The Holy Spirit is the personal link between Christ's prayer and ours. Pneumatology offers us a theological bridge between Christology and ecclesiology that helps us to locate the significance of prayer in the economy of salvation and see it as a Trinitarian event.

The link between Christ's prayer and his suffering, which we see most intensely at Gethsemane, is anticipated in his anointing at the Jordan: "Now when all the people were baptized, and when Jesus also had been baptized and was praying, the heaven was opened, and the Holy Spirit descended upon him in bodily form like a dove. And a voice came from heaven, 'You are my Son, the Beloved; with you I am well-pleased" (Luke 3:21–22). Jesus' prayer to the Father, the descent of the Holy Spirit from the Father upon him, and the response of the Father to Jesus are brought together in the Jordan as three interrelated aspects of the mystery of sonship. At the same time, Luke links the mystery of sonship to the mystery of the Son's suffering, for the Beloved is also the Suffering Servant upon God has put his Spirit, the one to whom the Father says "with you I am well-pleased" (one of Isaiah's Servant Songs).[36]

---

36. The reference is to Isa 42:1. The Servant shall be exalted and the nations will

Under a discussion of prayer as a dimension of the Father's anointing of Jesus with the Spirit into the office of priest, Cantalamessa provides various passages, where explicitly or implicitly, Jesus withdraws to deserted places such as the mountain or the wilderness to pray privately before major events in his life.[37] Considering these pericopes and the fact that Jesus' public prayer must have looked like that of any devout Jew of his time who prayed three fixed times a day, Cantalamessa argues that "the overall picture of Jesus that emerges is of a contemplative who every so often goes over into action, rather than of a man of action who every so often allows himself periods of contemplation."[38] We have an *ora et labora* Jesus (in that order, first prayer, then work), a picture of Jesus that is highly suggestive precisely because is so foreign to us in an era where the church often seems to rush and work in all kinds of projects without first taking the time to pray to the Father, who alone can guide her in carrying out his will in this or that situation and give her the strength to do it.[39] In our busy world today, we are a bit uncomfortable with the Jesus who "would withdraw to deserted places to pray," even when "many crowds would gather to hear him and to be cured of their diseases" (Luke 5:15-16). We protest. How can Jesus do such a thing? What can be more critical than doing God's work for the crowds? Jesus confounds us. Yet his determination is "not to let Himself be overwhelmed by them and so have to give up his dialogue with the Father."[40]

Cantalamessa's portrayal of Jesus, for whom prayer to the Father is "the continuous fabric" of his life, helps us to see that, just as the Spirit moves him to pray, so does the same Spirit urge us (the church) to pray. We are led by the same Spirit in whom Jesus "was led . . . in the wilderness, where . . . he was tempted by the devil" (Luke 4:1-2; cf. Mark 1:12-13). In the desert we find a place of struggle with Satan, the place where the devil puts the Son's

---

see the salvation of God (Isa 52:10, 13), but only after and through the Servant's humiliation and suffering (Isa 52:14-15 and 53).

37. See Luke 5:15-16; for example, Jesus prays before the choosing the twelve disciples (Luke 6:12-13), before the transfiguration (Luke 9:28-29), and—more suggestively—before beginning his public ministry because the wilderness where he is tempted by the devil is assumed to be a place of prayer (Luke 4:1-2ff.). He also prays before the descent of the Holy Spirit upon him at the Jordan (Luke 3:21-22) and at the garden of Gethsemane before his imminent death on Golgotha (Luke 22:41-44). Cantalamessa, *The Holy Spirit in the Life of Jesus*, 51-52.

38. Ibid., 52.

39. Cantalamessa does not merely mean that work must follow prayer (juxtaposition), but rather that work itself must flow out of prayer (subordination). He offers some provocative applications of this principle for the way the church should conduct her everyday business. Ibid., 61-62, cf. 57-58.

40. Ibid., 52.

faithfulness to the Father to the test ("If you are the Son of God..."). But the garden is the ultimate and most intense place of struggle against Satan. As Luke shows, there the Son wrestles intensely with the Father's will, but also asks the Father to give him the strength to do it:

> "Father, if you are willing, remove this cup from me; yet not my will but yours be done." Then an angel from heaven appeared to him and gave him strength. In his anguish he prayed more earnestly, and his sweat became like great drops of blood falling down on the ground" (Luke 22:42–44).

The Son entrusts his mission to the Father. The Spirit who dwells in the Son accompanies him in every prayer spoken and every struggle faced on the road to the cross. Luke tells us that "Jesus rejoiced in the Holy Spirit and said, 'I thank you, Father, Lord or heaven and earth . . . ' " (Luke 10:21). Yet for Jesus this joy and prayer in the Spirit does not occur in the absence of but rather in the midst of pain, persecution, rejection, and death. The presence of the Holy Spirit in the Son does not make him immune to the cross, but does sustain him in that filial trust that leaves one's life in God's hands—in the God who can raise the dead—even in the worst hour of struggle and suffering.

It is important to see Jesus' prayer as a defining expression of his being Son, his relationship to the Father in the Spirit. To affirm, within a substantialist framework, that Jesus does not need to pray because he is God is a penultimate statement. Because of its revelatory function, this affirmation highlights the discontinuity between Jesus and us. He is God the Logos. We are not. Indeed, we cannot share in the presence of the *Logos* in his assumed humanity, for that identity is unique to Jesus. Only Jesus is the Logos, the only-begotten Son of God. Not us. If we are to share in the mystery of the Son, in his prayer life, we must instead share in it according to the presence of the Holy Spirit (not exactly the Logos) in his humanity. For that we have in common with the Son, namely, a Spirit-indwelt humanity and history. We share in the Son's prayer life according to his Spirit in whom he prayed to the Father and whom he has given to us to do the same.

The notion of indwelling is particularly important here, for it implies that the Spirit has given the incarnate Son and us not only his external gifts but also himself. In other words, indwelling is a *personal* reality. As we said before in the case of the Logos, it is not the one divine essence that, by God's causality, is communicated to his assumed humanity. Rather, it is the person of the Logos alone who assumes a human nature (not the Father, not the Spirit). Similarly, in the case of the indwelling of the Holy Spirit, it is not the one divine substance that by God's efficient causality—and thus without personal differentiation—is given to the incarnate Logos *and* to us. Rather, it is the *person* of the Holy Spirit who indwells both the incarnate Son in all fullness and also the sons of God by grace, bringing them into an intimate relationship with their common Father. Indwelling is thus not a substantial reality, but a personal one. Prayer is not something merely external to Christ and to us, but rather constitutive of our common sonship in the Spirit. In the case of Christ, this sonship is grounded in a prior eternal relation to his Father; in our case, we speak of sonship by adoption, grace, or participation. Notwithstanding this distinction, the presence of the Holy Spirit in Christ and Christians, in the Son and the sons, makes it possible to speak of a human sharing in the Son's life of prayer to his Father.

It is in this Spirit of God who dwells in the Son that we sons not only pray to the Father, but are also helped in our "weakness . . . for we do not know how to pray as we ought . . ." (Rom 8:26a). Prayer is a Trinitarian event into which we are brought to express with the Spirit's boldness (with or without words) our filial trust in the Father: "But that very Spirit intercedes [for us] with sighs too deep for words. And God, who searches the heart, knows what is the mind of the Spirit, because the Holy Spirit intercedes for the saints according to the will of God" (Rom 8:26b-27). Not only does Paul show that the Spirit of the Son moves us to address God as our Abba Father, but he also teaches that the same Spirit moves us to pray "according to the will of God." Paul is proclaiming to us a promise for all who like himself (and his Lord Christ before him) cry out Abba as they go through the sufferings of this age and the struggles and pains that come from living in a tragic world. The groaning of the intercessor Spirit of the Son in us, in accordance with God's will, is an evangelical promise precisely because we do not always know how to pray in the midst of tragedy.

The groaning of the Spirit in us is also an evangelical promise because the Spirit of the Son in whom we pray is ultimately the Spirit of redemption and bodily resurrection: "We know that the whole creation has been groaning in labor pain until now; and not only the creation, but we ourselves, who have the first fruits of the Spirit, groan inwardly while we wait for adoption, the redemption of our bodies" (Rom 8:22-23). The mystery of prayer is linked to our sharing in the Son's sufferings, but also in our sharing in the Father's designation and establishment of Jesus "as Son of God in power according to the Spirit of holiness through resurrection from the dead" (Rom 1:4). The presence of the Spirit in the Son and in the sons may not make us immune to suffering in this world, but it does bring us now into the eschatological hope of the resurrection that is to come:

> If the Spirit of the one who raised Jesus from the dead dwells in you, the one who raised Christ from the dead will give life to your mortal bodies also, through his Spirit that dwells in you" (Rom 8:11).

In prayer, whether spoken or not, we put our very lives in God's hands because the Spirit of the crucified and risen Christ who dwells in our hearts moves us to put our trust, as the Son once did at Gethsemane, in the God who can raise the dead.

To speak of prayer as an expression of sonship, of filial trust (both Christ's and ours), we must ground prayer in the identity of the triune God. Prayer is an *address* to a personal God—more specifically, the person of the Father—who is not only in a rational relation with his creatures, but who is relational in his own being and therefore hears and responds to his children. There is a manner of speaking in which relationality can be posited in God in a *sui generis* way, in a manner that applies only to God. Can we speak of an intrinsic relationality in the triune God that is expressed in the economy of salvation by God's entering into communion with us freely and out of love, but that at the same time does not compromise God's radical distinction from creation?

John Zizioulas has argued that relationality in God was affirmed by the Cappadocians not to make God change in his relation to the world, but precisely to safeguard the distinction between God and the world over against Greek ontological monism (i.e., the substantial and non-personal unity of God with the cosmos). As we noted earlier in our discussion of Trinitarian theology, Zizioulas has shown that the Cappadocians countered the monists, who made God's substance dependent on the world's process, by grounding divine being in the free person of the Father. Because person is the hypostasis of being, hypostasis (concrete manner of being) is essentially relational (being-in-relation). Since the concrete existence of the divine substance (*ousia*) is to be found in the person (= hypostasis), the cause (*aitia*) of the divine existence must also be found in a particular person (not in the common divine essence per se). God is personal because he is, in the first place, the *person* of the Father (not God in general), and as the Father, he is the personal cause of the generation of the Son and the procession of the Holy Spirit. In Greek theology, "cause" is not understood in terms of cause and effect, but rather in a *sui generis* manner to refer to the Father's personal uniqueness as the fountain of divinity in a non-temporal, non-spatial sense (immanent Trinity), and thus as the fountain of love towards us through the Son and in the Holy Spirit (economic Trinity). If Zizioulas's thesis about the Cappadocian anti-monistic argument for the intrinsic relational nature of the triune God *ad intra* and *ad extra* is true, we have in our toolbox an explicitly Trinitarian way of acknowledging the subtantialist concern of the classical theist to preserve the Creator-creature distinction. At the same time, the Cappadocian focus on God's being-in-relation opens the way for addressing the concern of the open theist for adequately speaking of God's relation to the world in a way that goes beyond Thomas's merely rational relation.

We learn from the Cappadocians that the notion of *person* carries with it the ideas of an intra-Trinitarian being-in-relation and a Trinitarian relating-to-another in freedom and love in the economy of salvation. The idea of openness in freedom and love in turn points to a perichoresis or interdependence of persons in communion with one another that is expressed historically in the Father's loving outreach to his creatures through the Son and in the Holy Spirit. We are reminded that person or hypostasis can never precede relation in the Eastern-Cappadocian system. For "to be" is "to be in relation to another," both in the immanent Trinity (*theologia*) and the economic Trinity (*oikonomia*). Therefore, it is intrinsic to the divine persons to relate to each other and to us in such a way that God neither falls prey to us nor becomes apathetic to our cries. If we were to use Thomistic categories to fulfill these requirements, we could perhaps speak of a relation between God and the world that is "real" to us and "quasi-real" (as opposed to simply rational) to God.[41] Such language would affirm that God is relational intrinsically and therefore responsive in relation to the world (a concern of open theists), while also stating that God's responsiveness to the world cannot compromise his radical distinction from the world (a concern of classical theists).

We have yet to reflect briefly on the Trinitarian implication of prayer as a reality intrinsic and not simply external to the person of the Son. In Christ's prayer life, in his address to or dialogue with God the Father in and by the Spirit, we see Christ's filial trust of his Father. The prayer at Gethsemane, "Abba, Father, not what I want, but what you want," presents us

---

41. Similarly, Rahner uses the notion of "quasi-formal" causality (instead of efficient or formal causality) to speak of the triune God's self-giving or self-communication to the creature in indwelling without doing away with the ontological distinction between God and the graced creature. See *The Trinity*, 36, 77; in distinction from classical theism, Pinnock writes: "The open view sees God as self-sufficient, ontologically other trinitarian being who voluntarily created the world out of nothing and graciously relates to it in self-limiting ways out of respect for the freedom that he has bestowed on the creatures he made." *Most Moved Mover*, 145. I have no problem with the notion of relationality in God, which open theists develop, but with the extent to which the notion of divine self-limitation can be used to affirm such relationality to the detriment of God's ontological distinction from creation.

with a faithful Son who is finally total openness, perfect "Yes!" to the Father. As an economic expression of sonship, this filial trust is grounded in a prior eternal reality, namely, in the Son's own personal relation to his Father, of whom he is the perfect image, towards whom he faces, and from whom he exists in an eternal "I-Thou" reciprocal relation of love in the Spirit. Therefore, prayer is not accidental to Jesus. It is not external to the person of the Logos. Christ's prayer life tells us something about who he *is* as Son. In and by the Spirit of the Son, the church can also face towards the Father through the intercession of his Son, who is his perfect image, and confidently dialogue with her Father before setting out to work both to know the Father's will in this or that situation and receive the strength to do it and live (even struggle) with it in a tragic world.

Summary

First, my study has shown that Jesus' prayer life is an expression of his being Son. This means that Christ's prayer must not be discussed as a reality *external* to his person, even if his prayer is, as Thomas argues, revelatory of his essential sonship and instructive for us. Prayer is ultimately a Trinitarian event that is centered in the mystery of filiation or sonship. In the Spirit, the Son prays Abba. Prayer, therefore, is an expression in the economy of salvation of the Son's eternal "I-Thou" relation to the Father in the Spirit. Because we pray in and by the same Spirit, in the Spirit of the Son, our prayer must not be seen as something *external* to ourselves—that is, as something that we do but tells us nothing about who we *are*. Rather, prayer is for the church a Trinitarian event into which she is brought to share by the indwelling of the Spirit of the Son (and his Father) in her.

Practically speaking, this means that our prayer life must be seen as a *gift* from God. It is a dimension of sonship, central to who God has made us to be, *intrinsic* to our human identity as his children. From baptism, the Father has promised to us that the gift of his Holy Spirit, who alone searches and knows his thoughts (1 Cor 2:10b–11), will also intercede for us in accordance with divine will because we do not always know how to pray. This is a great promise for those living in the midst of tragedy and suffering great pain. Faith does not look into either God's immutability or his self-limitation—those divine attributes privileged respectively by classical and open theists—in the moment of anguish and numbness and speechlessness. Rather, faith looks trustingly to God's *promise* that we have received the Spirit of his Son at our little Jordan to pray (with or without words, with or without eloquence) as the Son once did: "Abba, Father, Thy will be done!"

Otherwise stated, our personalist approach to prayer does not direct anxious consciences to divine attributes for the assurance of God's love, but rather to the Father's promise that he listens and responds to his dear children.

Second, and related to the point above, prayer is above all an expression of *filial trust*, not of speculation into what God might have already decided or might be deciding in the future. We simply do not know the mind of God. Only the Spirit does. It becomes an unbearable burden to wonder if I have prayed in accordance with God's immutable will (classical theism) or if I have prayed enough to make God change his mind (open theism).[42] This can only lead to self-security or despair. Since we have been given the Spirit to lead us to pray according to God's will, we are therefore free to put our lives in the Father's hands.

Practically speaking, this means that we should not think either that our prayers are not necessary because God already knows what he is going to do anyway, or that our prayers are necessary for God to change his mind about something which is yet to happen and he may or not know anything about. These formulations miss the point that prayer is an expression of filial trust, of self-giving to a merciful Father who knows what is best for his children. Filial trust does not allow us to say, "I won't pray because God already knows what is going to happen to me." Nor does filial trust allow us to say, "I'll pray because God needs my prayers to direct his course of action in the future." Both types of responses betray a sinful arrogance, an unwillingness to be faithful to God, to put trust back in God and not in ourselves. Filial trust says, "Abba, Father, I put my life and work into your hands." Filial trust is not a matter of submitting to an apathetic God or persuading a self-limiting God. It is a matter of trusting in a loving Father who has given us the Spirit of his Son to enter a reciprocal I-Thou relation with him characterized by faith on our side and love on his side.

Finally, prayer as an expression of sonship implies a participation of the church in the sufferings and glorification of the Son. Practically speaking, we must remember that the indwelling of the Spirit in us does not make us immune to suffering—as Christ's own anointing with the Spirit to be the Suffering Servant shows. The church's prayer is an instance of her

---

42. Even Sanders's affirmation that God may at times not do something "because we fail to ask for ourselves or for others" or that "we have not because we ask not" (Jas 4:2) can be a burden to the one who feels he or she has not prayed enough to change God's mind. See Sanders, *The God who Risks*, 268–74; Sanders's statements can be used to promote boldness in prayer for those who feel as if their prayers are useless in the face of God's sovereignty and foreknowledge. Unlike Sanders, however, I prefer to speak of such a call for bold prayer in terms of filial trust in the Father's promise without speculating on the power of such prayers to persuade him or the nature of his knowledge of the future.

sharing in the Spirit of the Son who prayed to his Abba at Gethsemane, the place of struggle and agony, which means prayer not in the absence of but in the midst of and in spite of suffering and death. This is the reality of the situation.

However, we must also remind the suffering church today that her prayer in this tragic world is, in and by the Spirit in her, a *proleptic eschatological groaning* of trust in the God who raises the dead to life precisely because he raised his Son to life by the power of the same Spirit. As in the case of the Son, the sons' prayer life in and by the Spirit will be joined to the mystery of suffering and final trust in God's eschatological deliverance.

9

Living in the Spirit of Christ
Models of Sanctification as Sacramental Pneumatology

WHAT DOES LIFE IN the Spirit of Christ look like in our own lives? In this chapter, I argue for a sacramental or incarnational approach to the theology of the Holy Spirit that in turn yields three models of the sanctified life. We use the term "sacramental" in the broad sense to speak of the Spirit's work in salvation history through material means in creation—above all, through the Son's own *human* life and history. Such a pneumatology focuses on the identity of the *incarnate* Christ as the privileged locus of the Holy Spirit, as the bearer and giver of the Spirit of God. Over against a highly spiritualized view of "spirit" grounded in the Greek philosophical dualism of spirit over matter, our sacramental pneumatology affirms the close association of the Holy Spirit with the Son in his life, death, and resurrection. It is an incarnational pneumatology.

We also employ the term "sacramental" in a narrow sense to refer to God's work through instituted means of grace such as baptism and the Lord's Supper.[1] The Holy Spirit dares to work through ordinary and seemingly insignificant means or signs in creation (such as water, or bread and wine)

---

1. "The word 'sacramental' . . . may be understood in the narrow sense and simply mean the two sacraments, baptism and the Lord's Supper. And it may be understood in the broader sense as a designation of a fundamental religious view, which seeks to find God, not in pure spiritual ideas, but in the small outward things of the world which are used by God as a means of manifesting himself in the visible and physical world." Prenter, *Spiritus Creator*, 152.

to deliver God's word of forgiveness, life, and salvation to a broken world. Such a material view of the Spirit has implications for our life together. If the grace God delivers through common appointed means directs us to the benefit (Lat. *beneficium*) of the sacraments in what pertains to our communion with God, the actual life in the Spirit Christ that flows from receiving such gifts of grace refers us to the daily use (Lat. *usus*) of the sacrament in our lives and relationships. A sacramental pneumatology draws attention to the Spirit's sanctifying presence and activity in the lives of ordinary human vessels, and thus speaks directly to the Spirit's shaping of the believer after Christ's own life in the Spirit.

Our argument proceeds in three stages. First, we show that a Nicene approach to the doctrine of the Holy Spirit, while interested in drawing the third person's ontological distinction from us, ultimately points to his sanctifying works on our behalf as the basis for acknowledging and confessing his divine equality with the Father and the Son. In a creedal hermeneutic, an important shift is made from the immateriality to the materiality of the Spirit, from ontology to soteriology, that sets the stage for conceiving the Spirit's work through means in creation to bring about God's saving and sanctifying purposes.

Second, we argue that a sacramental or incarnational view of the Holy Spirit finds its basis in a Spirit Christology, namely, in the affirmation of the Spirit's inseparable connection to Christ's own flesh, the incarnate Word's life and mission. Our approach does not only look to the Spirit who comes *after* Christ, but sees the Spirit already *in* Christ. In a prominent patristic reading of the Jordan event, Christ's receiving of the Spirit for us in baptism paves the way in the Father's plan of salvation for Christ's giving of the Spirit to us in our baptism.[2] There is a chain of salvation, a pneumatological link, between Christology and ecclesiology.

Third, we offer three models of life in the Spirit—namely, baptismal, dramatic, and eucharistic models of sanctification—and highlight how these ways of conceiving the Christian life are inspired in biblical narratives and corresponding sources in the Western Lutheran tradition. By showing the link between Christology and ecclesiology in these narratives and sources, we demonstrate how Christ's own cruciform life in the Spirit shapes the Christian's life in the Spirit. Finally, we suggest how these models, though they complement each other, may function practically in addressing particular issues faced in the life of the Christian, while directing him in some way towards the use or appropriation of the sacraments in everyday life. In

---

2. For a survey of various patristic reflections on the Jordan event, see McDonnell, *The Baptism of Jesus in the Jordan*.

short, our brief study yields three models of sanctification grounded in an incarnational and sacramental pneumatology.

FROM THE WORKS TO THE PERSON: THE NICENO-CONSTANTINOPOLITAN FOCUS ON THE MATERIALITY OF THE SPIRIT

In his classic treatise on the Holy Spirit, Basil the Great speaks of the third person of the Trinity according to both his divine nature and his grace towards us. Against the Arianizing pneumatomachians ("Spirit-fighters" or "Spirit-deniers") who subordinated the Holy Spirit ontologically to the Father and the Son, reducing his nature to that of a "ministering spirit,"[3] Basil shows that the Holy Spirit shares the same dignity with the Father and the Son because he shares with them the divine name into which catechumens are baptized according to the Lord's command and teaching in Matthew 28.[4] The pneumatomachians made a big deal of a particular doxology in use at the time (i.e., "Glory to the Father, *through* the Son, *in* the Holy Spirit"), which they interpreted in Arian fashion, claiming that the difference in the prepositions (i.e., "through" and "in") revealed a dissimilarity of natures among the three persons.[5] To buttress their argument, the pneumatomachians argued that another doxology also used at the time in the churches under Basil's pastoral care (i.e., "Glory to the Father, *with* the Son, *together with* the Holy Spirit") was an innovative liturgical rubric that should not be allowed in worship. Basil noted that the doxology in question was not innovative at all. It was established by the Lord's own instruction in Matthew 28 and preserved in the church's longstanding practice of Trinitarian baptism, which assumed and confessed "the union and fellowship" of the Holy Spirit with the Father and the Son.[6]

Basil's influence is felt in many churches to this day, each time we speak or sing the common doxology, "Glory be to the Father, and to the Son, and to the Holy Spirit."[7] Yet Basil does not deny the proper use of the

---

3. "Our opponents . . . divide and tear away the Spirit from the Father, transforming His nature to that of a ministering spirit." Basil, *On the Holy Spirit* 10.25 (trans. Anderson).

4. Ibid., 10.24.

5. Ibid., 1.3, 2.4.

6. Ibid., 10.24; Basil insists that "we follow the teaching of the Lord as our rule . . . He [i.e., the Spirit] is numbered *with* Them in the baptismal formula, and we consider it necessary to combine Their names in the same way when we profess our faith, and we treat the profession of faith as the origin and mother of the doxology." Ibid., 27.68

7. "We have already said that as far as our understanding is concerned, to say 'Glory

other doxology, where God's people say "Glory to the Father through the Son in the Holy Spirit," as long as the same is not understood in an Arian subordinationist manner. Both doxologies are ultimately Trinitarian, even if each one highlights something distinct about the Holy Spirit. One doxology ("Glory to the Father, with the Son, together with the Holy Spirit") speaks of the Holy Spirit according to his divine nature, who he is in communion with the Father and the Son. As Basil explains, the preposition "*with* proclaims the communion of the Spirit with God."[8] Those who share in the same divine nature deserve the worship due to God alone. In the Council of Constantinople's expanded version of the third article of the Nicene Creed, the confession of the divinity and lordship of the Holy Spirit, "who with the Father and the Son together is worshiped and glorified," bears the marks of Basil's teaching against the pneumatomachians. The equal glory of the Holy Spirit with the Father and the Son confessed at Constantinople amounts to an extension of the argument for the consubstantiality (*homoosious*) of the Son with the Father confessed earlier at Nicea.

In spite of its potential abuse by Arian sympathizers, Basil still accepts the other doxology ("Glory to the Father, through the Son, in the Holy Spirit"), which properly understood speaks of the Holy Spirit in accordance with what he does for us and for our salvation in history, according to "the grace we have been given."[9] As Basil puts it, in response to the pneumatomachian linguistic argument, "the preposition *in* expresses the relationship between ourselves and the Spirit."[10] If the first doxology points to the divine person of the Spirit *ad intra* (*theologia* or immanent Trinity), the second one points to the works of the Spirit for our benefit or *ad extra* (*oikonomia* or economic Trinity).[11] Vestiges of this economic type of doxology are still present in our churches each time we ask God the Father to hear our prayers "*through Jesus Christ, our Lord.*" Since such prayers occur "in" or "by" the Holy Spirit in any case, we do not typically articulate in the rubric itself what the Spirit is doing. In this case, we do not talk explicitly *about* the Holy Spirit, though we recognize he is at work in the background, behind the scenes. We simply pray *in* the Spirit, the one in whom we worship the Son and cry out to the

---

to the Father *and* to the Son *and* to the Holy Spirit' means the same as 'Glory to the Father *and* to the Son *with* the Holy Spirit.' We have received the word *and* from the very words of the Lord." Ibid., 27.68.

8. Ibid.

9. Ibid.

10. Ibid.

11. "Therefore, when we consider the Spirit's *rank*, we think of Him as present *with* the Father and the Son, but when we consider the working of His grace on its recipients, we say that the Spirit is *in* us." Ibid., 26.63.

Father through the intercession of the Son.[12] We pray in the Spirit of sonship, of Christ.

When Basil teaches about the Spirit in the immanent Trinity, he distinguishes the Spirit from God's creatures. As "holy" Spirit, the third person is not a ministering spirit, like angels, but rather the source of their holiness.[13] Likewise, the Spirit is the source of the sanctification or holiness of the saints.[14] When speaking of the Holy Spirit according to his divine attributes, Basil can also refer to his immateriality for "God is Spirit" and cannot be reduced to time or space.[15] As "spirit," the Holy Spirit is utterly distinct from creation and cannot be bound to any place. At this level, discourse on the Holy Spirit aims at safeguarding his divine *nature*, an important move against the Arians. In the larger scheme of things, however, this necessary move is a penultimate one. For Basil is more interested in discussing the *works* of the Holy Spirit in our midst in order to lead us to the confession of his lordship. There is a Nicene hermeneutic at work in these efforts, grounded in Athanasius's earlier claim against the Arians that the Word was not a human creature who was later anointed and exalted to become deified on the basis of his virtues or obedience. Rather, the Word, who is God with the Father, was anointed and exalted according to the flesh *for our sake*, so that we might be exalted through him. In Athanasius's own words: "Therefore He was not man, and then became God, but He was God, and then became man, and that to deify us."[16]

Athanasius and Basil share a theology from below, which moves from the sanctifying works of the Son and the Spirit in the economy of God's salvation to a recognition of the divine nature they have (are) in common with the Father. For Athanasius, we come to know, confess, and worship the Son as God, *homoousios* with the Father, on the basis of his works for us. In the same way, Basil shows that we come to know who the Holy Spirit *is* on the basis of what he *does* on our behalf. In Basil's pastoral application of the

12. "He who rejects the Spirit rejects the Son, and he who rejects the Son rejects the Father . . . It is impossible to worship the Son except in the Holy Spirit; it is impossible to call upon the Father except in the Spirit of adoption." Ibid., 11.27.

13. Ibid., 16.38 (cf. 19.49).

14. Ibid., 9.22–23, 19.49.

15. "His first and most proper title is Holy Spirit, a name most especially appropriate to everything which is incorporeal, purely immaterial, and indivisible." Ibid., 9.22.

16. Athanasius, *First Discourse* 11.39 (*NPNF*[2] 4:329). By deification, Athanasius does not mean that man becomes God by nature, but rather that man becomes deified by grace through the Holy Spirit. For Athanasius, such deification is an all-encompassing Spirit-driven saving work that begins with the Christian's anointing in baptism and thus includes his participation in Christ's own resurrection, immortality, incorruptibility, and being in the Father's presence (cf. ibid, 11.41 [*NPNF*[2] 4:330]).

Nicene hermeneutic to the third person, the soteriological move to the story of the Spirit in our sanctification, the desire to speak of what the Spirit does freely in time and space for us and for our salvation, drives the show. While the ontological distinction between God and his creatures is foundational, the soteriological claims of the creeds and the fathers concerning the joint mission of the Son and the Spirit in the Father's salvation of the world were determinative for the church's Trinitarian confession. What matters most is the Holy Spirit's in Christ's saints.

THE SPIRIT AND THE WORD: TOWARDS AN INCARNATIONAL AND SACRAMENTAL PNEUMATOLOGY

In his major work on pneumatology, Congar reflects on the bodily character of the Spirit's activity. After discussing the work of the Holy Spirit in the Scriptures as the life-giving breath who carries out or fulfills God's plans in history, Congar concludes that the Holy Spirit's identity should be described not so much in terms of immateriality as much as "subtle corporeality."

> Ruah-breath is not in any sense opposed to 'body' or 'corporeal.' . . . It is a subtle corporeality rather than an incorporeal substance. The ruah-breath of the Old Testament is not disincarnate. It is rather what animates the body. . . . The Greeks thought in categories of substance, but the Jews were concerned with force, energy, and the principle of action. The spirit-breath was for them what acts and causes to act and, in the case of the Breath of God, what animates and causes to act in order to realize God's plan).[17]

The bodily or material trajectory of the Holy Spirit's movement, starting in creation and reaching its fulfillment in the new creation, becomes the focal point of pneumatology. While Basil can speak of the immateriality of the Holy Spirit in order to distinguish the third person from creation (ontology), we have seen that Basil's greatest interest lies in the works of the Spirit for our sake (soteriology). The overriding reason for safeguarding the divinity of the Holy Spirit lies in the church's confession of the saving or deifying work of the Spirit in baptism. Through the regenerating grace of baptism, humans become Spirit-bearing souls, and many blessings follow.[18]

---

17. Congar, *Holy Spirit*, 1:3.

18. "Through the Holy Spirit comes our restoration to the kingdom of heaven, our adoption as God's sons, our freedom to call God our Father, our becoming partakers

In view of the sanctifying deeds of the Spirit from the beginning of our adoption in baptism to our final redemption at the resurrection, we confess the Spirit to be God.

Basil moves from the works of the Spirit to the worship of the Spirit: "Remission of sins is given through the gift of the Spirit.... Through the Spirit we become intimate with God.... Resurrection from the dead is accomplished by the operation of the Spirit.... Understanding all this, how can we be afraid of giving the Spirit too much honor?"[19] By locating the Holy Spirit's action in baptism and its benefits, Basil moves decisively towards a material and thus sacramental view of his work. Such an approach assumes an incarnational view of the Spirit, which flows from a broader Spirit-oriented approach to the mystery of Christ, and thus highlights his inseparability from the Son, the Word made flesh, who bears and gives the Spirit.[20]

The christological basis for a sacramental pneumatology requires that one look for the Holy Spirit not simply *after* Christ, but already *in* Christ, in his fleshly existence, his human life and mission. Accordingly, Basil locates the Holy Spirit not only in the saving baptism that Christ commanded for our sake *after* completion of his mission on earth, but *in* Christ's own incarnation. Referring to texts on the baptism of Jesus (John 1:33, Matt 3:17, and Acts 10:38), Basil asks:

> But when we speak of the plan of salvation for men, accomplished in God's goodness by our great God and Savior Jesus Christ, who would deny that it was all made possible through the grace of the Spirit . . . Everything that happened since the Lord's coming in the flesh, it all comes to pass through the Spirit. In the first place, the Lord was anointed with the Holy Spirit, who would henceforth be inseparably united to His very flesh."[21]

---

of the grace of Christ, being called children of light, sharing in eternal glory, and in a word, our inheritance of the fullness of blessing, both in this world and the world to come." Basil, *On the Holy Spirit* 15.36 (trans. Anderson; cf. 9.23).

19. Ibid., 19.49.

20. Rogers has argued for a bodily pneumatology, where the Spirit befriends and sanctifies matter because the he has made Christ his resting place in the incarnation. I am in basic agreement with his thesis: "Each of the bodies on which the Spirit rests depends analogically on the body of Christ: the body of Christ in the church, the body of Christ in the Christian, the body of Christ in the sacramental element. In each case, the Spirit befriends the body, because it is the body of Christ: in each case the Spirit gives a body to Christ, because Christ bade a body by the Spirit from the Father, that those with bodies might also receive the Spirit." Rogers, *After the Spirit*, 210, cf. 14.

21. *On the Holy Spirit* 16.39, 65.

Basil shows the defining action of the Spirit in the mystery of the incarnation, being "present in every action He [i.e., Christ] performed," "there when the Lord was tempted by the devil," "united with Jesus when He performed miracles," and also never leaving Him "after His resurrection from the dead."[22]

Before Basil, in the aftermath of the Council of Nicea, Athanasius shows a bit more clearly this pneumatological link between the baptism of Jesus and Christian baptism. The Word of God made flesh was anointed with the Holy Spirit at his baptism so that we might receive the Spirit through him [i.e., the Word] in Christian baptism. Athanasius argues that "no otherwise should we have partaken the Spirit and been sanctified, but that the giver of the Spirit, the Word Himself, had spoken of Himself as anointed with the Spirit for us."[23] The Word receives the Spirit in the flesh in order to give the Spirit to humanity. The Spirit's presence in Christ has a sacramental trajectory.

In the West, Luther's pneumatology acknowledges that the Holy Spirit cannot be bound to the spoken, sacramental, or written forms of the word. The Holy Spirit cannot be manipulated through the mere human performance of rites (Lat. *ex opere operato*), as if he were our personal possession or could be reduced to being a mere instrument of the word. At the level of ontology, "the Spirit is not bound *in* the Word" because he "has his own existence in God's eternal glory, away from the Word and from our world."[24] On the other hand, the Holy Spirit, "as the revealing Spirit," comes to us freely and out of love through the spoken and sacramental word, binding himself to the word not for his own sake but for our benefit.[25] The Holy Spirit is thus intimately linked to the written word that is heard and spoken in proclamation, as well as the word at it is seen, felt, and tasted in the sacraments. By drawing attention to the self-effacing character of the Spirit's free descent in our lives, Luther in his own way applies a Nicene creedal hermeneutic to the question of the relationship between the Spirit and the Word, privileging soteriology (the economy of salvation) over ontology in the formulation of pneumatology.

22. Ibid., 16.39.
23. *First Discourse* 12.50 (*NPNF*[2] 4:336).
24. Prenter, *Spiritus Creator*, 122.
25. "But as the revealing Spirit, as the Spirit which is come to us, he cannot be without the Word. For it is the Spirit's work to make risen Christ real and present among us. And the risen Christ can only be present among us in his humanity. But the risen Christ's humanity in our midst now is the Word, a contemporary and sacramental Word, which gives Christ as gift, and in which he is the acting subject." Ibid., 122–23.

Luther's affirmation of the Holy Spirit's work through the *external* word (Lat. *verbum externum*) that comes to us in God's promises is not merely a polemic move against enthusiasts who look *first* for the Spirit internally (or in the heart), but an approach to pneumatology that assumes *first* the Spirit's inseparable connection to Christ and his words of life. For this reason, a proper spirituality or view of life in the Spirit will not seek God *outside* his word, which points us to Christ in the flesh. The inseparability of the Spirit and the Word does not take away from the Spirit's work in the heart or even his hiddenness, but gives priority to the unity of his life-giving Breath with the creative Word that addresses us in the here and now. In paradoxical fashion, the Holy Spirit is both free from the word and yet freely bound to the word. Similarly, the Lutheran confessors note that the Holy Spirit works faith "where and when He wills," and then immediately add that the Spirit does so only "in those who hear the gospel."[26] There is a recognition of the hidden Spirit (Lat. *spiritus absconditus*), and paradoxically, of the revealed Spirit (Lat. *spiritus revelatus*) who ordinarily comes to us hidden in, with, and under the bodily Word.

The ultimate move towards the material or sacramental view of the Holy Spirit depends entirely on Luther's christological understanding of the word. Scripture, oral proclamation (including absolution), and the sacraments of baptism and the Lord's Supper point to and deliver Christ to sinners. Since "all Scripture tends toward him," Christ, the Word made flesh, is the object or aim of the word.[27] Moreover, Christ speaks his promises today when the Scriptures are delivered to us in the proclamation. Christ is thus the subject or agent of the word.[28] The inseparability of the Holy Spirit and the word of God that is heard and spoken in the proclamation, as well as felt and tasted in, with, and under the water and the bread and wine, is entirely dependent upon the inseparable fellowship of the Spirit and the Word made flesh.[29] There is no greater sacrament and sign of salvation than the incarnate Christ in whom the Spirit dwells and through whom the Spirit is given. In Luther's view, the Holy Spirit is united to Christ's promise (Lat. *promissio*) under sure signs (Lat. *signa*) of grace or sacraments, thereby revealing

---

26. CA V, 3, in *BC*, 40.

27. Luther, *A Brief Instruction on What to Look for and Expect in the Gospels*, 122.

28. "For the preaching of the gospel is nothing else than Christ coming to us, or we being brought to him." Ibid., 121.

29. The inseparability of the Holy Spirit and the Word (both as command and promise) drives Luther's critique against "enthusiasm," namely, "'God within-ism' or the human attempt to play god by seeking God's Spirit or living a spiritual life apart from or without reference to God's own Word." Sánchez, "Pneumatology," 125; cf. SA III, 8.3–5, in *BC*, 322.

"his own manifestation in the humanity of Christ" today and making these sacraments the "concrete means for the work of the risen Christ" on our behalf.[30]

The early Lutheran theologians, almost in passing, point to this Christ-centered character of the Holy Spirit's work in the particular framework of a Spirit Christology. They draw attention to the pneumatological continuity, shape, and function of the proclamation of the word from Christ to the church.

> Therefore, the *Spirit of Christ* must not only comfort but through the function of the law must also 'convict the world of sin' [John 16:8]. Thus, in the New Testament, the Holy Spirit must perform . . . an alien work—which is to convict—until he comes to his proper work—which is to comfort and to proclaim grace. *For this reason Christ obtained the Spirit for us and sent him to us.*"[31]

Because the Holy Spirit is inseparably united to the Word made flesh and his words, and therefore to his Scripture, absolution, baptism, and Supper, we can posit the materiality and incarnational character of the Spirit and thus a sacramental view of life in the Spirit of Christ. If Christ is the privileged locus of the Spirit, the definitive bearer and giver of the Spirit, then, we must also look to Christ to know what life in the Spirit looks like in our own lives. Let us turn now to the shape of the sanctified life. In doing so, we seek to offer not only a conceptual presentation of sanctification, but also images or narratives that might help us to get a handle on three forms of Christlikeness the Spirit shapes in us.

THE SPIRIT IN CHRIST AND CHRISTIANS: SPIRIT CHRISTOLOGY AS A LENS FOR MODELS OF SANCTIFICATION

Basil's statement that the Holy Spirit is "inseparably united to His [Christ's] very flesh" succinctly highlights an incarnational view of the Spirit's work and guides us as we look more specifically at three dimensions of our

---

30. Prenter, *Spiritus Creator*, 166; Luther's views assume that a sacrament is only a visible sign (*signum*) of God's promise (*promissio*) because Christ in his humanity is God's sacrament, God's own visible sign and promise given to us in the proclamation of the Word. Luther also notes that only the Holy Spirit is able to bring together in a salvific way the promise and the sign offered in the sacrament by creating the faith that holds on to Christ in the sacrament. For a deeper study of these connections, see *Spiritus Creator*, 101–72.

31. FC, SD V, 11, in *BC*, 583; italics mine.

incarnate Lord's life in the Spirit that in turn shape the Christian's life in the same Spirit. These christological narratives yield three approaches to the Christian life, which we name the baptismal, dramatic, and eucharistic models of sanctification.[32] An operating assumption of our project is that, while Christ's life in the Spirit is unique from that of the saints, there are still aspects or configurations of such life that are in continuity with the Spirit's work in Christ's saints. The Spirit whom Christ receives and bears in the flesh for our sake is the same Spirit whom Christ gives to his saints in order to shape or conform their lives after his own.

In this section, we sketch our three models of sanctification, grounding them in a Spirit-oriented Christology, and showing how these forms of life in the Spirit of Christ correspond to various ways in which Lutherans have spoken of the Christian life. In the process, we will show how each of the models presented flow from a sacramental view of the Spirit's work in the church, one that highlights the continuous use or appropriation of the sacraments in the life of the saints during their pilgrimage in the world. We should note that all three models anchor the Christian life in a cruciform or cross-shaped reading of the Father's anointing of the Son with the Spirit at the Jordan. In the waters of the Jordan, the obedient Son receives the Spirit in the flesh to begin his ministry as our suffering Servant (Matthew 3:17, Mark 1:9–11, Luke 3:21).[33] Christ's reception and bearing of the Spirit gives his life a cruciform trajectory, setting him on a path to the cross.

At the Jordan, Christ was anointed to suffer unto death on our behalf. From this cruciform reading of Christ's baptism, we gather some implications for the Christian life. The Father's anointing of the Son at the Jordan for his mission as the Servant becomes paradigmatic for conceiving the sanctified life as a daily: 1) return to baptism, where we die with Christ in the waters and are raised with him from the waters to new life (baptismal model); 2) struggle in the deserts of life against the attacks of the devil, a battle the Christian must vigilantly stand firm and fight in with the word and prayer as his weapons (dramatic model); and 3) act of worship or thanksgiving to God for his gifts, a life where one becomes the servant of many, a living sacrifice unto the Lord (eucharistic model).[34]

32. For a fuller description of the three models, see Sánchez, *Teología de la santificación*, 75–147.

33. The Synoptic Gospels cite Isaiah 42:1, "with you I am well pleased," from the first Servant Song (cf. Isaiah 49:1–7, 50:4–11, 52:13—53:12). In John's Gospel, some manuscripts make an allusion to Isaiah 42:1 through the use of the title "God's chosen one" (1:34). In John, the Lamb of God who takes away the sin of the world (1:29) is the One on whom the Spirit remains and who baptizes with the Holy Spirit (1:33).

34. For a Catholic reflection on the Christian life as the church's participation in

The Baptismal Model: Dying and Being Raised with Christ

We have already seen how Athanasius links the church's reception of the Holy Spirit in baptism to the anointing or sanctification of Christ. The Word received the Spirit in the flesh in order to save the flesh. The Jordan reveals that, through our baptism, we are anointed and sanctified in Christ. Before Athanasius, Irenaeus had placed both the incarnation of the Word and his reception of the Spirit in baptism at the center of salvation history, as events through which the Word recapitulated or did over again for the human race the failed history of sinful Adam through his incarnation, death, and resurrection. As a result of the Fall, the Spirit had departed from Adam. In order to restore the Spirit to the race of Adam, the Word not only took upon himself the nature of Adam (human nature) at the incarnation but also received the anointing of the Spirit at his baptism.[35] The Spirit's resting on the Son in the waters of the Jordan inaugurates the Spirit's return to corrupted humanity. By descending upon the Son of God at the Jordan, the Holy Spirit once again becomes "accustomed in fellowship with Him to dwell in the human race, to rest with human beings," restoring them to fellowship with God.[36]

A prominent theme in Luther's catechesis is his instruction on baptism as a daily death and resurrection with Christ, a daily drowning of the Old Adam and raising of the new creature in Christ.[37] These images assume the church's participation in Christ's life, his death and resurrection, but also his baptism, which is the entry point in his ministry towards the cross, the way of obedience unto death, as well as his exaltation and giving of the Holy Spirit to others. The faithful Son descends to the waters of the Jordan on behalf of sinners, anticipating his role as the Servant who will take upon himself our sins. In Scripture, the waters signify both judgment and new life. Jesus goes down to the waters of God's judgment on behalf of sinners,

---

Christ's threefold office, see Cantalamessa, *The Holy Spirit in the Life of Jesus*. He uses a methodology that is similar to mine, one that draws an account of the church's life in the Spirit on the basis of a pneumatological Christology.

35. Alluding to Gen 2:7, Basil speaks of the Spirit's return to the race of Adam through Christ's breathing of the same in the new creation. Referring to John 20:22-23, Basil writes: "When the Lord renewed mankind by breathing the Holy Spirit into His Apostles' faces (thus restoring the grace which Adam lost, which God breathed into him in the beginning), what did He say?" *On the Holy Spirit* 16.39.

36. Irenaeus, *Against Heresies* 3.17.1 (ANF 1:444); "The Word of God . . . dwelt in man, and became Son of man, that He might accustom man to receive God, and God to dwell in man, according to the good pleasure of the Father." Ibid., 3.20.2 (ANF 1:450); "God recapitulated in Himself the ancient formation of man, that He might kill sin, deprive death of its power, and vivify man." Ibid., 3.18.7 (ANF 1:448); cf., ibid., 3.18.1 (ANF 1:446).

37. SC, the Sacrament of Holy Baptism, 11-14, in *BC*, 360.

drowning our sins with him in our place, and then rises from the waters so that through him we might become a new creation.

In his Flood Prayer, Luther picks up on the patristic image of the sanctification of the waters. Through the baptism of his Son at the Jordan, God "hallowed and set apart the Jordan and all water to be a blessed flood and a rich washing of sins," in order that the baptized child may be blessed "with true faith in the Holy Spirit so that through this same saving flood all that has been born in him from Adam and whatever he has added thereto may be drowned in him and sink."[38] One may add to these catechetical uses of Romans 6 and the narrative of Jesus' baptism in the Flood Prayer, the image of the righteousness of Christ as the robe he clothes his saints with daily (cf. Eph 4:22–24, Rom 13:14). As Christ comes out of the waters of the new creation, he leaves his robe of righteousness and holiness in the waters for sinners to pick up, so that they might be clothed with his righteousness in the waters of baptism and receive his Holy Spirit.[39] Implications for the daily use of baptism follow.

> Therefore let all Christians regard their baptism as the daily garment that they are to wear all the time. Every day they should be found in faith and with its fruits, suppressing the old creature and growing up in the new.[40]

In the baptismal model, the Christian life is cyclical, a daily dying to sin in order to be raised to new life through the forgiveness of sins. Sanctification becomes a daily return to one's baptism to receive the blessings of justification promised therein. The model corresponds to the life of daily repentance, of contrition and faith, where the gospel alone provides the power and motivation to fight sin and do God's holy will in accordance with his word and for the neighbor's sake. The baptismal model avoids a fatalistic view of the Christian life where the reality of the sinful nature paralyzes the believer and prevents him from fighting against the power of sin in his life. This view of life in the Spirit also avoids a perfectionist or utopian view of sanctification where the believer thinks progress in sanctification is inevitable and thus lives under the illusion that he has nothing or little to repent of. The model encourages us to go back each day to the waters, where we see a reflection of our guilt and shame, but finally where we are cleansed of our sins and our filthy rags are replaced with Christ's holiness.

---

38. LC, Baptismal Booklet, 14, in *BC*, 374.

39. For a discussion of patristic reflection on the taking of Christ's robe of glory from the Jordan, see McDonnell, *The Baptism of Jesus in the Jordan*, 128–44 (cf. 145–55).

40. LC, Fourth Part: Concerning Baptism, 84–85, in *BC*, 466.

The Dramatic Model: Battling in the Desert and the Garden

Immediately after his baptism, the Son is led by the Holy Spirit into the desert where he is tempted by the devil (Mark 1:12-13 and par.). The Son's faithfulness to the Father and his mission to be our Servant is put to the test. In the Garden of Gethsemane, as the hour of the Passion approaches, the Son suffers God's will in a tragic world where the devil tempts (Mark 14:32-42 and par.). The desert and the garden are places of spiritual attack. The Son knows what is like to be tempted, and sympathizes with our struggles, even as he has defeated the devil for us on the cross (Heb 2:14-18, 4:15). In the first desert, idolatrous Israel became an unfaithful son of his Father. In the second desert, Jesus, the new Israel, triumphed where old Israel failed, standing firm against devil's attacks (Matt 4:1-11). In the first garden, Adam became a disobedient son, transgressing the command and word of God. In the second garden, Jesus, the second Adam, said yes to the Father's will and was obedient unto death for our sake.

Christians too live in the desert and the garden. Their lives are a spiritual battle or struggle against the evil one, a dramatic conflict between God and devil, where the need for vigilance through prayer and the word becomes the weapon of choice. A biblical image that corresponds to this vision of the Christian life are that of the gladiator who stands firm against the attacks of the devil with "the sword of the Spirit" (the word of God) in hand to defend himself (Eph 6:10-20). Another image is that of the disciplined athlete who prepares to run the good race of the faith through the deserts of life with his eyes on the prize of eternal life at the end of the finish line (1 Cor 9:24-27—10:1-13, cf. Phil 3). In his catechesis, Luther envisions the baptism of the child as a little exorcism, the moment where a child of wrath becomes a child of God, where the Spirit enters the child and drives away the evil spirit.[41] Baptism brings one into a struggle with the devil, hanging "around the child's neck a mighty, lifelong enemy," and provides the baptized with spiritual strength "so that the child might resist him valiantly in life and death."[42]

In his sermons on the temptation of Christ, Luther explicitly links the experience of the Son to the temptations his saints undergo.[43] Just as Christ

---

41. "The baptizer shall say: 'Depart, you unclean spirit, and make room for the Holy Spirit.'" Baptismal Booklet, 11, in *BC*, 373; "I adjure you, you unclean spirit, in the name of the Father (+) and of the Son (+) and of the Holy Spirit (+), that you come out of and depart from this servant of Jesus Christ, N. Amen." Ibid., 15, p. 374.

42. Ibid., 3-4, p. 372.

43. For two sermons on Matthew 4 for the first Sunday in Lent (Invocavit), see Luther, 1/2:133-47, and 5:312-20.

suffered physical, spiritual, and crass forms of temptation, so also Christians suffer attacks that aim at leading them to doubt God's care for their bodily needs, tempt God by choosing to be spiritual or holy apart from his word (his commands and promises), or turn away altogether from God in unbelief.[44] Reflecting on Luther's teaching, Bonhoeffer speaks of the temptations of the flesh (i.e., the body), spiritual temptations (i.e., spiritual aspirations above God's word) and the last temptation.[45] While the temptations of the flesh incite many kinds of sinful desires or lead to doubting God's power and love in the midst of suffering, spiritual temptations amount to tempting God by demanding that he manifest himself outside of his commands and promises. This attempt to be spiritual apart from God's word leads to carnal security (Lat. *securitas*) or despair (Lat. *desperatio*), which are forms of alienation from God as the sole source of help and comfort. In the end, Bonhoeffer places all our temptations in the "two stories of temptation," in the context of the Adam-Christ story.

> Either we are tempted in Adam or we are tempted in Christ. Either the Adam in me is tempted—in which case we fall. Or the Christ in us is tempted—in which case Satan is bound to fall.[46]

In the dramatic model, the Christian life is seen as a battle between God and the devil, between the Holy Spirit and the whole person in opposition to God. Luther speaks of life in the Spirit as a cycle where God forms his children through the attacks of the devil (*tentatio, Anfechtung*), leading them to put their lives in God's hands through prayer (*oratio*) and find strength in his word (*meditatio*) in the midst of the attacks.[47] We have another cyclical view of life in the Spirit of Christ, one in which the Holy Spirit drives Christians into the desert. Life is like a wilderness, the place where the evil spirit attacks (*tentatio*), but also like the garden—or the mountain and the temple, for that matter—the place of prayer (*oratio*) and the word (*meditatio*) where one receives the Spirit's strength to stand firm in the battle. This model of the sanctified life acknowledges that we all have deserts or gardens—our Achilles' heels, as it were—where we especially struggle with sin and thus are more easily tempted to fall. We think of those thoughts, words, attitudes, behaviors, and even places that incite us to transgress God's word most often, where we are most vulnerable. The dramatic model encourages vigilance in the face of recurring, habitual sins, through forms of external or

---

44. Ibid., 1/2:137–47.
45. Bonhoeffer, *Creation and Fall, Temptation*, 130–42.
46. Ibid., 115.
47. For a succinct account of Luther on *tentatio*, see Kleinig, "*Oratio, Meditatio, Tentatio*," 255–67.

corporal discipline and even accountability (e.g., fasting, rest, less Internet time, support groups), but ultimately through daily prayer and meditation on the word. The athlete runs the race and the warrior stands firm. Both learn to be alert, disciplined and well prepared, mindful of dangers and challenges along the way, as they look forward to the end of all struggles and the joy of triumph in the life of the world to come.

The Eucharistic Model: Spreading the Aroma of Christ in the World

At the Jordan, Jesus is anointed to be our suffering Servant. Christ's servanthood has soteriological and ethical significance. Jesus teaches his disciples what a disciple looks like, one that, like his Lord, does not come to be served but to serve and give his life for others (Mark 10:45). The apostle Paul places his christological hymn in the context of a moral exhortation to members of the church to serve one another as the Lord served us by becoming our suffering Servant (Phil 2). Just as Christ's entire cruciform life in the Spirit may be seen as a living sacrifice and pleasing worship to the Lord for the sake of the world, so also Christians are shaped by the Spirit to be living sacrifices unto the Lord for the sake of the neighbor (Rom 12). Through their faithful witness and good works, Christians spread the aroma of Christ throughout the world.

The Lutheran tradition speaks of the Christian life as a "eucharistic sacrifice" that is rendered to God by those who have been justified "to give thanks or express gratitude for having received forgiveness of sins and other benefits."[48] Through "the work of the Holy Spirit within us," Christians become living sacrifices unto the Lord and therefore practice the true worship of the New Testament, that "spiritual worship" which includes "the righteousness of faith and the fruits of faith."[49] Life in the Spirit is an act of worship, the living out of justifying faith through good works. It is a daily thanksgiving to God in service to others. Such "sacrifices of praise" encompass "the preaching of the gospel, faith, prayer, thanksgiving, confession, the afflictions of the saints, and indeed, all the good works of the saints."[50] These statements teach us about the benefit and use of the sacrament, or the "twofold effect" of the Lord's Supper, which consoles consciences by delivering

---

48. Ap XXIV, 19, in *BC*, 261.
49. Ibid., 26–27, pp. 262–63
50. Ibid.,

the benefits of Christ's atoning sacrifice but also empowers them with the gospel to love their neighbors everywhere.[51]

Similarly, Luther teaches about the spiritual fellowship between Christ and his saints that the sacrament brings about, a communion where two happy exchanges take place. Christ takes our sins and gives us his righteousness, and the saints in turn take each other's joys and burdens. Holy Communion signifies "a fellowship and a gracious blending of our sin and suffering with the righteousness of Christ and his saints."[52] Christ comes to the needy in and through his saints with gifts of love, or the saints bring the face, hands, and feet of Christ to the needy through their acts of love. When one partakes of the sacrament, Luther explains:

> [D]o not doubt that you have what the sacrament signifies, that is, be certain that Christ and all his saints are coming to you with all their virtues, sufferings, and mercies, to live, work, suffer, and die with you, and that they desire to be wholly yours, having all things in common with you.[53]

The eucharistic model of sanctification focuses on faith and its fruits, including the exercise of the gifts of the Spirit in accordance with the fruit of the Spirit, the works of missions/evangelization and mercy/justice in the world, and everything that concerns our vocations in this life. Because the eucharistic model assumes the Christian's personal dying to self and being raised to new life (baptismal model), and his dealing with the devil's personal attacks in his life (dramatic model), it will tend to focus on the outward, centrifugal, social, or neighbor-oriented dimensions of the sanctified life. By doing so, the model moves away from a potentially individualistic conception of holiness towards a more vocational approach that encourages Christians to find joy and give thanks to God by serving the neighbor through ordinary tasks. Being spiritual (of the Spirit) amounts to fulfilling God's commands through the exercise of one's gifts and vocation in the world.

Summary

We can now gather some lessons from our look at the productivity of a Spirit Christology for reflection on the Christian life. First, our approach to

---

51. Ibid., 74–75, p. 271.

52. Luther, *The Blessed Sacrament of the Holy and True Body of Christ, and the Brotherhoods*, 60.

53. Ibid., 61.

pneumatology is rooted in the Nicene creedal tradition, which highlights the material or corporeal dimension of the Spirit in his works for us as the basis for confessing his divine majesty. This approach to pneumatology may be called sacramental because it teaches us that, in God's plan of salvation, the privileged locus of the Holy Spirit is the incarnate Word who receives the Spirit in the flesh in order to give the same Spirit to humanity through his word in, with, and under visible signs or means of grace.

Second, our approach to sanctification flows from an incarnational view of the Spirit that links the baptismal, dramatic, and eucharistic models to Christ's own life in the Spirit. In other words, Christ's life in the Spirit determines and shapes what life in the Spirit looks like for the Christian. In particular, the Lutheran sources for a biblical doctrine of sanctification bear witness to the sacramental framework of the Christian life, since all three models are linked to some appropriation or use of the sacraments of baptism and the Lord's Supper for daily life. This is most evident in the baptismal and eucharistic models, but also in the dramatic model. The latter describes Christian baptism as a little exorcism where the Holy Spirit drives away the evil spirit, the entry point for the Christian's lifelong battle against Satan, and the go-to place where the Christian holds on to God's promises to help him stand firm against Satan's attacks.

Third, each model of sanctification offers a particular set of images or narratives that gives us not only a conceptual but also a visual handle on what life in the Spirit of Christ (or Christlikeness) looks like in daily life. In the baptismal model, the Spirit conforms us to Christ in his death and resurrection, bringing us into the rhythm of daily repentance. In the dramatic model, the Spirit brings us into the story of Christ's battle against the evil spirit in the desert and the garden, where we face spiritual attacks with the word of God and prayer to God. In the eucharistic model, the Spirit shapes us to be living sacrifices or the pleasing aroma of Christ in a hurting world, renewing in us the mind of Christ the Servant so that we might reflect in our lives the fruit of the Spirit.

Even though these models intersect in real life, we may relate to one model more than another at particular times depending on the situations we are experiencing. Those dealing with guilt and shame can especially find comfort in the baptismal model and its view of life as a daily return to the cross, where all condemnation is taken away and we are unconditionally accepted. Those dealing with habitual sins, addictions, fear, or areas of vulnerability to the devil's attacks can find strength and courage for the journey in the dramatic model and its realistic image of life as a battlefield where we depend on God for strength and security. Others will find meaning in life through service, focusing on the needs of neighbors as they carry out their daily vocations and labors in the world.

Finally, our brief study on the contribution of a Spirit Christology in Lutheran key to the theology and practice of sanctification should cast suspicion, and put to rest, the popular claim that the centrality of the doctrine of justification by faith prevents Lutheran churches from taking sanctification seriously. What emerges from the Lutheran sources is a robust theology of sanctification, closely linked to the Spirit's justification of sinners through word and sacrament, and thus to the daily use or living out of one's baptismal and eucharistic identity in the world where the devil attacks and the saints pray to God, die to sin, hear God's promises, give thanks for his blessings, and serve their neighbors. Having said this, our focus on the Lutheran tradition does not exhaust reflection on the shape of life in the Spirit. Christians from other traditions are welcome to see how their own theological sources foster a pneumatology that prepares the ground for, inspires, paints a picture of, and fosters life in the Spirit of Christ.

Conclusion

"No Christology without pneumatology and no pneumatology without Christology."[1] So succinctly did Congar state the Trinitarian basis and framework for Christian theology. A systematic theology could be elaborated under the theme of the *joint mission* of the Word and the Spirit of God in the economy that spans from creation to incarnation and from the paschal mystery to the eschaton. In this project, I have focused on the place of the Spirit of the Father in the life and mission of the Son. I set out on a journey to dis-cover (or unmask) the relativized pneumatological dimensions of Christian reflection on the mystery of Christ in order to re-discover and then revitalize or invigorate what had been forgotten and at times neglected. Faithfulness to the biblical story of Jesus, the incarnate Son who receives, bears, and gives God's Spirit, as well as the witness of church fathers and contemporary theologians to the constitutive place of the Spirit in defining Jesus' identity, required nothing less.

The problem of the secondary role of pneumatology in the West has virtually become an axiom in contemporary theology.[2] The legitimate centrality that Scripture (especially the Gospels) and the great Christian tradition ascribe to Jesus Christ in the church's discourse and piety also points to a broader Trinitarian reality that has often been implicitly assumed more than explicitly articulated. When this occurs, as far as pneumatology goes, one gets the impression that the mission of the Holy Spirit becomes somewhat

---

1. Congar, *The Word and the Spirit*, 1.

2. "In the West, we think essentially in Christological categories, with the Holy Spirit as an extra, an addendum, a 'false' window to give symmetry and balance to theological design. We build up our large theological constructs in constitutive Christological categories, and then, in a second, non-constitutive moment, we decorate the already constructed system with pneumatological baubles, a little Spirit tinsel." McDonnell, "The Determinative Doctrine of the Holy Spirit," 142; cf. McDonnell, "Reconceiving the Trinity as the Mystery of Salvation," 9; see also Vischer, *Spirit of God, Spirit of Christ*, 18; and Zizioulas, *Being as Communion*, 123–32.

accidental in relation to that of the Son. Much reflection on the Spirit has taken as its implicit or explicit starting point Jesus' sending, as risen Lord, of the Spirit of the Father to the church. From this moment forward, one can speak of a *christologically-informed* pneumatology. Here the Spirit comes *after* Christ. No pneumatology without Christology. In the framework of a Logos Christology, a christological pneumatology typically assumes that the Son gives the Spirit because he is personally God and the Holy Spirit proceeds from the Father and him (*filioque*) or through him (*per filium*).

I have argued that more attention must be given to a *pneumatologically-informed* Christology that grounds Jesus' identity as dispenser of the Spirit to others in the Father's giving of the same Spirit to him: "He on whom you see the Spirit descend and remain is the one who baptizes with the Holy Spirit" (John 1:33). The Spirit must first be found *in* Christ, in his life and mission, before we look for the Spirit *after* Christ in his word and sacrament, and in the prayer and holiness of his saints. No Christology, or life in Christ, without pneumatology. The risen Messiah and Lord gives the Spirit from the Father to the church in his Spirit-glorified humanity because he first receives and bears the same Spirit throughout his life and work. Through the last or second Adam, in whom the fullness of the Spirit dwells in the new creation, the Father gives back to the human race the Spirit whom the first Adam lost in the old creation. By resting on or dwelling in the incarnate Son, the Spirit becomes accustomed to dwell once again in the human race. The incarnate Son's economic existence in faithfulness to his Father and for us in the Spirit points to and thus has its immanent ground in the eternal Son's reciprocal love for the Father in the same Spirit. The Son gives the Spirit, not only as one through whom the Spirit proceeds (*per filium*), but also as one upon whom the Spirit rests and thus is begotten from the Father in the Spirit (*in spiritu*).

In spiritu. In the Spirit. This expression sums up the thesis of this work, namely, that a Spirit Christology, which highlights the role of the Spirit in Jesus' life and mission, complements classic Logos-oriented accounts of Christology, soteriology, Trinitarian theology, and the Christian life. A Logos Christology serves as a critical lens to approach Spirit Christology, making sure that any Spirit-oriented proposals take full account of the Son's divine preexistence and incarnation. While our Spirit Christology at times has also served as a critical lens and corrective economic-Trinitarian trajectory for certain Logos-oriented readings of events in the life of Christ, our main goal has been to bring Logos and Spirit Christologies into constructive dialogue with one another, seeking integration of these aspects of the mystery of Christ.

Lutheran Christology in particular has offered us an ecumenical approach to the complementarity of Logos and Spirit Christologies. From the Eastern Alexandrian tradition, Lutheran Christology gathers that the divine majesty of the Logos is communicated to and through his human nature (*genus maiestaticum*). Therefore, the Logos acts through his own human nature, each nature doing what is proper to each (*genus apotelesmaticum*). There is also a Western scholastic side to Lutheran Christology that, with some development of its notion of supernatural created gifts or effects that inhere in Christ's humanity, allows us to reflect on the active role of the Spirit in the holy life and salvific work of the incarnate Logos. My proposal for a *genus habitualis* or *genus pneumatikon* is an attempt to account more systematically for the Spirit-oriented trajectory of a Logos Christology, or the shape of the Son's life in the Spirit (*in spiritu*).

Such a *genus* also lays a foundation for speaking about the presence of the Spirit in Christ's saints, highlighting the pneumatological link between Christ's and the Christian's life in the Spirit. Because the only-begotten Son gives the Spirit whom he bears in the flesh to the adopted sons of his Father, we speak of the Christlike shape of the church's life in the Spirit. Since the Son is anointed with the Spirit unto death, we speak further of the cross-shaped form of such life. To know what life in the Spirit means one looks to Christ, the privileged locus or dwelling place of the Spirit. In the Spirit, the Son speaks words that convict of sin and give life even as he experiences rejection. In the Spirit, the Son prays to the Father with trust and in hope even as he suffers his abandonment on the cross. In the Spirit, the Son is anointed to make us participants of his death and resurrection, his life of prayer and trust in God's promises in the midst of spiritual attacks, and his life of sacrificial service to neighbor. Such reflection on the relative continuity between the presence of the Spirit in Christ and his church for understanding and promoting the Christian practices of proclamation, prayer, and sanctification brought our project to completion, showing once again that there is no christological pneumatology without a robust pneumatological Christology.

Appendix
A Comparison of Logos and Spirit Christologies

THE TABLE BELOW OFFERS, under a few concise headings, a brief comparison of various themes, concerns, and arguments that characterize Logos- and Spirit-oriented dimensions of Christology. I have distributed these contributions into seven categories: 1) locus of reflection, 2) primary definition of Jesus' identity, 3) defining states and/or events in Jesus' life and mission, 4) methodological point of departure, 5) functions of the biblical narrative, 6) view of the incarnation, and 7) understanding of the person of Christ.

Category	Logos Christology	Spirit Christology
1) Locus of reflection	The relationship between Jesus and God (against Arianism), and between Jesus and the Word (against Nestorianism).	The relationship between Jesus and the Spirit of God.
2) Primary definition of Jesus' identity	Jesus as the divine Word made flesh, or God-man.	Jesus as the receiver, bearer, and giver of God's Spirit.
3) Defining states and/or events in Jesus' life and mission	Eternal preexistence of the divine Word, incarnation (personal or hypostatic union).	Conception, anointing for mission (at the Jordan), and glorification—the mysteries of Jesus' life in the Spirit.

4) Methodological point of departure	Assuming the true divinity and true humanity of Christ, this approach begins "from above." It argues from the divinity of the Word to his humanity. It asks, "How is the divine Word a true and particular human being?"	Assuming the true humanity and true divinity of Christ, this approach begins "from below." It argues from the man Jesus and his works to his divinity. It asks, "How is this particular man, Jesus of Nazareth, true God?"
5) Functions of the biblical narrative	Jesus' story as an epiphany, revelation, confirmation, or proclamation for others of his prior identity as God; salvation through the work of the Son of God in and through the flesh; baptism and prayer as exemplary or pedagogical for us (church), but not ontologically necessary for the Son.	The Christian story as a drama of God's deeds in and through Jesus by the power of the Spirit in him; salvation through the work of the Son as the receiver, bearer, and giver of God's Spirit; baptism and prayer as defining events for the identity of the Son and the adopted sons (church).
6) View of the incarnation	The Word assumes a human *nature* (personal or hypostatic union) at a set point in time (Gk. *chronos*). A static and individual view of the incarnation.	The Word assumes a human *history* with special times (Gk. *kairoi*), in which the Spirit is at work. A dynamic and ecstatic view of the incarnation ("incarnating").
7) Understanding of the person of Christ	The person of the Word is self-subsisting from eternity. At the incarnation, this Word is made flesh, or constituted as the person of the God-man. The ontology focuses on the Son's "being-from-before" (static dimension) and "being-in-himself" (individual dimension).	Jesus does his life and work in loving obedience to the Father and for us in the Spirit. The Word acts and relates to the Father in the Spirit eternally and in the economy. The emphasis falls on the Son's "being-in-act" (dynamic aspect) and "being-in/with-another" (ecstatic aspect).

Glossary

Anfechtung: See **tentatio**.

Anointing: Among early church fathers and theologians, a metaphor for the begetting of the Son from God (Justin Martyr) in view of the creation or ordering of the world (Justin Martyr, Irenaeus), or a metaphor for the incarnation of the Son (Athanasius, Gregory Nazianzen, Augustine, John of Damascus). In biblical theology, the term refers to the Holy Spirit's descent upon Jesus at his baptism (Luke-Acts) or to the Holy Spirit itself (cf. 1 John 2:27). In Christian theology, the term includes reflection on the paradigmatic nature of the baptism of Jesus for the church's anointing in baptism, and his fulfillment of the offices of prophet, priest, and king (Christ's threefold office or anointing).

Appropriation: In Western-Augustinian thought, assigning or appropriating each person of the Trinity certain works (i.e., creation to the Father, redemption to the Son, sanctification to the Holy Spirit), even though all three persons of the Trinity share the same works in common due to their indivisible unity (see ***proprium***).

Baptismal model: The Christian life or life in the Spirit as a daily return to the waters of baptism, where one dies with Christ through contrition and is raised to new life with Christ through the forgiveness of sins (see **sanctification**).

Classical theism: A form of theism that stresses God's transcendence over his immanence in the world in the formulation of theology (see **open theism, theism**).

Communicatio idiomatum: The communication of divine and human attributes or properties (Gk. *idiomata*) in the person of Christ (see ***genera***).

Dramatic model: The Christian life as a struggle or battle in the desert against the forces of evil in our lives. Life in the Spirit as a drama between God and the devil that finds its resolution in Christ's victory over evil on our behalf through his death and resurrection (see **sanctification**, *tentatio*).

Economic Trinity: The persons of the Trinity as they relate to us in the world or *ad extra* (see **immanent Trinity**).

Eucharistic model: The Christian life or life in the Spirit as an act of worship or thanksgiving (Gk. *eucharistia*) to God for his gifts (see **sanctification**).

Explanation: A form of secondary discourse, usually in the third person. Talk *about* God in creeds, catechisms, or theological works (see **proclamation**).

Filioque: Model of the Trinity in which the Holy Spirit proceeds from the Father "and the Son" (see *per filium, spirituque*).

Genera: Types or kinds (Lat. *genera*) of communication of the divine and human attributes in the person of Christ (see *communicatio idiomatum*). In Lutheran Christology, there are three *genera* (see *genus apotelesmaticum, genus idiomaticum*, and *genus maiestaticum*).

Genus apotelesmaticum: Type or kind (Lat. *genus*) of the communication of attributes or properties according to which the whole person of Christ does all his works (Gk. *apotelesmata*) according to both natures, each nature contributing what is proper to each (see *genus idiomaticum*).

Genus habitualis: see *genus pneumatikon*.

Genus idiomaticum: Type or kind (*genus*) of the communication of attributes according to which the attributes or properties of either the human or the divine natures are ascribed to the one person of Christ (see *genus apotelesmaticum*).

Genus maeistaticum: Type or kind (*genus*) of the communication of attributes according to which the attributes or properties of the divine nature, majesty, and power are passed on, communicated to, or revealed (displayed) through the human nature of Christ.

Genus pneumatikon: Type or kind (*genus*) of the communication of attributes that focuses on the supernatural presence and activity of the Holy Spirit in, with, and through the human life and history of the Logos (see *genus habitualis, gratia habitualis*). The genus highlights the incarnate Logos's work of salvation through his Spirit-indwelt humanity and his identity as receiver, bearer, and giver of the Spirit.

Gratia habitualis: Habitual grace. A term used in scholastic theology to refer to the special holiness of Christ. The term may be used to refer to the presence and activity of the Holy Spirit in the life of Christ (see ***genus habitualis***).

Gratia unionis: Grace of union. A term used in scholastic theology to refer to the incarnation (see ***hypostatic union, personal union***).

Hypostasis: See **person**.

Hypostatic union: See **personal union, incarnating**.

Incarnating: The idea that, in assuming a human *nature* (incarnation, hypostatic or personal union), the person of the Logos also assumes a human *history* with special moments (Gk. *kairoi*) in which the Spirit has an active role in the incarnate Son's becoming our Servant and Lord for the sake of our salvation.

Immanent Trinity: The persons of the Trinity as they relate to one another in the Godhead or *ad intra* (see **economic Trinity**).

In spiritu: Model of the Trinity in which the Son is said to be begotten of the Father "in the [Holy] Spirit" because the Spirit of the Father eternally rests on his Son.

Logos Christology: Approach to Christology that focuses on the identity of Jesus as the divine Word made flesh, or the God-man. Some ante-Nicene Logos Christologies reflected on the preexistence of the Logos in God and his creative outward work in the ordering of the cosmos. Against Arius, Nicene Logos Christology defends the divinity of the Son, his consubstantiality with God the Father. Against Nestorius, Chalcedonian Logos Christology defends the unity of the person of Christ in two natures (see **Spirit Christology**).

Ontology: A statement about someone's "being." In Christology and Trinitarian theology, an ontology may be described as "static" if it refers to a person's "being-from-before." By contrast, a "dynamic" ontology highlights a person's "being-in-act." Moreover, an ontology may be described as "individual" if it refers to a person's inner-constitution, self-subsistence, or "being-in-himself." By contrast, a "relational," social, or ecstatic ontology highlights a person's "being-in-relation" (or "being-in/with/for-another").

Open theism: A form of theism that stresses God's immanence in the world over his transcendence in the formulation of theology (see **classical theism, theism**).

Ordo cognoscendi: Order of knowledge according to which a reality is acknowledged as existent after it is known. Approach to Christology in which the lordship and divinity of Jesus is confessed on the basis of our knowledge and experience of his works (see ***ordo essendi***).

Ordo essendi: Order of being according to which a reality is acknowledged as existent even before our knowledge of it. Approach to Christology in which the lordship and divinity of Jesus is confessed before discussing our knowledge and experience of his works (see ***ordo cognoscendi***).

Per filium: Model of the Trinity in which the Holy Spirit proceeds from the Father "through the Son" (see ***filioque***).

Perichoresis: A manner of describing the unity or communion of the three persons through the language of reciprocal or mutual indwelling or being in one another.

Per spiritum: Model of the Trinity in which the Son is said to be begotten of the Father "through the [Holy] Spirit" (see ***in spiritu, spirituque***).

Person (Lat. *persona*, Gk. *hypostasis*): Term that points to the three who are distinct in the Godhead or one divine substance (see **personal union, substance**).

Personal union (Lat. *unio personalis, unio hypostatica*): The union of the divine and human natures in the one person of Christ (see **person, incarnating**).

Personalist language: A way of speaking about God that gives ontological priority to what is proper to each of the divine persons, over the essential attributes all three persons have in common (see ***proprium*, substantialist language**).

Prayer: Talk *to* God in petition, confession of sins, praise, and thanksgiving. A form of primary discourse, usually in first-to-second person address (see **proclamation**).

Proclamation: Talk *for* or *on behalf of* God to the hearer in preaching or teaching, with particular reference to the speaking of God's promises or gospel. A form of primary discourse, usually in first-to-second person address (see **explanation**).

Proprium: That which is proper and not merely appropriated to each person of the Trinity in the economy of salvation. A non-transferable property or characteristic of a particular person of the Trinity that makes such person unique, either in the economy (e.g., the person of the Son alone becomes incarnate), or in the inner-life of God (e.g., the Father is unbegotten, the Son is begotten of the Father, and the Holy Spirit proceeds from the Father and the Son); see **appropriation**.

Rational relation (Lat. *relatio rationis*): In Thomistic thought, a manner of describing the God-world relationship in such a way that the world changes in relation to God, but God only has a rational ("in the mind") relation to the world due to his immutability and thus is not affected ontologically by the relationship (see **real relation**).

Real relation (Lat. *relatio realis*): In Thomistic thought, a manner of describing the God-world relationship in such a way that only the world changes in relation to God due to its mutable nature, though God is aware of the relationship (see **rational relation**).

Relation: In Latin (Western-Augustinian) theology, a term that describes distinction in God through an "opposition in relation" (Lat. *oppositio relationis*)—e.g., Father is *not* Son, Son is *not* Father—without doing harm to the one divine essence. In Greek (Eastern-Cappadocian) theology, a term that best describes how the persons of the Son and the Holy Spirit relate to the Father as their origin (Gk. *archē*), source (Gk. *pēgē*), and cause (Gk. *aitia*) in the Godhead or divine substance (Gk. *ousia*). In scholastic theology, the term also describes ways of speaking about the relationship between God and creation (see **rational relation**, **real relation**).

Sanctification: The holiness of Christ (see *gratia habitualis*) or his saints. In Lutheran theology, sanctification describes what life in the Spirit entails for the justified believer. Such life can be described in terms of daily repentance, vigilance against the devil's attacks, and a life of thanksgiving (see **baptismal model, dramatic model, eucharistic model,** *tentatio*).

Spirit Christology: Approach to Christology that focuses on the identity of Jesus as the receiver, bearer, and giver of God's Spirit. Adoptionist Spirit Christologies see Jesus as a Spirit-indwelt man adopted by God. Some orthodox ante-Nicene Spirit Christologies see "spirit" as a synonym for the preexistent Logos or the divine nature of Christ. Post-Chalcedonian (post-Trinitarian) Spirit Christologies see "spirit" as the power of God operative in the man Jesus. A Nicene-Chalcedonian Spirit Christology speaks of Jesus' identity in the Spirit in a Trinitarian perspective and as a complement to two-natures Christology (see **Logos Christology**).

Spirituque: A model of the Trinity in which the Son is said to be begotten of the Father "and the [Holy] Spirit" (see *in spiritu, per spiritum*).

Substance (Lat. *substantia*, Gk. *ousia*): Term that points to the one divine nature or essence the three persons have (are) in common (see **person**).

Substantialist language: A manner of speaking about God that gives ontological priority to his essential attributes over what is proper to each of the divine persons (see **personalist language**).

Tentatio: Spiritual attack (Ger. *Anfechtung*). Luther's way of describing the Christian life as a cycle in which the Holy Spirit uses the devil's attacks to shape the Christian into conformity with Christ, leading him to die to sin and be raised to new life through dependence on the Word (Lat. *meditatio*) and prayer (Lat. *oratio*); see **dramatic model**.

Theism: A manner of speaking about God on the basis of his divine essence and attributes (see **classical theism, open theism**).

Bibliography

Abelard, Peter. "Peter Abailard: Exposition of the Epistle to the Romans (Exposition from the Second Book)." In *A Scholastic Miscellany: Anselm to Ockham*, edited and translated by E. R. Fairweather, 276–87. Library of Christian Classics 10. Philadelphia: Westminster, 1956.
Alfaro, Sammy. *Divino Compañero: Toward a Hispanic Pentecostal Christology*. Eugene, OR: Pickwick, 2010.
Althaus, Paul. *The Theology of Martin Luther*. Translated by Robert C. Schultz. Philadelphia: Fortress, 1966.
Anselm. *Cur Deus Homo?* In *St. Anselm: Basic Writings*, translated by S. N. Deane, 191–302. 2nd ed. Chicago: Open Court, 1962.
Aranda, Antonio. "Cristología y pneumatología." In *Cristo, Hijo de Dios y Redentor del Hombre*, edited by Lucas F. Mateo-Seco et al., 649–69. Pamplona: Universidad de Navarra, 1982.
Aulén, Gustaf. *Christus Victor: An Historical Study of the Three Main Types of the Idea of the Atonement*. Translated by Arthur G. Hebert. New York: Macmillan, 1969.
Badcock, Gary D. *Light of Truth & Fire of Love: A Theology of the Holy Spirit*. Grand Rapids: Eerdmans, 1997.
Barth, Karl. *Church Dogmatics*. Vol. 1/1, *The Word of God*. Edited by Geoffrey W. Bromiley and Thomas F. Torrance. Translated by G. T. Thomson. Edinburgh: T. & T. Clark, 1936.
———. *Church Dogmatics*. Vol. 2/2, *The Doctrine of God*. Edited by Geoffrey W. Bromiley and Thomas F. Torrance. Translated by Geoffrey W. Bromiley et al. Edinburgh: T. & T. Clark, 1957.
Basil the Great, St. *On the Holy Spirit*. Translated by David Anderson. Crestwood, NY: St. Vladimir's Seminary Press, 1997.
Basinger, David. "Practical Implications." In *The Openness of God: A Biblical Challenge to the Traditional Understanding of God*, 155–76. Downers Grove, IL: InterVarsity, 1994.
Benoît, Pierre. "Préexistence et Incarnation." *Revue Biblique* 77 (1970) 5–29.
Berkhof, Hendrikus. *The Doctrine of the Holy Spirit*. Richmond, VA: Knox, 1964.
Bobrinskoy, Boris. "The Filioque Yesterday and Today." In *Spirit of God, Spirit of Christ*, edited by Lukas Vischer, 133–48. Geneva: WCC, 1981.
———. "The Indwelling of the Spirit in Christ: 'Pneumatic Christology' in the Cappadocian Fathers." *St. Vladimir's Theological Quarterly* 28 (1984) 49–65.

———. *The Mystery of the Trinity: Trinitarian Experience and Vision in the Biblical and Patristic Tradition.* Translated by Anthony P. Gythiel. Crestwood, NY: St. Vladimir's Seminary Press, 1999.

Boff, Leonardo. *The Trinity and Society.* Translated by Paul Burns. Theology and Liberation Series. Maryknoll, NY: Orbis, 1988.

Bonhoeffer, Dietrich. *Creation and Fall, Temptation: Two Biblical Studies.* New York: Simon & Schuster, 1997.

Bouyer, Louis. *The Eternal Son: A Theology of the Word of God and Christology.* Translated by Simone Inkel and John F. Laughlin. Huntington, IN: Our Sunday Visitor, 1978.

Breck, John. "'The Two Hands of God': Christ and the Spirit in Orthodox Theology." *St. Vladimir's Theological Quarterly* 40 (1996) 231–46.

Bulgakov, Sergius. *Le Paraclet.* Translated from the Russian by Constantin Andronikof. Paris: Aubier/Montaigne, 1946.

Cantalamessa, Raniero. *The Holy Spirit in the Life of Jesus: The Mystery of Christ's Baptism.* Translated by Alan Neame. Collegeville, MN: Liturgical, 1994.

———. "'Incarnatus de Spiritu Sancto ex Maria Virgine.' Cristologia e Pneumatologia nel Simbolo Constantinopolitano e nella Patristica." In *Credo in Spiritum Sanctum*, 1:101–25. Vatican City: Libreria Editrice Vaticana, 1983.

Cavadini, John C. *The Last Christology of the West: Adoptionism in Spain and Gaul, 785–820.* Philadelphia: University of Pennsylvania Press, 1993.

Chemnitz, Martin. *De Duabis Naturis in Christo.* 1653. Reprint, Chelsea, MI: Lutheran Heritage Foundation / Sheridan, 2000.

———. *The Two Natures in Christ.* Translated by J. A. O. Preus. St. Louis: Concordia, 1971.

Childs, Brevard S. *Biblical Theology of the Old and New Testaments: Theological Reflection on the Christian Bible.* Minneapolis: Fortress, 1992.

Coffey, David. *Deus Trinitas: The Doctrine of the Triune God.* New York: Oxford University Press, 1999.

———. *Did You Receive the Holy Spirit When You Believed? Some Basic Questions for Pneumatology.* Milwaukee: Marquette University Press, 2005.

———. "Spirit Christology and the Trinity." In *Advents of the Spirit: An Introduction to the Current Study of Pneumatology*, edited by Bradford E. Hinze and D. Lyle Dabney, 315–46. Milwaukee: Marquette University Press, 2001.

Congar, Yves. *I Believe in the Holy Spirit.* Translated by David Smith. 3 vols. 1983. Reprint, New York: Crossroad, 1997.

———. "Pour une christologie pneumatologique: note bibliographique." *Revue des Sciences Philosophiques et Théologiques* 63 (1979) 435–42.

———. *The Word and the Spirit.* Translated by David Smith. San Francisco: Harper & Row, 1986.

Cullmann, Oscar. *The Christology of the New Testament.* Translated by Shirley C. Guthrie and Charles A. M. Hall. Philadelphia: Westminster, 1959.

Cyril of Alexandria. *Commentary on John.* Vol. 1, *Book 1–Book 5, John 1:1 through John 8:43.* Translated by David R. Maxwell. Edited by Joel C. Elowsky. Ancient Christian Texts. Downers Grove, IL: InterVarsity, 2013.

Dalton, William Joseph. *Christ's Proclamation to the Spirits: A Study of 1 Peter 3:18—4:6.* 2nd rev. ed. Analecta Biblica 23. Rome: Editrice Pontificio Istituto Biblico, 1989.

Davies, W. D., and Dale C. Allison. *A Critical and Exegetical Commentary on the Gospel according to St. Matthew.* Vol. 1. International Critical Commentary. Edinburgh: T. & T. Clark, 1988.

Davis, Leo Donald. *The First Seven Ecumenical Councils (325–787): Their History and Theology.* Collegeville, MN: Liturgical, 1990.

Del Colle, Ralph. *Christ and the Spirit: Spirit-Christology in Trinitarian Perspective.* New York: Oxford University Press, 1994.

Dunn, James D. G. *Christology.* Vol. 1 of *The Christ and the Spirit.* Grand Rapids: Eerdmans, 1998.

———. *Jesus and the Spirit: A Study of the Religious and Charismatic Experience of Jesus and the First Christians as Reflected in the New Testament.* Grand Rapids: Eerdmans, 1975.

———. "Jesus—Flesh and Spirit: An Exposition of Romans 1:3-4." In *Christology,* 126–53. Grand Rapids: Eerdmans, 1998.

———. *Pneumatology.* Vol. 2 of *The Christ and the Spirit.* Grand Rapids: Eerdmans, 1998.

———. "Rediscovering the Spirit (1)." In *Pneumatology,* 43–61. Grand Rapids: Eerdmans, 1998.

———. "Rediscovering the Spirit (2)." In *Pneumatology,* 62–80. Grand Rapids: Eerdmans, 1998.

———. "Spirit and Holy Spirit in the New Testament." In *Pneumatology,* 3–21. Grand Rapids: Eerdmans, 1998.

———. "Spirit and Kingdom." In *Pneumatology,* 133–41. Grand Rapids: Eerdmans, 1998.

———. "2 Corinthians 3:17 'The Lord is the Spirit.'" In *Christology,* 115–25. Grand Rapids: Eerdmans, 1998.

Durrwell, François-Xavier. *Jesús, Hijo de Dios en el Espíritu Santo.* Salamanca: Secretariado Trinitario, 2000.

Dziuba, Andrzej F. "El Espíritu Santo como don del Señor glorificado." In *El Espíritu Santo y la Iglesia,* edited by Pedro Rodríguez et al., 157–70. Pamplona: Universidad de Navarra, 1999.

Evdokimov, Paul. *L'Esprit Saint dans la tradition orthodoxe.* Paris: Cerf, 1969.

Fairweather, Eugene R., ed. and trans. *A Scholastic Miscellany: Anselm to Ockham.* Library of Christian Classics 10. Philadelphia: Westminster, 1956.

Fee, Gordon D. *God's Empowering Presence: The Holy Spirit in the Letters of Paul.* Peabody, MA: Hendrickson, 1994.

Fitzmyer, Joseph A. *The Gospel according to Luke.* Vol. 1, *I–IX.* Anchor Bible 28. Garden City, NY: Doubleday, 1970.

———. *Scripture and Christology: A Statement of the Biblical Commission with a Commentary.* New York: Paulist, 1986.

Forde, Gerhard O. *On Being a Theologian of the Cross: Reflections on Luther's Heidelberg Disputation, 1518.* Grand Rapids: Eerdmans, 1997.

———. *Theology Is for Proclamation.* Minneapolis: Fortress, 1990.

Forte, Bruno. *The Trinity as History: Saga of the Christian God.* Translated by Paul Rotondi. New York: Alba House, 1989.

Fortman, Edmund J. *The Triune God: A Historical Study of the Doctrine of the Trinity.* 1982. Reprint, Eugene, OR: Wipf and Stock, 1999.

Frei, Hans W. *The Eclipse of Biblical Narrative: A Study in Eighteenth and Nineteenth Century Hermeneutics*. New Haven: Yale University Press, 1974.
García-Moreno, Antonio. "El Espíritu Santo, fruto de la Cruz." In *El Espíritu Santo y la Iglesia*, edited by Pedro Rodríguez et al., 71–77. Pamplona: Universidad de Navarra, 1999.
Garrigues, Jean-Miguel. "A Roman Catholic View of the Position Now Reached in the Question of the *Filioque*." In *Spirit of God, Spirit of Christ*, edited by Lukas Vischer, 149–63. Geneva: WCC, 1981.
Gibbs, Jeffrey A. "Israel Standing with Israel: The Baptism of Jesus in Matthew's Gospel (Matt 3:13–17)." *Catholic Biblical Quarterly* 64 (2002) 511–26.
González, Justo L. *A History of Christian Thought*. Vol. 1, *From the Beginnings to the Council of Chalcedon*. Rev. ed. Nashville: Abingdon, 1987.
González de Cardedal, Olegario. "Un problema teológico fundamental: la preexistencia de Cristo. Historia y hermeneútica." In *Teología y mundo contemporáneo: Homenaje a K. Rahner en su 70 cumpleaños*, edited by A. Vargas-Machuca, 179–211. Madrid: Universidad Pontificia Comillas y Ediciones Cristiandad, 1975.
Granado, Carmelo. "El Don del Espíritu en san Hilario de Poitiers." *Estudios Eclesiásticos* 57 (1982) 436–45.
———. "Pneumatología de San Cirilo de Jerusalén." *Estudios Eclesiásticos* 58 (1983) 421–90.
Grenz, Stanley J. "The Spirit and the Word: The World-Creating Function of the Text." *Theology Today* 57 (2000) 357–74.
Gunton, Colin. "Two Dogmas Revisited: Edward Irving's Christology." *Scottish Journal of Theology* 42 (1988) 359–76.
———. "Using and Being Used: Scripture and Systematic Theology." *Theology Today* 47 (1990) 248–59.
Habets, Myk. *The Anointed Son: A Trinitarian Spirit Christology*. Eugene, OR: Pickwick, 2010.
———. "Spirit Christology: Seeing in Stereo." *Journal of Pentecostal Theology* 11 (2003) 199–234.
Haight, Roger. "The Case for Spirit Christology." *Theological Studies* 53 (1992) 257–87.
Hansen, Olaf. "Spirit-Christology: A Way Out of Our Dilemma?" In *The Holy Spirit in the Life of the Church: From Biblical Times to the Present*, edited by Paul D. Opsahl, 172–203. Minneapolis: Augsburg, 1978.
Hardy, Edward R., ed., in collaboration with Cyril C. Richardson. *Christology of the Later Fathers*. Library of Christian Classics 3. Philadelphia: Westminster, 1954.
Hook, Norman. "A Spirit Christology." *Theology* 75 (1972) 226–32.
Hunter, Harold. "Spirit Christology: Dilemma and Promise (1)." *Heythrop* 24 (1983) 127–40.
———. "Spirit Christology: Dilemma and Promise (2)." *Heythrop* 24 (1983) 266–77.
Illanes Maestre, José Luis. "Cristología 'desde arriba' y Cristología 'desde abajo.' Reflexiones sobre la metodología cristológica." In *Cristo, Hijo de Dios y Redentor del Hombre*, edited by Lucas F. Mateo-Seco et al., 143–56. Pamplona: Ediciones Universidad de Navarra, 1982.
Imbelli, Robert P. "The New Adam and Life-Giving Spirit: The Paschal Pattern of Spirit Christology." *Communio* 25 (1998) 233–52.
Jenson, Robert W. *The Triune God*. Vol. 1 of *Systematic Theology*. New York: Oxford University Press, 1997.

Kasper, Walter. *The God of Jesus Christ*. Translated by Matthew J. O'Connell. New York: Crossroad, 1984.

———. *Jesus the Christ*. Translated by V. Green. New York: Paulist, 1976.

Kelly, J. N. D. *Early Christian Doctrines*. 5th rev. ed. London: A. & C. Black, 1977.

Kingston Siggins, Jan D. *Martin Luther's Doctrine of Christ*. New Haven: Yale University Press, 1970.

Kittel, Gerhard, and G. Friedrich, eds. *Theological Dictionary of the New Testament*. Translated and edited by Geoffrey W. Bromiley. 10 vols. 1964–1976. Reprint, Grand Rapids: Eerdmans, 1999.

Kleinig, John W. "*Oratio, Meditatio, Tentatio*: What Makes a Theologian?" *Concordia Theological Quarterly* 66 (2002) 255–67.

Kolb, Robert, and Timothy J. Wengert, eds. *The Book of Concord: The Confessions of the Evangelical Lutheran Church*. Minneapolis: Fortress, 2000.

LaCugna, Catherine Mowry. *God for Us: The Trinity and Christian Life*. San Francisco: HarperCollins, 1991.

———. "Re-conceiving the Trinity as the Mystery of Salvation." *Scottish Journal of Theology* 38 (1985) 1–23.

LaCugna, Catherine Mowry, and Killian McDonnell. "Returning from 'The Far Country': Theses for a Contemporary Trinitarian Theology." *Scottish Journal of Theology* 41 (1988) 191–215.

Ladaria, Luis F. "El bautismo y la unción de Jesús en Hilario de Poitiers." *Gregorianum* 70 (1989) 277–90.

———. *La cristología de Hilario de Poitiers*. Analecta Gregoriana 255. Rome: Università Gregoriana, 1989.

———. "Cristología del Logos y cristología del Espíritu." *Gregorianum* 61 (1980) 353–60.

———. "El Espíritu Santo en San Hilario de Poitiers." In *Credo in Spiritum Sanctum*, 1:243–53. Vatican City: Libreria Editrice Vaticana, 1983.

———. Interview by Leopoldo A. Sánchez M. Tape recording, December 2, 2002. Università Gregoriana, Rome.

———. "Jesús y el Espíritu Santo según Gregorio de Elvira." *Gregorianum* 81 (2000) 309–29.

———. *La Trinidad, misterio de comunión*. Salamanca: Secretariado Trinitario, 2002.

———. "La unción de Jesús y el don del Espíritu." *Gregorianum* 71 (1990) 547–71.

Lampe, G. W. H. *God as Spirit*. Oxford: Clarendon, 1977.

———. "The Holy Spirit and the Person of Christ." In *Christ, Faith and History*, edited by S. W. Sykes and J. P. Clayton, 111–30. London: Cambridge University Press, 1972.

Leontius of Byzantium. "Extracts from Leontius of Byzantium." In *Christology of the Later Fathers*, edited by Edward R. Hardy and Cyril C. Richardson, 375–77. Library of Christian Classics 3. Philadelphia: Westminster, 1954.

Lotz, David W. "The Proclamation of the Word in Luther's Thought." *Word & World* 3 (1983) 344–54.

———. "*Sola Scriptura*: Luther on Biblical Authority." *Interpretation* 35 (1981) 258–73.

Luther, Martin. *The Blessed Sacrament of the Holy and True Body of Christ, and the Brotherhoods*. Translated by Jeremiah J. Schindel. In *Luther's Works*, edited by Helmut T. Lehman, 35:45–73. Philadelphia: Muhlenberg, 1960.

———. *A Brief Instruction on What to Look for and Expect in the Gospels.* Translated by E. Theodore Bachmann. In *Luther's Works*, edited by Helmut T. Lehman, 35:117–24. Philadelphia: Muhlenberg, 1960.

———. "First Sunday in Lent (Invocavit)." Translated by John Nicholas Lenker. In *The Complete Sermons of Martin Luther*, edited by John Nicolas Lenker, 1/2:133–47. Grand Rapids: Baker, 2000.

———. "Invocavit Sunday—First Sunday in Lent (1534)." Translated by Eugene F. A. Klug. In *The Complete Sermons of Martin Luther*, edited by Eugene F. A. Klug, 5:312–20. Grand Rapids: Baker, 2000.

———. "Sunday after Pentecost, or Trinity Sunday." Translated by John Nicholas Lenker. In *The Complete Sermons of Martin Luther*, edited by John Nicholas Lenker 3:406–21. 1907. Reprint, Grand Rapids: Baker, 1995.

Mateo-Seco, Lucas F., et al., eds. *Cristo, Hijo de Dios y Redentor del Hombre: III Simposio Internacional de Teología de la Universidad de Navarra.* Pamplona: Universidad de Navarra, 1982.

Matera, Frank J. *New Testament Christology.* Louisville: Westminster John Knox, 1999.

McCormack, Bruce L. *For Us and for Our Salvation: Incarnation and Atonement in the Reformed Tradition.* Studies in Reformed Theology and History. Princeton: Princeton Theological Seminary, 2003.

McDonnell, Kilian. *The Baptism of Jesus in the Jordan: The Trinitarian and Cosmic Order of Salvation.* Collegeville, MN: Liturgical, 1996.

———. "The Determinative Doctrine of the Holy Spirit." *Theology Today* 39 (1982) 142–61.

McGuckin, Paul. "Spirit Christology: Lactantius and His Sources." *Heythrop* 29 (1983) 141–48.

Moltmann, Jürgen. *The Crucified God: The Cross of Christ as the Foundation and Criticism of Christian Theology.* Minneapolis: Fortress, 1993.

———. "The Fellowship of the Holy Spirit—Trinitarian Pneumatology." Translated by Margaret Kohl. *Scottish Journal of Theology* 37 (1984) 287–300.

———. *The Spirit of Life: A Universal Affirmation.* Minneapolis: Fortress, 1992.

———. "Theological Proposals toward the Resolution of the *Filioque* Controversy." In *Spirit of God, Spirit of Christ*, edited by Lukas Vischer, 164–73. Geneva: WCC, 1981.

———. "The Trinitarian History of God." *Theology* 78 (1975) 632–46.

———. *The Trinity and the Kingdom: The Doctrine of God.* Minneapolis: Fortress, 1993.

———. "The Unity of the Triune God." Translated by O. C. Dean. *St. Vladimir's Theological Quarterly* 28 (1984) 157–71.

———. *The Way of Jesus Christ: Christology in Messianic Dimensions.* Minneapolis: Fortress, 1993.

Montague, George. *Holy Spirit: Growth of a Biblical Tradition.* Peabody, MA: Hendrickson, 1976.

Mühlen, Heribert. "Das Christusereignis als Tat des Heiligen Geistes." In *Mysterium Salutis*, edited by J. Feiner and M. Löhrer, 3/2:513–44. Einsiedeln: Benziger, 1969. Translated into Spanish by Guillermo Aparicio and Jesús Rey under the title "El acontecimiento Cristo como acción del Espíritu Santo," **3**:960–84. Madrid: Cristiandad, 1992.

———. *Der Heilige Geist als Person: In der Trinität, bei der Inkarnation und im Gnadenbund: Ich—Du—Wir.* 2nd ed. Münster: Aschendorff, 1966.

———. *Espíritu. Carisma. Liberación. La renovación de la fe cristiana.* Translated by Luis Artigas. 2nd ed. Salamanca: Secretariado Trinitario, 1975.

———. *Una Mystica Persona: Die Kirche als das Mysterium der Identität des Heiligen Geistes in Christus und die Christen: Eine Person in Vielen Personen.* 2nd ed. Munich: Schöningh, 1967.

Nafzger, Peter H. *"These Are Written": Toward a Cruciform Theology of Scripture.* Eugene, OR: Pickwick, 2013.

Newman, Paul W. *A Spirit Christology: Recovering the Biblical Paradigm of Christian Faith.* Lanham, MD: University Press of America, 1987.

Nissiotis, Nikos A. "Pneumatological Christology as a Presupposition of Ecclesiology." In *Oecumenica: An Annual Symposium of Ecumenical Research*, edited by Friedrich Wilhelm Kantzenbach and Vilmos Vajta, 235–52. Minneapolis: Augsburg, 1967.

O'Carroll, Michael. *Veni Creator Spiritus: A Theological Encyclopedia of the Holy Spirit.* Collegeville, MN: Liturgical, 1990.

Odero, José Miguel. "La Unción de Cristo según S. Cirilo Alejandrino." In *Credo in Spiritum Sanctum*, 1:203–8. Vatican City: Libreria Editrice Vaticana, 1983.

———. "La Unción y el Bautismo de Cristo en S. Cirilo de Alejandria." In *Cristo, Hijo de Dios y Redentor del Hombre*, edited by Lucas F. Mateo-Seco et al., 519–40. Pamplona: Universidad de Navarra, 1982.

O'Donnell, John J. "In Him and Over Him: The Holy Spirit in the Life of Jesus." *Gregorianum* 70 (1989) 25–45.

———. Interview by Leopoldo A. Sánchez M. Tape recording, December 4, 2002. Università Gregoriana, Rome.

———. *The Mystery of the Triune God.* New York: Paulist, 1989.

———. *Trinity and Temporality: The Christian Doctrine of God in the Light of Process Theology and the Theology of Hope.* London: Oxford University Press, 1983.

———. "The Trinity as Divine Community." *Gregorianum* 69 (1988) 5–34.

Orbe, Antonio. "El Espíritu Santo en el bautismo de Jesús (en torno a san Ireneo)." *Gregorianum* 76 (1995) 663–99.

———. *Introducción a la teología de los siglos II y III.* Vol. 2. Analecta Gregoriana 248. Rome: Università Gregoriana, 1987.

———. *La unción del Verbo.* Analecta Gregoriana 113. Rome: Università Gregoriana, 1961.

Owen, John. *The Holy Spirit.* Grand Rapids: Sovereign Grace, 1971.

Pannenberg, Wolfhart. *Jesus—God and Man.* Translated by Lewis L. Wilkins and Duane A. Priebe. 2nd ed. Philadelphia: Westminster, 1977.

———. *Systematic Theology.* 3 vols. Translated by Geoffrey W. Bromiley. Grand Rapids: Eerdmans, 1991–1998.

Photios, Saint. *The Mystagogy of the Holy Spirit.* Translated by Joseph P. Farrell. Brookline, MA: Holy Cross Orthodox Press, 1987.

Pikaza, Xabier. *El Espíritu Santo y Jesús: Delimitación del Espíritu Santo y relaciones entre Pneumatología y Cristología.* Salamanca: Secretariado Trinitario, 1982.

Pinnock, Clark H. *Flame of Love: A Theology of the Holy Spirit.* Downers Grove, IL: InterVarsity, 1996.

———. *Most Moved Mover: A Theology of God's Openness.* Grand Rapids: Baker, 2001.

Pinto da Silva, Alcides. "L'interpretazione di Giov. 7, 37–39." In *Credo in Spiritum Sanctum*, 2:855–64. Vatican City: Libreria Editrice Vaticana, 1983.

Porsch, Felix. *El Espíritu Santo, defensor de los creyentes: La actividad del Espíritu según el evangelio de san Juan*. Translated by Severiano Talavero Tovar. Salamanca: Secretariado Trinitario, 1983.

Potterie, Ignace de la. "L'Onction du Christ." *Nouvelle Revue Theologique* 80 (1958) 225–52.

Prenter, Regin. *Spiritus Creator: Luther's Concept of the Holy Spirit*. Translated by John M. Jensen. Philadelphia: Muhlenberg, 1953.

Rahner, Karl. "Christology Today?" In *Theological Investigations*, translated by Margaret Kohl, 7:24–38. New York: Crossroad, 1981.

——————. "Current Problems in Christology." In *Theological Investigations*, translated by Cornelius Ernst, 1:149–200. Baltimore: Helicon, 1961.

——————. "Remarks on the Dogmatic Treatise 'De Trinitate.'" In *Theological Investigations*, translated by Kevin Smith, 4:77–102. Baltimore: Helicon, 1966.

——————. "Theos in the New Testament." In *Theological Investigations*, translated by Cornelius Ernst, 1:79–148. Baltimore: Helicon, 1961.

——————. *The Trinity*. Translated by Joseph Donceel. With an introduction, index, and glossary by Catherine Mowry LaCugna. 1970. Reprint, New York: Crossroad, 1998.

——————. "The Two Basic Types of Christology." In *Theological Investigations*, translated by David Bourke, 13:213–23. New York: Crossroad, 1975.

Rice, Richard. "Biblical Support for a New Perspective." In *The Openness of God: A Biblical Challenge to the Traditional Understanding of God*, by Clark Pinnock et al., 11–58. Downers Grove, IL: InterVarsity, 1994.

Richard de Saint-Victor. *La Trinité*. Translated by Gaston Salet. Sources Chrétiennes 111. Paris: Cerf, 1959.

Richard of St. Victor. *On the Trinity*. In *A Scholastic Miscellany: Anselm to Ockham*, edited and translated by E. R. Fairweather, 324–31. Library of Christian Classics 10. Philadelphia: Westminster, 1956.

Roberts, Alexander, et al., eds. *The Ante-Nicene Fathers: Translations of the Fathers down to A.D. 325*. 10 vols. 1885–1897. Reprint, Peabody, MA: Hendrickson, 1994.

Rodríguez, Pedro, et al., eds. *El Espíritu Santo y la Iglesia: XIX Simposio Internacional de Teología de la Universidad de Navarra*. Pamplona: Universidad de Navarra, 1999.

Rogers, Eugene F., Jr. *After the Spirit: A Constructive Pneumatology from Resources outside the Modern West*. Grand Rapids: Eerdmans, 2005.

Rosato, Philip J. Interview by Leopoldo A. Sánchez M. Tape recording, December 4, 2002. Università Gregoriana, Rome.

——————. *The Spirit as Lord: The Pneumatology of Karl Barth*. Edinburgh: T. & T. Clark, 1981.

——————. "Spirit Christology: Ambiguity and Promise." *Theological Studies* 38 (1977) 423–49.

Sánchez M., Leopoldo A. "God against Us and for Us: Preaching Jesus in the Spirit." *Word & World* 24 (2003) 134–45.

——————. "The Holy Spirit in Christ: Pneumatological Christology as a Ground for a Christ-Centered Pneumatology." In *Propter Christum: Christ at the Center*, edited by Scott Murray et al., 343–56. St. Louis: Luther Academy, 2013.

——————. "Life in the Spirit of Christ: Models of Sanctification as Sacramental Pneumatology." *LOGIA* 22 (2013) 7–14.

———. "A Missionary Theology of the Holy Spirit: The Father's Anointing of Christ and Its Implications for the Church in Mission." *Missio Apostolica* 14 (2006) 28–40.

———. "More Promise than Ambiguity: Pneumatological Christology as a Model for Ecumenical Engagement." In *Critical Issues in Ecclesiology: Essays in Honor of Carl E. Braaten*, edited by Alberto García and Susan K. Wood, 189–214. Grand Rapids: Eerdmans, 2011.

———. *Pneumatología. El Espíritu Santo y la espiritualidad de la iglesia*. St. Louis: Concordia, 2005.

———. "Pneumatology: Key to Understanding the Trinity." In *Who Is God? In the Light of the Lutheran Confessions*, edited by John A. Maxfield, 122–42. St. Louis: Luther Academy, 2012.

———. "Praying to God the Father in the Spirit: Reclaiming the Church's Participation in the Son's Prayer Life." *Concordia Journal* 32 (2006) 274–95.

———. "Receiver, Bearer, and Giver of God's Spirit: Jesus' Life and Mission in the Spirit as a Ground for Understanding Christology, Trinity, and Proclamation." PhD diss., Concordia Seminary, 2003.

———. *Teología de la santificación. La espiritualidad del cristiano*. St. Louis: Concordia, 2013.

Sanders, John. *The God Who Risks: A Theology of Providence*. Downers Grove, IL: InterVarsity, 1998.

Saraiva Martins, José, ed. *Credo in Spiritum Sanctum: Atti del Congresso Teologico Internazionale di Pneumatologia*. 2 vols. Vatican City: Libreria Editrice Vaticana, 1983.

Scaer, David P. *Christology*. Confessional Lutheran Dogmatics 6. Ft. Wayne, IN: International Foundation for Lutheran Confessional Research, 1989.

———. "*Homo Factus Est* as the Revelation of God." *Concordia Theological Quarterly* 65 (2001) 111–26.

Schaaf, Philip, and Henry Wace, eds. *A Select Library of the Christian Church: Nicene and Post-Nicene Fathers*. 28 vols. in two series. 1886–1900. Reprint, Peabody, MA: Hendrickson, 1994.

Scharlemann, Martin H. "'He Descended into Hell': An Interpretation of 1 Peter 3:18–20." *Concordia Theological Monthly* 37 (1956) 88–94.

Schoonenberg, P. J. A. M. "Spirit Christology and Logos Christology." *Bijdragen* 38 (1977) 350–75.

———. "Trinity—The Consummated Covenant: Theses on the Doctrine of the Trinitarian God." Translated by Robert C. Ware. *Studies in Religion* 5 (1975–1976) 111–16.

Schwöbel, Christoph. Introduction to *Trinitarian Theology Today: Essays on Divine Being and Act*, edited by Christoph Schwöbel. Edinburgh: T. & T. Clark, 1995.

Silanes, Nereo. *La santísima Trinidad, programa social del cristianismo: Principios bíblico-teológicos*. Salamanca: Secretariado Trinitario, 1991.

Simonetti, M. "Note di cristologia pneumatica." *Augustinianum* 12 (1972) 201–32.

Spence, Alan. "Christ's Humanity and Ours: John Owen." In *Persons, Divine and Human*, edited by Christoph Schwöbel and Colin E. Gunton, 74–97. Edinburgh: T. & T. Clark, 1991.

Staniloae, Dumitru. "The Procession of the Holy Spirit from the Father and His Relation to the Son, as the Basis of Our Deification and Adoption." In *Spirit of God, Spirit of Christ*, edited by Lukas Vischer, 174–86. Geneva: WCC, 1981.

Tábet, Miguel Ángel. "El Testimonio 'del Espíritu, y del agua y la sangre' (1 Jn 5, 8)." In *El Espíritu Santo y la Iglesia*, edited by Pedro Rodríguez et al., 79–90. Pamplona: Universidad de Navarra, 1999.

Thomas Aquinas. *Summa Theologiae: Latin Text and English Translation, Introductions, Notes, Appendices, Glossaries*. Translated by the Fathers of the English Dominican Province. 61 vols. London: Blackfriars / New York: McGraw-Hill, 1964–1980.

Thomsen, Mark. "A Christology of the Spirit and the Nicene Creed." *Dialog* 16 (1977) 135–38.

Valliere, Paul. *Modern Russian Theology: Bukharev, Soloviev, Bulgakov: Orthodox Theology in a New Key*. Grand Rapids: Eerdmans, 2000.

Vanhoye, A. "L'azione dello Spirito Santo nella Passione de Cristo secondo l'Epistola agli Ebrei." In *Credo in Spiritum Sanctum*, 1:759–73. Vatican City: Libreria Editrice Vaticana, 1983.

van Rossum, Joost. "The 'Johannine Pentecost': John 20:22 in Modern Exegesis and in Orthodox Theology." *St. Vladimir's Theological Quarterly* 35 (1991) 149–67.

Vischer, Lukas, ed. *Spirit of God, Spirit of Christ: Ecumenical Reflections on the Filioque Controversy*. Faith and Order Paper 103. Geneva: WCC, 1981.

Weinandy, Thomas G. "The Case for Spirit Christology: Some Reflections." *Thomist* 59 (1995) 173–88.

———. *The Father's Spirit of Sonship: Reconceiving the Trinity*. Edinburgh: T. & T. Clark, 1995.

———. "Review of Ralph De Colle's *Christ and the Spirit*." *Thomist* 59 (1995) 656–59.

Welker, Michael. *God the Spirit*. Translated by John F. Hoffmeyer. Minneapolis: Fortress, 1994.

Wong, Joseph H. P. "The Holy Spirit in the Life of Jesus and of the Christian." *Gregorianum* 73 (1992) 57–95.

Wright, John H. "Roger Haight's Spirit Christology." *Theological Studies* 53 (1992) 729–35.

Zizioulas, John D. *Being as Communion: Studies in Personhood and the Church*. Crestwood, NY: St. Vladimir's Seminary Press, 1985.

———. "The Teaching of the Second Ecumenical Council on the Holy Spirit in Historical and Ecumenical Perspective." In *Credo in Spiritum Sanctum*, 1:29–54. Vatican City: Libreria Editrice Vaticana, 1983.

Subject Index

Adoptionism, xi, xix, xxi, xxiii, 1–3, 5, 10, 31–32, 42, 44n42, 48, 50, 58, 61, 74, 86, 97, 100, 109, 144, 147, 158, 161–62, 169, 187, 247
Alexandrian tradition. *See* Christology—Eastern-Alexandrian
Anointing of Jesus, views of
  constitutive (defining), x, xxi, 1, 8, 19–20, 22, 27–28, 30–31, 33, 38n26, 39, 48, 62, 69, 76, 100, 106, 123, 127–28, 133, 147, 149, 153, 161–62, 180, 190, 212, 226, 238, 242, 264
  cosmic, 4, 6, 11, 19, 22, 27–28
  ecclesial, 9–12, 15–20, 27–29, 43, 45–47, 59, 66–69, 74, 129, 169, 179, 190–92, 217–18, 229–30
  eternal (preexistent), 4–11, 12n34, 19, 22, 27–28, 41
  exemplary, xxi, 30, 39, 41, 43, 45, 99, 204–6, 209, 216, 242
  incarnational, 9, 21–22, 24–29, 39–44, 190
  revelatory (confirming, declarative, epiphanic, proclamatory), xxi, xxiv, 1, 8, 10, 15, 21, 28–30, 39, 43, 46, 48, 55, 76, 98–99, 153, 163, 204–5, 212, 216, 242
  titular (threefold), 4, 6–7, 11, 27, 212, 230n34
Apollinarianism, 114–15, 158, 165
Appropriation(s), 91, 124, 243
Arianism, ix, xx–xxi, 1–2, 4n7, 21–24, 27, 31n2, 32, 41–42, 49n60, 50, 74, 102n49, 112, 118, 122, 134, 136, 142, 164, 169, 178, 187, 208, 221–23, 241
Atonement, views of
  actual (Forde), 193n30
  classic (Aulén), 79–83, 166
  exemplary (Abelard), 77–79, 165
  Latin (Anselm), 76–79, 81–84, 165, 182, 186

Christology
  Adoptionist (*see* Adoptionism)
  Apollinarian (*see* Apollinarianism)
  Arian (*see* Arianism)
  Docetic, 14, 16, 18, 58, 61, 158
  Eastern-Alexandrian, xxiv, 26, 42–43, 56, 156, 167, 171, 174–75, 179–80, 240
  Ebionite, 2–3, 14, 16–17, 61, 158, 160n36, 187
  Eutychian (*see* Eutychianism)
  From above, xx, 6–7, 13, 15–18, 57, 157–59, 162–63, 186, 242
  From below, xx, 57, 157–59, 162–63, 186–87, 223, 242
  Gnostic (*see* Gnosticism)
  Monophysite (*see* Monophysitism)
  Monothelite (*see* Monotheletism)
  Nestorian (*see* Nestorianism)
  Western-scholastic, xxiv, 38n26, 148, 167, 171, 173–76, 179–80, 240, 245
Christus Vicar. *See* Atonement, views of—Latin (Anselm)
Christus Victor. *See* Atonement, views of—classic (Aulén)

260 Subject Index

Classical theism, xxiv, 94n34, 194, 197–99, 200–201, 215, 217, 243
Communicatio idiomatum, 148, 170–71, 243

Deification, 22, 24, 27, 49n60, 166, 169–71, 191, 223

Eastern (Greek) tradition. *See* Trinity, models of—Eastern (Greek) Cappadocian
Economic Trinity, x, xii, xxii, 49, 58, 61n82, 86–88, 93–96, 99–106, 109, 111, 116–17, 119, 124–26, 128–29, 132, 139n78, 141, 144, 147, 156–57, 164, 201, 214–15, 222, 244
Ecumenical Councils
  Nicea I (AD 325), 21, 31–32, 40n29, 98, 112–14, 142, 222, 226
  Constantinople I (AD 381), xxi, 32n5, 35–36, 38, 40n29, 98, 142, 221–22
  Ephesus (AD 431), 112
  Chalcedon (AD 451), 112
  Constantinople II (AD 553), 3n5, 112, 115
  Constantinople III (AD 680–81), 164–66
Enhypostatic union, 58, 96, 115
  anhypostatic union, 58, 115
  "reciprocal enhypostasis" (Schoonenberg), 59–60
Eutychianism, x, xx, 3, 114–15
Explanation, 182–84, 187, 191

Genera (sing. *genus*), types of definition, 244
  genus apotelesmaticum, 170, 172, 240, 244
  genus idiomaticum, 170, 172, 244
  genus maiestaticum, 171–72, 175–79, 240, 244
Genus habitualis (*See genus pneumatikon*)
Genus pneumatikon (Sánchez), xxiii, 148, 167, 170, 176n64, 179–80, 240, 244

Gnosticism, xxi, 1–3, 12–18, 20, 28, 32n4, 98
Gratia habitualis (habitual grace), 38, 47, 57, 61n83, 98, 128, 148, 161–62, 174–75, 245
Gratia unionis (grace of union), 37–38, 47, 57, 61n83, 98, 128, 148, 161–62, 174–75, 245

Holy Spirit. *See* Spirit
Homoousios (consubstantial, of the same substance), ix, xx, 21–22, 31–32, 100, 112, 114, 136, 185, 204, 222–23
Hypostasis. *See* person
Hypostatic union. *See* personal union

Immanent Trinity, x, xii, xxii–xxiii, 61n82, 85–88, 90–91, 93–96, 99–106, 109–11, 118–19, 123–25, 128–30, 132–47, 156–57, 164, 180, 201, 214–15, 222–23, 245
Incarnating, xxii, 45, 52, 57, 94, 97, 104–5, 109, 130n65, 147, 155, 162, 242, 245

Jesus Christ
  as giver of the Spirit, 7, 11, 18, 21, 23–24, 26–27, 31, 33, 41n34, 42, 46, 65–85, 87, 94–95, 129, 160, 163, 169, 177–79, 186, 192, 219, 226, 228, 239, 241–42, 244, 247
  as person (subject), xxii, 21, 26, 29–30, 37, 39, 42, 53, 55–56, 113–15, 153, 227
  as receiver and bearer of the Spirit, 7, 11, 21, 23, 30–64, 66, 76, 94–95, 129, 160, 162–63, 175, 179, 186, 219, 241–42, 244, 247
  "births" (Hilary), 49–52, 74, 100, 105, 156
  created (habitual, Spirit's, supernatural,) gifts in his humanity, 4–5, 7, 9–10, 38n26, 57, 161, 171–79, 207n30, 212, 240
  habitual grace (*see gratia habitualis*)
  kairoi (special times) in the economy, 25, 38, 40–41, 45, 48–49,

Subject Index 261

51–52, 62, 74, 105, 111, 154, 158, 166, 242, 245
sinlessness, 60, 83, 99n41, 174n60, 175n62
uncreated attributes of the Logos (and the Holy Spirit) in his humanity, 172–75
Jesus Christ, life and work of
anointing (*see* Anointing of Jesus, views of)
ascension, 7–8, 10, 31, 33, 46, 48–49, 65, 69–70, 83, 91, 106–8, 175n61
atonement (*see* Atonement, views of)
baptism (*see* Anointing of Jesus, views of—constitutive, revelatory)
birth, conception, xxiii, 2n3, 20, 34–41, 43n41, 45–46, 48, 58–59, 63, 74, 95–100, 104–7, 141, 153, 156, 159n34, 174n50, 176, 189–90, 241
death, 12, 15, 19, 53, 56, 66–72, 76–84, 95n37, 105, 129, 156n25, 165, 176, 184, 190–91, 193, 212, 218, 229–30, 232, 240
descent into hell, 80, 83
exaltation, xxi, 23–24, 33, 46–49, 56, 63, 66, 70–72, 74, 83–84, 106, 108, 156, 159–60, 162n39, 169–70, 175–76, 191, 223, 230
exorcisms, 50n64, 52–56, 58, 62–63, 80, 82–83, 150, 190
glorification, xx, 31, 41–44, 47–50, 52, 55–56, 60, 66 –70, 73–74, 76, 84, 98, 104, 106–8, 156, 170, 175, 186, 191, 196, 206–7n30, 217, 239, 241
healings, 18, 40, 52, 55–56, 58, 62–63, 82–83, 107, 150n8, 190, 193
miracles, 14, 32, 50n64, 55–56, 226
paschal mystery, xx, xii, 31, 65, 69–70, 74, 76, 80, 84–85, 107–8, 131, 159–60, 163, 183, 187n18, 190, 193, 195, 238
prayer (*See* prayer—in the life of Christ)
preaching, proclamation, 14, 18, 52–53, 56, 58, 62–63, 81, 83, 150, 156, 178, 190
resurrection, 24, 49–52, 63, 70–74, 106, 159–60, 162n39, 176, 230
session at God's right hand, 31, 33, 46, 65, 83, 108, 192
teaching, 53, 56, 58, 62, 221
temptation, 59, 80, 106, 211n37, 232–33
Justification by faith, xxv, 93n32, 231, 237

Logos Christology (Logos-oriented Christology)
comparison with Spirit Christology, 241–42
definition, 245
static and individual ontology, xx, 45, 57, 106, 109, 111–15, 121, 131–32, 147, 149, 153, 155–57, 163, 189
view of the incarnation (*see* personal union)

"Mere monotheism" (Rahner), 88–89, 109, 134
Modalism, 60–61, 116–18, 122, 134, 187
Monophysitism, 58, 61, 99, 100, 115, 158, 161–62, 165
Monothelitism, 158, 164–65

Nestorianism, x, xx, 3, 39, 42, 58, 61n83, 97, 113–15, 158, 161, 165, 187, 241

Ontology, xx, 57, 85, 114–15, 120–21, 126–28, 135n69, 159, 220, 224, 226, 245
Open theism, xxiv, 194, 197–200, 215, 217, 245

Ordo cognoscendi (order of knowledge), xxi, xxiii, 57, 103, 148, 157, 159–60, 162–63, 180, 188n21, 246
Ordo essendi (order of being), xx, xxiii, 57, 101–2, 128, 142–43, 148, 157, 159, 161–64, 180, 246
Ousia. *See* substance

Perichoresis, 110, 119, 122, 132–35, 139, 141, 146, 215, 246
Person(s), Trinitarian
 definition(s), xi–xiii, 246
 in economic Trinity, 30, 33–34, 43, 60–63, 73, 86, 88–109, 121, 124–28, 149–57, 164, 166, 168, 189–90, 207–8, 214–16, 221–24
 in immanent Trinity, xxiii, 33–34, 60–61, 88, 90–109, 116–47, 164, 166, 189, 204n17, 205n22, 214–16
Personalist language (personalism), xxv, 121–23, 125, 126n52, 130, 142, 202, 209–17, 246
Personal union, xx, xxii–xxiii, 9, 17, 30, 37–38, 42–48, 52, 55–58, 61, 94–98, 105–6, 109–11, 113–15, 128, 130n65, 144, 147–48, 155, 161–62, 172–77, 179, 186, 188, 191, 201, 207, 241–42, 246
Prayer
 Luther's Flood Prayer, 231
 in the life of Christ, xxiv–xxv, 150n8, 194–218, 240, 242
 in the life of Christians, xiii, xx, xxiv–xxv, 168–69, 194–203, 209–19, 222, 229, 232–34, 236, 239–40, 242, 246
Proclamation, ix, xx, xxiv, 56, 58, 62–63, 83, 150, 168, 181–94, 226–28, 240, 246
Proprium (proper work of divine persons), xxiii, 38, 47, 57, 83, 86, 90–94, 96–98, 104, 109, 121, 130n65, 134, 144, 153–55, 157–58, 161–62, 164, 166, 173, 201, 205, 208–9, 228, 246–47

Recapitulation (Irenaeus), 19–20, 75, 230 (cf. 53)
Relation (God-world), types of
 quasi-real, 215
 rational (*relatio rationis*), 200–1, 204, 207, 214–15, 247
 real (*relatio realis*), 200–202, 204, 207, 215, 247
Relation (Trinitarian), types of
 opposition in relation (*oppositio relationis*), 90, 118–19, 126n52, 135–36, 138n76, 145
 relation of origin, 34n8, 35, 97–98, 106, 120, 130–31, 134, 136–38, 167

Sacrament(-al), xiii, xxv, 74n27, 178–79, 182, 185n9, 192, 194, 219–21, 224–30, 234–37, 239
Sanctification, models of
 baptismal, 25, 220, 229, 230–31, 235–36, 243
 dramatic, 25, 220, 229, 232–34, 235–36, 243–44
 eucharistic, 25, 220, 229, 234–36, 244
Self-communication (self-giving), divine
 God the Father's, 48, 57, 89–90, 92–93, 96, 101–2, 104–6, 108, 128, 157, 167, 180, 188
 the Logos's, 38n26, 40, 48, 60, 93–94, 96, 101, 104–6, 108, 128, 152–53, 157, 161, 173–74, 177, 178n69, 180
 the Spirit's, 46, 48, 57, 59, 93, 96, 101, 104–6, 108, 157, 161, 178n69, 180
Spirit
 as bond of love (communion), xiii, 63, 119, 123–27, 129–33, 139n78, 143–45, 147, 167
 as divine nature (*see* Spirit Christology—pre-Chalcedonian)
 as person (personal agent), xii–xiii, xix–xx, xxiii, 35, 37n23, 38–39, 42, 44, 48–51, 56–58, 60, 62–63, 72–73, 86–111, 116–47, 149–57,

161–64, 166, 171–74, 179–80, 187–88, 210, 212–17, 221–24
  in holiness (indwelling, sanctification) of Jesus, xxiii, 3, 25–27, 34–41, 43n38, 47, 49–52, 55, 57–59, 61–63, 69, 86, 95–100, 104–9, 128, 139, 144, 147–48, 156, 161–62, 173–78, 187–89, 212–13, 230–31, 245, 247
  in indwelling (holiness) of saints, 19–20, 24, 55, 59, 62, 93, 96–97, 101, 107, 109, 124, 139, 189, 210, 212–13, 215–17, 247
  in sanctification of saints (*See* sanctification, models of)
Spirit Christology (pneumatological, pneumatic, Spirit-oriented Christology)
  comparison with Logos Christology, 241–42
  definition, 247
  dynamic and relational (ecstatic) ontology, xx, 45, 52, 57, 63, 106, 109, 111, 119–21, 125–28, 132–33, 147, 151, 155–57, 162–63, 167, 189–90
  post-Chalcedonian (post-Trinitarian), xix, xxiv, 150–53, 155, 161, 187, 247
  pre-Chalcedonian (ante-Nicene, early orthodox), xix, 26, 35–36, 49–51, 149, 153, 155
  view of the incarnation (*see* Incarnating)
Substance, xi, 5n7, 21–22, 24n85, 31–32, 36, 56, 89, 91, 96, 98, 112–13, 117, 122, 124–25, 134, 137, 142, 145, 198, 200, 202, 208, 212, 214, 224, 248

Substantialist language (substantialism), xxiv, 34n8, 121–23, 142, 197–209, 213–14, 248

Tentatio, 196, 233, 248
Trinity, models of
  Eastern (Greek) Cappadocian, 33–34, 64, 89–90, 108, 120–23, 126, 128, 130–39, 141–42, 209, 214–15, 247
  filioque, xxiii, 34n9, 42n36, 99, 105–6, 108–9, 111, 133, 135–42, 144–47, 157, 179n73, 239, 244
  in spiritu, x, xxiii, 99, 105–7, 109, 111, 131, 133, 135, 139, 141, 144–47, 157, 162, 239–40, 245
  patreque, 166
  per filium, xxiii, 50n61, 99, 105–6, 108–9, 111, 133, 135, 137–40, 142, 144–47, 157, 239, 246
  per spiritum, 108, 133, 139–40, 144–46, 246
  processional, xxiii, 21, 26, 28, 34, 42–43, 47n55, 50n61, 56, 58, 90, 92, 98–102, 107–8, 110, 122–25, 128, 132–33, 135–47, 157, 162, 164, 180, 201–2n9, 205n22, 214
  social (community-oriented, ecstatic, perichoretic), xxiii, 45, 63, 110–11, 115, 117–20, 123, 128, 131–34
  spirituque, 109, 133, 135, 139–41, 144–46, 247
  Western (Latin) Augustinian, xi, 34, 64, 88–92, 118–20, 125–38, 141, 201n9, 243, 247

Western (Latin) tradition. *See* Trinity, models of—Western (Latin) Augustinian
Western-scholastic tradition. *See* Christology—Western-scholastic

Name Index

ANCIENT

Abelard, Peter, xxii, 76–81, 84–85, 165
Alcuin of York, 3
Anselm, Saint, xxii, 76–85, 90n19, 119, 136n71, 165–66, 182, 186
Apollinaris, 114–15, 165n42
Aquinas, Thomas. *See* Thomas Aquinas
Arius of Alexandria, 3, 22, 31, 113, 245
Athanasius, Saint, xxi, 21–29, 32, 41–42, 44, 50, 55n71, 74–75, 98, 112, 134, 138n78, 156, 169–71, 223, 226, 230, 243
Augustine, Saint, xiii, 34n8, 43, 44n42, 50, 63, 89–92, 116, 118–20, 122–25, 129, 131–32, 135–37, 145, 201n9, 204n20

Basil, Saint, 31–33, 40, 43–44, 100, 120–21, 145, 164, 221–28, 230n35

Cerinthus, 3, 14–16
Chemnitz, Martin, 38n26, 97–98n39, 99n41, 170–79
Cyril of Alexandria, 4n7, 41–43, 55–56, 75, 97n39, 98, 114, 156, 171
Cyril of Jerusalem, 37

Elipandus of Toledo, 3n6

Epiphanius, 40n29, 138n78
Eutyches, x, 114–15

Felix of Urgel, 3n6

Gregory Nazianzen, 43n38, 44, 75, 166, 243
Gregory of Cyprus, 146n94
Gregory Palamas, 138n78

Hilary of Poitiers, 49–52, 74, 100, 149, 156, 204n20
Hippolytus of Rome, 116, 117n21

Irenaeus, Saint, xxi, 2, 12–21, 26, 28–29, 32, 44, 74–75, 98, 100, 155, 156n22, 230, 243

John of Damascus, 37, 44, 138n78, 243
Justin Martyr, xxi, 2, 4–12, 15, 19, 21, 27–28, 36–37, 41, 50, 74–75, 243

Leontius of Byzantium, 115–16
Leo of Rome, 55n71, 114n7
Luther, Martin, 82n58, 160n37, 184, 187nn17–18, 192, 196, 226–27, 228n30, 230–33, 235, 248

Maximus the Confessor, 138n78

Nestorius, x, 41n34, 42, 55nn72–73, 75n34, 97n39, 113–15, 245

Noetus of Smyrna, 116

Paul of Samosata, 2
Photius of Constantinople, 139, 140n80
Pope Agathos, 165n43, 166
Pope Vigilius, 3n5
Pope Zacharias, 138n78
Pseudo-Cyril of Jerusalem, 138n78

Richard of St. Victor, 120, 123–25, 131–32

Severus, 165n42

Tertullian, 36, 116–17, 122, 149
Theodore of Mopsuestia, 3n5, 144n6
Thomas Aquinas, xxiv, 37–39, 43, 47, 57, 89, 92, 98, 103n52, 105, 174n59, 200–209, 215–16
Trypho, 2–5, 7–8, 10, 12, 27, 74

MODERN

Alfaro, Sammy, 33n7
Allison, Dale C., 35n12, 53n67, 66n3
Althaus, Paul, 82n58, 187nn17–18
Aulén, Gustaf, xxii, 76, 79–82, 84–85, 166

Badcock, Gary, 34n10, 57n74
Barth, Karl, 87–88, 93, 140n81, 157
Basinger, David, 198n2
Benoît, Pierre, 166n81
Berkhof, Hendrikus, 151n11
Bobrinskoy, Boris, 43n38, 75n35, 145n93, 146n94
Boff, Leonardo, 134n68, 140–41
Bolotov V., 139n80
Bonhoeffer, Dietrich, 233
Bouyer, Louis, 140n81
Breck, John, 139n78, 146n94
Bulgakov, Sergius, 37n23, 139n79

Cantalamessa, Raniero, 1, 32n4, 36n16, 112, 113n5, 186n14, 211, 230n34

Cardedal, Gonzalo de, 149n1
Cavadini, John, 3–4n6
Coffey, David, 61n83, 93n31, 95n37, 96, 100n42, 126n52, 128n62, 129–32, 146n95
Congar, Yves, xiiin5, 33n7, 35n11, 40, 43n41, 45n47, 47nn50–51, 49, 61n83, 68n7, 71n15, 73n27, 86, 90n19, 102–106, 109, 120, 125n46, 136nn70–71, 137–38, 139n78, 140nn80–81, 147, 162n39, 164, 224, 238
Cullmann, Oscar, 140n81

Dalton, Wiliam Joseph, 71n17, 72, 83n60
Davies, W. D., 35n12, 53n67, 66n3
Davis, Leo Donald, 114nn6–7, 115n12, 165n42
Del Colle, Ralph, 61n83, 155n20
Dunn, James D.G., 53–54, 71nn15–16, 73, 149–50, 153, 190n25

Evdokimov, Paul, 139–40, 142

Fee, Gordon, 71n17, 72–73
Fitzmyer, Joseph, 35n11, 157n26
Forde, Gerhard, xxiv, 182, 184–85, 187n18, 193n30
Forte, Bruno, 104
Fortman, Edmund, 116n18
Frei, Hans, 183

Garrigues, Jean-Miguel, 138n76
Gibbs, Jeffrey, 66n4
González, Justo, 2n3, 116n18
González de Cardedal, Olegario, 149n1
Granado, Carmelo, 37n22, 50n64, 75n33
Grenz, Stanley, 184n5
Gunton, Colin, 176n64, 179n71, 185

Habets, Myk, 33n7, 157n26
Haight, Roger, xixnn8–9, 151n12, 152n14, 187n18
Hansen, Olaf, 152n15, 189n23
Hook, Norman, 178n16

Name Index   267

Hunter, Harold, 152n15

Illanes Maestre, José Luis, 157n26
Imbelli, Robert, 159n34, 187n18
Irving, Edward, 178n71

Jenson, Robert, 81n57, 136n71

Kasper, Walter, 33n7, 57, 61n82,
   102, 103nn53–54, 114n10, 120,
   126–28, 131–32, 160n36, 161,
   188
Kelly, J. N. D., 35–36n15
Kleinig, John, 233n47

LaCugna, Catherine Mowry, xi, 31,
   90–91, 92n25, 93n32, 101–3,
   113n4, 201n8, 202n9
Ladaria, Luis F., 15, 33n7, 40n32,
   44n43, 49nn59–60, 50n61–64,
   51n65, 60n80, 75n33, 95n36,
   100n43, 102n48, 128n62,
   142n90, 143n91, 149n3, 153–56,
   161n38, 167
Lampe, G. W. H., xixnn8–9, 150–53,
   155n20, 187–88
Lotz, David, 184n4

McCormack, Bruce, 176n64
McDonnell, Kilian, 9–10, 12n34,
   39n28, 75n33, 220n2, 231n39,
   238n2
McGukin, Paul, 36n15
Moltmann, Jürgen, 33n7, 66n1,
   94, 104n55, 134n68, 135n69,
   138n76, 158n27, 159, 160n35,
   191n27
Montague, George, 46n49, 70, 72n18,
   73–74
Mühlen, Heribert, 47, 57, 125–26,
   199n4

Nafzger, Peter, 190n24
Newman, Paul W., 152n16
Nissiotis, Nikos, 47n51

Odero, José Miguel, 41n33

O'Donnell, John J., 15, 33n7, 94n34,
   123n41, 136n72, 151n12, 201n5
Orbe, Antonio, 6nn13–14, 7n16,
   9–11, 12n34, 15n48, 16n54, 17,
   18n62, 74n28
Owen, John, 176n64, 178n71

Pannenberg, Wolfhart, xix$n$7, 115n14,
   116n14, 157n26, 159, 160n36
Pikaza, Xabier, 141
Pinnock, Clark, 33n7, 200n5, 215n41
Porsch, Felix, 54n70, 68n6, 190n25,
   191nn26–27
Potterie, Ignace de la, 44n46
Prenter, Regin, 219n1, 226nn24–25,
   228n30

Rahner, Karl, xxii, 35n13, 59n75,
   86–90, 92–94, 97, 101–5, 109,
   128, 134, 157, 158n29, 161n38,
   188, 201n8, 207–8, 215n41
Régnon, T. de, 120
Rice, Richard, 198n3
Rogers, Eugene F., 225n20
Rosato, Philip J., xix$n$7, 3n4, 15,
   160n36, 187n18

Sánchez M., Leopoldo A., xxiv$n$10,
   154, 156n22, 161n38, 171n54,
   179nn72–73, 227n29, 229n32
Sanders, John, 217n42
Scaer, David P., 79n50, 80n55, 83n59
Schoonenberg, Piet, xix$n$9, 59–61,
   103n52
Schweizer, Eduard, 71–72
Schwöbel, Christoph, 89n13
Silanes, Nereo, 134n68
Simonetti, Mario, xix$n$6, 35n15, 149
Spence, Alan, 176n64, 179n71
Staniloae, Dumitru, 138n76, 145n93

Tábet, Miguel Ángel, 68n8, 192n28
Thomsen, Mark, 154n19

Valliere, Paul, 37n23
Vanhoye, A., 70
van Rossum, Joost, 69n9

Name Index

Weinandy, Thomas, 61n83, 141–44, 146n95, 151n12
Welker, Michael, 33n7
Wong, Joseph, 33n7

Wright, John H., 151n12

Zizioulas, John D., 32n5, 34n8, 43n39, 112–14, 120–22, 137n74, 142, 214, 238n2

Scripture Index

OLD TESTAMENT

Genesis
2:7	230n35

Deuteronomy
32	53

2 Samuel
7	35n11

Psalms
2:7	9, 49, 49n59, 50, 75
22:1ff.	195–97
31:5	196
45:6ff.	5–7, 22, 40, 41n34, 156n24, 172n58, 176n65
68:18	7
72:5	176n13
89:3–4	35n11
89:34–37	35n11
101:1	49
110:3–4	6n13
132	35n11

Isaiah
7:10ff.	5, 8n22, 38
9:6–7	35n11
11:1ff.	4, 7, 18, 35n11, 172n58
42:1	39, 66n2, 191, 229n33
49:1ff.	xi, 66n2, 229n33
50:4–11	66n2, 229n33
52:10ff.	211n36
52:13—53:12	66n2, 229n33
53:4	53, 191
61:1ff.	15, 18, 27, 40, 53
66:13	xi

Joel
2:28ff.	7, 18n66, 192
3:1–5	65

Micah
5:2	8

Zechariah
9:9	8n24

NEW TESTAMENT

Matthew
1:16ff.	35, 36n16, 37–38
2:11	8, 35
3:7ff.	54
3:13ff.	39, 66, 191, 225, 229
4:1ff.	52, 232

Matthew (continued)

6:9ff.	xi, 196
8:14ff.	53, 82
12:22ff.	53–54, 107, 193
16:15	ix, 186
26:37–39	195n1
28	18n66, 221

Mark

1:9ff.	39, 52, 106, 211, 229, 232
5:8	53
10:38ff.	66, 82, 191, 234
14:16ff.	xi, 195, 232
15:34	195

Luke

1:15ff.	54
1:32ff.	35, 35n11, 37, 40
1:35	10, 34–39, 50–51, 59, 95–96, 106–7, 149, 174n60, 189
1:41ff.	54
2:11ff.	40, 54
2:40	172n58
2:52	172n58
3:16ff.	190
3:21ff.	9, 39, 50, 191, 210, 211n37, 229
4:1ff.	52–53, 107, 191, 211n37
4:14ff.	18, 27, 40, 50, 52–53, 107, 191, 193, 211n37
5:15–16	211
6:12–13	211n37
8:29	53
8:46	107
9:28–29	211n37
10:17	54
10:21	107, 212
11:2	xi
11:14ff.	53, 193
12:28	107
12:50	66, 191
13:34	xi
18:31–33	82
22:41ff.	82, 195n1, 211n37, 212
23:34	82
23:46	196
24:26	160
24:46ff.	38, 46, 107, 160, 190

John

1:1ff.	35, 36n16, 37–38, 60n80, 95–96, 153
1:29ff.	32n6, 39, 42n37, 54, 66–67, 69, 75n35, 75n36, 107, 190, 225, 229n33, 239
3:5	105
3:13ff.	34, 42, 54, 67, 69, 107, 172n58, 177n68, 191
4:7ff.	55, 67–68, 107
7:37ff.	42, 55, 68–69, 75n35, 107, 156n24, 191
10:18	82, 193
11:42	204n20
13:31–32	69, 191
15:26	34n9, 108
16:1ff.	xii, 55, 228
17:1ff.	xi, 69, 191, 206n30
17:19	25
19:30ff.	68–69, 107, 191
20:17ff.	xi, 32n6, 34n9, 67–69, 107, 160, 191, 230n35

Acts

1:1ff.	38, 46, 53, 107, 160, 190
2:16ff.	7n19, 18n66, 46, 49, 52, 65, 70–71, 82, 108, 192–93
5:30–32	70
10:30ff.	32n6, 38, 40, 53, 107, 191, 225
13:32ff.	49–50, 74
16:6ff.	35, 70

Romans

1:3–4	35, 36n16, 71–73, 83, 108, 150, 192, 213
5:12–21	71
6:3ff.	192
8:11ff.	xi–xii, 51, 71–74, 83, 108, 192, 196, 213–14
10:17	184
12	169n48

1 Corinthians

1:24	37
2:10-11	216
9:24—10:13	232
10:16-17	192
11:27-29	192
12:3	103, 160
15:20ff.	71, 73, 108, 192
15:45	70n14, 71, 73, 150, 192

2 Corinthians

1:22	71
3:17-18	70n14
5:18ff.	83, 174n60

Galatians

3:13ff.	83
4:4ff.	74, 83, 196

Ephesians

4:7ff.	xii, 7n19, 70, 231
6:10-20	232

Philippians

2:4ff.	23, 84, 191, 234
3	232

1 Timothy

3:16	71-73, 83, 107-8, 192

Hebrews

1:5	49n59
1:13	49
2:14ff.	175n60, 232
4:15	189, 232
5:5ff.	49n59, 155
7:26	174n60
9:11ff.	66n1, 70, 71n16, 82, 107, 193n30

James

1:17	33
4:2	217n42

1 Peter

1:20ff.	82, 84
2:20-21	84
3:18	71-72, 83, 192

1 John

4:9-10	69
5:6-8	191

Revelation

13:8	82

www.ingramcontent.com/pod-product-compliance
Lightning Source LLC
Chambersburg PA
CBHW061434300426
44114CB00014B/1678